D. L. Moody

D. L. MOODY

AND HIS WORK.

BY

REV. W. H. DANIELS, A.M.

With Portraits and Illustrations.

SOLD ONLY BY SUBSCRIPTION.

HARTFORD:
AMERICAN PUBLISHING COMPANY.
1876.

PUBLISHER'S ANNOUNCEMENT.

In view of the earnest desire of Mr. Moody to escape personal notoriety, the first two chapters of this book, as published in the English Edition—having reference to his early life—have been revised and brought within the smallest compass consistent with a fair record of essential facts. In other portions of the book, some matters relating to the personal life of Mr. Moody have also been omitted, and others connected with his evangelical labors substituted. Several new engravings and much matter have been added, embracing Mr. Moody's Farewell Sermon at London, which materially enhance the interest of the book. All of the facts and incidents regarding Mr. Moody and his work, which the volume now contains, are of the author's own knowledge, or have been related to him by the personal and intimate friends and co-laborers of Mr. Moody, but not by Mr. Moody himself, as the latter feels it his duty to abstain from any participation in giving this form of publicity to matter connected with himself—however gratifying and profitable the information thereby conveyed might be to the thousands of Christian sympathizers throughout the land—or in any other way doing that which might give ground for the slightest suspicion that he is directly or indirectly interested in the publication, sale, or profits of this or any other book. The Publishers have therefore endeavored to remove from the pages of the volume everything which could in any way give cause for such comment on Mr. Moody, or conflict with his wish to escape personal notice.

INTRODUCTION;

By Rev. C. H. Fowler, D.D., LL.D.,

PRESIDENT OF THE NORTH-WESTERN UNIVERSITY.

THE best teachers of humanity are the lives of great men.

As, in the nature of things, it is true that "wherever McGregor sits, there is the head of the table," so wherever there is a McGregor, he is sure to have something to tell us.

Men become great only by representing some profound, productive, forceful idea.

Things in this world go by majorities; and each man has dominion just in proportion as he carries the majority under his own hat and coat. A man with a great truth in him has only to bide his time, and the multitude will come to sit at his feet and learn of him. If the centre of gravity falls without his base, no matter how high he is, he topples over into disorder and obscurity: if the centre of gravity falls within him, he stands, a way-mark for mankind.

Truths, to be felt, must be incarnated.

The eternal purposes of salvation were moving in a plane out of our sight: God incarnated them in a

Man, and thus brought them within range of our vision, our sympathy, and our faith.

The Bible is largely made up of biographies; and men see the value of faith and righteousness by seeing the men who believed and obeyed. Abstractions are feeble; but, when a man causes things to come to pass, by studying him we find out some great secret of power.

Truths need bodies; therefore God puts them into men, that they may have feet to run, hands to strike, and elbows to crowd their way to the front. They must have personality, outline, experience; then they reach and move us.

Religions which depend upon argument are failures. A religion, to be aggressive, must be experimental: men must be something and do something by means of it, which would be otherwise impossible; then they become both rhetoric and logic—persuasion and proof.

D. L. Moody is one of the men who stand for great truths. The study of his life and work will help the world to believe in a Divine Redeemer, and in the supernatural power of saving grace.

May God give this book a million readers, and many converts to Christ!

C. H. FOWLER.

Evanston, Ill., May 1st, 1875.

PREFACE.

THIS record of the life and work of D. L. Moody, the American evangelist, who, with his sweet-voiced companion, Mr. Sankey, has made such a deep impression upon the Christian world, is a work b .th of love and duty.

It is almost entirely from original materials, obtained from first sources, by the author in person; who was, for years, a neighbour of Mr. Moody in Chicago, both before and after the great fire.

Learning the plan and purpose of this volume, some of his relatives, as well as many of his best friends both in America and Europe, have gladly adopted it as the medium through which to correct sundry wrong impressions; and of publishing such information as, in their judgment, would least conflict with his desire to avoid mere *personal* notoriety; at the same time, placing before the public such an account of his early life and work as might properly be demanded concerning a religious teacher so widely known and trusted.

Having finished the record in America, the author took ship for England; where, in the midst of the great London revival, the account of that signal work of grace has been prepared.

In order that this volume might be more complete, the author has made a tour of the chief cities where Messrs. Moody and Sankey have laboured; with a view to learning, not only the facts concerning those wonderful services, but also the results which, thus far, have followed them.

It has been presumed that the Church and the world would like to know how these evangelists have been brought out and trained for their mission, by the providence and grace of God; and what are the real sources of their power. A grouping of the leading facts and incidents of this great awakening, exhibiting it in some degree of unity, would, doubtless, also be acceptable. To meet these wants, and to add a helpful volume to the literature of Christian work, has been the author's prayerful and earnest endeavour.

If it is found to be somewhat out of the usual style of religious portraiture, let it also be kindly borne in mind, that the purpose has been to make it as nearly like its subject as a book can be like a man.

It should also be distinctly stated, that Mr. Moody is in no way responsible for the preparation of this book; and that neither he, nor any of his family, have any interest whatever in its sale.

River Forest, Chicago, April 28th, 1875; *and* W. H. Daniels.
14, *Queen Square, Bloomsbury, London, July 12th,* 1875.

CONTENTS.

PART I.

PART II.

CONTENTS.

PART II.—*continued.*

LIST OF ILLUSTRATIONS.

PART I.

PART II.

THE OLD FARM HOUSE.

PART I.

D. L. MOODY AND HIS WORK.

CHAPTER I.

THE BOY IS FATHER TO THE MAN.

A CERTAIN family Bible, in an old farm-house in Northfield, Massachusetts, has the following record:—

"Edwin Moody was born November 1st, 1800. Betsy Holton was born February 5th, 1805. Were married January 3rd, 1828."

Both the Moodys and the Holtons were old families in the little mountain town. The latter were among the first settlers of the "plantation of Northfield," which was purchased of the Indians in 1673, and laid out by a committee of the General Court of Massachusetts, of which committee William Holton was a member. This man was of English descent, born in the colony of Massachusetts Bay, and from him Betsy Holton is a lineal descendant of the fifth generation.

Of the nine children (seven sons and two daughters) born of this marriage, Dwight Lyman was the sixth, born on the 5th of February, 1837.

On the 28th of May, 1841, his father died. In the morning of that day he was at his usual work—that of a mason; but feeling a pain in his side, caused by over-exertion, he went home to rest. At about one o'clock in the afternoon he felt the pain suddenly increasing, staggered to the bed, fell upon his knees beside it, and in this posture of prayer death seized upon him, before any one knew he was seriously ill.

All that was left to the widow for her support was the little home on the mountain side, with an acre or two of land; and even this was encumbered with debt. Of her seven children the eldest was but thirteen years of age; and a month after her husband's death another boy and girl were born.

Some of her worldly-wise neighbours advised her to give away or bind out her children, all except the twin babies; but this she was determined not to do. God had endowed her with unusual strength both of body and mind, and, trusting in Him, she bravely lifted her burden of poverty and toil, and carried it patiently, hopefully, and at length cheerfully, until the little ones were able to help her bear it, and at last to fill her hands with plenty as they had filled her heart with love and care.

Her brothers, in Boston, helped her to pay the interest of the mortgage on her home, the eldest boys helped to take care of the little farm, the mother took care of the house and the children, and God took care of them all.

The minister of the parish, Rev. Oliver Everett, was a faithful shepherd to this little flock. From the first he counselled the widow not to part with the children, but to keep them together as best she could; to trust in God, and to bring them up for Him: promising to help her in their education, and, if need be, in their support.

Pastor Everett was a Unitarian. It must however be borne in mind that, in those days, the name had not become associated with all sorts of heresies, as at present. His differences with his orthodox neighbours were mostly concerning certain points of speculative theology. He believed in the Bible as the inspired word of God, in Jesus Christ as the saviour of all sinners who would try to save themselves, in the Sabbath, and in the Church and its sacraments.

The Apostles' creed would doubtless have been acceptable to him as a fair summary of the Gospel, if such a document had been known in his region at that time; but that other creed, named after St. Athanasius, would probably have worried him a good deal, as indeed it does a great many other good people.

In those days sectarian controversy was the chief business of many of the clergy, and great doctors of divinity belabored one another with logical cudgels, attacking and defending extra-Scripture dogmas whose very existence has now been almost forgotten.

To Mrs. Moody these controversies were peculiarly distasteful. The pressing cares and heavy burdens of her life led her to seek for a Friend and Helper in the Lord, and not to speculate about His secret will. She was determined to do all she could to save her children in this life, and she insisted on believing in a God who would do the same for them in the life to come; but this was not at all the manner of the orthodox theology of those days, which taught that God had foreordained, for His own good pleasure, the destruction of a large portion of the human race, and that, without respect to their character. To some of her neighbours this seemed a wholesome doctrine, a warning to unbelievers, but a great comfort to the saints, who were thus assured of a small and select society in the great hereafter; but to the widow it was the gall of bitterness.

Another theological invention of those times which had a considerable run was the duty of being willing to be damned if God in his secret will had so determined. Great stress was laid upon it in certain parts of Massachusetts and Connecticut, and the orthodox neighbours of Mrs. Moody did not fail to exhort her to the attainment of this rather mournful state of mind. Against this the soul of the widow rebelled. She was not at all willing to be damned, and more especially was she unwilling that any of her little children should be. Her Calvinistic friends reproved her for her rebellion against the divine decrees; but if there were any decrees which shut out any of her household from a fair chance of Heaven, she determined, at least, not to be tormented by them in prayers and sermons, and she placed herself and her family under the instructions of Pastor Everett, who was for giving all sinners the best possible chances of salvation; and they were all baptized together, and received into the Unitarian Church of Northfield, after the fashion of those days.

The successor of Pastor Everett was of the worst rationalistic school, and Mr. Moody sometimes quotes one of his sayings with horror; but the widow held fast to the hand of the Lord, and brought up her children to read the Bible and to believe in the grace of God whereby she hoped they would all be brought into His kingdom.

True to his promise, Pastor Everett used to help the widow in the care of her children. He would visit them betimes, cheer them up with some pleasant words, settle quarrels among the boys, give the little ones a bright piece of silver all round, and bid the mother keep on praying, telling her God would never forget her labour of love. At one time he took little Dwight into his family to do errands and go to school—a work of charity which, by all accounts, must have sorely tried his patience. The good man was often perplexed what to do with the boy, being forced to laugh at his pranks in spite of himself, when he felt it his duty to be stern and severe.

But his chief instructor in religion, as well as in everything else, was his mother. Great sorrow and years of toil and privation had drawn her heart very close to the Saviour, and when the care of her great family of little children grew so heavy as almost to overwhelm her, she learned to cast her burden on the Lord. Sometimes, when the boys were quarrelsome and rebellious, and the household was in utter confusion, she would go away to her own room and pray for wisdom and patience. "And when I would come back," said she, "they would all be good children again."

As fast as they came to be old enough, they were sent to the Unitarian Church in the village—a little more than a mile away; the elder boys, who were out at work, coming home on Saturday night, to go with their little brothers and sisters. They used to take their dinners and stay all day, hearing the two sermons, and attending the Sunday-school which was sandwiched between them; and then they would all come home again for supper, before going to their places of work. Thus the mother kept her family together. In spite of the poverty which parted them during the week, the home life of the Sabbath preserved their unity.

After supper the mother would gather them all around her on an old settle in the porch, or under one of the great sugar-maple trees in the front yard, if it were summer time, and read to them out of the books which they brought home from the Sunday-school library.

It was no small wonder how these little books always knew so much about that particular family. If Dwight had been unusually proud and mischievous, or if George had been out of patience with him, or if anything had gone wrong in the household, the library book was sure to have some account of it, or of something wonderfully like it; and also to contain just the sort of good advice adapted to each particular case. It was sometimes rather difficult for them to "find the place" afterwards; but they were none the less interested in the reading. And had not Mrs. Moody as good a right to revise and adapt the Sunday-school books as anybody else had to make them? Surely the things she read out of her own heart for the good of her little flock were of just as high authority as if they had actually been printed between those little speckled covers with the red backs and corners, and bearing the name of the famous old American Sunday-School Union.

At the table the mother would repeat a text of Scripture or a verse of a hymn, and the children would say it in chorus after her. That table, as may well be supposed, was not always very well supplied; but the mother, though toiling day and night to feed and clothe her children, and not always knowing to-day where the food was to come from for to-morrow, kept up a brave heart and wore a cheerful face. The shadow of poverty and death was over them, but the love of the Great Father above, and of the godly mother below, kept the little ones from want and gloom, and made their home a happy one in spite of all their misfortunes.

But another sorrow fell upon that home on the mountain side. One of the elder sons, with a boyish ambition to make his fortune in the great world, suddenly disappeared.

For years no tidings of the lost boy reached the widowed mother. It seemed sometimes as if her heart would break for him. "Oh! if I could only know he was dead, it would be better than this! Maybe he is sick and in want!—maybe he has fallen in with wicked men, who will make him like themselves!"

They would all sit in a semicircle about the fire of a stormy winter's night, and listen to stories of their dead father: what he did, what he said, how he looked, how he was kind to a friend and lost a great deal of money by him, and so their little home was mortgaged; and they were poor. But if by chance any one spoke the name of the absent brother, a great silence fell upon them ; the tears would come into the eyes of the mother, and then they would steal away to bed, whispering their "good-nights," and walking softly as they went; for that name was like a sword-thrust to the mother's heart. Then they would lie awake listening to the roar of the wind among the mountains, thinking maybe *he* was out in the cold somewhere ; or, worse than that, perhaps he had gone to sea, and while they were snug in bed was keeping watch on a wave-beaten deck, or climbing a reeling mast in just such darkness and storm.

Now and then, between the gusts, a sound would be heard like the wail of the summer wind when it used to make harpstrings of the leaves and branches of the great maple trees in the yard: low and gentle now, and again rising into louder and stronger tones. Then they held their breath and listened. Mother was sitting up to pray for her lost boy.

Next morning perhaps she would send them down to the post-office in the village, a mile and a half away, to ask for a letter—a letter from *him*, though the mother never said so. But no letter ever came.

Long years after, when the widow was growing old, and her soft dark hair was turning white, one summer afternoon a tall, swarthy man, with heavy black beard, was seen coming in at the gate. He came up under the porch, and, the door being open, he stopped and looked in, with an eager, anxious face, as if he were afraid he might not find the one he was seeking, though he had stopped at the church-yard on his way through the village to see whether there were two graves instead of one where his father had been laid so many years ago. Surely his mother was not dead, but was she still at the old home?

The widow came to the door to bid the stranger in. The eyes that had watched so long for his coming did not know him now. He was only a boy when he ran away; years of hardship and exposure to sun and storm had made him strange even to his mother.

"Will you come in?" said she, in her courteous and kindly way.

But the stranger did not move or speak. He stood there, humbly and penitently, in the presence of her whose love he had slighted, and whose heart he had broken; and, as a sense of his ingratitude began to overwhelm him, the big tears began to find their way over his weather-beaten face.

By those tears the mother recognised her son. He had come at last! There was so much of the old home in him that he could not always stay away. But he would not cross its threshold till he had confessed his sin against it, and heard from the same lips which had prayed for him so often and so long, the sweet assurance that he was forgiven.

"No! no!" said he; "I cannot come in till my mother forgives me."

Weeping upon his neck, forgetting all the sorrow he had caused her in the joy of seeing him once more, she forgave him because he asked it, and because she loved him.

"And that is just the way," says Moody,—who sometimes tells the story to his great congregations,—"that is just the way God forgives all the prodigal sons who come back to Him. Do you think mother kept her long-lost boy out there in the porch till he had gone through with a string of apologies, and done a list of penances, and said ever-so-many prayers? Not at all! She took him to her heart at once. She made him come right in. She forgave him *all*, and rejoiced over his coming more than over all the other children. He had been lost, and now he was found!"

A lovelier spot than that old homestead would be hard to find. It stands on the eastern slope of the valley of the Connecticut river, which here flows through narrow meadows, with grand hills on either side, rising here and there into peaks, which, if there were not so many of them in that part of the State, would be called mountains, and honoured with separate names. Whatever advantage there is in glorious natural scenery, the boy Dwight enjoyed it in great perfection. Certain it is that in after life his manners came to be quite suggestive of bold peaks, mountain torrents, and hurricanes sweeping over woods and hills.

The air of that region is the very elixir of life. One of his Chicago friends went to visit him at his old home, being just ready to die of consumption; but in a little while he inhaled so much health from the breezes of the Northfield mountains, that he gave up his immediate prospects of heaven and went back to business once more.

Among the rich inheritances of this poor boy were a vigorous constitution, boundless ambition and animal spirits, and a will strong enough to break

VIEW FROM THE OLD HOMESTEAD.

down all opposition and drive him on to success. His pride was all the time leading him to undertake things far beyond his years. His mother says, "He used to think himself a man when he was only a boy." The fatherly authority was wanting, and he soon came to feel himself his own master. Anything was easier than submission.

He had little faith in prayer. Once when he was creeping under a heavy fence, it fell down upon him and caught him, so that he could not get away. He struggled till he was quite exhausted, and then began to cry for help; but he was far from any house, and no one heard him. At last he got safely out; and this was the account he gave of his escape:—

"I tried and tried, and I couldn't lift them awful heavy rails; then I hollered for help, but nobody came; and then I began to think I should have to die away up there on the mountain all alone. But I happened to think that, maybe, God would help me, and so I asked Him. And after that I could lift the rails, just as easy!"

During these years Dwight went through as many as a dozen terms at the little district schoolhouse; but very little of the school ever went through him; in fact, the boy was so amazingly *full*, that there was really no room in him for the sciences and arts.

There were few things he would not do for his mother: at her urgent entreaty he would even do a little studying. He would usually obey her; but she was the only person in all the world who ever was able to manage him. He was proud and wilful to the last degree, but full of generous impulses. He was ungovernable, partly because he was a natural leader himself. Still there was nothing vicious in his disposition. If he could be made to see that he had wronged any one, he was ready to beg his pardon for it, and do better in future.

His last term of school was in the winter of his seventeenth year. He was the leading spirit among the boys, and so much mischief did he lead them into that at length the teacher was in despair, and threatened to turn him out. At this his good mother was sorely grieved. She told him how much ashamed she should be to have one of her sons turned out of school, and directed him to go to the teacher, ask forgiveness for his bad conduct, and try to be a credit to his mother rather than a disgrace. This he did in all sincerity, and the rest of the term, for the first time in his life, applied himself faithfully to study.

But it was too late for him to become a scholar The time had come when he felt called to the hard work of life ; and, with such little learning as had accumulated in him, he hardly knew how, he must go out and boldly face the world.

Whatever religious impressions he had felt in childhood seem to have been covered out of sight, and he grew up to be a young man, or rather, a big boy, with no other piety in him than the love of his mother, and a sturdy determination to be an honest and successful man. He had muscles like steel, and the courage of a young lion. More than this,—he had the courage to take his place among educated people, in spite of his own deficiencies, though he sorely regretted the

THE OLD HOME, 1875.

wasted opportunities of the years which would come again no more. He was determined to "make the best of it" now. Of course he would have to labour at a disadvantage all his life; but then, he had always succeeded *somehow*, and this he always expected to do.

If he came to a hard word in reading, he did not stop at it, but made a rough guess what it might be, from the sense of the passage; or, if it was altogether out of his reach, he would invent a word which might sound something like it in the more prominent syllables, and drive on all the faster for the excitement caused by his desperate vocal spring.

So in emergencies of every kind. A bold push, aided by ready wit, carried him over many a difficulty before which a wiser but less courageous lad would have set himself down in despair. Like the eagle which springs from the mountain crag into the air above the abyss, safely trusting to its power of flight, young Moody plunged into many a desperate situation, strong in the sense of power which he felt within him, on which he seemed upborne like the eagle on its wings.

There was evidently "something in him," but that "something" seemed to be almost anything else rather than a preacher of the Gospel.

His mother still lives in the old home at Northfield, and to that cherished spot Mr. Moody hastened upon his arrival from England; his name known and blessed throughout the whole civilized world. Surely that mother has met a great reward for her faithfulness and love;—the bread she cast upon the waters years ago has been found again.

CHAPTER II.

OUT INTO THE WORLD, AND UP INTO THE CHURCH.

SOON after his seventeenth birthday, the winter school being over, young Moody started to seek his fortune in the great world. He went first to Clinton, where he had a brother, clerk in a store; but finding no business to his mind, he pushed on to Boston—then, as now, the Mecca of all Bay State boys ambitious of a business career.

His uncle, Samuel Holton, had visited the old home a little while before, and Dwight had asked him for a place in his boot and shoe store in Boston; but learning what a wild young colt he was, he had refused, fearing to take him to a great city, where there seemed to be ninety-nine chances in a hundred that he would go straight to ruin. But the young man was determined to show his uncle that he could find or make a place for himself, without help from any one. Accordingly, much to that excellent man's surprise, his nephew one day made his appearance in his store,—not to ask for a place, oh no! but just as a visitor acquainted with his sister in the country. Her younger brother Lemuel had a house in the city, and here he was made welcome while, relying on himself as usual, he began to beat about the city for a situation.

But fortune did not seem to favour him. He was fresh from the farm, and had far more of the mountains than of the schools in his conversation and manners; his clothes were seedy, and not of the most fashionable style; and, by way of a climax to his difficulties, a big boil came out on his neck, which forced him to go about with his head turned down over one shoulder, in a way which did not at all improve his personal appearance or help his prospects for business.

At the end of a week he was disgusted, but not discouraged. Nobody in Boston appreciated him; and he announced his purpose of shaking off its dust from his feet and trying what he could do in New York,—to which place he must have travelled on foot, for his money was all gone, and he had nothing he could sell to raise any more.

"Have you asked your Uncle Samuel to help you to a situation?" inquired Mr. Lemuel Holton.

"No," said Dwight; "he knows I am looking for a place, and he may help me or not, just as he pleases."

But his pride was beginning to bend a little, though it was by no means ready to break. He was adrift in the world, which seemed to care no more for him than the ocean waves care for a floating spar. Taking advantage of this state of mind, for which he had been waiting, his uncle ventured to offer him a little sound advice; telling him that his self-will was greatly in his way, that modesty was sometimes as needful as courage, and suggesting that his Uncle Samuel would no doubt be glad to do something for him if he should show himself a little more willing to be governed by people who were older and wiser than himself. Acting upon this advice, he was kindly received by that gentleman, who consented to give him a place as salesman in his store, on the following conditions: First, he was to board at a place to be selected by his uncle; second, he was not to be out in the streets at night, or go to places of amusement which his uncle did not approve; third, he was regularly to attend the Mount Vernon Church and Sunday-school.

Mr. Holton was and is a successful business man, who came to Boston himself looking for a situation when about his nephew's age, and who, by strict attention to duty and religion, had come to wealth and honour. Knowing how many young clerks are lost through the carelessness of their employers, he resolved on making a right beginning with this one, hoping that his own good sense would keep him in the straight road when once he was fairly started in it. Before his removal to the suburban village of Winchester he had been a long time member of the Mount Vernon Church, where he knew the young man would be sure to find good companions—a matter which he regarded as of vital importance. To these three conditions another general one was added; viz., that Dwight was to be governed by the judgment of his uncle rather than his own,—which was a mild way of stating the, to him, exceedingly irksome duty of obedience to his superiors.

In his extremity the young man agreed to all things required of him, and, what was more, he kept his agreement. A home was found for him in a Christian family who lived in very humble style, and he entered upon his duties on a very small salary, though with a sure foothold in the world of trade; where his future would depend upon the use he made of himself and his opportunities.

It may be imagined that his country life and his misuse of the country school had not fitted him to shine in the city. His pride and poverty kept him from feeling at home among the well-bred, well-dressed people to whom he was introduced. For a time he was unhappy; but he steadily held to his purpose of conquering a place for himself high up in the circles of wealth and influence. He felt sure of ultimate success, and for it he laboured night and day.

He was a sharp observer of human nature, quick to take advantage of everything in his favour, always on the alert, and ready for any emergency. His pride did not admit of his asking too many questions, and, as the business was new to him, he was often in doubt about prices and qualities; but what he lacked in knowledge he would make up in shrewd guessing, and within three months after his entering the house, he sold more boots and shoes than any other man in it. His idea of business was, a struggle with mankind, out of which the hardest heads and the sharpest wits were sure to come with the largest influence and the longest purse. The quiet manners of his uncles he could never learn, nor did he desire to learn them. He went about his duties in the store in much the same way as he would have swung a scythe in a field of tangled clover, or broken a yoke of wild steers. If any one offended his sense of honour, he would fly into fury at once; but the tempest of passion soon passed by.

His habit of striking out right and left sometimes raised an uproar in the whole establishment; and there was no little difficulty in keeping the peace. It was difficult for him to get rid of the notion that he must fight his way through the world; and, a long time afterwards, when he became famous as a Christian teacher and leader, he seemed to enjoy the service of the Lord all the more because, at the same time, he could be valiantly fighting the devil.

The Mount Vernon Church was one of the most excellent and exact of all the orthodox Congregational Churches of New England. Its pastor was magnificent—physically, mentally, and spiritually; just the sort of man to captivate this high-spirited youth, who, at that period, was older and wiser than at any other time in his life, and to whom only the greatest heroes and the grandest ideas were of any particular importance. An ordinary preacher would have failed to reach him or win his respect: he would have spent the hour of church service in criticizing him, and would have mimicked his weaknesses and made fun of his faults when he came home. But Dr. Kirk was a prince among ministers; and young Moody, having at last found a man whom he believed to be wiser and stronger than himself, sat reverently at his feet and learned of him.

In the Sunday-school he was placed in the Bible-class of Mr. Edward Kimball. Here he attended, at first, perforce of his agreement with his uncle, and sat out the lesson with evident weariness and impatience. His teacher says he felt as if he were not getting any hold of the young man, and was even failing to interest him. But one Sunday, when the lesson happened to be about Moses, he listened with considerable attention, and at length broke out with this question, which was the first remark he had ventured to make,—

"That Moses was what you would call a pretty smart sort of a man, wasn't he?"

Glad at last to hear a word from his unpromising scholar, Mr. Kimball received the question with much favour, and enlarged upon it, greatly to young Moody's satisfaction. He soon began to warm towards his teacher, though for the church and school in general he had an increasing dislike. The men and women were so rich and proper and pious, that they seemed to live in a world almost out of his sight. The young people wore good clothes and spent a good deal of money, in which he could not imitate them; therefore he felt himself a victim of misfortune, and revenged himself, as people often do in such cases, by denouncing his more fortunate brethren and sisters for their pride; when, if he could have looked into his own heart, he might have seen it was the proudest of them all.

But presently the Spirit of the Lord began to work upon him. Under the plain and loving sermons of his pastor, and the personal instructions of his Sunday-school teacher, his heart began to soften; and, remembering the lesson taught him by his mother, he began again to pray the Lord to help him to be good.

One day Mr. Kimball called upon him at his place of business; and, putting his hand kindly on his shoulder, inquired if he would not give his heart to Christ. That question awakened him. He began to seek the Saviour in earnest, and in a little while he felt the assurance of the pardon of his sins and of his acceptance as a child of God.

Years afterwards he used to say, "I can feel the touch of that man's hand on my shoulder even yet."

With the same enthusiasm in religion as in everything else, he soon began to speak in the meetings of the church, telling what God had done for his soul, sometimes adding a little piece of exhortation, which was not always flattering to the elegant believers around him, and which was received with evident marks of disfavour.

One good lady called upon his Uncle Samuel, and requested him to advise the young convert to hold his peace until he should become more able to edify the meetings. But Mr. Holton replied that he was glad Dwight had the courage to profess his faith in the Saviour in such presence, and declined to put a straw in his way.

In due time he applied to be received into the Mount Vernon Church, and went before the deacons to be examined as to his faith and doctrine. His home training in religion, as it appeared, had not very well qualified him to pass that strict examination. He had a good deal of faith, but in doctrine he was lamentably wanting. The Spirit of God had begun the work of sanctification in him, but as yet the leaven of orthodox theology had made but little impression upon the lump. He could not answer the questions the good deacons put to him ; but, as far as he knew his duty to Christ, the church, and the world, he was willing and anxious to do it.

There was no such sudden and complete transformation in him as is sometimes wrought in the experience of conversion ; but the work of saving grace went on in him gradually, and his piety deepened by slow degrees, having so much of the old Adam in its way. But he had set his face as a flint in the direction of duty and heaven, and so sturdily did he resist the devil, and so hopefully did he get up and go on again whenever that enemy managed to trip him up, that, in the judgment of his friends, and especially of his aunt, Mrs. Holton, to whom he opened his heart, it became fully evident that he was one of the elect.

The cautious and conservative deacons, however, were not quite clear in their minds about receiving a convert into that church with such a meagre supply of doctrine in him. At length they proposed to put him upon a kind of probation, advising him to go on towards heaven by himself for a while—an arrangement which Deacon Ward reported to his uncle, and to which all parties agreed.

After a time he made a second application, and at the May Communion, in the year 1855, he was received into the church at whose portal he had waited half a year, not for want of faith, but for want of doctrine.

Some years afterwards Dr. Kirk was in Chicago,

attending the anniversary of the American Board of Commissioners for Foreign Missions; and lodged at the house, and preached in the pulpit, of his former parishioner. On his return he called upon Mr. Holton and said,—

"I told our people last night that we ought to be ashamed of ourselves. There is that young Moody, who we thought did not know enough to be in our church and Sunday-school, exerting a greater influence for Christ than any other man in the great North-West."

The Rev. Dr. Savage, of Chicago, relates an incident which occurred during Mr. Moody's second visit to England, when he took a good-natured revenge upon one of those very deacons.

At one of his great meetings in Exeter Hall he espied his old friend sitting in a corner away back under the gallery. The good man, travelling for his health, had seen the notice of the meeting, and, partly out of curiosity to see what the man could do, he attended the service, taking a seat where he felt sure Moody would not see him. But just before closing the meeting Mr. Moody exclaimed,—

"I see in the house an eminent Christian gentleman from Boston. Deacon Palmer, come right forward to the platform; the people want to hear from you!"

The deacon shook his head, but Moody was inexorable; so there was nothing for it but to accept the situation and face the audience. He commenced by saying that he had known Mr. Moody in Boston in early life; had been, in fact, a member of the same church with him, and was very glad of his great success in the service of the Lord: when Moody suddenly burst out with the remark,—

"Yes, Deacon, and you kept me out of that church for six months, because you thought I did not know enough to join it."

The effect of such a speech under such circumstances can be better imagined than described. But the deacon was too old a speaker to be silenced by such a retort, though he found it difficult to be heard on account of the laughter which followed it. The audience, he said, must agree with him that it was a great privilege to have received Mr. Moody into the church at all, even though with great misgivings and after long delay.

To his teacher, Mr. Kimball, Mr. Moody has always felt under the deepest obligations; for it was his personal and affectionate interest in his soul's welfare which, under God, was the means of his conversion. One of the sweetest experiences of his after life, when he had become a successful evangelist, was to find his own exhortations blessed to the awakening and conversion of a daughter of his old teacher, whose care of the rough young stranger was thus rewarded in a way to make his heart for ever glad.

But this was not all. Some years ago he was holding some meetings in Boston, when a young man came to him after service and introduced himself as a son of Mr. Kimball.

Mr. Moody was glad to see him, and at once inquired if he were a Christian. He answered that he was not.

"How old are you?"

"Seventeen."

"Just my age when your father led me to the Saviour; and that was just seventeen years ago this very day. Now I want to pay him by leading his son to Christ."

The young man was deeply impressed. They went into a pew together; Mr. Moody prayed with him, and received his promise to give his heart to Christ. Soon after, he heard by a letter from his father that the young man had found peace in believing.

After his reception into the church, young Moody became more and more zealous, and spoke with still greater freedom, but did not become any more acceptable to his quiet and cultivated brethren and sisters. The love of God and the longing to be useful was "as a fire shut up in his bones," and, like other fires, it sometimes gave out smoke as well as heat. Like too many other young believers, he also came to think he must speak or pray in every meeting,—an opinion which he acted upon so persistently that even good Dr. Kirk himself was a little out of patience with him, and felt obliged to put on an extinguisher now and then.

A more careful study of this young steam-engine convert would have shown the pastor that what he needed was not to put out his fires, but to help him to make some connection with the work of God which would allow him to use his surplus energy and zeal. But no one made this discovery; no one set him at work. The type of religious life in the churches of that order, at that time, was passive rather than active; no one felt in a hurry about the salvation of sinners, or the sanctification of believers. God's processes of grace were presumed to be slow and gradual. Everything would come right in God's own time. Their patience came to be almost a vice.

Young Moody was at the opposite extreme. He desired to rush into the kingdom of heaven himself, and was impatient of the apparently slow pace of his neighbours. He reached out blindly, yet eagerly, for "the powers of the world to come." He wanted to hurry on the Millennium.

During the rest of his stay in Boston, which was about five months after his reception into the Mount Vernon Church, he seems to have felt like a caged bird. The settled and finished condition of everything around him was a constant restraint. There seemed to be no room for him anywhere. His brethren cherished the hope that longer experience would tone down his impetuous spirit, and make him at length a quiet and orderly Christian, after their own hearts. Against all this young Moody's soul rebelled; but finding the pressure of society too strong for him, he began to dream of the West, where fortunes were awaiting those who had the courage and genius to strike for them, and where, above everything else, an irrepressible young man like him would be sure to find plenty of room.

CHAPTER III.

SMALL BEGINNINGS IN MISSIONARY WORK.

IN September 1856 young Moody struck out for the West, full of ambition to make his fortune.

On his arrival in Chicago, where God had such a glorious mission awaiting him, he found a situation as salesman in the boot and shoe store of Mr. Wiswall, in Lake Street, to whom he had been recommended, but who received him with great misgivings, on account of his unfinished appearance and impetuous manner.

In a little while he was in high favour with his employer. His bluff and hearty style made him very popular with the rough class of customers, and at length it was the established custom in the house, when sharp or unmanageable men or women came in to buy, to turn them over to Moody, who took great delight in dealing with them on that very account.

Mr. Wiswall says, "His ambition made him anxious to lay up money. His personal habits were exact and economical. As a salesman he was just the same zealous and tireless worker that he afterwards became in religion."

A jobbing department being presently opened,

Moody was promoted to a situation in it, where he seemed to be quite in his element; its duties, partly inside and partly outside, giving him an opportunity to beat up the hotels, depôts, and all other public places, for customers; and having found persons who had come to town to make purchases in his line, he, as his employer says, "used almost literally to 'compel them to come in' and buy."

In those early days Chicago merchants realized large profits. Business was brisk, and times were good; and the young man seemed in a fair way to realize his dreams of a fortune. A gentleman, who was then a clerk in the same house, says, "Moody was a first-rate salesman. It was his particular pride to make his column foot up the largest of any on the book, not only in the way of sales, but also of profits. He took particular delight in trading with notional or unreasonable people; especially when they made great show of smartness and cunning, and thought themselves extraordinarily wise. Nothing was ever misrepresented in the smallest particular; but when it came to be a question of sharpness of wit between buyer and seller, Moody generally had the best of it."

Some of the clerks had their lodgings in the store —an arrangement which served the double purpose of economy and security; and it became one of the standard amusements of the young men, after their day's work, to turn the place of business into a hall of debate. The clerks from several neighbouring establishments would come in of an evening, and thereupon a fiery discussion would ensue, on some question of politics or theology. This served to develop their powers of oratory, and did not weary or confuse their audience, which consisted, for the most part, of boxes of boots and shoes.

The slavery question, on which the nation was already dividing, was a prolific source of argument. Moody, true to his Boston notions, was a violent abolitionist; but some of his fellow-salesmen took the Southern view of the peculiar institution, and thus the tides of excitement rose to an exceeding height. A still greater interest was imparted to these discussions by the presence of the porter, a smart young negro who had formerly been a slave, and whose eloquence, inspired by sorrow, was sometimes touching, and even sublime.

In theology the chief subject of discussion was foreordination *versus* free-will.

For some reason, in spite of his early trainings, Moody had come to be an ardent Calvinist; while young Wiswall, a fellow-clerk, was a Methodist. These two theologians, therefore, kept up the "Conflict of Ages" in the Lake Street store, and were about as much advantaged by it as the most of their famous predecessors. They exercised their wits to good purpose, but were not materially assisted in religion.

The vexed question of amusements also gave them good practice in debate. Moody was a Puritan. He hated theatres, billiards, cards, and all such pastimes,—counting them so many enticements of the devil. One of his fellow-clerks tells of his coming into the store one night from some religious meeting, and finding a game of checkers going on. In an instant he seized the board, dashed it to pieces, and before a word could be spoken, dropped upon his knees and began to pray.

But notwithstanding his opposition to all time-wasting amusements, he was fond of a blood-stirring frolic or a good-natured trial of strength. He would plan and execute the most ingenious practical jokes, and laugh uproariously over their success; but at the same time holding himself ready to laugh no less heartily at the pranks which were played upon him.

On his arrival in Chicago he joined the Plymouth Congregational Church, of which the Rev. J. E. Roy was pastor, and at once commenced his career as a home missionary. This he did partly because he was lonesome and uneasy on the Sabbath, and felt the necessity of having something to do.

His first effort was to hire four pews in Plymouth Church and keep them full of young men every Sunday. He also opened his mouth in speech and prayer at the social meetings, with a freedom which, even in the West, soon brought him into trouble again.

He had never heard of Talleyrand's famous doctrine that speech is useful for concealing one's thoughts. Like Anthony, he only spoke "right on." There was frequently a pungency in his exhortations which his brethren did not altogether relish. Sometimes in his prayers he would express opinions to the Lord concerning them which were by no means flattering; and it was not long before he received the same fatherly advice which had been given him in Boston—to the effect that he should keep his four pews full of young men, and leave the speaking and praying to those who could do it better.

Partly on this account, and partly because no one church could furnish him enough to do, he began to attend a Sunday morning class in the First Methodist Church. Here he found congenial fellowship and labour with its Mission Band,—a company of young men who used to visit the hotels, saloons, etc., etc., on Sunday mornings, distributing tracts and inviting people to attend divine service.

It must have been a pleasant sight to see this sturdy young Congregationalist standing at the door of a Methodist church, at an hour when there was no meeting in his own, eagerly giving out printed and verbal invitations to the passers-by to join in the worship there.

His success with the four pews in the little church gave him the clue to a line of work in which he afterward became famous. He was interested in Sunday-schools; but the position of scholar was too quiet for him, and for that of teacher he was not very well qualified; as a recruiting-officer, however, he was a marvel. Finding, in his missionary explorations, a little Sunday-school in North Wells Street, he offered to take a class in it. The superintendent replied that he could find plenty of teachers, and had, indeed, almost as many teachers as pupils; but offered him the privilege of teaching any new scholars he might bring. The next Sunday, when the school opened, the new teacher appeared, followed by eighteen bare-headed, bare-footed urchins, ragged and dirty; but, as the new teacher said, every one of them having a soul to be saved, which to him was the chief item of interest.

Mr. J. B. Stillson, a Presbyterian elder from Rochester, New York, was at that time building the Chicago Custom House. Feeling himself impelled to do some kind of missionary work, he began, in the spring of 1857, to visit the ships in the river on Sunday mornings, giving tracts and Testaments to the sailors, and sometimes holding little meetings on deck, or at some street-corner in the neighbourhood of a sailors' boarding-house. One morning he met a stout, hearty-looking fellow doing the same thing. The two at once joined company, and, having worked pleasantly together through the morning, the young man, feeling attracted by the fatherly ways of Mr. Stillson, begged the privilege of further work with him,—saying he wanted to do something for Christ, but did not very well know how. From that meeting commenced a friendship, which was of great advantage to the young enthusiast, and which is still remembered by his senior ally with ever-increasing pleasure. These two men, Moody and Stillson, thenceforth laboured and prayed together among the shipping, in the hospitals and jails, and in the homes of the poor and destitute. During that summer they also helped to recruit no less than twenty mission Sunday-schools.

It was not long before Moody projected a mission of his own. Finding a deserted saloon, near the North Side Market, he rented it for his school on Sunday, and occasional service in the evenings of the week. The region in which this school was opened may be understood from the fact that, standing on the steps of the old Market House near by, their voices could be heard in two hundred drinking and gambling dens. It swarmed with young barbarians—just the kind of scholars he wanted. He had a kind of instinct that his mission, like that of his Master, was to save those who were lost; an idea simple enough in itself, but hard to understand by members of comfortable churches, who shrink from contact with all who are not a good deal saved already. This man had read the parable of the Shepherd who left the ninety-and-nine safe in the fold, to go out into the mountains in search of the one that was lost; and, without stopping to think whether the work would be hard or easy, popular or unpopular, he began looking for lost sinners on "The Sands."

This was a section on the Lake shore, north of the river, which was to Chicagc what the Five Points were to New York, Old Ann Street to Boston, or St. Giles's to London. It was a moral lazaretto. Disorder, and even crime, was regarded as a matter of course on "The Sands," which would have been checked and punished in any other part of the city. To this abandoned region flocked the bad women and worse men, who had fallen too low to feel at home anywhere else; and it was proverbially dangerous for any decent person to walk those streets after nightfall.

Thither went Moody to recruit his Sunday-school.

A more difficult field of labour could hardly be conceived; but to him this was rather an attraction than a discouragement. The same ambition which led him to take pleasure in managing the roughest people in trade, made it also his great delight to bring the worst sinners to Christ. He had begun to be conscious of the defects in his education, and to mourn over them; but here were people whom even he could teach; here were souls whom he could exhort, without giving offence; for they accepted the statement that they were sinners and in danger of perdition; and thus, with perfect freedom, as well as with earnest tenderness, he plunged into the work of bringing these neglected people to the knowledge of Christ and His cross.

His success as a Sunday-school scout assured him any number of wild boys and girls he might choose to bring in; but his want of knowledge of the Scriptures and the methods of Sunday-school work led him to distrust himself, and to seek the assistance of the wisest and best Christian men among his acquaintance. He had indeed been accustomed to read the Bible as other people read fiction, poetry, biography, and travel—*i.e.*, because he liked it. He would spend hours together in this way, reading chapter after chapter, spelling out the hard words and skipping those he could not make out, but managing somehow to find the Lord in His Word; and, having found Him, he was eager to show Him to all who had never made His acquaintance; but how to do it, he did not very well know.

"The contrast," says Mr. Hazard, in a recent number of the *Sunday School Teacher*, "between Mr. Moody as he now is and Mr. Moody as we first knew him is simply amazing. Those who have known him from his earliest beginnings as an evangelist find it next to impossible to realize the change that has taken place in him, even though their memory shows a faithful portrait of his former self not the least dimmed by time. Those whose acquaintance with him is but recent can hardly conceive of the difficulties and apparent limitations through which Mr. Moody has struggled up to his present wonderful power."

His old friend Mr. Reynolds, of Peoria, Illinois, related the following incident at a recent convention in Canada:—

"The first meeting I ever saw him at was in a little old shanty that had been abandoned by a saloon-keeper. Mr. Moody had got the place to hold a meeting in at night. I went there a little late; and the first thing I saw was a man standing up, with a few tallow candles around him, holding a negro boy, and trying to read to him the story of the Prodigal Son; and a great many of the words he could not make out, and had to skip. I thought, If the Lord can ever use such an instrument as that for His honour and glory, it will astonish me. After that meeting was over Mr. Moody said to me, 'Reynolds, I have got only one talent: I have no education, but I love the Lord Jesus Christ, and I want to do something for Him; and I want you to pray for me.' I have never ceased from that day to this, morning and night, to pray for that devoted Christian soldier. I have watched him since then, have had counsel with him, and know him thoroughly; and, for consistent walk and conversation, I have never met a man to equal him. It astounds me when I look back and see what Mr. Moody was thirteen years ago, and then what he is under God to-day—shaking Scotland to its very centre, and reaching now over to Ireland.

The last time I heard from him, his injunction was, 'Pray for me every day; pray now that God will keep me humble.'"

The ideal Sunday-school of the present day is in a spacious hall, seated with chairs, or Booth benches; the walls covered with maps or mottoes, or frescoed with texts and Scripture scenes; a piano, or organ; a blackboard; object-lesson charts; several hundred dollars' worth of light literature, and a considerable income to spend in picture-papers, lesson-leaves, teachers' journals, prizes, etc.; to say nothing of fountains, bouquets, banners, and other luxuries, designed to civilize rude sinners, while the Gospel is saving them.

But none of these things were within Mr. Moody's reach. He himself was poor, and as yet had no rich friends; but he possessed certain qualities of mind and heart by means of which he at length commanded all things needful for a great and efficient Sunday-school.

One important qualification for his work was an intense and almost womanly love for children. He never seemed happier than when in the midst of a crowd of boys and girls, with whom he romped in the wildest fashion, beating them at their own sports and games, until he won their fullest confidence, and came to be regarded by them as the biggest and jolliest boy of them all.

The first difficulty in the way was to make the acquaintance of those neglected little heathen—who, passing their lives in a constant struggle, amid kicks and blows, starvation and drunkenness, were savage and suspicious to the last degree. A Sunday-school pure and simple would not be likely to attract such children; it was useless to distribute tracts and Testaments among them, for they could not read. But Moody had taken counsel of the great apostle who used to catch unbelievers "with guile." Accordingly, he approached the enemy's works by strategy. Casting about to find some weak point favourable for his assault, he remembered that children were fond of sweets, and thereupon he invested quite a large sum of money, out of his small savings, in maple sugar, which appeared to give the largest value for the money of anything in that line; and then, with his pockets full of the missionary sugar, and his heart full of zeal and love, he proceeded to attack The Sands.

Very soon Moody was the most popular man in all that region. At first the little people would run away when he approached, but the sweetness of his manners and his gifts were sure to bring them back again; and, having disarmed the hostility which those young gutter-snipes naturally felt towards any well-dressed person, it was not difficult to induce them to attend his school.

If any one is inclined to take exception to Mr. Moody's missionary sugar, let him bethink himself of the various sweet enticements offered to more elegant sinners by the ministers and managers of fashionable congregations. Fine architecture, fresco and gilding; inlaid pulpits, and upholstered pews; three-bank organs; quartette choirs, whose music costs a dollar a stave; chimes of bells; elaborate vestments; rhetoric, poetry, and all manner of literary and social attractions, as used in the higher circles of society,—are so many arguments in favour of that missionary sugar, which, better than any of the aforementioned persuasions, was adapted to coax these young barbarians to attend the means of grace. It was an argument which even the most ignorant could understand, and by its help it is said that Moody made the acquaintance of every child within reach of his Mission ; and, through the children, he was known by almost every man and woman on The Sands.

But what was to be done with such a crowd of small ruffians, when once they were brought together in the ex-saloon? The question was one to appal a man of less faith and courage ; but he was equal to the occasion. Of one thing he felt sure : namely, that these children would enjoy Sunday-school singing; his musical friend, Mr. Trudeau, was therefore installed in the office of chorister. Mr. Stillson came also, to make himself generally useful. This was the entire organization. Moody was Constitution, Stillson and Trudeau were By-laws. Each man was superintendent in such matters as forced themselves on his attention—all three being worked to their fullest capacity, in quieting several simultaneous scuffles and fights in different corners of the room, rescuing little boys from the clutches of big ones, and keeping down the noise among this mob of children, who, between the prayers and hymns, would pull each other's hair, and black each other's eyes, in a manner which left no doubt of the strictly missionary character of the school.

It was a great blessing to Moody that he had a perfect contempt for trifles. These slight disorders among his scholars gave him little trouble. His school was a religious institution,—strictly so, intensely so. He felt certain it would help to save some of those neglected little sinners; therefore, in the midst of confusion, he was hopeful and happy. It was so much clear gain to bring them to a place where they would hear a few words of Scripture, a few Christian hymns, and a few words of godly counsel (provided the speaker had good lungs, and was not modest about using them), and a few words of prayer, which they were almost certain not to hear anywhere else.

A Sunday-school martinet would have fretted himself out of patience, and out of the school, in a very short space of time. But Moody had worked hard to bring those children together; he had spent his money to buy the sugar that coaxed them; he had promised the Lord to do his best to save them; and he had persuaded some of his friends to help him. He was committed to the enterprise before God, angels, men and women, and a good many bad children; therefore, if it took a superintendent for every boy and an assistant superintendent for every girl, that school was foreordained to go on.

CHAPTER IV.

THE NORTH MARKET MISSION.

IT was not long before the increasing crowd needed a larger room; and, by permission of Mayor Haines, the school was removed to the great hall over the old North Market. This hall was generally used on Saturday nights for a dance; and it took most of the forenoon of Sunday to sweep out the sawdust, and wash out the tobacco and beer. There were no chairs or benches, so that the school was compelled to stand, or else sit on the floor. After enduring this state of things for some time, Moody constituted himself a committee of finance, and started to raise money for seating the place—making his collections on the general principle of asking money of those whom he thought most likely to have it.

Among those to whom he applied was Mr. J. V. Farwell, already a prominent man of business. After getting his money, he inquired what Mr. Farwell was doing in the way of personal work for Christ; and, finding him not fully occupied, he invited him over to see his mission school. Knowing the quality of this man, whom he used to meet at the Sunday morning class, in the Methodist Church block, he determined to press him into service.

The next Sunday Mr. Farwell appeared as a visitor at the North Market School. The scene was a new one. All his previous Sunday-school notions were put to flight. That riotous crowd seemed to be following the example of the Israelites in the time of the Judges, with one essential difference—namely, that each one was doing what was *wrong* in his own eyes, with the evident purpose of mischievous enjoyment. The seats had not yet arrived. The school was leaning up against the walls, and scattered over the floor in ever-varying forms, like the figures in the kaleidoscope; jumping, turning somersaults, sparring, whistling, talking out loud, crying, "Papers!" "Black your boots!" "Have a shine, mister?"—from which state of confusion they were occasionally rescued by a Scripture reading from Mr. Stillson, or a song from Mr. Trudeau, or a speech from Mr. Moody; only to relapse again into clamour and uproar, before the speaker or singer was fairly through. The emotions of Mr. Farwell, on being introduced to make a speech, were vivid rather than pleasing. He ventured a few words, and only a few, lest he should weary the patience of his audience. But what was his horror, at the close of his remarks, to hear himself nominated by Moody as superintendent of the North Market Mission Sunday School!

Before he had time to object, the school had elected him with a deafening hurrah.

Many honours have fallen to that gentleman since that day; and none of them ever came more unexpectedly, were bestowed more heartily, or brought with them more embarrassment; but he accepted the office to which he was thus suddenly called, and entered at once upon its duties, which for more than six years he faithfully continued to perform. The outside work he left to his younger partner, while he managed the internal affairs of the school; sometimes adding to his other duties those of treasurer—at least, so far as to make up any deficiency in the funds.

The North Market Mission speedily became popular, partly as a means of grace, and partly as a curiosity. Before this time no mission school in the city had numbered more than one hundred and fifty; but the school of Moody, Farwell, and Company increased by such rapid strides, that in three months it was two hundred strong; in six months, three hundred and fifty; and within a year the average attendance was about six hundred and fifty; with an occasional crowd of nearly a thousand. It is estimated that about two thousand children annually passed through the school; many, of course, staying but a few weeks; but in those few weeks a revelation opened to their blinded souls which changed the whole course of their lives.

Let it not be supposed that all these children came to Sunday-school of their own accord. It was necessary to hunt them up and bring them in, one by one. In this work Moody and his friend Stillson were steadily engaged every evening in the week, from the close of business until ten and eleven o'clock at night. On Sunday morning also they made a grand excursion through The Sands, and other lost regions; from which they would return, bringing their spoils with them, in the shape of a dozen or so of the wild boys and girls they had found.

Of course a work on this scale consumed large quantities of Moody's missionary sugar; but when his funds ran low, he begged the sinews of war from his friends, which he invested, not only in this sweet attraction, but also in clothing and provisions, for the poorest of the poor, and in little luxuries for the sick, to whom he gave special attention, devoting a part of every evening to visiting and praying with them.

Not content with capturing such children as he might find in the streets—whom he would sometimes chase into alleys and cellars, up and down ladders, and over piles of lumber, for the purpose of making their acquaintance—he also searched for them in their homes, making the acquaintance of their parents also, a good many of whom followed their children into the mission, and into the kingdom of heaven.

At such times he often came across a Roman Catholic family, and sometimes narrowly escaped with a whole head. The enraged father, having previous knowledge of that heretical sugar, and being exceedingly mad at Moody for coaxing his young papists away with it,—on seeing his beaming face and sturdy form coming upstairs, or in at the door, would sometimes seize a club, and rush at him with oaths and curses. At this Moody would obey the exhortation given by Highest Authority to certain earlier missionaries: "If they persecute you in one" place, "flee ye into another." At such times, he used to say, his legs were his best friends. But though they served so well to take him out of danger, they

SCHOLARS AND TEACHERS, NORTH MARKET MISSION SCHOOL.

always brought him back into it again; till, at last, his patience and good-nature conquered all opposition. He adopted the Fabian policy, and wore out or wearied out his adversaries by constant light skirmishing, never venturing a battle; and in most cases this method was so successful that he not only overcame his enemies and captured their children for his mission, but generally won them over to be his friends.

The school presently became a wonder. Some of the leading members of prominent churches volunteered to teach classes in it, and some wealthy persons, who did not give themselves, gave of their fortune to help on the fortunes of the school. The name of one gentleman is mentioned, who would occasionally make the evening round of visits with Moody and Stillson—at which times he would provide himself with a quantity of one-dollar notes, folded separately, of which he sometimes gave away forty or fifty in a single evening, among their sick and poor parishioners.

It was not long before the city missionary, who had divided the city into districts, began to make objection to the wide range of Mr. Moody and his workers for the North Market School. But this man never could understand ecclesiastical geography. Its dividing lines, like those on all other maps, were purely imaginary; and if he crossed them freely in his search for children to teach, or sinners to save, it must be set down to the fact that, to his eyes, such lines were never visible. He would as soon have thought of marking out parishes for the sunshine, or parcelling out the air. The only authority he asked for doing good was the opportunity; and so vigorously did he use that authority, that, for a little while, he seemed in danger of monopolizing it. Neighbouring schools, working under a lower pressure, began to lose their scholars; but, being exercised by this light affliction, it worked out for them a far more exceeding weight of success. Their zeal was provoked by the brilliant example of the Market Hall Mission, which thus became a still greater blessing, by reflecting its own light and spirit into all the other mission schools of the city. Of the school at this period Mr. Stillson says, "The city missionary began to be alarmed for it, lest, being worked at such high pressure, it should some time blow up." But this fear was never realized. Mr. Moody was guilty of all sorts of vagaries, and would follow an impulse, without waiting for judgment,—frequently shooting off at a tangent from all recognised circles of propriety; but, in spite of all this, the school increased in vigour and in numbers, and, what was better, it gradually improved in order and in true religious life. Of its leader it may be said, as of Hezekiah, "And in every work that he began in the service of the house of God, and in the law, and in the commandments, to seek his God, he did it with all his heart, and prospered."

For the seventy or eighty classes there was no lack of teachers. Every Sabbath the school was visited by people from all parts of the city, attracted by its growing fame as a curiosity of grace; and from among these visitors there were many volunteers for work, so that every post was filled. But the management of such a band of teachers was a task of the utmost delicacy. Coming from different churches, with wide variety of training and experience, the strict uniformity of method now insisted on was quite out of the question. In those days there was no International Series of Sunday School Lessons, selected and wrought out, ready to the teacher's hand. But there was a book with which every teacher and scholar was supplied—namely, the New Testament; and this was the one point of uniformity in the school.

The New Testament was Moody's sheet anchor. It held his craft from drifting into any serious heresy, and kept it from being wrecked on the shoals of mere amusement, towards which so many schools are carried with the tide. A teacher might have all sorts of notions of his own; but, so long as he was willing to teach a class of such children out of the New Testament, Moody felt certain that the man or woman could do but little mischief, while the book was certain to do much good. Thus, with a great and irregular band of teachers—Methodists, Calvinists, Liberals, rich and poor, high and low, learned and unlearned—the Gospel, which was its great theme and inspiration, made the school a unit and held it close to Christ.

Safe in the New Testament as the common textbook, the school was made to depend for its further compactness upon the spirit and order of each individual class. Thus the fitness of the teachers for their work became a vital question; and when one was found to be a failure,—a discovery by no means uncommon, since this kind of teaching was the most difficult of all,—it became an immediate necessity that he should be removed. Those young Arabs of the street were wild as colts, and cunning as foxes, and were certain to run away with their teacher if they detected any weakness in him. At the same time it would have been a painful task to say to a kind-hearted Christian, "You cannot teach; you must make way for another." But Moody and his privy council hit upon a plan which brought them through every such difficulty. Scholars were permitted, on applying to the superintendent, to remove from one class to another; and being quick to find out what teachers were alive and well up to their work, they applied the doctrine of natural selection in a manner that would have made Mr. Darwin's heart glad; for it notably resulted in "The survival of the fittest." A teacher who was a failure would in two or three Sundays be left without a class; for the children had the instinct of bees for finding out where the honey was; and so, his occupation being gone, he would quietly and regretfully disappear, making room for a more fortunate successor.

Under the administration of Messrs. Moody and Farwell this principle was maintained—namely, the school is for the scholars and not the scholars for the school. The rights of every child were respected.

This unusual freedom of choice, though often abused, at length developed a spirit of pride, which helped to keep the classes in order. The school was *their* school; the teacher was *their* teacher; the superintendent was *their* superintendent; and, above all, Moody was *their* Moody. Of this latter fact they never had any doubt; and because of their absolute faith in him, more than for any other reason, they submitted to be ruled by him, helped him to find new scholars, defended him against slanders, and sometimes even suffered punishment and abuse at home, because they would attend his heretical school.

One of the larger boys came to Moody one Sunday afternoon, seeming to be in great trouble, and asking for confidential advice. It appeared that his father was a violent Roman Catholic, and a miserable drunkard besides; kind enough to his family when not in liquor, but almost certain to be drunk every Sunday, and equally certain to give his son an unmerciful flogging on his return from the North Market School. The boy, who had outgrown his wild ways, and learned something of Christian duty, had endured this treatment for a long time rather than run away from home, and leave his poor mother and his little sisters, whom he hoped some time to lead into a better way of life.

On hearing the case, Mr. Moody replied, "You must take advice of Some One who is strong,"—by which the boy at once understood that he should ask help of the Lord. This he did; and then, going home, was met at the door by his father, in a drunken rage, ready to give him the customary beating.

Deliberately taking off his coat, he said,—

"Father, you have always been kind to me when you are not in liquor: it is not my father, but whisky, that beats me every Sunday; so now I am going to fight the whisky."

The old man, by no means cooled by such a response, fell upon him with fury; but in the struggle which followed, whisky was so thoroughly beaten that from that time the father left his son to go to his mission school in peace.

But his elder brother, also a papist, took the matter in hand, and, for a change, proposed to thrash Mr. Moody, whom he had never seen, as he had lately returned to the city after a long absence; but before a convenient opportunity arrived he was taken sick with a fever, and for some time lay dangerously ill.

Among those who came to watch with him were some of the teachers of that hated North Market School; and presently, Moody himself, who sat up with him a night or two, watching for a chance to help the poor fellow's soul. On learning who the warm-hearted stranger was, all his anger passed away, and the promised beating was referred to no more.

The history of the North Market School for its six years in the hall which gave it its name is full of the proofs of God's favour, and of the faith and devotion of the men and women who sustained it. The great purpose always kept in view was the salvation of souls. To reach this result every possible means was tried. Mere literary and social advantages were never regarded as important. A free evening school was, indeed, established, where such children as pleased to attend were taught a little reading and writing; but it was believed by Moody and his brethren that the shortest road to education and refinement was the road which led to the cross of Christ and the gate of heaven. The words of the Saviour, "Seek ye first the kingdom of God and this righteousness, and all these things shall be added unto you," formed the basis of its hope and its success. If he could make Christians of these wild boys and girls, Moody believed they would make gentlemen and ladies of themselves. With this thought in view little time was spent on the geography or archæology of the Bible, but the Gospel of the Son of God, pure and simple, was impressed upon the minds of the children in every possible way. Thus, while other kindred organizations might properly be called Bible schools, the North Market Mission was, above everything else, a Gospel school. It naturally took this direction, from the spirit and experience of its leader, who was determined to know nothing among them but "Christ, and Him crucified"; a determination easy for him to carry out, for he was thoroughly converted to, and quite well acquainted with, Christ; while his other "knowledges" were, for this purpose, conveniently few and small.

His friend, Mr. Stillson, declares that during those years he does not know of Moody's owning any other book except a copy of the New Testament. No man was more hungry for learning than he, but his taste was wholly in the direction of learning how to work for Christ. A history was of interest to him chiefly as a source from which to draw illustrations of Gospel truth; a poem was very little to him unless it could be sung in his school; of the sciences and polite arts he had no knowledge whatever. But in methods of work he was largely learned; indeed, so fully was this recognised, that many profound scholars and Doctors of Divinity, though shocked by his bad rhetoric and worse grammar, came to him for instruction in the ways of reaching and saving the great

neglected mass of sinners who continually swarmed around them.

"He that winneth souls is wise," the Scriptures say; and, measured by that standard, there was not to be found among the learned laity or clergy, in the whole United States, a wiser man than the rough, impetuous leader of the North Market Mission School.

In order to bring his work to a religious focus, he established week-night prayer-meetings in the old saloon. In one respect these prayer-meetings were peculiar,—namely, they were nothing else than an assembly of people who wanted something of God, and who came together expecting to get it by asking. The going through with a set of appropriate religious exercises was to them a thing wholly unknown. They came together, a company of penitent sinners, not because they ought to come, but because they wanted to come. To this rude place, seated with rough boards placed upon empty nail-kegs, lighted by a few candles, and protected from violence by the police, came those children and older persons whose hearts the Gospel had reached, to inquire of Mr. Moody and his New Testament what they must do to be saved. There was a charming freshness in the praying and speaking at these meetings, which was just what might be expected from the previous training of the school. These inquirers believed in God, not as an "unknown and unknowable Force," but as the Maker and Governor of heaven and earth. They believed in Jesus Christ not as "a reforming Jew," but as the Son of God who came into the world to save sinners; and, though they had no clear conception of the Holy Spirit, they were greatly under His influence —going about the work of repentance and prayer for themselves, and for their friends, with the same simple directness with which they would have entered upon any other work. The best praying was that which brought the greatest blessing, no matter how rude and uncouth the language; the best exhorting, that which brought souls soonest to the Saviour.

Here Mr. Moody began to learn the true work of the Christian pastor. He was brought face to face with the sins and sorrows of immortal souls, laid open before him, for sympathy and instruction, as confidingly as he laid them before God for pardon and comfort. According to his theory, the penitent sinner might immediately become a Christian on the terms laid down by the apostle: "Believe on the Lord Jesus Christ, and thou shalt be saved."

To his mind nothing could be easier than this; and to these poor people, uninstructed in the mysteries of systematic theology, it also appeared easy. They had never heard the distinctions between intellectual faith, historic faith, and saving faith; but they did as they were taught,—reached out their dirty hands to take Christ, and attended to the washing of the hands afterwards.

It was with inexpressible joy that Moody received and instructed the inquirers who came to this little meeting. If no new cases appeared from week to week, he became anxious, as if something were going wrong. He would scan his crowd of boys and girls with the greatest eagerness, watching for signs of heavenward purpose or softening of heart; and when he found them he felt as if God owned his work, and so was happy.

The duties thus laid upon him made him increasingly sensible of his deficiency in knowledge of the Word of God. The light and comfort he might give from his own experience of grace were not enough without some appropriate text of Scripture.

Up to this time his method of reading the Bible had been to open the book at random, and begin with the first chapter that caught his eye. He had none of those helps to the study of the Scripture in the form of notes, commentaries, Bible dictionaries, and the like: he did not even own a concordance. His preparations for his work from day to day, and from Sunday to Sunday, were made on this wise;—He would go over to Mr. Stillson's lodgings, some distance from his own, and together they would have a little season of prayer for God's blessing upon the work they were about to do. Then they would go out to visit the sick, search for new scholars, read the New Testament, exhort, sing, and pray, as occasion offered; trusting to the Lord to give them words to speak.

One day Mr. Stillson, who from the first was strongly impressed that his young friend had a great career before him, said,—

"Moody, if you want to draw wine out of a cask, it is needful first to put some in. You are all the time talking, and you ought to begin to study."

To this Moody assented; and Mr. Stillson proceeded to mark out for him a course of reading, intending to assist him in enlarging his education.

Among the books selected was Müller's "Life of Trust"; But before he had fairly entered upon this short road to learning, his preceptor, through some sudden change in business matters, left the city, and returned to his home in Rochester. Thus narrowly did Moody escape becoming a bookish man.

CHAPTER V.

INCIDENTS OF THE WORK AT THE NORTH MARKET MISSION.

LEFT now to himself, he went on in his old ways, reading his Testament, telling his experience, working up the scenes of every-day life into effective exhortations and addresses, and absorbing knowledge from everybody and everything around him.

His beloved mission school went on with increasing power and interest. Nothing was left untried which could help to save these neglected people,—who, in their turn, loved and trusted him for his patient and earnest work in the Saviour's name.

The Rev. Dr. Savage, then the Western Secretary of the Boston Tract Society, gives an account of a jubilee held in an old rookery opposite Market Hall, on a certain thanksgiving night. The "old rookery" was none other than the ex-saloon, now Moody's prayer-room, which he describes as a most forlorn and wretched place, dimly lighted, and with no fire, where thirty or forty children had assembled to hold the jubilee; every one of them bearing marks of poverty, if not of actual want.

The name, jubilee, and the time, Thanksgiving evening, would naturally suggest a festival, or supper; but such a thing being quite beyond their means, Moody had appointed a kind of love-feast, at which every one was to tell what he was most thankful for.

One little fellow, who had no other relative in the world but a decrepit old grandfather, with whom he lived in the greatest poverty, had become a Christian some time before, and, like others of the children, was trying to do a little home-missionary work on his own account. When his turn came to tell what he was most thankful for, he said,—

"There was that big fellow, 'Butcher Kilroy,' who acted so bad that nobody would have him, and he had to be turned out of one class after another, till I was afraid he would be turned out of the school. It took me a long time to get him to come, and I begged for him to stay. I used to pray to Jesus every day to give him a new heart, and I felt pretty sure He would if we didn't turn him out. By-and-by Butcher Kilroy began to want to be a Christian, and now he is converted; and that is what makes this Thanksgiving the happiest one in all my life."

Mr. Stillson mentions another desperate case, of a boy they found on The Sands. He was a sort of chief of a gang of gutter-snipes, who, partly because they admired him and partly because they were afraid of him, allowed him to be a perfect tyrant over them. It was a long time before they could get near enough to this young ruffian to speak to him; but even he at last was caught with the missionary sugar, and invited to come to the mission school.

It was a cold day in February; but the only garment he had was a man's old overcoat, so ragged that it had to be stitched together around his body, giving him the appearance of being sewed up in a great dirty bag. A big pair of shoes, and papers wrapped around his legs, completed his winter costume. In this outfit he made his appearance one Sunday, at the door of the North Market School. Moody, catching sight of him, gave him his hand, pulled him in, and, marching with him the whole length of the room, gave him a place in a class, with the same kindness and attention he would have shown to the best dressed boy on the North Side.

At sight of this wretched waif, a stranger visiting the school was moved to tears. After the exercises were over, he took him to his house, and gave him a full suit of clothes belonging to his own son.

The wild lad, thus civilized in appearance, continued to attend the school; and at length, one by one, brought all his followers with him. "That lad," said Mr. Stillson, "is now a Christian gentleman, in receipt of a large salary, and superintendent of a Sunday-school in one of our large cities."

Many were the exciting scenes through which Moody passed, as month after month he continued the work of visitation. Sometimes he was "shamefully entreated"; and on more than one occasion he was actually in danger of becoming a martyr to the cause. One Sunday morning he was visiting some Roman Catholic families for the purpose of bringing their children to his school, when a powerful man, who had sworn to kill him, sprang upon him with a heavy club, before he knew he was in danger. It was a run for dear life. The Sands were in an uproar. Some of the papists cheered on their man, knowing if he caught the heretic it would be all over with him; while those who were friendly dared not come to his rescue, for fear of his wrathful pursuer. But it was all lost labour to drive Moody away from a place where there were any children whom he felt ought to come to his school. On this occasion, as on others, he escaped by being very swift-footed; but he was sore pressed by his enemy, who seemed really in hopes of putting an end to his heretical labours by putting an end to his life. Not at all discouraged, he went back the next Sunday, and kept on going again and again, till at last his gentleness and patience disarmed his adversary, who gave him no further trouble.

In his explorations one Saturday evening, he found a jug of whisky in a house, which the men had brought home to drink next day. They were all away from home; but Moody gave the women a rousing temperance lecture, and persuaded them to let him empty the whisky into the street. Early on Sunday afternoon he returned, as he had promised, to take the children with him whom the women had consented to send to his school. But the men of the house were lying in wait to give him a pounding. He had touched them at a tender point, and they thirsted for revenge. The situation was desperate. One of them had stepped between him and the door before he was aware of it, and all were about to pounce upon him, when Moody arrested proceedings on this wise,—

"See here, now, my men, if you are going to whip

me for spilling the whisky, you might at least give me time to say my prayers."

So unusual a proposal attracted their attention, and they agreed to let him pray before they thrashed him, thinking it would add just so much to their sport. Moody at once dropped upon his knees and began to pray. Such praying those rough fellows had never heard. At first they were astonished, then they were interested, then they were softened; and when he had finished his prayer they gathered around him, gave him their hands, declared he was a good fellow, —and in a few minutes Moody was triumphantly marching towards the North Market Hall, with all the children of the house at his heels.

No class of persons was neglected, except those who had no need of attention. The great majority of those people, whatever other qualifications they lacked for being saved, had at least this one—they were sinners. The worst as well as the best who came to the great school, or the little prayer-meeting, found Mr. Moody, or some of his workers, holding the door open for them, and inviting them to enter the kingdom of heaven. Among his scholars were the daughters of prostitutes and keepers of brothels, who begged him to take them away from the place in which they seemed destined to certain ruin; and, in more instances than one, he has sent them to places of safety, in which they have become honoured members of Christian families.

No matter how repulsive the person might be, Moody was always ready to help him; he seemed to take the most interest in those who were most wretched and needy. Instances enough to fill volumes might be given of his successful work for those who had always been considered beyond the reach of grace and salvation.

Among the worst places in this field was a sailors boarding-house, which was continually haunted by a rough, quarrelsome crowd. This place, vile and dangerous to the last degree, Moody and his friend ventured to enter. They were set upon, and threatened with broken heads if they did not leave immediately; but remembering that "a soft answer turneth away wrath," they gently replied that they meant no harm, and, as proof of their kind intentions, offered to sing a song. This task, of course, fell to the lot of Stillson; for Moody never could sing a note: and he immediately struck up the hymn commencing—

"O how happy are they
Who the Saviour obey,
And have laid up their treasures above!"

The crowd listened to the singing with evident enjoyment; it was better singing than they were accustomed to. When the hymn was finished, Moody followed with prayer. From that day they were privileged characters in that house, and were held in high respect by all the inmates. They captured the children of the keeper of the den for the North Market Mission,—every one of whom was afterwards brought to Christ.

It was not often that their visits to saloons resulted so favourably as in the following case. Going into a drinking den one Saturday night, when the carousal was at its highest, they asked permission to leave some religious papers for the men who were drinking at the little tables around the room. This being done, they entered into conversation with the keeper of the place, and presently drew out the fact that his parents were Christian people. The question instantly followed, " Do they know you are selling liquor ? "

The man hesitated, and seemed deeply affected. They gave him a kindly word, and then bade him good-night. But they had not gone far before one said to the other,—

"We have neglected our duty ; let us go back and pray with that man."

They immediately turned back, re-entered the saloon, begged the keeper's pardon for having neglected to pray with him, and, kneeling there in the sawdust, Moody offered a prayer which seemed the direct inspiration of the Holy Ghost. Mr. Stillson says,—

"I never heard Moody pray like that before; it seemed as if the baptism of the Holy One was upon him."

Two weeks afterwards one of them met the man in the street, who informed him that he had given up the saloon business, had left off drinking, and would die in the poor-house rather than sell any more liquor.

The most miserable of the many wretched families they met in all their visitation was one which they found one Sunday morning in an attic. The husband, who was just on the verge of *delirium tremens*, had become half idiotic from drink, while the wife and children were half dead from starvation. The first thing done was to give them something to eat. Next they held a temperance meeting, and persuaded the man to sign the pledge, a copy of which they usually carried with them; and by way of impressing it upon his stupid senses, they made him kneel down and place his hand upon the pledge, while they prayed to God to give him strength to keep it. The next Sunday the whole family, decently clad, came to the mission school.

An evening or two afterwards, passing by the same house, the man hailed them from his attic window, and threw them down a piece of silver, saying, "I believe in that Sunday-school, and I want to take a little stock in it."

On Mr. Stillson's return to Chicago, six years afterwards, he was saluted by a gentlemanly stranger, who proved to be none other than the poor man who had thrown him the money out of the attic window—now a prosperous man of business, with a beautiful home of his own, and himself a leading member in a thriving church.

One of Moody's strong points was his ability to keep every one around him hard at work. His method may be described in a single word—*leadership.* He was not skilful in giving minute directions, but he was always ahead, and they learned to follow him, and to do as he did. He was as ready to go down, as to go up, to find and save a sinner; indeed, he was always ready to go anywhere or do anything which gave promise of such a result. It was impossible to be with him and not feel the contagion of his energy and faith. Scholars as well as teachers caught it from him, and began to be missionaries on their own account, searching out and bringing in new scholars, and keeping the enthusiasm of the school always at fever heat.

Prizes were sometimes offered for the largest number of new scholars brought in. On one occasion he presented the most successful young missionary with a pet lamb,—a somewhat unusual gift at a Sunday-school, but one which served as a striking and valuable object-lesson, which Moody was not slow to use.

Among the band of young converts, which all the time increased around him, was a little girl, whose father owned a small vessel, with which he freighted lumber. Having given her own heart to the Saviour, she tried to persuade her father to do the same. But he was a man having no taste for religion, though he was very fond of the child—whom he took with him on a certain voyage, during which she tried in vain to establish a prayer-meeting in the little cabin, and to convert some of the crew. On arriving at the lumber camp, this little missionary commenced a Sunday-school, as nearly as possible like the North Market Mission. Not content with this, and hearing of another encampment of woodcutters similar to their own, she opened a second school among them also. During the severe northern winter she presided personally over both these institutions; riding on horseback through the woods every Sabbath, after the manner of the early Methodist pioneers.

It may be supposed that these two schools in the woods were of a very simple character, since the little girl herself was the entire force of officers and teachers; and all the library and literature in use among them was her own little copy of the New Testament. The results of her labour cannot now be given; but it is easy to imagine the tender interest with which those rough woodsmen sat at the feet of their child-missionary, charmed by her Christian courage, and cheered by her simple faith.

The lumber season being over, the little vessel started for Chicago. During the voyage a terrible storm arose, disabling the craft, and driving her rapidly toward a lee shore. The crew being completely exhausted, and expecting in a few minutes to be drowned, begged the little girl to pray for them, —which she did, with the greatest composure. When she had told the good Lord all about them, and asked Him to take them out of their danger, if He thought best, and, above all things, to forgive their sins and make them ready for heaven, she began, in a clear, sweet voice, to sing that little Sunday-school hymn,—

> "We are joyously voyaging over the main,
> Bound for the evergreen shore."

With the song new strength and hope seemed to come to the arms and hearts of the crew; and renewing their efforts to weather the point which threatened their destruction, and aided, perhaps, by some slight change in the wind or abatement of the storm, the little craft weathered the rocks of the headland close enough to toss a biscuit ashore, and then swung out safely on the open course for home.

The visit of President Lincoln was a notable fact in the history of the school.

Mr. Farwell, hearing that the President-elect was in the city, and being all the time on the look-out for something to keep up the spirit of the school, called at his hotel, and obtained from Mrs. Lincoln a promise, on the President's behalf, to visit the mission on the following Sunday. At the appointed time a carriage was sent for him, to the house of a prominent citizen, who had made a dinner-party for his distinguished guest. On being told that the carriage had come, the great man left his half-finished dinner, took a hasty leave of the elegant company, and started for the North Market Hall.

As they drove along, Mr. Lincoln said that talking to Sunday-schools was out of his line, and requested that he should not be asked to make a speech. But on his being introduced as the President-elect of the United States of America, the enthusiasm of those wild embryo citizens broke out beyond all bounds; and, yielding to their rough persuasions, Mr. Lincoln, for the first and only time in his life, made a Sunday-school address. He told them they were in the right place, and learning the right things. What they learned out of the Bible would certainly be of use to them, if they practised it; and their chances of coming to be honourable men and women, he said, would very much depend upon the attention they gave to the lessons which were taught them in that Sunday-school.

In all the address there was no word about religion, —for it was not until overwhelmed with the cares of office, and heart-broken with the horrors of war, that the great man himself learned what religion was; and he was too honest to speak in that presence, or any other, on a subject he did not understand.

A few months after, Fort Sumpter was fired upon; and when the call was issued for an army of seventy-five thousand men, about sixty of the big rough boys who listened to him that day answered to the President's call. They had seen the man; his fatherly face and lofty form was still before them, and his calm, earnest words still echoed in their hearts: it was *their* President who was calling for them; and they were quite ready to go.

To keep such an assembly in order was of course impossible; though a degree of confusion which would have been fatal to an ordinary Sunday-school was no serious objection here. But sometimes a wild young barbarian would make his appearance, defying all authority, and actually disturbing the meeting!

There was one big fellow in particular who insisted on bringing his street manners into the schoolroom. All kinds of moral suasion seemed to be wasted on him. He was too big to be frightened, and too ignorant to be shamed. After bearing with him for a long time, during which he continued to grow worse instead of better, Moody and his friends began to fear that they had at last found one boy for whom nothing could be done. A great many evil spirits had been cast out by the influence of that school, but this one seemed determined to stay. To turn a scholar away as hopelessly bad would be a disgraceful confession of failure; besides, it was contrary to all their ideas of the Gospel to shut this young ruffian out from the means of grace, when he was in such evident need of them.

A solemn council was held one Sunday, but no one could think of any new method of reaching this desperate case. All the week it lay heavy on Moody's mind. The next Sabbath the big fellow appeared, more uproarious than ever;—there was actual danger of his breaking up the school.

On this memorable day Mr. Moody determined to try the last remedy. His ample physical endowment for missionary work has already been mentioned, —of which on this day he made a very effective use. Coming suddenly upon the fellow, in the middle of the crowded hall, he seized him with both hands, fairly lifted him off his legs, carried him into a little ante-room, locked the door, and proceeded to apply the treatment recommended by Solomon. This was by no means an easy task, for the culprit was as strong and active and savage as a wolf. The noise of the struggle awakened the most lively interest of the school, and by way of diversion Mr. Farwell started a song. Thus on the two sides of that bolted door two widely different means of grace were in simultaneous operation.

In due course of time Moody and his pupil emerged from the ante-room, both greatly flushed, and one completely subdued.

"It was hard work," said Moody; "but I think we have saved him."

Only a little while ago Mr. Farwell met this very

boy, now grown to a man, at the noon prayer-meeting. They recognised each other, and heartily agreed that Moody was right in applying desperate remedies for desperate diseases.

After that his school was no more disturbed by such ruffians. He had shown a new claim to their admiration and respect. Order thus enforced became sacred in the opinion of all.

A lad—the one nicknamed "Indian" in the picture—coming into the school one day, found a raw recruit sitting with his cap on. Instantly he drew it off, and hit the offender a blow between the eyes which laid him sprawling on the floor. "I'll learn you better than to wear your hat in this school," said he; and then he passed quietly to his place, feeling the high satisfaction of having done his duty.

One of Moody's friends reported a family to him where there were several children who were "due" at the North Market School, but whose father was a notorious infidel rum-seller, and would not let them come.

The missionary at once called upon him; but as soon as he made known his errand he was obliged to "get out of that place" very quickly, in order to save his head. Again and again he called, only to be driven away with curses and blasphemies. "I would rather my son should be a thief, and my daughter a harlot, than have you make fools and Christians of them over there at your Sunday-school," said the desperate man. But still Moody would not give up the case.

One day, finding the man in a little better humour than usual, he asked him if he had ever read the New

Testament,—to which the publican replied that he had not, and on his part inquired if Moody had ever read Paine's "Age of Reason." Finding he had never done so, the man proposed to read the Testament if he would read the "Age of Reason." To this Moody at once agreed.

"He had the best of the bargain; but it gave me a chance to call again to bring him the book," said Moody.

After wading through that mass of infidel abominations, he called on the publican again, to see how he got on with the Testament; but found him full of objections and hot for debate.

"See here, young man," said he; "you are inviting me and my family to go to meeting: now you may have a meeting here if you like."

"What! will you let me preach here in your saloon?"

"Yes."

"And will you bring in your family, and let me bring in the neighbours?"

"Yes. But mind, you are not to do all the talking. I and my friends will have something to say."

"All right. You shall have forty-five minutes, and I will have fifteen."

The time for the meeting was set, but when Moody reached the place he found that the company had removed to a larger house in the neighbourhood, where a great crowd of atheists, blasphemers, and wild characters in great variety, were waiting for a chance to make mincemeat of the young missionary, and use up the New Testament for ever.

"You shall begin," said Moody.

Upon this they began to ask him questions.

"No questions!" said he. "I haven't come to argue with you, but to preach Christ to you. Go on and say what you like, and then I will speak."

Then they began to talk among themselves; but it was not long before they quarrelled over their own different unbeliefs, so that what began as a debate was in danger of ending in a fight.

"Order! Your time is up," said Moody. "I am in the habit of beginning my addresses with prayer. Let us pray."

"Stop! stop!" said one. "There's no use in your praying. Besides, your Bible says there must be 'two agreed' if there is to be any praying; and you are all alone."

Without attempting to correct this false quotation, Moody replied that perhaps some of them might feel like praying before he got through; and so he opened his heart to God.

When he had finished, a little boy who had been converted in the Mission School, and had come with his friend to this strange meeting, began to pray. His childish voice and simple faith at once attracted the closest attention. As he went on telling the Lord all about those wicked men, and begging Him to help them to believe in Jesus Christ, the Holy Ghost fell upon the assembly. A great solemnity came over those hard-hearted infidels and scoffers; there was not a dry eye in the room. Pretty soon they began to be frightened. They rushed out, some by one door and some by the other—did not stop to hear a word of the sermon, but fled from the place as if it had been haunted.

As a result of this meeting, Moody captured all the old infidel's children for his Sunday-school; and, a little while after, the man himself stood up in the noonday prayer-meeting, and begged them to pray for his miserable soul.

Striking out in all directions, taking no thought of the prejudices or passions of those he met, but urging them all to come at once to Christ, and to the North Market Mission, it was impossible but that he should make a good many enemies. One old Roman Catholic woman, whose children he was inviting to his Sunday-school, seized a butcher's knife and rushed out to kill him. But he easily got away.

Three ruffians, who had threatened him with a beating, came into his prayer-room one night just after the meeting was over, when there was no one present but himself and a lad. Knowing their errand, he invited them to sit down till he had gathered up his hymnbooks and Testaments, at the same time motioning the lad to leave.

Unlike his first place of meeting, this room was lighted with gas, a single jet of which was burning. Towards this he made his way, picking up his books as he went along; and then, as quick as a flash, he turned out the light, sprang over the benches in the darkness, and was off before his enemies suspected his design.

Such slight annoyances as these, however, soon ceased to disturb his mind. He became accustomed to them. But what did really worry him was the

Catholic boys disturbing his meetings and breaking the windows of the place in which they were held.

When the strain on his patience came to be too severe, Moody determined to strike at the root of the matter; and accordingly went to Bishop Duggan, the Romish prelate of Chicago, and laid his grievance before him. He told the bishop that he was trying to do good, in a part of the city which everybody else had neglected; and that it was a shame that the members of the bishop's church should break the windows of his schoolroom.

The zeal and boldness of the man surprised and delighted the bishop; who promised that the lambs of his flock should hereafter be duly restrained. Moody, thus encouraged, went on to say that he often came upon sick people who were Roman Catholics; he should be very glad to pray with them and relieve them, but they were so suspicious of him that they would not allow him to come near them. Now, if the bishop would give him a good word to those people, it would help him amazingly in his work of charity.

Such a request from a heretical Protestant was probably never made of a Catholic bishop before. But he very kindly replied that he should be most happy to give the recommendation if Mr. Moody would only join the Catholic Church; telling him at the same time he seemed to be too good and valuable a man to be a heretic.

"I am afraid that would hinder me in my work among the Protestants," said Moody.

"Not at all," answered the bishop.

"What! do you mean to say that I could go to

the noon prayer-meeting, and pray with all kinds of Christian people—Baptists, Methodists, Presbyterians, all together—just as I do now?"

"Oh yes," replied the bishop; "if it were necessary, you might do that."

"So, then, Protestants and Catholics can pray together, can they?"

"Yes."

"Well, bishop, this is a very important matter, and ought to be attended to at once. No man wants to belong to the true Church more than I do. I wish you would pray for me right here, that God would show me His true Church, and help me to be a worthy member of it."

Of course the prelate could not refuse; so they kneeled down together, and the bishop prayed very lovingly for the heretic, and when he had finished, the heretic began to pray for the bishop.

From that day to the day of his death Bishop Duggan and Mr. Moody were good friends. The bishop made no progress in converting him, it is true; but he stopped his wild young parishioners from breaking the prayer-room windows; and if only Moody would have joined the Church of Rome there is no telling to what high dignities he might have come!

This incident was published recently in London, and a Catholic priest who read it called on Mr. Moody, and actually laboured with him for a long time, with the utmost zeal and earnestness, in the hope that he might be persuaded into the Church of Peter and Mary.

"If you would only join the true Church," said the priest, "you would be the greatest man in England."

But, as may easily be supposed, this kind of argument made no impression upon a man who is more honoured in bringing thousands of lost sinners to Christ than he would be by a seat in the chair of St. Peter himself.

According to his idea, it is of little consequence whether a man is Catholic or Protestant, so long as he is not truly converted; and, as will be seen hereafter, in the account of his work in Ireland, penitent sinners of both these great classes are alike invited to the blessings of salvation, and come, under his ministry, to an experience of grace by the same simple faith in Christ.

CHAPTER VI.

MOODY JOINS THE YOUNG MEN'S CHRISTIAN ASSOCIATION.—THE END OF HIS BUSINESS CAREER.

THE great revival of 1857-8 led to organizing the Young Men's Christian Association of Chicago. Like many other similar bodies, it was largely made up of elderly persons, who managed its affairs for the benefit of the young men till they should be able to manage them for themselves.

Its first important work was the establishment of a daily noon prayer-meeting, after the manner of the Fulton Street prayer-meeting in New York; which, during the winter and spring, was very well attended. But after a while the revival impetus was lost, and the meetings grew smaller and smaller, till at last they seemed likely to die. From the first Moody had made himself conspicuous in these meetings by his blunt manners and bold attacks upon fashionable sins, such as tippling, the use of tobacco, going to the theatre, playing billiards, and other loaferish games. He was very severe against professors of religion who wish to enjoy as many of the pleasures of sin as possible, without spoiling their hopes of heaven—Christians who are so nearly like the people of the world that, except on Sunday, it is very hard to tell the difference.

On this account he came to be looked upon with disfavour. Many sensitive people left off attending the noon prayer-meetings for fear of this bold brother, in whose eyes sin was sin wherever it might be found, and who was so insensible to the dignities of wealth, fashion, station, and age, that no offender was safe from being held up on the point of his spear.

But Moody was eminently fit for the kingdom of heaven in this respect: viz., having once put his hand to the plough, he never looked back. Therefore the coldness of some of his brethren produced no discouragement in his mind. A man who had achieved such success in the North Market Mission, which had been started against the advice of every clergyman in the neighbourhood, was not likely to be troubled by criticisms on his rhetoric or his manners.

The waning interest in the noon prayer-meeting roused him to new efforts on its behalf. When the attendance fell to half a dozen he was one of the six; and when there were but three he was one of the three,--the other two very likely being his good friends J. V. Farwell and B. F. Jacobs.

One day, all these brethren being out of town, nobody went to the prayer-meeting but one old Scotchwoman. This excellent person set great store by the noon meeting, and, when no one else appeared, she determined to hold it herself rather than have it fail even for a single day. So, after waiting a long time, she put on her spectacles, went forward to the leader's desk, read a passage of Scripture, talked it over to herself, for the comfort of her old heart, and then offered prayer for the languishing meeting, and for the outpouring of the Holy Spirit upon it, and upon the city. Prayer being ended, she sung a psalm, and, the time having thus been all improved, she went comfortably home, feeling that she had done her duty, gained a blessing, and saved the noon prayer-meeting from utter extinction.

On relating her solitary experience, some of the brethren were deeply impressed by it. Mr. Moody at once set about the business of bringing in recruits; and so well did he succeed, that very soon there was a large and regular attendance, and the meeting began to be marked with the presence of the Spirit of the Lord.

All this time he had steadily pursued his purpose of making his fortune in business. His energy had secured for him an increase of salary and a percentage on his sales. The same tactics which he used so successfully in the Young Men's Christian Association and the Sunday-school worked equally well in the store. He was always on the outlook for buyers; he was never idle. Other salesmen in his line complained that he captured their customers, and pushed himself forward, regardless of established business etiquette. But, for the life of him, he never could see why a country merchant, with money in his pocket to be invested in boots and shoes, was not the rightful customer of the first man who could persuade him to buy; so he paid no more attention to the traditional courtesies of business than he did to denominational lines in religion. Nevertheless, his employers, during all his business life, testify to his rigid truthfulness and his earnest Christian character, though he was so ambitious of success as to be liable to frequent errors in judgment. One of them says:—

"We regarded him as an excellent salesman, but a poor judge of credits. In one particular instance he sold goods, amounting to over two hundred dollars, to a man whom we found rated as 'doubtful' in the Mercantile Directory, and therefore refused to send the goods. But Moody at once came to the rescue of his customer, declared him to be 'as good as the Bank of England,' and offered to be responsible for the bill. On this we sent the goods; and when the money was due, sure enough it was Moody who paid it."

Another of his old employers, in speaking of his last year in business, says:—

"His habits were economical, and he might have saved money if he had not spent so much on his Mission. I have seen as many as twenty children come into the store at once, to be fitted out with shoes."

Of course all the money for this purpose did not come out of his moderate earnings; but what he did not give himself he obtained from others for this purpose, and thus a great deal of his time, as well as money, was spent on his Mission School.

During such hours as he devoted to business he gave himself up to it with the greatest interest. One gentleman says:—

"He would never sit down in the store, to chat or read the paper, as the other clerks did when there were no customers; but as soon as he had served one buyer he was on the look-out for another; if none appeared, he would start off to the hotels or depôts, or walk the streets, in search of one. He would sometimes stand on the side-walk in front of his place of business, looking eagerly up and down for a man who had the appearance of a merchant from the country; and some of his fellow-clerks were accustomed laughingly to say, 'There is the spider again, watching for a fly.'"

He was silent and preoccupied in manner, when not closely engaged in business; and seemed to have an undercurrent of thought concerning his Mission School, into which he instinctively fell at every moment of leisure. His business neighbours seem to have thought him unsocial, except those who, like him, were interested in Christian work; but with his friends at the Young Men's Christian Association, and at the Mission, he was reckoned the very soul of good fellowship.

After two years with his old friend Wiswall, he entered the house of Mr. C. N. Henderson, who had become acquainted with him at his Mission, and had taken great interest in him and his work. He now became a commercial traveller, making long excursions into the country; but, to whatever distance his travels might lead him, he was sure to be at home every Sunday. This large amount of extra travel—for he was only allowed his expenses in returning once a month—would have been a serious matter for his slender purse, but for the kindness of his friend Colonel Hammond, the distinguished Railway Manager, who at that time was superintendent of the Chicago, Burlington, and Quincy railroad. The Colonel especially delighted to clear his brain of business, and warm his great and tender heart, by helping Moody in his school on Sunday afternoons; and, finding that his presence was essential to its success, he gave his young friend a free pass over the lines of his road, to bring him home three Saturdays out of the four.

On the death of his good friend Henderson, Moody at once removed to the house of Messrs. Buel, Hill, and Granger, with whom he remained about a year. During all this time he was more and more a missionary and less and less a merchant, until, not suddenly, but by degrees, he came to be so full of his religious work as to lose all interest in everything else.

This was his last connection with the world of business. Following the leadings of the Holy Spirit, whereby he had now become dead to the world, he gave up his long-cherished hope of making his fortune, and thenceforth devoted himself to the work of saving souls.

"I met him one day," says Mr. Hill, "soon after he left our house, and said to him, 'Moody, what are you doing?'

"'I am at work for Jesus Christ,' was the reply.

"His answer shocked me a little at first; but on thinking it over, I felt that it was a fair statement of the facts in the case. That was just what he was doing; and his work for the Lord was just as real and as vigorous as it had always been for his other employers.

"He left our house," says Mr. Hill, "under the

pleasantest circumstances, having maintained his Christian character unblemished; and we all bade him God-speed in the work to which we believe he was called."

Mr. C. M. Henderson, the nephew and successor of Mr. C. N. Henderson, and clerk with him during his uncle's life, speaks of Moody thus:—

"For fifteen years since Mr. Moody left us, I have watched him, assisted him, and believed in him."

Having bidden the last good-bye to business, he said to his friend Mr. Jacobs,—

"I have decided to give God all my time."

"But how are you going to live?" asked his friend.

"God will provide for me, if He wishes me to keep on, and I shall keep on till I am obliged to stop," was Moody's reply.

That resolution has never been broken. From that day to this he has never received a salary from any society or individual, or engaged in any business or speculation. God has provided for him and his family; sometimes, indeed, sorely trying his faith, and bringing him even in sight of actual want, but never suffering him to come quite into it. He had laid by a small sum of money out of his earnings, a part of which he invested for future use, reserving about a thousand dollars to pay his first year's expenses. He was now the happiest man in Illinois. He was rich; he was free; his hands and heart were full of work for Christ; he could devote as much time as he chose to his Mission, week-days as well as Sundays, and still do something for his second love—the Young Men's Christian Association.

MR. MOODY'S MISSIONARY PONY.

Not to lighten his labours, but only to increase their amount, he invested part of his thousand dollars in a pony.

Recognising his pre-eminent ability in that direction, the Young Men's Christian Association had appointed him Chairman of the Visiting Committee to the sick and to strangers. In the duties of this office he scoured the city in all directions; and very soon Moody on his pony became a familiar sight, especially in the regions of The Sands, the Association Rooms, and the North Market Hall. An old resident on the North Side, who was familiar with him in those days, declares that he would chase the wild small-fry up the streets and down the alleys, and; after a Sunday morning's search for new scholars, would emerge from some dirty lane, or court, his pony literally covered with ragged urchins, followed by others of the same sort, holding on by the tail, catching by the stirrups, or clinging to each other's rags; and these he would march in grand procession down to the North Market Sunday School.

The thousand dollars, which had seemed so large to him, were soon consumed by the Mission, the Association, and the various works of charity which multiplied on his hands. The rest of his small fortune took some kind of wings and flew away; and, before long, he found himself obliged, like Müller, whose life was one of the few books he had read, to rely solely on the promise, "Trust in the Lord and do good; so shalt thou dwell in the land, and verily thou shalt be fed."

The increasing attendance at the noon prayer-meeting had occasioned its removal to a large back room, in the Methodist Church block. To this place Moody removed his residence,—that is, removed himself. Having no longer any money, he determined fully to test the question whether God would really take care of him in his new work. At length he was brought to the necessity of sleeping on the benches of the prayer-room, and living on crackers and cheese. But he kept on with his work all the same. He collected considerable sums of money for the poor, and for the various works of charity and religion carried on by the Association; but he would not use a penny of it for himself, because not given for that specific purpose.

Under these privations a faith less firmly fixed on God must have begun to fail. But the Lord had not forgotten His servant, who, like Peter of old, had "left all and followed Him"; He was preparing a confirmation of His promise, "And all things whatsoever ye shall ask in prayer, believing, ye shall receive."

In the days when the noon prayer-meeting languished, and was ready to die, a Mr. Field, from Wisconsin, came to Chicago to perfect a certain mechanical invention. He was one of the recruits who rallied to its standard in that crisis of the battle; and, being "full of faith and of the Holy Ghost," he became at once a valuable helper in the work of the Association, and also connected himself with the North Market School.

For many years he had suffered from a disease in one of his legs: it had become stiff and crooked, and thus practically shorter than the other—obliging him to walk with a crutch, or cane; but the work of the Mission so absorbed him that, forgetting his lameness, he searched the highways and byways, after the fashion of his leader, till excessive use aggravated the disease, and he began to suffer great pain. Becoming alarmed, he applied to a physician one Friday evening, who appointed an examination of the case for the following Monday morning.

On Sunday it was noticed that Mr. Field came to the school without his cane. At the close of the exercises he took Mr. Moody and Mr. Farwell up to his room, bounding up the stairs two steps at a time, and told them his wonderful experience, as follows:—

"You know how lame I have been, and that my leg had become so painful that I had decided to go to a doctor. Last night I crept out to the nearest bath-rooms, and returned to bed in great distress. While I lay there, the idea seemed impressed upon me that the Lord could cure me as well as the doctor. I called to mind how He healed the man sick with the palsy; and I said to myself, 'I will ask Him to cure me in the same way.' Committing my case wholly to the Lord, I soon fell asleep; and dreamed that I went to the surgeon, as he had appointed, and that he cut open my leg, performed some operation which I did not comprehend, and immediately closed the wound again—not hurting me in the least, or even leaving a scar.

"My first thought, on awaking in the morning, was that all the pain was gone. The lame leg felt strangely well. Throwing off the bedclothes, I was astonished to find it straightened, so as to be of equal length with the other. Leaping from the bed, I found I could use it with freedom ; and, remembering my dream, I began to praise God for answering my prayer and working on me a miracle of healing.

"While I thought upon this wonderful experience, I observed that the muscles of the leg were still shrunken, as before. Then I said to myself, 'There must be some mistake; this cannot be God's work, for when He does anything He does it thoroughly and well.' But, presently, I remembered that it is not God's plan to do for us what we can do for ourselves. Those muscles had withered from disuse; by using them they would become full and strong, like the others. Then all doubt departed ; and I have called you to join me in praising God, who is able to save people in these days just as He did in the days of His flesh."

"Since then," says Mr. Farwell, "he has walked upon two good legs, like any other man ; and the shrunken muscles, by means of proper exercise, have, as he expected, returned to their normal proportions."

This sight of God's healing hand on the body of his friend came, like a vision of light and hope, to cheer the heart which was almost faltering, and to strengthen the hands which were beginning to hang down. It was evident that God did not forget His people: prayer was still a power; the promises still held good; and, in the strength of this vision, Moody seemed to overleap all difficulties,—he reached out his hand to grasp the hand of the Lord. Presently, without a word from him, some of his friends began to wonder how he was living; and, finding out the poverty of his bed and board, they insisted on supplying him with abundant comforts of life.

So it was evident that the Lord still intended him to "keep on."

Mr. S. A. Kean, for the last fifteen years treasurer of the Chicago Young Men's Christian Association, says:—

"Moody found a congenial field of labour in the Association. When we joined, it had but few members; and, though it was called a Young Men's Association, it was composed and managed almost entirely by middle-aged or elderly men. As a consequence, its methods and policy were quiet and conservative. Moody's advent among them was like a stiff northwest breeze. His zeal and devotion were the life and hope of the Association; but he shocked the nice sense of propriety of some of these gentlemen by carrying its work among a class of people who had hitherto been neglected, under the impression that its proper line of effort was among the higher classes of young men.

"Under Moody's leadership the Young Men's Christian Association became, like the North Market Mission, a free and popular institution,—extending its influence to all classes of society, and bringing the cultured and wealthy to the assistance of the ignorant and the poor.

"Mr. Moody was fertile in schemes and expedients for raising money for the Lord's work; but of the many tens of thousands of dollars which he secured for the Association, he received nothing whatever for himself.

"He always refused a salary, saying it would embarrass him, and limit his freedom to go at a moment's notice wherever the Lord might call him. I was treasurer of the Association from the time of his first connection with it; and I do not remember* to have paid him a dollar, either for his services or the expenses incidental to his work. Neither do I remember any appropriation being made for his assistance, though he often needed and always deserved it."

To his friends, who sometimes blamed him for his neglect of his worldly interests, he would say,—

"God is rich, and I am working for Him."

His favourite text of Scripture was, "This one thing I do; forgetting those things which are behind, and reaching forth unto those things which are before, I press toward the mark, for the prize of the high calling of God in Christ Jesus."

It must not be inferred from this that his whole life thereafter was one of privation. His faith was severely tried again and again; but, taking the years together, the Lord supplied His servant comfortably, and sometimes bountifully. His life of faith became a rest and a luxury to him; for, being absolutely sure of his daily bread, all care for the morrow was banished, and, with a single eye and a perfect heart, he was able to give himself to the work of the Lord.

It was not long before the Young Men's Christian Association began to make itself felt in all the mission work of the city. Moody, the acknowledged chief in this department, devised a system whereby each mission school should be visited by, and make

* Mr. Kean is obliged to speak from memory, as all the Young Men's Christian Association books were burned in the great fire.

reports to, the Association; and also for bringing it under the care and patronage of some strong church and congregation. This plan secured two benefits: the feeble missions were strengthened and encouraged, and the churches and their home schools were aroused to new activity.

Another good result from the plan of the Association was the development of a great deal of lay talent. Hitherto, by far the larger part of the work of the churches, had been left to clerical hands. The ministry was generally understood to be a special and exclusive office.

To this rule Moody was a notable exception.

While yet a man of business, as we have already seen, the most important spiritual work of the pastorate fell to his hands; and it is safe to say that he was the minister of Christ to more souls and bodies than any ordained clergyman in the city. Certain eminent divines regarded him as an intruder into the holy office; the Young Men's Christian Association appeared to them as a sort of fifth wheel to a coach, or, worse than that, a harmful diversion of money and labour from the old-established, traditional channels. Some of the lay brethren attained a skill in explaining the Scriptures, and a power of exhortation, which was dangerously similar to preaching; and, if this were permitted to go on, who could tell how long it might be before the Association would attempt to set itself up as a new denomination?

On the other hand, the brethren of the Association felt that the Church had crystallized around certain forms, and that some new means must be brought into use to do that work among the poor and the outcast which the Church was leaving undone. Their success in bringing into Christ's kingdom large numbers of persons who had seemed to be utterly reprobate caused a great deal of astonishment, and stirred up sluggish Christians to duty. Like the influence of the North Market Mission on other Sunday-schools, the Association became a blessing to all the evangelical churches in the city; and at length it was able to command the confidence and co-operation of almost the entire Christian community.

The report of the first year's work of the Committee of Visitation, of which Mr. Moody was chairman, gives the number of families visited 554, and the amount of money bestowed in charity $2350. Of the spiritual results there is no record this side of heaven; but, in many cases, "man's extremity was God's opportunity." Many souls came into Christ's kingdom, at the invitation of Mr. Moody and his relief committee, who had stayed outside for years because they could not go to church in respectable style, and so did not care to go at all.

The poor now had the Gospel preached unto them, sometimes almost in spite of themselves. All the missions were active and thriving; the noon prayer-meeting, though not always select, was generally forcible; and the blessing of Heaven rested on the man whose faith and zeal had roused the whole evangelical brotherhood to a higher sense of their power and privilege as believers in Christ and His Gospel, and set so many of them at work.

CHAPTER VII.

THE WAR COMMITTEE.—CAMP AND FIELD.

WAR is the carnival of hell. Its legions march with every army, and bivouac in every camp. It does, indeed, furnish brilliant figures of speech, with which the apostle stirs the blood of laggard soldiers of Christ; and such a man as Hedley Vicars, or such a regiment as Havelock's Saints, may help to relieve its awful record of death and crime. But wars waged for personal or national pride have always been flames in which God permitted bad men to burn themselves. Rarely has the world been made substantially better by mankind killing one another.

But the war which saved the American Union and crushed out slavery was the occasion for a grand system of Christian helpfulness, whereby unnumbered thousands of sick and wounded men were saved from death, and unknown thousands of souls were saved from a life of sin.

No thoughtful person can study the history of the Sanitary and Christian Commissions without feeling sure that, while the devils were making "a long pull, a strong pull, and a pull altogether," Jesus Christ, the

Captain of salvation, had His forces also in the field. Christian men in camps and battles, Christian women in hospitals and prisons, and good angels everywhere, were working with might and main together, to save the souls and bodies of the soldiers—gathering in the great harvest which death was constantly ripening. In the midst of the horrors of war God was working miracles of grace, the like of which no other war-history has ever seen. Every campaign was begun and ended with a revival.

In the work of the Christian Commission Mr. Moody, already well known at home, was first brought into public notice. At the breaking out of the war, in 1861, the devotional committee of the Young Men's Christian Association, of which Mr. Moody was chairman, found a new line of work made ready to their hands. The first 75,000 volunteers were under way so quickly that very little could be done in the form of religious work among them. But when the second call, for 300,000 more, was made, and a camp of rendezvous was established near the southern limits of the city of Chicago, Moody and his brethren saw their great opportunity, which they instantly and eagerly improved. On the arrival of the first regiment, ordered to Camp Douglas for instruction, the committee was on the ground, and before the tents were fairly pitched a camp prayer-meeting was in progress. Other regiments arriving, and encamping in various portions of the city, were promptly visited and supplied with religious reading. Public worship on the Sabbath and prayer-meetings during the week were established within easy reach of every boy in blue.

It was a matter of no little surprise and joy to the soldiers, many of whom had come from churches, Sunday-schools, and Christian homes, to hear themselves saluted in the name of Christ almost before they could stack their arms, and to have the very first tent which was pitched in their camp put to its first use as a place for prayer. Christian zeal kept pace with patriotism. Mr. Moody and his committee were obliged to call for help: a hundred and fifty clergymen and laymen promptly responded to the call. Every evening eight or ten meetings were held in different camps; and an almost continual service, within reach of every regiment, on the Sabbath. Over fifteen hundred of these services were held in and around Chicago by the Association during the war.

Mr. Jacobs says:—

"In these meetings Mr. Moody seemed almost ubiquitous; he would hasten from one barrack and camp to another, day and night, week-days and Sundays, praying, exhorting, conversing personally with the men about their souls, and revelling in the abundant work and swift success which the war had brought within his reach."

The chapel of the Young Men's Christian Association at Camp Douglas was the first camp chapel in existence—being built in the October of 1861.

Meanwhile many of the soldier converts had been sent to the field, in Kentucky; and, feeling the want of the means of grace which they had left behind, they sent repeated calls to the Chicago brethren to come down and establish similar meetings among them. In response to this invitation Mr. Moody was sent to the army, near Fort Donelson—being the first regular army delegate from Chicago. Similar labours by other Associations led to a convention in Norfolk, Virginia, on the 16th of November, 1861, where the United States Christian Commission was projected, of which Mr. George H. Stuart, of Philadelphia, was president. Mr. J. V. Farwell was made the chairman of Mr. Moody's War Committee; and when the Christian Commission was organized, he was placed on its managing board.

The news of the battle of Fort Donelson, on the 15th of February, 1862, was the signal for sending to the field a special committee of relief, composed of the Rev. Robert Patterson, D.D., Mr. Moody, and Mr. Jacobs. With them went a number of other brethren from Chicago, eager to minister to the sick and wounded and dying.

On board the steamer from Cairo a discussion arose as to the most efficient way of doing the new work before them. Mr. Moody, full of the idea of saving souls, urged that the very first business in every case was to find out whether the sick or dying man were a child of God; if so, then it was not necessary to spend much time on him—he being safe enough already. If not, he was to be pointed at once to the Saviour.

Robert Collyer, the Unitarian, took the sanitary view of the question. He declared that the first comforts to be administered to these men who were ready to perish were whisky, brandy, milk-punch, and the like. "Brace up the nerves of the poor fellows," said he, "and help to keep them alive, rather than begin by trying to prepare them for death."

The Rev. Dr. Patton, Congregationalist, thought that both the brethren were right, and both were wrong. He was in favour of a double treatment, varied to suit each particular case; though agreeing with Mr. Moody that, if the poor fellow were actually dying, the thing to be done was to offer him a short and swift salvation, by telling him the story of the thief on the cross.

Mr. Collyer was on his feet in a moment. "What!" said he, "are we to tell our dying heroes, who have gone forth to fight our battles and save our flag, while we stay comfortably at home,—are we to talk to them about thieves?"

The storm of applause which greeted this patriotic speech showed that the crowd on the boat, the most of whom knew but little, and cared still less, about questions of theology, were full of that strange belief common to both armies in all battles, that patriotism is one form of piety, and that, somehow or other, though in a way not laid down in the Bible, to die for one's country is a quick way of getting to heaven. This doctrine was taught by the ancient heathen orators and poets; later by Mohammed; still later by Joseph Smith, the Mormon. The Russian priests and officers taught it to their soldiers in the Crimea; while the leaders of the Southern army are reported to have been in the same faith. But the wide experience of the Christian Commission with thousands of brave men at the point of death proved that Mr. Moody was right; for there is no record of a soldier dying with heaven in sight, unless by faith he first had seen the Saviour on the cross. No man, be he soldier or civilian, is redeemed by his own death.

Back and forth, between Chicago and the various camps and battle-fields, with tireless vigour and jubilant faith, Mr. Moody toiled and travelled, during the four terrible years of war; which, by the work of the Christian Commission, were transformed from four great harvests of death into four great harvests of souls for the garner of the Lord in heaven. Wave after wave of patriotism and Christian devotion swept over the land. Love of country and love of Christ were mingled, so that no one could tell where one ended and the other began.

Like the men who go down to the sea in ships, Moody and his brethren saw God's wonders, in camp and field. Having so many sinners to point to the Saviour, and so little time in which to do it, they prayed to the Lord to do His "short work." So many men found the Saviour, and died while they were praying for them, that they came to have a strange familiarity with heaven. These souls seemed to be messengers between them and God, carrying up continually the fresh and glowing record of the work they were doing in His name. And so simple and easy did it become for them to "ask and receive," that they were rather surprised if the penitent for whose conversion they prayed was not blessed before they reached the Amen.

One of the Christian Commissioners gives the following instance of another kind of answer to prayer:—

"A party of our men found themselves one night

on a battle-field, in charge of a great many wounded soldiers, who, by reason of the sudden retreat of the army, were left wholly without shelter or supplies. Having done their best for the poor fellows—bringing them water from a distant brook, and searching the haversacks of the dead for rations—they began to say to themselves, and one another, 'These weak and wounded men must have food, or they will die. The army is out of reach, and there is no village for many miles: what are we to do?'

"'Pray to God to send us bread,' said one.

"That night, in the midst of the dead and dying, they held a little prayer-meeting, telling the Lord all about the case, and begging Him to send them bread immediately; though from whence it could come they had not the most remote idea. All night long they plied their work of mercy. With the first ray of dawn the sound of an approaching waggon caught their ears; and presently, through the mists of the morning, appeared a great Dutch farm waggon, piled to the very top with loaves of bread.

"On their asking the driver where he came from, and who sent him, he replied:—

"'When I went to bed last night I knew that the army was gone, and I could not sleep for thinking of the poor fellows who always have to stay behind. Something seemed to say to me, "What will those poor fellows do for something to eat?" It came to me so strong that I waked up my old wife, and told her what was the matter. We had only a little bread in the house; and while my wife was making some more I took my team and went around to all my neighbours, making them get up and give me all the bread in their houses, telling them it was for the wounded soldiers on the battle-field. When I got home my waggon was full; my old wife piled her baking on the top, and I started off to bring the bread to the boys, feeling just as if the Lord Himself were sending me.'"

No wonder that men working year after year amid such scenes as these should have learned how to claim the promises in prayer! They acquired the habit of talking to God with the same simplicity and directness as with one another; their faith increased continually by the sight of the swift procession of Divine mercies which was all the time sweeping by.

These wonders of grace in camp and field were reported at the Chicago noon prayer-meeting by Mr. Moody and his co-labourers, on their return from their frequent excursions to the front. By this means a very intimate connection was kept up between the work in the army and the work at home, and the meeting became intensely interesting—especially to those whose husbands, sons, and brothers, were fighting for the Union.

Strangely enough, as though no other place were so near to heaven, and no other believers had such access to the ear of the Lord, people from all over the State, and even from neighbouring States, used to send requests for prayer to be read at the Chicago noon prayer-meeting. These requests were received by thousands; and often, in quick succession, came the tidings of glorious answers to prayer, with offerings of glad thanksgiving, and sometimes gifts of money and supplies for helping on the work of the Commission.

In this way the Chicago noon meeting became the very centre and heart of the religious life of the whole North-West.

One of the marvels of those days was the revival of religion among the rebel prisoners,—about ten thousand of whom had been taken at Fort Donelson and brought to Camp Douglas, which was transformed from a camp of instruction into a prison. Mr. Moody was impressed with the thought that these poor men needed the means of grace fully as much as the Union soldiers; but to gain access to them was a matter of extreme difficulty. One day he succeeded in obtaining a permit to visit them, which he gave to his friend Mr. Hawley, the Young Men's Christian Association Secretary; and himself took a can of kerosene oil to light up with, it being towards evening, —hoping, in the capacity of a servant, to be allowed to pass the guard along with his more clerical-looking friend. But it was of no use; the guard would not let in two men on one permit, though Mr. Moody exhibited his can of oil, and declared he was only going with the other gentleman to help along the meeting.

The earnest discussion was overheard by the officer of the day, who came up to see what was the matter; and, recognising Mr. Moody, he took him to headquarters, vouched for his being all right, and obtained a pass for him to go in and hold meetings with the prisoners as often as he liked. In a few minutes he rejoined his friend Hawley in the prison. They announced the purpose of their visit; and the men, being both surprised and pleased, gathered around them while they read the Scriptures, exhorted, and prayed.

At the very first meeting the power of God was manifest, and a large number of the prisoners were inquiring what they must do to be saved. Meetings were held with them every afternoon and evening. The flame of revival spread throughout their entire camp. The tidings flew over the whole city and county, and produced the most intense excitement. Great numbers of clergymen and lay workers begged for the privilege of assisting in the meetings. It was held to be a peculiar honour to lead one of those enemies to Christ. Great numbers were soundly converted; and, as it was not thought expedient to establish a church among them, they were organized into a Young Men's Christian Association. Bibles, Testaments, and other religious books and papers, were bountifully supplied to them. They were treated as brethren in Christ: and when their time came to be exchanged, they went to their Southern homes thanking God for their bonds, in which His servants had found them out, and where they, though prisoners of war, had found peace and liberty in the Saviour.

The report of the Army Committee for the year 1865 shows a distribution of 1537 Bibles, 20,565 Testaments, 1000 prayer-books, 2025 hymn-books, 24,896 other religious books, 127,545 religious newspapers, and 43,450 pages of tracts, besides 28,400 literary papers and magazines. The Camp Douglas chapel was erected at a cost of $2300, and a soldiers' library and reading-room were furnished by the Association, in a building erected by the Christian Commission. This was all in addition to the regular home work.

An Employment Bureau was established this year, chiefly for the benefit of the many wounded soldiers who were continually applying to the Association for assistance. Situations were found for 1435 men, 124 boys, and 718 girls, besides transient employment for many persons who were unable to go out to service.

In all this work Mr. Moody bore an important and honourable part. His frequent excursions to battle-fields and camps made him, more than any other man, the medium of communication between the work in the army and the work at home. He was on the field after the battles of Pittsburgh Landing, Shiloh, and Murfreesboro', with the army at Cleveland and Chattanooga, and was one of the first to enter Richmond, where he ministered alike to friend and foe.

On the 23rd of April, 1865, was held, in Mr. Crosby's splendid new Opera House—then thrown open to the public for the first time—the memorable third anniversary of the north-western branch of the Christian Commission. To describe the enthusiasm of that meeting would be as impossible as for those who were present to forget it. The report of the year's work, partially given above, surprised and delighted the vast assembly; while, to those who had been chiefly engaged in it, well-earned praise and honour were not wanting. Among other honours conferred, a committee of clergymen presented to Mr. J. V. Farwell, chairman of the War Committee, an elegantly bound copy of the Holy Scriptures, accompanied by an address, expressing their high estimate of the value of his services as chairman of the north-western branch of the United States Christian Commission.

To Mr. Moody, on this occasion, very high compliments were paid, which, to a man more mindful of worldly glory, must have been inspiring. But compliments were of no value to him. He regarded them as temptations and snares. He would sometimes say, "Strike me rather than praise me." So long as his omnivorous appetite for work was satisfied, nothing else was needed to make him one of the happiest men alive.

But it is easy to see, in the light of his subsequent history, that the Lord was training him in this school of the war for still greater victories in the name of Jesus. In prisons and battles, in the midst of blood and agony and death, the Holy Spirit taught him God's own simple method of salvation, and the short, straight road to Christ and heaven.

CHAPTER VIII.

MR. MOODY'S CHURCH.

THE work of the Christian Commission, in which Mr. Moody was so greatly blessed, and by reason of which he began to be had in reputation, was, after all, only incidental. His chief care and labour was still his dear North Market Mission.

The new impulse given to every Christian enterprise by the army work of the Association was notably felt in Mr. Moody's school. During the first two years of the war its rapid increase demanded increased accommodation ; and its leader set about the task of building an edifice suited to its wants.

In 1863 a commodious chapel, with tower and spire, was erected in Illinois Street, not very far from the old Market Hall, at the cost of about $20,000—which money was collected by Mr. Moody himself.

The school now numbered nearly a thousand ; and from among the scholars and their parents about three hundred persons had given their hearts to the Saviour. As the number of converts increased, it began to appear that, within this school, the Lord was building up a church. At first Mr. Moody urged them to give their names to some orthodox pastor, with which they might hold their membership and celebrate the sacraments, though, for the most part, worshipping and working with their brethren of the Mission. It was the custom here, as well as at the Young Men's Christian Association, to inquire of converts in what communion they had been brought up. If the young believer were of a Methodist family, some brother at the Mission, connected with a Methodist church, would introduce him to its pastor; in the same way, if he had been a Presbyterian, Baptist, etc., etc., he was introduced to some church of his own denomination.

Thus was avoided the difficulty so often arising out of union services; and no church had any reason to complain that those who were due at its communions were improperly led elsewhere. This plan was moderately successful in connection with the noon prayer-meeting, and other services of the Association, in which a good many sinners were all the time coming to Christ; but it was by no means a success with the converts at the North Market Mission. The most of these had no religious antecedents whatever. Some of them came from a depth of heathenism so far below the Church of God that, of its forms, orders, and divisions, they knew and cared absolutely nothing. But there was a strong tie binding them to each other which it was found impossible to transfer to any other body of worshippers. They had come up together out of poverty and ignorance; they had learned their duty in the same school, and under the same teacher; and thus their fellowship of suffering, as well as their fellowship of faith, was something with which no stranger might intermeddle.

It must also be confessed that, of all the Christian congregations then in Chicago, there was not one to whose care these persons, who had nothing to commend them except the fact that they were saved sinners, could safely be confided. The very reasons for which they needed sympathy and attention were those which would prevent them from receiving it. Thus the necessity for a church of their own became increasingly evident.

Before the war—in which tears had softened their hearts, and fires had melted them together—the clergy of the city stood aloof from Moody and his Mission. But working side by side with him among the wounded and dying, they learned to love him more as they came to know him better, and so began to give him their counsel and fellowship, which he had all the while so greatly desired. That religious conceit, whose father is Zeal and whose mother is Ignorance, and which is so often found in the heads of men who come to sudden success outside of the organized Church, was not found in Mr. Moody. He never doubted the value of the Church or the ministry, in any of the forms they had adopted. But none of these forms could meet the needs of his particular congregation. Therefore, after much prayer for Divine guidance, he invited all the city ministers of his acquaintance, with a number of prominent laymen, to meet in council, at the Illinois Street chapel, for the purpose of organizing a Christian communion for the three hundred people who had been converted under his ministry.

This council is remembered with peculiar interest.

There was a goodly attendance, and all the evangelical denominations were represented.

Prayer having been offered, Mr. Moody arose, and stated the business on which he had called them together. He gave a vivid picture of the Mission, and of its success in bringing sinners to Christ; told how he had failed in all his efforts to lead them to unite with other congregations; and explained the evident necessity for organizing them into a church by themselves, of which he, who had been the means of saving them, should be the pastor, recognised as such by the Christian world. He desired to form an orderly congregation of believers, among whom the ordinances of the Gospel should be celebrated and the work of the Lord carried on.

As he proceeded with his remarks, one after another of the prevailing forms seemed to disappear from among the possibilities of the case. First of all, his good friend, Dr. ——, rector of the Episcopal church, felt compelled to withdraw from the council, though expressing his pleasure in the good work which he could not officially recognise. Next, an excellent Presbyterian D.D. announced his sympathy with Mr. Moody and his Mission, but of course, if he were to assist in organizing a church, it must be a Presbyterian church. A Baptist brother laboured under a similar difficulty; for the proposed pastor of this congregation had not gone down into the water, or come up out of the water; the ordinance in his case having been administered by Dr. Kirk after the manner suggested by the text, "I will sprinkle clean water upon you, and ye shall be clean." A Methodist pastor, a fast friend and fellow-worker with Mr. Moody, was sorry that these good people, who showed so strong a "desire to flee from the wrath to come," could not be organized into a Methodist church, with class-meetings, love-feasts, quarterly meetings, and camp-meetings; all of which seemed so well suited to their spiritual needs. But Mr. Moody could not be persuaded to join Conference; neither did he propose an itinerant ministry for his church, though he was so great a traveller himself. Besides, there were still some strong points of Calvinism in his creed, which the Methodist brother regretted; therefore, he could not give him his hand officially, though, as a friend and brother, he sat the council through.

All the factors of the problem had now been eliminated but the Congregationalists, to whom the duty fell of organizing "The Illinois Street Church"; a fact which they still recount with no little satisfaction, since their method excelled all others on this notable occasion, in being the only one simple enough to meet the wants of this peculiar people, whose only notion of a church was a company of saved sinners, with Mr. Moody for their pastor and Jesus Christ as the Head over all.

After their manner, then, the church was duly established; and the candidates for membership, who had been examined concerning their experience of grace, received the ordinance of baptism at the hands of the ministry present, and then celebrated their first communion together with tears and songs of joy.

Afterwards, when members were to be received by

baptism, a neighbouring pastor was usually invited to perform the service. But at the Lord's Supper, where Christ alone is Master of the feast, all established forms were dispensed with, and the company of brethren and sisters broke the bread and drank the wine together, the pastor reading or reciting, out of the Gospel, the history of the last supper of the disciples with their Lord.

This church, though organized by Congregationalists, has never been reckoned a Congregational church. Its minister has received no ordination, save that of the Spirit and Providence of God; his name has never been published in the Minutes of that body or any other; and the statistics of the society have never been published at all. It is a strictly independent organization, asking no authority of men, but abundantly blessed of the Lord. It endeavours to keep the unity of the Spirit in the bond of peace; and, with this end in view, everything which could debar from its fellowship any lover of the Lord Jesus Christ has been carefully excluded from its form of discipline and confession of faith. The following is its Manual complete, as revised by Mr. Moody and his brethren a short time previous to his last departure for England. The change in name to "The Chicago Avenue Church" suggests the destruction of the first edifice in the Great Fire, and the building of a new and spacious house of worship at the point above indicated.

ARTICLES OF ADMISSION.

On Lord's Day morning, such believers as have been previously examined by the Committee and accepted by vote of the Church will be publicly received into fellowship; they having subscribed to the following

ARTICLES OF FAITH.

(MEMBERS STAND WHILE THE ARTICLES ARE BEING READ.)

I. We believe in the only true God (John xvii. 3), the Father, the Son, and the Holy Ghost (Matt. xxviii. 19). Who created all things (Rev. iv. 11), and upholds all things by the word of His power (Heb. i. 3), in whom we live, and move, and have our being (Acts xvii. 28). A God of truth, and without iniquity, just and right is He (Deut. xxxii. 4); and He shall judge the world (Psalm ix. 8).

II. We believe all Scripture is given by inspiration of God, and is profitable for doctrine, for reproof, for correction, for instruction in righteousness: that the man of God may be perfect, throughly furnished unto all good works (2 Tim. iii. 16-17).

III. We believe that by one man sin entered into the world, and death by sin, and so death passed upon all men, for that all have sinned (Rom. v. 12), and judgment came upon all men to condemnation (Rom. v. 18). For the wages of sin is death, but the gift of God is eternal life, through Jesus Christ our Lord (Rom. vi. 23).

IV. We believe there is none other name under heaven, given among men, whereby we must be saved (Acts iv. 12). For other foundation can no man lay than that is laid, which is Jesus Christ (1 Cor. iii. 11). We also believe that Christ died for our sins according to the Scriptures, and that He was buried, and that He rose again the third day according to the Scriptures (1 Cor. xv. 3-4), and sat down on the right hand of the Majesty on high (Heb. i. 3), now to appear in the presence of God for us (Heb. ix. 24).

V. We believe God so loved the world that He gave His only-begotten Son, that whosoever believeth in Him should not perish, but have everlasting life (John iii. 16); and he that believeth not God hath made Him a liar; because he believeth not the record that God gave of His Son, and that is the record, that God has given to us eternal life, and this life is in His Son. He that hath the Son hath life, and he that hath not the Son of God hath not life (1 John v. 10-12).

VI. We believe that Christ, the Head over all to the Church (Eph. i. 22), hath commanded us to baptize in the name of the Father, and of the Son, and of the Holy Ghost (Matt. xxviii. 19); and the same night in which He was betrayed, took bread; and when He had given thanks, He brake it, and said, Take, eat: this is my body, which is broken for you; this do in remembrance of me. After the same manner also He took the cup, when He had supped, saying, This cup is the New Testament in my blood. This do ye, as oft as ye drink it, in remembrance of me; for as often as ye eat this bread, and drink this cup, ye do show the Lord's death *till He come* (1 Cor. xi. 23-26).

In accepting and subscribing to the above articles of faith, we by no means set aside or undervalue any of the Scriptures of the Old and New Testament, but believe all to be equally God's own written Word, given to us through the inspiration of the Holy Spirit; but the knowledge and belief of the truth, as stated in our articles of faith, we deem necessary to salvation and sound doctrine, and thereby requisite for Christian fellowship.

ADDRESS.

And you hath He quickened, who were dead in trespasses and sins. Wherein in time past ye walked according to the course of this world, according to the prince of the power of the air, the spirit that now worketh in the children of disobedience: among whom also we all had our conversation in times past in the lusts of our flesh, fulfilling the desires of the flesh and of the mind; and were by nature the children of wrath, even as others. But God, who is rich in mercy, for His great love wherewith He loved us, even when we were dead in sins, hath quickened us together with Christ (by grace ye are saved); and hath raised us up together, and made us sit together in heavenly places in Christ Jesus; that in the ages to come He might show the exceeding riches of His grace in His kindness toward us through Christ Jesus. For by grace are ye saved through faith; and that not of yourselves: it is the gift of God. Not of works, lest any man should boast. For we are His workmanship, created in Christ Jesus unto good works, which God hath before ordained that we should walk in them.

But now in Christ Jesus ye who sometimes were far off are made nigh by the blood of Christ. For through Him we both have access by one Spirit unto the Father. Now, therefore, ye are no more strangers and foreigners, but fellow-citizens with the saints, and of the household of God. And are built upon the foundation of the apostles and prophets, Jesus Christ Himself being the chief corner-stone; in whom all the building, fitly framed together, groweth unto an holy temple in the Lord; in whom ye also are builded together for an habitation of God through the Spirit. (Eph. ii. 1-10, 13, 18-22.)

Praying that the Lord God of peace that brought again from the dead our Lord Jesus, that great Shepherd of the sheep, through the blood of the everlasting covenant, make you perfect in every good work, to do His will, working in you that which is well-pleasing in His sight, through Jesus Christ; to whom be glory, for ever and ever. Amen. (Heb. xiii. 20-21).

PRINCIPLES OF ORGANIZATION AND GOVERNMENT.

This body of believers desire to be known only as Christians, without reference to any denomination; yet regarding all who hold and preach the truth contained in our articles of faith as equally belonging to the same Head; and are thereby free to co-operate and unite with them in carrying on the work of our common Master.

GOVERNMENT.

The government is vested in the body of believers of which the Church is composed.

OFFICERS.

The officers of this Church shall consist of Deacons, a Clerk, Treasurer, Trustees, and Finance Committee. Other officers than those named may be appointed if required. All officers shall be members, and shall be elected by ballot. All officers of the Church shall be members of the Examining Committee, and shall constitute the Executive Committee, and shall adopt such measures as they deem advisable, subject to the action of the Church at its business meetings.

DUTIES OF OFFICERS.

The officers shall take the oversight of the flock, caring for their spiritual interests.

EXAMINING COMMITTEE.

This Committee shall examine all candidates for membership, and report to the assembly the names of such as they approve of, for their acceptance. It shall be the duty of the Committee to gather information concerning the spiritual condition of the members; and upon learning anything amiss, to deal with them according to Matt. xviii. 16-18. The action of the Committee in matters of discipline shall be final.

CLERK.

The Clerk shall keep a record of the doings of the Church, which record shall be read at each annual meeting. He shall also keep a record of the membership, and make an annual report.

TREASURER.

The Treasurer shall receive all moneys due or contributed, and disburse the same under the direction of the Finance Committee, and report at each annual meeting.

FINANCE COMMITTEE.

This Committee shall adopt methods for collecting funds for the Church, and shall have the general management of the finance, subject to the action of the Church.

TRUSTEES.

The title of all the property belonging to the Church shall be vested in its Trustees—they to keep the same in repair. The edifice shall be under the control of the officers of the Church for all meetings.

Calls for Mr. Moody to attend religious meetings, revivals, and conventions, became more and more frequent; but his chief work was with his own congregation, which rapidly increased in numbers and interest, and soon came to be one of the most thriving and useful bodies of believers in the city. At present it has about four hundred and fifty members, a large and vigorous Sunday-school, and an honourable place in the community.

Its success seems largely due to Mr. Moody's admirable appointment and division of labour. All the members have something to do. The bell in the tower of the first church edifice—the gift of a friend in New York—was said to ring every night in the year for some kind of religious assembly. There were not only the ordinary services common to all churches, but also men's meetings, young men's meetings, boys' meetings, women's meetings, mothers' meetings, girls' meetings, Bible meetings, strangers' meetings, Gospel meetings, praise meetings, and testimony meetings,—each with some distinct character of its own. Sometimes, in different parts of the chapel on Sunday, and at private houses during the week, there were three or four of these in progress at once. It was Mr. Moody's habit to attend them all, dividing the day or evening between them—thus establishing a wonderful unity in all the various sections of the work.

The amount and fervour of religious exercises, all the time carried on at this church, could seldom be found elsewhere except during a season of revival; in which, if it continued for several weeks, both pastor and congregation would be completely exhausted; a reaction would follow, attendance would drop below the average, and the minister be forced to ask for a vacation, or possibly make a tour for his health.

Not so with Mr. Moody and his church. They are like old soldiers, hardened by long campaigning, or like old sailors, who are so well acquainted with hurricanes as not to mind them; while their captain with the nerve and steadiness of a veteran joins the enthusiasm of a boy.

It was impossible that weariness should not sometimes overtake him; but he possessed the faculty of throwing off all care, and regaining his accustomed spirits, in a wonderfully short space of time.

His old friend Col. Hammond mentions this instance:—

"Mr. Moody came to see me one Sunday, after his morning service, seeming to be quite tired out. He threw himself into a chair and burst out with the following exclamations:

"'I am used up—can't think, or speak, or do anything else. There is my meeting at the church tonight—you must take it. I have absolutely nothing left in me.'

"Knowing that Mr. Moody never asked help unless he needed it, I promised to take the service off his hands. When the time came I went down to the Illinois Street Church, and found the house quite full. I was about to commence the service, when the door opened, and in walked, or rather rushed, Mr. Moody, followed by a long procession of young men whom he had picked up in saloons and at street corners, and brought with him on an errand which, to them, was evidently a new one.

"Mounting the platform with a bound, he seized the hymn-book and commenced, and from beginning to end of that service I had nothing to do but to keep out of the way.

"It appeared that he had taken an hour or two of rest; and then, having no care about the evening service on his mind, he took up his old familiar work of bringing in recruits, at which he was this time more than usually successful. As he led the way to church some happy thought struck him, and between the street corner and the pulpit he arranged a sermon, which was one of the most effective I ever heard him preach."

As a pastor Mr. Moody was a success. He was acquainted with all his people, and all his people felt acquainted with him. All the poor and unfortunate who lived in his vicinity were quite familiar with the number on the door of his modest little house. He was able to say continually with Job, "The blessing of him that was ready to perish came upon me; and I caused the widow's heart to sing for joy. I was eyes to the blind, and feet was I to the lame. I was a father to the poor, and the cause which I knew not I searched out."

Mr. Hitchcock, for some time a member of his household, gives an account of two hundred calls which Mr. Moody made one New Year's Day:—

"At an early hour the omnibus, which was to take him and several of his leading men, was at the door; and, with a carefully prepared list of residences, they began the day's labour. The list included a very large proportion of families living in garrets, and the upper stories of high tenement houses. On reaching a family belonging to his congregation, he would spring out of the 'bus, leap up the stairways, rush into the room, and pay his respects as follows :—

"'You know me: I am Moody; this is Deacon De Golyer, this is Deacon Thane, this is Brother Hitchcock. Are you all well? Do you all come to church and Sunday-school? Have you all the coal you need for the winter? Let us pray.' And down we would all go upon our knees, while Mr. Moody offered from fifteen to twenty words of earnest, tender, sympathetic supplication, that God would bless the man, his wife, and each one of the children.

"Then, springing to his feet, he would dash on his hat, dart through the doorway and down the stairs, throwing a hearty 'good-bye' behind him, leap into the 'bus, and off to the next place on his list; the entire exercise occupying about one minute and a half.

"Before long the horses were tired out, for Moody insisted on their going at a run, from one house to another; so the omnibus was abandoned, and the party proceeded on foot. One after another his companions became exhausted with running upstairs and downstairs, and across the streets, and kneeling on bare floors, and getting up in a hurry; until, reluctantly, but of necessity, they were obliged to relinquish the attempt, and the tireless pastor was left to make the last of the two hundred calls alone; after which feat he returned home in the highest spirits, and with no sense of fatigue, to laugh at his exhausted companions for deserting him."

The next year Mr. Moody would not take a carriage, but went through with a similar social and religious work on foot—reminding his friends that, on the previous New Year, they had often felt obliged to leave the carriage before reaching the house, lest the sight of it should grieve or offend the poor whom they visited, to whom it would seem a needless and extravagant use of money, and who might therefore give their pastor and his friends a less sincere and affectionate welcome.

Mr. Moody always liked to have his preaching-places decorated with Scripture mottoes. The walls of his Illinois Street chapel were profusely ornamented with texts; and even the gas-burners above the pulpit were so arranged as to spell out, in great letters of light, the precious words, GOD IS LOVE.

One Sunday night in winter a poor shivering fellow was passing the place, and seeing the vestibule door open, went in to shelter himself from the cold. The inner door also was ajar; and being curious to see for once the inside of a place of worship, he looked cautiously in. The strange light above the pulpit at once attracted his notice, and the holy words were soon imprinted on his heart. He entered the meeting, gave himself to Christ, was soon happily converted, and became a useful member of Mr. Moody's church.

The Yokefellows have already been mentioned. These young men, organized into a band by Mr. Moody, continued their work year after year, distributing printed invitations to the service at the Illinois Street Church in the morning, and to those at Farwell Hall in the evening. They would stand at the street corners, on the bridges, and in other places where strangers were to be met in crowds; and so successful were they as to send quite a procession of persons to these meetings, some of whom had seldom, if ever, entered a house of worship before. One of this band gives the following account of how he was captured and thrust into the work:—

"I was a stranger in Chicago. One Sunday morning I was standing at a street corner, not very far from Mr. Moody's church, staring about, not knowing what to do with myself, or which way to go. Mr. Moody, who was just then sending out the Yokefellows to their morning stations, came up to me, and said, familiarly, 'Here, take this pile of papers, stand at that corner, and give one to everybody who goes by!'

"Glad to hear a friendly voice, and to have something to do, I took the papers, and gave them out as directed; and I have been a member of that band ever since."

It may well be believed that Mr. Moody's system of giving every one something to do for Christ has brought his church up to a high degree of efficiency.

Some of those wild lads who once were so troublesome in the old North Market Hall have grown to be highly respectable and useful men, well trained in the Bible and in the conduct of all sorts of religious meetings.

There are eight or ten of the deacons and leading members who are acceptable preachers, and who during his long absences from home regularly conduct the Sunday services, unless some visiting clergyman is at hand. There are others who, by twos and threes, are accustomed to hold public worship; and very many of the older members of the church are effective Bible readers, prayer leaders, and exhorters.

Mr. Moody's relations to his church are of the closest and tenderest character. Most of them have been led to Christ by his ministry, and they feel towards him as one might feel towards a man who had plunged into the water to save him from drowning, or climbed into a burning house to pull him out of the fire.

He is more completely *with his people,* even at four thousand miles' distance, than many pastors are who are at home all the while. His wishes are regarded with the greatest attention. His parting instructions to the Sunday-school teachers still ring in their ears. His way of doing things is copied—even to a fault, sometimes; and for his sake his people toil and suffer, if need be, to prove their love for the man who came down to them in their sins and poverty, and brought them up into the light and joy of the fellowship of the saints.

Of course the congregation is not all made up of the humbler classes of society. Some of the best people of Chicago are identified with the church. Wealthy and cultivated ladies and gentlemen, though not all of them belonging to his communion, are among the teachers and workers; and some of these, it is but just to say, are among the most active and useful Christians of the whole North-West.

Mr. Hitchcock, superintendent of Mr. Moody's Sunday-school,—one of the strangers whom he brought in and set about the work of the Lord, and who has kindly furnished some of the facts in this volume, says:—

"If it is announced that a letter is to be read from Mr. Moody, we are sure to have a crowded school.

He really holds us in his hand, though he has been nearly two years absent; and if he would only come home and wind us up again, with a few weeks' work among us, we could run on like a clock for a long time to come."

It is a noticeable fact that a very large proportion of that congregation are Britons. The English and Scotch elements are particularly numerous. These persons, away from home and country, find so much heartiness and good cheer in that society, and, withal, so many familiar methods in the meetings, which Mr. Moody has learned abroad, that, more than at any other church in the city, they feel attracted here. Thus Mr. Moody's church is, like himself, cosmopolitan, catholic, and free.

CHAPTER IX.

FARWELL HALL.

THE rapid growth of the Young Men's Christian Association, and the great increase of its work during the war, called for largely increased accommodation. Their rooms in the Methodist Church block were small and over-crowded, and the new departments which had been added needed separate offices of their own.

Mr. Moody had removed his residence from the benches of the prayer-room, having married, and set up housekeeping in a little cottage on the North Side. But he had lost none of his interest in the place, which had become the headquarters of a wide-spread and powerful work of salvation. There was a certain dark closet, under a stairway, used for the storage of wood and coal; and, every other nook and corner of the building being fully occupied, this was the only place he could use as a closet for prayer. Here, sometimes alone, and sometimes in company with Mr. Jacobs and one or two other kindred spirits, he would shut himself up with the Lord, for those personal communings which were to him the very breath of life.

The pressing need of a new building led them to make it a subject of prayer. Various plans for securing it had been discussed, prayed over, and abandoned. The difficulties in the way were too great; the amount of money which would be required, it seemed impossible to raise. But while other friends of the Association despaired, Mr. Moody and his comrades kept on praying for a new hall.

One day, when the need of more spacious rooms had been most painfully evident, a great many people having been turned away from the noon prayer-meeting for want of room, Moody and two of his young friends made a solemn covenant with each other—which they set forth in writing, and to which each one signed his name—pledging continuous efforts for a hall till the Lord should give them success.

At length one of the brethren said:—

"The only way for us to obtain a new building is to elect Mr. Moody president of the Association."

His recent success in erecting the Illinois Street Church, and his well-known boldness and devotion in the performance of any duty which the Lord might lay upon him, seemed to give great force to this suggestion. The proposal, however, met with determined opposition.

The Young Men's Christian Association was now the strongest Christian society in the whole North-West. Its membership comprised many a scholarly, influential, and reverend man, whose name and influence as president would add to its dignity and popularity. To place in the chair a blunt and unlearned man like Mr. Moody, seemed strangely radical and inappropriate, to those conservative members, whose pride would be sorely wounded in following such a leader. Nevertheless he was put in nomination for the office.

The canvass and election were marked with great excitement. The respective friends of Mr. Moody and the opposing candidate laboured night and day, persuading old members and bringing in new ones; and, when the result was reached, Moody was elected by a small majority, which event was hailed by his friends as the prelude to the ultimate success of their building scheme.

The list of officers and committees of the Association for the year 1865 comprises the names of many honoured gentlemen, some of whom have won a national fame; but of all those scholars, philanthropists, and divines, none have come to be so widely known and so greatly honoured as this rough but devoted man, who reached his office with difficulty because of his want of education.

To the long list of committees a new one was added—namely, the Building Committee, of which Mr. J. V. Farwell was chairman, assisted by Mr. T. M. Avery and Mr. W. L. Lee.

Mr. Moody's plan of operations was, to organize a stock company, with twelve trustees, who should erect and hold the building in trust. Subscriptions to the stock were to be solicited under the following conditions:—

The stock was to bear six per cent. interest, from the completion of the building. The interest on this stock was to be paid out of the rentals of such portions of the building as were not needed for the use of the Association, and also from the rents of the great hall. The excess of the rentals above the interest was to be used by the Association to buy up the stock, at par value, until the whole amount should be called in; thus leaving the building the unincumbered property of the Association. Its revenues were then to be used in carrying forward its various benevolent operations, and in establishing and maintaining a free public library and reading-room, to be managed by the Association on strictly Christian principles.

The placing of this stock, to the amount of $101,000, was the great financial success of Mr. Moody's life. It demonstrated the wisdom, if not the inspiration, of those who had put him in charge of the work, and secured the erection of a magnificent structure, whose name and fame is known throughout the English-speaking world.

The trustees of the building were as follows: T. M. Avery, B. F. Jacobs, J. V. Farwell, William L. Lee, E. W. Blatchford, H. E. Sargeant, C. H. McCormick, George Armour, E. D. L. Sweet, Horace Hurlbut, A. R. Scranton, and E. B. McCagg. Of this board Mr. Avery was chairman, Mr. Jacobs secretary, and Mr. Farwell treasurer.

The building was located in Madison Street, between Clarke and La Salle Streets, in the heart of the business portion of the city. It contained a public hall capable of seating three thousand persons; a large room for the noon prayer-meeting, about one-third that size; a library; a reading-room; offices for the tract and publication department, the relief department, and the employment bureau; private rooms for some of the officers who were to live in and have charge of the building; and, last but not least, a worthy successor to the little coal-hole closet for prayer.

There were also several fine stores and offices, on the rental of which, as has been seen, the ultimate financial success of the scheme depended; but so large a portion of the building was devoted to religious uses, that subscriptions to its stock had a sweet savour of Christian liberality. It might possibly pay for itself; but probably the investment would bring larger returns in heaven than on earth.

The completion of this long-contemplated building opened a new era in the history of the Association.

On Sunday evening, September 29th, 1867, the new hall was dedicated to the worship and service of Almighty God. An immense assembly, representing not only the city, but the whole country round, gathered to celebrate the event. The great platform was filled with ministers of all denominations, and with distinguished visitors from several neighbouring States, After the opening devotional exercises, President Moody delivered an address, of which the following is a brief synopsis:—

"If there is one thing more than another for which Chicago is distinguished, it is the rapidity of its growth in size, wealth, and in the extent of its trade. But of all the great and swift successes which have come to us, none is more striking than that of the Young Men's Christian Association.

"During the last month, while we have been getting

in sight of the end, many a man has said to me, 'Don't get proud.'

"That is good advice. I feel, more than anything else, and more than ever before, that Jesus has accomplished this great result for us. And for this wonderful blessing I want you all to praise Him.

"A few years ago this Association was growing weaker and weaker, and at one time it came very near dying. Those who organized it made the mistake of supposing that if they opened some rooms, and gave notice of meetings to be held in them, sinners would come there of their own accord to be saved. But they were not long in finding out that if they would save the lost they must search for them in the byways and dark places, where they are hidden away from the light of Christ and His Gospel.

"Then we began to go out and bring in. That was just what Christ told us to do. And now, because we have obeyed Him and gone to work in His way, Christ has helped us to build this hall.

"But it seems to me the Association has just commenced its work. There are those, indeed, who say we have reached the limit of our power. But we must rally round the Cross; we must attack and capture the whole city for Christ.

"When I see young men, by thousands, going in the way to death, I feel like falling at the feet of Jesus, and crying out to Him with prayers and tears to come and save them, and to help us to bring them to Him.

"His answer to our prayers, and His blessing on our work, give me faith to believe that a mighty influence is yet to go out from us, that shall extend through this county and every county in the State; through every State in the Union; and, finally, crossing the waters, shall help to bring the whole world to God.

"We have been on the defensive too long. It is time we went into the conflict with all our might: straight into the enemy's camp.

"It has been said that the Association is now fairly established, and has all the money it needs; but if we should begin to think so, it would be the death of us. When we stop trying to enlarge our work for the Lord and raise more money for it, we shall become stale and stupid, like some of the rich institutions of the Old World, which are settling down into indolence, and dying of dry rot, because they are 'full and have need of nothing.' We must ask for money, *money*, MORE MONEY, at every meeting; not for the support of the Association—as it now is—but to enlarge its operations.

"We want to build homes for young men and for young women; mission schools; Magdalen asylums; reformatory institutions of various kinds; as well as places of resort for innocent amusement, and mental and social culture; so that there may be no excuse for our young people being caught in the traps which Satan sets for them all over the city."

Mr. Moody closed his remarks by showing the unsectarian character of the Young Men's Christian Association—a society in which people of all Christian creeds could live and labour harmoniously together, and which, for the first time since the days of the apostles, opened up a prospect for the substantial and practical unity of all Christ's disciples.

Standing on the summit of such a splendid success, with the light of God's favour shining so brightly on him, no wonder he looked out toward the future, seeing in it the still greater glory of the Lord! But, at this distance of time, and with his recent record in view, one part of Mr. Moody's speech that night seems to have been inspired by the spirit of prophecy. The grand vision which then rose up before him has already taken the form of history, even in the very order in which he declared it.

By its admirable system the Association first made itself felt in every part of the city. Presently its members began to be invited to hold meetings in suburban villages and neighbouring towns; then, by means of the Sunday School Conventions, which were awakened into new spiritual life by Moody and his brethren, every county in the State was visited by organized bands of Christian workers, whose labours, as we shall see hereafter, were wonderfully blessed of God. Next came the State Young Men's Christian Conventions, in which the influence of the Chicago brethren came to be felt through almost every State of the Union. And now, fulfilling the prophecy of that impressive hour, the work and power of which he spoke have, in his own person, crossed the waters, and are sweeping grandly onward to bring the whole world to Christ. From Christians of all creeds in all parts of Great Britain, from France, and even from Australia, come pressing invitations to this servant of God to bring the Gospel and come to them. Surely the spirit of prophecy was in these hopeful words!

The next speaker was Mr. Farwell, treasurer of

the Board of Trustees, and chairman of the Building Committee.

"Twenty-five years ago," said he, "there might have been seen, wending their way through the dirty streets of Chicago, a number of casks on wheels, distributing the waters of the lake at the houses of the people. A little later a few favoured ones were supplied with water, by means of wooden pipes, from a small tank, which was filled from the lake by the surplus power of the engine in the only flour-mill at that time in the place.

"Then some enterprising capitalists conceived the idea of a mammoth reservoir, large enough to supply the whole city, and the lot on which this building stands was bought by the 'Chicago Hydraulic Company' as a location for it. But the rapid growth of the city rendered this plan inadequate, and the municipal government, taking the matter into their own hands, built huge reservoirs in each division, still taking the water from near the shore, where it was always more or less impure.

"This system, in its turn, has been supplanted by the tunnel, through which pure water from the depths of the lake—an inexhaustible supply—is brought to the homes of our people.

"I have thought, since these walls were commenced on the very spot once selected for our central reservoir, and now to be dedicated as a spiritual centre, whence we trust the pure Water of Life shall flow in every direction, of which if a man drink he shall never thirst again—I have thought that God's hand was in all this, and that, while we bless Him for the pure water from the depths of the lake, we should also magnify His goodness, which has taught us how to pass beyond the shores of shallow and turbid sectarianism, and draw our spiritual life from the pure depths of the heart of Christ, and, by means of a Christian union which knows no differences of church or creed, to send out that tide of blessing all over this great city.

"This building is a practical demonstration of the unity of Christ's Church. Here we are not Baptists, nor Methodists, nor Presbyterians; we are simply Christians; and as soon as the Lord wills it, nothing will delight me more than to see, as the result of such enterprises as this, a complete and hearty union of all who love our Lord Jesus Christ,—such a union as will sweep away sectarian distinctions, and make His Church a unity in diversity, with one pasture, one flock, and one Shepherd.

"This enterprise, whose successful issue we celebrate to-night, has long been in contemplation. But only of late has any one had faith enough to conceive of its present proportions. It is well this project was delayed, or it might have been only a water-cart, instead of a great central reservoir."

Mr. Farwell then read his treasurer's report, in which it appeared that the cost of the land, building, and appurtenances was $199,000. Stock to the amount of $135,000 had been subscribed; $50,000 had been loaned on mortgages, leaving a floating debt of $14,000, which he proposed to meet by a subscription, then and there. The annual rentals were estimated at $32,000; the expenses and interest at

$17,000, leaving an annual net surplus of $15,000, with which the Association would be able to buy in the stock, pay off the mortgages, and ultimately come into full possession of the building and its handsome income, with which to continue and extend its work.

Among the other speakers was Mr. George H. Stuart, president of the United States Christian Commission, than whom no man living could have been more welcome. He was rapturously received by the vast audience, by whom he was loved and honoured for his admirable management and brilliant leadership in the Commission during the war.

He commenced his speech by saying,—

"I have travelled eight hundred miles expressly to be present at the dedication of the first hall ever erected for Christian young men. * * * *

"Let me take you, in thought, to a store in St. Paul's Churchyard, London, and introduce you to a modest business man, Mr. George Williams, who, in 1844, was a clerk in that house. In those days he used to invite his fellow-clerks to his own little room for prayer,—I too have prayed in that room,—and the result of those meetings, on the 6th of June, 1844, took the form and name of the "London Young Men's Christian Association." From thence the organization has spread through Europe and America; and its work, by all kinds of good men on behalf of all kinds of unfortunate and bad men, has demonstrated its usefulness and power.

"The Chicago Young Men's Christian Association was revival-born. Springing into life after the great awakening of 1857-8, it was among the first in existence. It was also among the earliest and most successful missionary organizations brought into use in connection with the war. God has been with you. You have had the 'God bless you!' of thousands of soldiers; and, now that the war is over, untold thousands of sinners out of Christ wait for your peaceful ministry in His name.

"In the year 1865 your Association attained its majority; and now, with the hope of youth, and the vigour of manhood, it commences a new and splendid career, blessed with the confidence and supported by the beneficence of all branches of the Christian Church. Therefore, inscribe upon your banners the words of the heroic missionary Carey:

"'Attempt great things for God, and expect great things from God.'"

The following statistics of the Young Men's Christian Association, which Mr. Stuart read on that occasion, are not without interest now: In England there were sixty-five organizations, in Scotland twenty-three, in Ireland six, in the Channel Islands two, in France fifty-four, in Germany two hundred and fifty-five, in Holland seventy-one, in Belgium ten, in Switzerland ninety-seven, in Italy five, in Asia five, in Oceanica six, and in America two hundred and forty-two.

The enthusiasm of that occasion it is impossible to describe. There were shouts of ecstasy, and tears of joy; generous sentiments, and liberal gifts; loving congratulations, and renewing of vows to Christ; the mighty voice of singing, and the solemn words of prayer; and, above all, and better than all, was the manifest presence of the Spirit of the Lord, cheering the hearts and strengthening the faith of those whose toil and offerings had achieved such grand success.

But, as yet, this splendid auditorium was without a name. Mr. Moody, near the close of the service, rose and said:—

"It was the generous subscription of thirty thousand dollars, by the chairman of our Building Committee, which purchased this land, and gave us at the outset a good hope of all we see to night. Now, by way of giving honour to whom honour is due, I propose that we name this building FARWELL HALL. All in favour say 'Aye!'"

The shout which greeted this proposal must have reminded Mr. Farwell of that other rousing "aye" by which he was once elected superintendent of the North Market School. And now once more was he honoured, in a way which any man might covet.

Acting on his own advice, President Moody then called for "more money."

A handsome subscription was raised on the spot, sufficient to relieve the Association from all present embarrassment; and thus, in evident favour both with God and man, it started on its new career.

CHAPTER X.

MR. MOODY BECOMES THE APOSTLE OF THE YOUNG MEN'S CHRISTIAN ASSOCIATION.

THE Association being now established in the finest Christian workshop in the world, the question arose how best to use it, and by whom its uses should be directed.

In order to insure the co-operation of all the city churches, and prevent the appearance of any conflict with their services, a meeting of all the evangelical pastors was called—where, after full and free discussion, it was voted to give over the entire direction of the meetings in Farwell Hall to Mr. Moody, the president of the Association. Thus, the humble clerk who, twelve years before, had started his little mission in an abandoned saloon, with a score of ragged and dirty street Arabs for his scholars, had at his command one of the finest halls in America, and the most complete appointment and outfit for city missionary work which could be found in all the world.

A small man, or a vain man, lifted to such a pinnacle of prosperity, would have been almost certain to lose his head. But to Mr. Moody there was in all this no temptation to pride. It was, indeed, a splendid opportunity, and to make the most of it for the salvation of men was his ceaseless ambition and his tireless toil. Under his management Farwell Hall became a people's institution. Its meetings were attended by large numbers of strangers from all parts of the country; and Moody himself became the recognised leader in this particular line of work—his zeal being honoured and his methods copied throughout the Northern States, and in Canada as well.

The noon prayer-meeting frequently filled the thousand seats in the prayer-room, and on special occasions was held in the great hall. It was still attended by proofs of the Divine favour; and requests for prayers, though fewer in number, still continued to come from abroad. A strangers' meeting was held on Monday evenings, at which Mr. Moody usually presided, where he talked and prayed with such point and freedom as few other men would have ventured to use. His first effort was to make strangers feel perfectly at home—in which he succeeded to a wonderful degree. He greeted them with the heartiness of an old friend. He would ask their names, where they came from, where they lived, what business they were doing, what churches they had attended; giving them such information and counsel as he thought would be of practical service. He would single out the new-comers, and call on them to speak. Thus:—

"You brother, over there by the first window, don't you love the Lord?"

"That red-haired man on the back seat, are you a Christian?"

And the timid brother thus addressed would rise

friendly manner

tremblingly to his feet, and give a reason of the hope which was in him, if he had one, whereupon Mr. Moody would immediately ask his name and residence, note it down in his book, and tell the new man that he was now to count himself one of the old members, and to begin to help in looking up and entertaining the strangers.

Sometimes he would walk up and down the aisles, looking into the faces of the congregation for signs of the work of the Holy Spirit on their hearts; and when he noticed a person who seemed to be thoughtful, or penitent, he would go straight to his side and say, "Are you a Christian?" If the answer was at all doubtful, he would instantly follow with, "Do you want to be saved? Do you want to be saved *now?*" And, before the half-penitent sinner had time to make objections, he would have him on his knees in prayer, kneeling himself beside him, while the whole congregation were kneeling around him. The man thus publicly brought out as a seeker of religion would generally give himself up to the Lord,—being, as it were, pushed headforemost into the kingdom of heaven; though under a less impetuous leader he might, for years, have dragged himself along at a snail's pace towards the entrance of the church.

It was his habit to spend the first three quarters of the hour from eleven to twelve in the little prayer-closet already mentioned, where he laid his personal wants before the Lord with the utmost plainness and confidence, asking, with equal faith, for blessings temporal and spiritual, and looking for immediate answers in both directions. From these communings with

God he would come down on the side walk in front of the entrance to the hall, his face fairly shining with the love and zeal of his soul, and, for a few minutes before the hour of meeting, would try to turn into it as many people as possible from the crowd which at that hour was always passing by.

One day he laid his hand on the arm of a powerful man who was hurrying along, and brought him up with the question—

"Are you for Jesus?"

"I am," was the reply.

"Then go right up to the noon prayer-meeting."

This was rather more than the stranger had looked for; besides, he had fallen out of the habit of going to prayer-meetings. To quote his own expression, he "used to be a Baptist, but had not worked at it any for a good while." He therefore tried to excuse himself, saying,—

"I cannot go up to-day."

"You can," said Mr. Moody, reading his man in an instant; and it was only by a pretence of anger, and a display of actual force, that the backslidden Baptist was able to shake off the grip of his captor, and get out of the way.

In ten or fifteen minutes of this vigorous kind of work he would send up a large number of people for prayers, who would not otherwise have attended. At the stroke of twelve he would leap up the stairway, three or four steps at a time, and rush to his place near the platform, to watch and help on the progress of the meeting.

The leadership of the noon prayer-meetings he

uniformly gave into other hands, securing the services of clergymen and prominent laymen in that capacity. But whoever occupied the platform, and read the Scriptures, and gave out the hymns, Mr. Moody was almost certain to take the meeting in hand before it was ended, especially if the prayers were dull and long, or there appeared any signs of prosy debate. Many a slow-moving service did he rouse into vigour by some sharp admonition; many a discourseful brother did he suddenly shut up by calling for a verse of a hymn, or quoting a text of Scripture.

So inexorable was his demand for point and brevity that, in these respects, the noon prayer-meeting became a model and a marvel. He, more than any other man, taught the Christian people of Chicago the art of speaking and praying in meetings; and, under his training, it was curious to see with what anxiety the speakers would plunge at once into the midst of what they had to say. His influence in this respect is not likely to be lost, at least by the present generation. It is said by those who are curious in these matters that you may detect a Farwell Hall man in a meeting in any part of the country, by the amount of speaking and praying which he can cram into three minutes—that being the time to which each of its exercises was limited.

Sometimes a slow-going brother from the country—a reverend brother, perhaps—would fail to notice the tinkling of the bell when he had just commenced his remarks; and if the one in charge of the meeting hesitated in his duty, Mr. Moody would jump to his feet and perhaps ask the stranger a question.

Catching the first word or two of his answer, he would use it as a rudder with which to bring the meeting up before the wind and send it off on its proper course again, leaving the bewildered brother out of sight behind.

The Farwell Hall services, under his administration, were always managed with a view to supplement, but never to supplant, the regular work of the churches. The noon meeting was a union service, at which most of them were represented; but the other appointments were made to meet the wants of such persons as would not have entered an ordinary place of worship. Most of the inquirers who came to ask advice of Mr. Moody would never have ventured into a pastor's study. His unpolished speech and manners were strong attractions for certain classes of people, who were glad enough of a chance to throw themselves into his sturdy arms, but would have been repelled by courtly manners and dignified address. He was a man of the people, and they opened their hearts to him accordingly.

He was conscious of his power over those who were out of the reach of other men; but he never used blunt words and phrases merely for sensational effect. A man more perfectly natural it would be a difficult matter to find.

Perhaps it was this which carried him triumphantly over his own mistakes, and prevented his being unduly mortified or cast down by reason of his many trifling blunders. In the saving power of rhetoric and grammar he had no faith at all; and the possession of these gifts by others never made him afraid of them, or hindered him from speaking his mind to them in his own plain and honest way. Rich men had given him money by thousands; wise men had asked him to show them how to save sinners; reverend men had begged him to come and help them in revivals. It was with good reason, therefore, that there was absolutely no fear of man before his eyes. He would familiarly inquire of a dignified Doctor of Divinity, "How does your soul prosper to-day, brother?" or thrust a stranger through, whom he had never seen before, with the sharp-pointed question, "Do you love the Lord?" Many were troubled by this, at first; but his earnest manner came at length to be so well understood, that people ceased to be offended or even surprised by it. It came of love and not of pride.

A merchant from a distant city was one day passing along a street in Chicago, when he was suddenly stopped by a person whom he had never seen before,—who, placing his hand upon his arm and looking him full in the face, startled him by the question—

"Do you belong to Christ?"

For a moment he was too much astonished to reply; but at length, remembering that he was in the neighbourhood of Farwell Hall, a broad smile broke over his countenance, and, looking kindly upon his questioner, he replied, "You must be Mr. Moody."

And so indeed it was.

"You must stop your impertinence," said one of his friends to him, one day: "you narrowly escaped a beating from a man whom you asked in the street whether he were a Christian or no. He said he would have slapped you in the face if he had not remembered you were a non-combatant."

"Do you remember his name?" inquired Mr. Moody.

It was given him.

"Have you seen him within a few days?"

"No."

"Well," said Mr. Moody, triumphantly, "that man has come to be one of my very best friends. He was baptized, and joined the church last Sunday; and he dates his first serious feelings from that impertinent question of mine."

In these direct appeals to strangers he was accustomed to act from impulse, which he believed was given him by the Spirit of the Lord. He held himself ready to obey, on the instant, any instructions which he might thus receive; and on such authority he would sometimes go directly contrary to the advice of his most judicious friends. But the event usually proved that he was right and they were wrong.

In the language of one who for many years has been in intimate relations with him,—

"He seems always to be carried along on a sea of inspiration. He passes his life tossing on its waves, where he is as perfectly at home as the stormy petrel on the ocean."

But in this he did not set himself up as a rule for others to follow. "To every man his work," was a favourite saying with him; and the fact that he was out of fashion in his way of serving the Lord seems seldom to have entered his mind.

Mr. Reynolds, one of his particular friends, mentions the following incident, related to him by a Christian brother from his own experience:—

"I shall always remember Mr. Moody," said he; "for he was the means of leading me to Christ. I was in a railway train one day, when a stout, cheery-looking stranger came in, and sat down in the seat beside me. We were passing through a beautiful country, to which he called my attention, saying,—

"'Did you ever think what a good Heavenly Father we have, to give us such a pleasant world to live in?'

"I made some indifferent answer; upon which he earnestly inquired,—

"'Are you a Christian?"

"I answered, 'No.'

"'Then,' said he, 'you ought to be one at once. I am to get off at the next station, but if you will kneel down, right here, I will pray to the Lord to make you a Christian.'

"Scarcely knowing what I did, I knelt down beside him there, in the car filled with passengers, and he prayed for me with all his heart. Just then the train drew up at the station, and he had only time to get off before it started again.

"Suddenly coming to myself out of what seemed more like a dream than a reality, I rushed out on the car platform, and shouted after him, 'Tell me who you are!'

"He replied, 'My name is Moody.'

"I never could shake off the conviction which then took hold upon me, until the prayer of that strange man was answered, and I had become a Christian man."

A nature so intense and active could not fail to provoke hostility; but the enmity excited by his manner often gave place to admiration on becoming better acquainted with him and catching a glimpse of his real life and love.

A certain Chicago physician once said to Mr. Jacobs,—

" I have no faith in your Mr. Moody ; I think him an impostor."

Some time afterwards he called at Mr. Jacobs' office, and said,—

" I once told you I did not believe in Mr. Moody. I have now come to say to you that I have greatly changed my mind."

Being asked to give the reason, he said,—

" I was called, the other day, to see a dying woman, who had led a life of shame. She gave me her watch and jewels, and asked me to send them to her only daughter, whom she had not seen for many years, and whose place of residence no one could give me but Mr. Moody.

" I obtained the address, and wrote to the daughter, —who came to Chicago, proved her identity, and received the articles her mother had left her. " Her respectable and lady-like appearance awakened my interest, and I ventured to inquire how she had managed to escape the life and fate of her mother.

" She answered, ' When I was a little girl, and we lived on the North Side, I used to go to Mr. Moody's Sunday-school. It was he who begged my poor mother to send me away where I might be safe ; and, by her consent, he took me to some friends of his in another State, who adopted me as their child. I grew up in a Christian home; and now I am blessed with a happy home of my own. All this good fortune I owe to the Lord, and Mr. Moody.'

"This man," said the doctor, "must be a Christian."

It may be proper to add that he was raised still higher in the doctor's estimation by another fact which afterwards came to his knowledge.

A year or two after the child had been given away, the wretched mother insisted on having her back again; and on Mr. Moody's refusal to return the child, or even to tell where she was, the woman threatened to destroy his good name by denouncing him, falsely, as guilty of gross crimes. But the man who could not be moved from his duty by poverty was also impervious to fear of black-mail. Remembering the words of Christ, "Blessed are ye when they shall revile you, and persecute you, and say all manner of evil against you, falsely, for my sake," he remained faithful to his precious trust, even though it should cost him the loss of what was dearer than his life; reaching the climax of Christian courage, and proving himself immovable as the everlasting hills. Finding her threats were of no avail, the woman resigned her child to a life of virtue; and, on her death-bed, rejoiced at the course of the faithful missionary of the North Market School, to whose fidelity and godly life she bore her dying testimony.

After the building of Farwell Hall, Mr. Moody became the chief apostle of the Young Men's Christian Association; and his services were in great request throughout the United States and Canada, where similar societies were to be organized, or special revival services were to be held under their direction.

Wherever he found these organizations too much given over to Constitution and By-laws, and a system of ceremonies, with respectable official forms and dignities, it was his delight to wake them up and bring them into active duty, in leading souls to Christ.

He would call the leading brethren together, and inquire what efforts they were making to save men from their sins. If he found them doing, in a slightly different fashion, the ordinary work of the churches, among the respectable classes of society, he would insist that they should at once become missionaries for Christ—going out into the wretched streets of the cities, to bring in the halt, the lame, and the blind, and down into saloons and gambling-houses, to invite their inmates to turn from their evil ways and be saved. In a word, he taught them to lay aside their fine notions of artistic religion, and plunge into the rapids which are sweeping souls to destruction, to pull them out and land them safely on the shores of Christ's kingdom.

More than any other man in America, God made use of Mr. Moody to save this new Christian organization from degenerating into mere social fraternities, or becoming merely another sect, still further to divide the Christian world.

It would have been easy for him to secure a very large following, and, after the manner of certain small reformers, to set up some kind of religious organization for the sake of being the head of it. But his humility was equal to his zeal—a combination seldom found—and on this account his leadership was safe, though often impetuous: he would sometimes rush along with apparently dangerous speed, but his direction was sure to be towards Christ.

CHAPTER XI.

THE SECOND FARWELL HALL.

THE new hall, which had given the Association such promise of future usefulness, was of very short duration.

Hardly were the various departments settled in their new offices, before the beautiful structure was laid in ashes. It was dedicated in September, 1867, and burned in January, 1868. The loss was a heavy one, for the building was only partially insured.

While yet the ruins were smoking, a new subscription was opened; and before the fire was fairly out the designs for the new hall were under way. It was to be built upon the old foundations; but in every other respect it was to be very much improved.

Of the first hall Mr. Farwell says,—

"It should have been named for Mr. Moody; for without his faith and devotion it never would have been built." Again Mr. Moody's talent in raising money for the Lord's work was called into exercise. To what extent the second Farwell Hall owed its existence to the unquenchable zeal and courage of the president of the Young Men's Christian Association, is not easy to determine. Both he and Mr. Farwell were pledged before God and man to this great enterprise; and most of the original stockholders being of the same mind, rallied nobly to its rescue. New stock was subscribed, new donations made, and the following year the second Farwell Hall, in all respects superior to the first, was finished and dedicated, with another shout of joy and another song of praise.

Mr. Moody's acquaintance with all sorts and conditions of men, and now more especially with rich men, was of great service to him in raising this second subscription. Considerable sums of money were given him for this purpose by persons who cared little or nothing for religion, but who liked his youthful heartiness and admired his boundless faith.

Many incidents are related of his aptness at taking advantage of circumstances and turning them to account. The following is one of the most pleasing:

Among the old, substantial citizens of Chicago, were two wealthy men with whom he was on the best of terms. Neither of them were religious men,—quite the reverse, indeed; but, for some reason or other, Mr. Moody had come to be particularly interested in their salvation. One of them had the misfortune to be thrown from his carriage, striking a curb-stone and receiving severe injuries. He was carried into an hotel near at hand, where Mr. Moody, on hearing of the accident, made haste to call upon him.

The wounded man was glad to see him; and Moody, taking a seat by his bed, opened upon him as follows:—

"I heard the other day that your old friend J——

was converted to God, and I said to myself, 'Now there is some hope of ——.' So I went right down to the noon-meeting, and had them pray for you. And now, don't you see, the Lord has answered our prayers by tipping over your buggy, and breaking your bones and laying you up here for awhile, in order to get you away from business and give you time to take care of your soul."

"That may be so," replied the wounded man, thoughtfully and kindly.

The doctor coming in just then, Mr. Moody took his leave.

Not long after, he called a second time, and offered to pray with his friend. The offer being accepted, he kneeled down at his bedside and opened his heart to the Lord, telling Him all about his afflicted friend, what a sinner he had been, and saying how much he wanted to have him saved. On rising from his knees, the wounded man, with tears trickling through his fingers, with which he had covered his face, said to him, as soon as he could command his voice, "Mr. Moody, I thank you. I have been prayed *for*, and prayed *at*, a great many times; but no one ever prayed *with* me until now."

A few days afterwards, the hall having been burnt in the meantime, Mr. Moody called again, and proposed that the patient should subscribe to the stock of the new hall.

"That's a matter of business," said Mr. ——. "If my manager says it's all right, I will take some of the stock. But you must take this for yourself," and he drew out a cheque for a considerable amount. Mr.

Moody refused the money, saying he was in need of nothing; but his friend forced it upon him. "While I have been here in bed," said he, "a great many charity agents have taken advantage of me to come and beg for money. You have come, once and again, asking for nothing, but trying to save my soul. And now I am doing for you what I would not do for them. Take the money, and use it for yourself and family."

At the date of this writing no further answers to prayer on this man's behalf have come to light. He is still a fast friend of Mr. Moody, who, when he comes back from across the sea, may yet realize his joyful prophecy, which seemed so improbable when he made it,—"We shall some time see ——— leading the noon prayer-meeting in the new Farwell Hall."

The intense orthodoxy of the Young Men's Christian Association, under Mr. Moody's administration, gave no little offence to certain Unitarian brethren, who had joined it by reason of their interest in its lectures, its proposed free library and reading-room, and its work of relieving the poor. But for the prayer-meetings and other religious services they had a strong dislike; and the Puritanical strictness with which all the affairs of the Association were managed roused their determined opposition. On one occasion some of them had hired the great hall for a fair; and, at a late hour of the evening, the tables were cleared away for a dance. This use of a place dedicated to the work and worship of the Lord roused Mr. Moody's conscience. He expostulated, but without producing any impression; and, finding them determined on this desecration of the hall, he turned off the gas, leaving them in darkness to find their way out into the street as best they might, and, as may be supposed, in no very amiable frame of mind.

No wonder that a policy so fearless and uncompromising should have roused the opposition of these easy-going religionists!

The pastor of one of the few Unitarian societies of Chicago was a recent pervert from orthodoxy, having backslidden from a leading evangelical pulpit to the platform of the liberal church, over the way. Desiring, no doubt, to signalize his new departure, he devised a rival society to the Young Men's Christian Association, based on the principles of a softer theology, and privileged with the indulgence of easier habits and a wider range of amusements.

One great objection against Mr. Moody's administration had been his use of the relief department as a missionary institution. It was alleged by the opposition, and confessed by Mr. Moody, that he never gave away a pair of trousers, or a load of wood, or a pound of tea, without an accompanying exhortation or prayer; and on all possible occasions the recipients were urged to give their hearts to Christ, devote themselves to a life of piety, and attend the prayer-meetings in Farwell Hall.

Many a family, deserted and poor, were by this means restored to society, and to the enjoyment of the means of grace: but it was noticeable that only the congregations at Farwell Hall, or at some orthodox church, were enlarged by the operation of this system ; which was, no doubt, an added reason for the zeal of Mr. Colier in his efforts to establish his rival "Christian Union."

The burning of the first Farwell Hall was the signal for the commencement of their enterprise. A great meeting at the Opera House, with all the clerical, financial, and social glory which this heterodox community could bring together, resulted in raising a subscription of several thousand dollars. With this they established the new organization. It was their intention to save young people from saloons and gambling-houses by means of innocent recreation, mingled with occasional instruction in literature and art; but by no means annoying them with psalm-singing, or disturbing them with prayers.

During the brief period in which the second Farwell Hall was rising from the ruins, of the first, the "liberal" association carried on a moderately thriving business. But presently, from some reason or other, it began to lose ground. Worldly amusements, with a mild flavour of religion, at the rooms of the Christian Union, were evidently less attractive to worldly people than those offered elsewhere, taken in the natural way. The attendance on its debates, amateur theatricals, gymnastics, games of dominoes, checkers, and chess, dwindled by slow degrees, until the whole scheme reached the point of absolute collapse ; and about the time that the new Farwell Hall was ready for use, its treasury was empty, its rooms abandoned, and the last checker-board and box of dominoes, with all the other furniture, was sold by auction, to help to pay its outstanding debts. Afterwards the "Union" took the form of a school, with classes and lectures, day and evening, at a moderate cost. In this way it has made itself useful; but as an "opposition" to the Young Men's Christian Association in methods of religious culture, it has been a conspicuous failure.

Through the relief work of the Association, the poor in all parts of the city came to know Mr. Moody. They would run after him, and stop him in the street, sometimes to ask assistance and sometimes to overwhelm him with thanks and blessings. If any one praised his charity, he would reply, "Don't praise me,—bruise me rather; but if you love me, love Christ for my sake." He was tender-hearted, and full of sympathy with those in distress; but he managed the relief of the poor not so much for the sake of comforting their bodies as with the hope of saving their souls. Everything was made to contribute to the work of bringing sinners to Christ.

For four years Mr. Moody held the office of president of the Young Men's Christian Association. He then declined re-election, but consented to act as vice-president, with his old friend J. V. Farwell in the chair.

The improvements in the second hall, the loss from inadequate insurance, and the interest upon borrowed money, left the Association in considerable financial embarrassment. Mr. Moody raised about $20,000, in donations and stock, while the hall was building. But, the treasury running low, he resorted to an ingenious expedient for replenishing it.

A sumptuous banquet was given at the Tremont House, to which the ministers of the city, the leading business men of their churches, and the stockholders of Farwell Hall, were invited. After supper the report of the financial condition of the Association was rendered, and an appeal made, first to the stockholders, to donate their stock to the Association, or to donate the interest due on it; and then to the other members of the company, to subscribe money for the current expenses of the year. The enthusiasm was great. Large amounts of stock were turned over, a considerable portion of the accrued interest subscribed, and the treasury largely replenished for the work of the coming year. The supper, which was free to the guests, was itself a donation secured by Mr. Moody's appeal. It may be said, therefore, that, under his generalship, the Association ate its way out of its difficulties.

The Sunday evening meetings in the new hall came to be a power and a blessing. It was Mr. Moody's custom to preach the same discourse in the evening which he had given to his Illinois Street congregation in the morning. This was always understood by his people; but they followed him in crowds to hear the sermon a second time, as well as to assist in the social meetings which followed it. With a single exception, it was the largest Protestant congregation in Chicago. At the close of the preaching-service, descending from the platform, he would stand at the door, greeting his friends, and watching for an opportunity to make acquaintance with strangers; after which he would lead the way to the prayer-room, on the floor below, where a meeting for inquiry and conference was held, for the purpose of following up and securing the results of the public services above.

Lewd fellows of the baser sort sometimes came into the meetings, and caused disturbances. On one occasion, there being no policeman at hand, the preacher was constrained to draw upon his own treasury of muscular force; and, almost before he was aware of it, he had repeated upon the disturber of the meeting the treatment which once before resulted so favourably at the North Market Mission. But notwithstanding such trifles as these, all classes and conditions of men and women continued to receive invitations to his services. He was glad to take the risk of annoyance if the bad fellows would only come.

It was no small attraction to those who were too poor to hire a seat in church, or even to clothe themselves suitably to attend it, to know that one of the finest audience-rooms in the State was open, every Sunday night, for their especial benefit; that a great organ and well-trained choir were in readiness to cheer their hearts with music; and that the most forcible and fervent, if not the most eloquent preacher in the whole North-West, was on the platform, to give them a sermon which was all the better for having been preached before.

The second Farwell Hall soon became a great religious centre. State and national assemblies, anniversaries, and conventions of various kinds, were held in it; ecclesiastical councils of various denominations met there; the great divines of England and America preached there; and the matchless temperance orator, Mr. Gough, would not speak anywhere else in the city.

If a mass-meeting was to be held, or a benefit to some charity was projected, the managers felt assured of success if they could secure the use of Farwell Hall. There was an atmosphere of spiritual fervour about the place, which was as evident as the atmosphere of reverence in Westminster Abbey, or of antiquity and mystery about the Pyramids and the Sphinx. It seemed to have a soul in sympathy with every godly work. It was a church which had taken down its spire, widened its pulpit, substituted chairs for pews, left its sectarian traditions behind it, thrown its doors wide open day and night, week-days and Sundays; and thus, with everything "cleared for action," as they say in the navy, had taken up a position in the midst of the world of business, as if to say,—Religion belongs everywhere: Christ and His Church are here, close to the Chamber of Commerce, and on 'Change. Again and again Mr. Moody organized revival campaigns in it: calling to his aid the best clerical talent of the city, and bringing together crowds of the most prayerful members of all the evangelical churches. The watchword was, UNION: union with Christ first, and in Him, union with one another. No controversies were permitted. No doctrines were preached but such as were believed by all intelligent Christians; and it was found by actual experiment that there was really no use for any other, so far as the work of saving sinners and edifying saints was concerned. The Gospel, pure and simple, was mighty to the pulling down of the strongholds of Satan; especially the one called sectarian exclusiveness.

God honoured His Word greatly in those Union

revival services, one result of which was to bring about more perfect harmony among the various denominations in Chicago than was ever seen in any large city before.

Here may be found another section of the path along which the Holy Spirit was leading this man. He was learning the true idea of Christian unity; and, out of the successes of those Union services, came the experience and skill which have made him the chief apostle, in our time, of co-operative work by all believers for bringing the world to Christ.

A library and reading-room were among the appliances included in the original plan of Farwell Hall. These were opened in due time; and so rapidly did this branch of the work increase, that in three years after the second hall was completed, the Chicago Young Men's Christian Association possessed a library equal in practical usefulness and value to almost any in the older cities of the Union.

It was a Christian library. All unchristian works were excluded; but it did not at all suffer thereby.

In the administration of the library, and of all the other departments of the Association, Mr. Moody, though no longer president, was the leading spirit. He had come to be recognised as a man of the people; his judgment was taken as a kind of thermometer of the judgment of the masses of ordinary Christians; and the inspirations and leadings of the Holy Spirit which sometimes came to him were often acted upon by his brethren contrary to their own opinions. He was, as they thought, better acquainted with the Lord than they, and therefore more likely to know His pleasure and will. "If any man lack wisdom," says the Scripture, "let him ask of God . . and it shall be given him." Mr. Moody, feeling his lack of the wisdom of the schools, was all the while asking instructions of God; and his simple faith in this promise was so greatly honoured that, in spite of his headstrong and impetuous manner, and his contempt of fashions and forms, he was listened to with respect whenever he said, "I feel that God wants us to do this."

He also had the grace to learn wisdom from his own mistakes. An accomplished Christian gentleman, and one of his faithful helpers, says of him, "Moody is impetuous, and all the time committing blunders; but he never makes the same mistake twice."

CHAPTER XII.

MR. MOODY'S CONVENTION WORK.

AS a platform speaker and a manager of crowds, this man, with none of the graces of oratory, but with a soul on fire with love and zeal, has come to be a master among men.

Early in his missionary life he was called to speak in small Sunday-school conventions, chiefly on account of his experience in ways of reaching the masses of neglected children in great cities. He knew this thing better than any other man in the West; and, in his blunt way, he could tell it, greatly to the instruction, and sometimes not a little to the amusement, of his audience. For several years he filled little niches in the programmes—willing to do anything, however small, to help on the cause of his Master.

But on a certain occasion in the spring of 1861, he was thrust to the front by the providence of God; and, in a sudden emergency, he learned more fully how to use the power which had so long been growing and slumbering in him.

The Committee of the Sunday-School Convention for Bureau County, Illinois, had written to Chicago for speakers, and it was arranged that several brethren should go down and help them. But when Mr. Moody reached the place, coming from some other appointment, he found that none of the "distinguished speakers from Chicago" were on hand, except his friend Mr. E. W. Hawley, the secretary of the Young Men's Christian Association, who, like himself, was reckoned one of the lesser lights in the Chicago constellation. Great things were expected from the Chicago men; and the whole of the afternoon on the great day of the meeting had been set apart to hear them. "If ever two poor fellows were frightened," says Mr. Hawley, "it was Moody and I."

It was about two o'clock on a cold March morning when they reached the city of Princeton, where the Convention was held,—too early to sit up, and too late to go to bed. Shivering with cold, and trembling under the load of responsibility thus suddenly laid upon them, they took a room, not for sleep, but for prayer. During the rest of the night they sought unto God for power and guidance, and in the morning both of them felt the smile of Heaven warming and gladdening their souls.

The morning session passed in humdrum style, with fussy debates on trifling questions; all of which led Mr. Moody and Mr. Hawley to see the importance of a more spiritual turn being given to the work of the afternoon.

In due time, happy in a sense of God's presence, they started for the large church where they were to fill the places of the "distinguished brethren from Chicago." Close to the church was a public schoolroom, which Mr. Moody engaged for the afternoon.

"What do you want with that?" asked his friend.

"I want it for an inquiry meeting after we get through," was the reply.

It was arranged that Mr. Hawley should speak first, while Mr. Moody prayed for him; they were then to change places, and Moody was to speak, while Hawley prayed; and so the meeting began. There was a great congregation, come to hear the "distinguished speakers"; but the two young men trusted in God and went ahead.

Mr. Hawley spoke for about twenty minutes with good effect; and then came Mr. Moody's turn. He seemed like one inspired. Before long he had the audience in tears. He pictured to them their need of Christ to help them as Sunday-school teachers; showed them the awful sin of doing their work in a careless or worldly manner; and, after an address of an hour or more, which was like a wild mountain torrent, he called for those who wanted to find Christ *now*, to meet him at once in the schoolroom, next door.

Great numbers of anxious inquirers accepted his invitation, about sixty of whom were blessed before leaving the place.

This was the beginning of a wide-spread revival in Bureau County; for the delegates carried the spirit of that wonderful meeting home with them, and gave their hearts and hands anew to their work. But it was also the beginning of a new life for Mr. Moody. He had taken hold of power; and from that day he went everywhere in the strength of God. With perfect *abandon*, he threw himself upon Christ and into his subject; and, carried on the tides of heavenly love and sympathy, he swept along towards the mercy-seat, taking multitudes of penitent sinners with him, and offering them in prayer to the Saviour as trophies of His grace.

This way of acting and speaking by special inspiration led him to do strange things sometimes, though afterwards they were generally seen to be useful and right.

On one of his rounds of meetings in the State of Indiana, he was riding in the waggon of a quiet Christian brother, who was taking him to his next appointment; when they passed a little school-house which was closed for the day. Telling his friend to stop at the dwelling nearest to it, he stood up in the waggon and hailed the house. A woman came to the door, and Mr. Moody asked if there were any religious meetings held in that school-house.

"No indeed," answered the woman; "we haven't any meetings anywhere about here."

"Well," said Moody, "tell all your neighbours there will be prayer-meetings in that school-house every night next week."

At the next house they found the teacher of the school, to whom he gave the same announcement, and bade her send the notice by all her scholars.

As they rode on, the brother who was conveying him seemed lost in amazement. He knew that this strange man had a long list of appointments in advance, and could not attend those meetings he was giving out. At length he said,—

"You are telling these people there are to be prayer-meetings in that school-house every night next week. I should like to know who is going to conduct them ?"

"You are," said Mr. Moody.

"I!" said the man in astonishment: "I never did such a thing in my life."

"It's time you had, then," said Moody. "I have made the appointment, and you will have to keep it."

Thrust out into the work in this strange manner, the good brother actually went and held the meetings, which filled the little school-house to overflowing, and resulted in a great revival of religion throughout all that neglected region of country.

An organization had existed for several years in the State of Illinois, a part of whose work it was to hold an annual State Sunday School Convention, to which every school was invited to send its superintendent and one delegate, for a four or five days' conference upon general Sunday-school interests. These conventions were somewhat cold and formal, devoting much time to parliamentary tactics, and discussions on the theory and art of teaching, to the neglect of spiritual questions: such as—How to bring the children to a saving knowledge of Christ: How to save the parents through the children: How to call more labourers into Christ's whitening harvest: How, in prayer, to get firmest hold on God's promises: How to become sanctified through the Truth.

From 1858 to 1865 the annual Conventions went on in this style. Mr. Moody, Mr. Jacobs, and Major Whittle—who, from being so much together in the work of the Lord, were called the "Chicago Trio"—

became deeply impressed with the need of more of the presence and power of the Holy Spirit.

The meeting for 1865 being at hand, the Chicago brethren laid a plan for lifting it out of its old formality, and making it a truly spiritual and godly assembly.

Four days previous to the time at which the meeting was to be held, in the city of Springfield, Mr. Moody, Mr. Jacobs, and one or two other brethren, started for the scene of action ; reaching the place at about four o'clock on Saturday morning. For an hour or two they walked the streets, talking of the ways and means by which the great Convention might, with God's blessing, be turned into a revival. After breakfast, Mr. Jacobs, feeling special liberty in that direction, sought out a Baptist church, climbed in at a window, followed by Moody and the rest ; went into the pulpit ; opened the Bible ; read a portion of Scripture, and commenced to hold a little prayer-meeting : when the pastor of the church, entering by the door, gave them hearty welcome to his church and city.

The Chicago brethren told him they were the advance-guard of the Sunday School Convention, and had come to hold revival meetings as a prelude to its exercises.

This church and other places of worship were gladly placed at their disposal. Meetings were held on the Sabbath, which attracted such multitudes that many were turned away for want of room. In the Presbyterian church, the meeting led by Messrs. Moody and Jacobs on Sunday afternoon resulted in the awakening of seventy persons, who arose for prayer in all parts of the house; of all classes of people, and all ages, from a child of six to a grey-haired infidel of seventy years. These revival meetings were continued through the session of the Convention, resulting in about two hundred conversions—one of the converts being the aged infidel above mentioned. But the most remarkable fruit of this effort was its influence on the Convention itself. Its sessions were made glorious by the presence of the Holy Ghost. No more wordy discussions; no strife for honours: but all hearts, thrilled by "power from on high," sought for a fresh baptism, and consecrated themselves anew to Christ and His work. The fire there kindled spread all over the State. The delegates, returning to their own homes and schools, stirred up their brethren to greater activity and devotion in the work of saving souls, with most encouraging results.

The next annual meeting, held in the city of Decatur, was a perfect jubilee. A record was brought up of about ten thousand conversions, most of them traceable to the baptism of power on the Convention of the previous year.

Encouraged by the blessing of the Lord, they determined on an effort for the complete and systematic canvass of the State, with a view to organize Sunday-schools in every neglected region.

The sum of five thousand dollars, which was the estimated expense of the work, was raised in about thirty minutes. Well-known brethren, from each of the one hundred counties, were appointed as a committee of exploration, who were to call in such aid as they could at home, by which means it was expected that every part of the State would be reached, and immense numbers of people brought under this simple means of grace.

The Convention held the following year, in the city of Du Quoin, in the southern part of the State, sometimes called "Egypt," was a still greater marvel of success.

Du Quoin was then a village of three thousand inhabitants; and about an equal number of Sunday-school delegates poured in upon them. But every one brought a benediction with him; the hearts of the people grew large with welcome, and the whole place, for those four days, was given over to rejoicing. The meetings were almost continuous, from early morning until eleven o'clock at night. No church or hall being large enough to accommodate them, they were held in an immense barn, used for baling and storing hay, but at this time, by good fortune, empty.

At the next annual Convention, held in Bloomington, the enthusiasm was unparalleled. Mr. Moody was elected president, and carried the great meeting along at the highest rate of speed. No long prayers or speeches were tolerated; and the meeting rolled on in an ever-increasing tide of power; reaching its climax in the moving address of its president on the memorable night of its closing.

The success of the organization in the previous year led to a call for volunteers, to canvass the counties over again; and in this manner every town in the State was brought into line.

Mr. Moody, and Mr. Reynolds of Peoria, pledged themselves to hold County Conventions through all the southern portion of Illinois.

These Conventions are remembered with great delight. The progress of these two brethren from one county to another was a sort of triumphal procession; large numbers of people accompanying them in waggons and on horseback; the interest of the meetings increasing as they went along. When no hall of sufficient capacity could be obtained, the services were held in the open air. There were also camp-meetings, field-meetings, street preaching in the towns on their route, from the court-house steps, and other public places. In one county—that of Gallatin—the conversions at these meetings reached the number of six hundred.

The State Convention of 1870 was held at Quincy,—where, it is estimated, five thousand Sunday-school delegates were present. The success of Messrs. Moody and Reynolds, and their co-labourers Messrs. Jacobs and Whittle, of Chicago, Tyng of Peoria, and Gillett of Jacksonville, had naturally made them prominent, and led to their being placed on the most important committees; and Professor Gillett, superintendent of the State Asylum for the Deaf and Dumb, had been placed in the chair, in opposition to a local candidate. It appears that the gentleman in question, though an excellent man, was also a candidate for some political office; and it was thought, by his friends, that the position of President of the State Sunday School Convention would greatly help his chances of election. Such a use of such an office was determinedly opposed by the brethren above mentioned, with the result already indicated.

Much ill-feeling was manifested by the friends of the losing candidate, as the Convention went on; and when Mr. Moody took the stand to "open the question drawer,"—that is, to give off-hand answers to impromptu questions on Sunday-school topics, (an exercise in which he particularly excelled,) the question was asked him whether "the ring" which controlled the State Sunday School Convention had any limit to its power.

Such a question in such an assembly, already somewhat disturbed, threatened to produce an open rupture, break up the Convention, and do irreparable injury to the cause it represented. Mr. Moody saw the situation at a glance. He knew the determined and organized opposition to the strictly religious methods introduced and carried out by himself and his friends. A less ready and courageous man would have suffered the meeting to drift into confusion; but, without the least apparent anxiety, he replied to this remarkable question by giving a full account of "the ring," and the blessing of God which, year after year, had attended their united labours all over the State. Having done this, he closed his remarks by tendering to the Convention the resignation of every office held by himself and the brethren at whom the question was aimed.

The scene which followed is indescribable. Thousands of people were weeping. Brethren from every part of the State earnestly defended Mr. Moody and his friends. The opposition was hushed in silence, and drowned in tears. A motion was made and carried by acclamation, refusing to accept the resignation offered by Mr. Moody on behalf of himself and his friends. The facts connected with their work were their only and sufficient defence.

When the motion had passed, Mr. Moody spoke a few words, full of tenderness and emotion, and then said, "Let us pray."

In speaking of the scene which followed, Mr. Jacobs says,—

"Many people have told me they never heard anything like that prayer." The whole audience was melted; sobs and cries drowned the leader's voice; and when he rose from his knees, Philip Phillips, the "sweet singer" of the Methodist Israel, struck up one of his tender and loving hymns, which was like oil upon the troubled waters.

At the close of the meeting, one of the friends of the gentleman in whose behalf the unhappy division had been made, spoke of his feelings thus:—

"We were sufficiently punished when Mr. Moody told us what he had been trying to do for Christ, and then offered to give up all his honours; but when he prayed for us, our punishment was greater than we could bear."

The storm had passed. Love and harmony reigned once more. The Convention went forward to its close, with the old-time vigour and success; and since that day no discord has marred its history.

Other States also sought the services of the "Chicago ring," and attempted to copy their plans.

The Young Men's Christian Association of Boston

invited Mr. Moody to attend a great Sunday-school meeting at Tremont Temple, in that city, to explain the Illinois method, and to help them to put it in operation throughout the State of Massachusetts. He went, and made a characteristic speech, setting forth his plan minutely, and awakening in the audience a high degree of interest. The motion was then made to put this plan in operation, without delay. But some of the more cautious brethren were not prepared to enter on so great a work without a large amount of argument. They spoke, one after another, of the difficulties in the way. What could be done easily enough in the Western State of Illinois might not be possible, they thought, in the Eastern State of Massachusetts. This line of remark so cooled down the enthusiasm of the meeting, that at last they actually voted to postpone the whole subject for a year.

Mr. Moody's genius in snatching victory from the jaws of defeat was notably manifest on this occasion. The Convention, having proved a complete failure, was about to adjourn, when he whispered to the chairman: "Call another meeting for this evening; tell the people I will speak."

The presiding officer did as he was directed, and in the evening the hall was filled; though the only attraction offered was another speech from the man whose views the Convention had set aside during the day. Cautiously and steadily Mr. Moody commenced his work. He spoke of his own North Market Mission School; gave them scenes and incidents, in which ragged and dirty children of the street had become cultivated and honoured Christian ladies and gentlemen; and, when he felt that his audience had become sufficiently impressible, he brought up again the discarded plan of the morning, for organizing the Sunday-school work of Massachusetts. Throwing all his power and energy into the subject, it soon became evident that he was carrying the audience with him; and, at the supreme moment, he opened the question again as follows:—

"Brethren and friends, I am not very much used to putting motions, and bringing them back again after they have been voted down; but we must do something to correct that wrong vote of this morning. Now everybody in the house who is not satisfied with that vote, and wants to go to work, at once, and organize this State after the Illinois pattern, let him stand on his feet, hold up his right hand, and say 'Aye!'"

As by a common impulse, the entire congregation rose to their feet, and answered "Aye," in a shout so hearty that before the close of the year its echoes were heard all over the old Bay State.

When the State Christian Convention of Missouri was held in the city of St. Louis, not long after the close of the war, it was found impossible to agree upon a candidate for presiding officer. The city was divided between the friends of the Union and the friends of the late Confederacy; and every prominent religious man in the State was known as a partisan on one side or the other.

Mr. Moody, who was present, was at length agreed upon by both sides as a suitable man to fill the chair;

for, though he was not a citizen of their State, and had been a staunch Union man through the war, yet there was so much Christianity in him as either to hide or glorify whatever opinions he might hold on any other subject.

It will readily be believed that the duties of the chairman, under such circumstances, were difficult and trying in the extreme. But Mr. Moody made an admirable presiding officer. He seemed to hold the Union men by one hand and the ex-Confederates by the other, thus constituting himself a tie of Christian brotherhood between them. When any confusion seemed likely to arise, he knew how, suddenly but gracefully, to bring the Convention around the dangerous point by the help of a prayer or a hymn; sometimes changing the whole order of services, to avoid a dangerous debate.

Thus, with a cool head, a warm heart, and a steady hand, all sanctified and empowered by Divine grace, he managed this dangerous combination of fire and gunpowder without an explosion: an achievement of which the speaker of the House of Representatives or Commons might be proud, and which would certainly be mentioned in their memoirs as a triumph of genius, good-nature, and parliamentary skill.

From Maine to Texas, from Montreal to San Francisco, from St. Paul to New Orleans, Mr. Moody went, year after year, preaching and praying, rousing the Christian Associations into activity, labouring with the pastors of churches in revivals; coming home, now and then, to give a few weeks' earnest labour to his own congregation, and finding a hatful of calls awaiting him. He thus gained experience of inestimable value, and received a training, better than that of the schools, for the still greater work which the Lord had in store for him across the sea.

During this time, as may be supposed, he had no leisure for books. One Book only had he time to study; but the Bible, as he learned to use it, answered every purpose. He is still unlearned, as that word is commonly understood; but the knowledge and training which he has obtained in his seventeen years of labour as a missionary and evangelist, with a continent for his college, and hundreds of the best men in it for his teachers and models, have made him a truly accomplished man in the line of his special duty: "a workman that needeth not to be ashamed, rightly dividing the Word of truth."

CHAPTER XIII.

BIBLE STUDY AND BIBLE WORK.

IN the earlier years of Mr. Moody's work for Christ, his sermons and addresses, though often founded upon a text of Scripture, were largely made up of personal incidents, arguments drawn from surrounding scenes and circumstances; fervid personal appeals to Christians, inciting them to greater activity; and earnest calls to sinners, urging them at once to repent and believe the Gospel.

The readiness with which he could appropriate every useful thought and thing which came within his reach, enabled him to do an amount of preaching which was marvellous for a man of his meagre attainments and his very limited time for study. He reckoned all sermons and addresses which he heard or read as so much lawful plunder. Of this he made no secret. He would sometimes say to a minister:—

"I heard you preach from such a text, at such a time; and I went home and preached that same sermon to my people."

Rev. Dr. Savage mentions a discourse which Mr. Moody found in a little tract, entitled, "Quench not the Spirit," and which he preached with such telling effect that twenty persons were converted by it. But it is doubtful whether the author himself would have recognised it in Mr. Moody's version.

When at a loss for a subject, he would go to his friends, at their offices or homes, and converse with them, until some remark started a train of thought in his mind; when he would rush with it to his study, or sometimes even to the platform. If he met any one from whom it seemed probable he might obtain an idea for use in his pulpit, he would salute him with,—

"Give me something out of your heart. Tell me something about Christ."

At table, in the Farwell Hall restaurant, where he and his *confrères* dined together, he would ask one and another, round the table,—

"What has been your best thought to-day?"

Being always surrounded by active, studious, and consecrated people, he thus possessed an almost unfailing source from which to draw the outlines and suggestions of his sermons and addresses. Thus, his widely-extended travels, his intense religious life, and the constant recurrence of striking conversions and other powerful incidents under his ministry or observation, enabled him to keep alive the interest of his great congregations at home, and made him a most effective platform speaker abroad.

But there was something still better in store for him: even the inexhaustible treasures of the Holy Scriptures. These he already read with intense delight, and on their promises he relied for his daily bread, as well as for the maintenance of his spiritual health and strength. But to the divine art of expounding them he had not yet attained.

"The words which I speak unto you, they are Spirit and they are Life," said the Saviour.

"The sword of the Spirit, which is the Word of God," said Paul.

"Man doth not live by bread only, but by every word that proceedeth out of the mouth of the Lord doth man live," said Moses, in his dying charge to Israel.

God was about to reveal this hidden wisdom to His servant, in a manner at once loving and impressive; and to a degree which should make him one of the most successful Bible teachers of his times.

One Saturday, as he was about leaving home to spend the Sabbath at a distant convention, he said to his wife: "I have received a letter from Harry Moorhouse, an Englishman who calls himself the 'Boy preacher,' saying he will be in Chicago to-day, and will preach for me if I wish it. It is too late to get any one else, and I suppose we must let him try it in the morning; but if he makes a failure, you must tell the deacons to find some one else for the evening, or let them hold a prayer-meeting."

On his return the next week, Mr. Moody anxiously inquired what sort of a preacher Harry Moorhouse had proved to be.

"He is a wonderful preacher," was the reply. "On Sunday morning he preached from the text, 'God so loved the world that He gave His only-begotten Son, that whoso believeth in Him should not perish but have everlasting life.' The people were so much interested, that a crowd filled the church in the evening, when he took the same text again; and so wonderfully did he explain it that the deacons have asked him to preach every night this week."

That week was a memorable one. Night after night Mr. Moorhouse preached to immense congregations, taking the same text every time; until he made the love of God appear the central truth of the whole Bible. At the close of the seventh sermon from the same words, he said,—

"If I were to die to-night, and go up to heaven, and there meet Gabriel, who stands in the presence of God; and if I were to ask him how much God loves sinners, this is what I think he would say: 'God *so* loved the world that He gave His only-begotten Son, that whoso believeth in Him should not perish but have everlasting life.'"

When the meetings were over, Mr. Moorhouse said to Mr. Moody,—

"You are sailing on the wrong tack. If you will change your course, and learn to preach God's words instead of your own, He will make you a great power for good."

The other results of these seven sermons from one text cannot now be reckoned up; but to Mr. Moody they were a revelation from heaven. He began to see that the Word of the Lord giveth light: he began to understand something about comparing Scripture with Scripture: the wonderful panorama of Divine truth, which he had seen unfolded, opened to him a new world. From this time he began, as never before, to study the Gospel of the grace of God, and to search for the hidden mysteries of His Word. The exhortation of Paul came home to him with tremendous force,—

"I charge thee, therefore, before God, and the Lord Jesus Christ, who shall judge the quick and the dead at His appearing and His kingdom; PREACH THE WORD."

But the great question was how to acquire such a knowledge of the Word as should enable him to preach it. He had no time to study books; neither had he the books to study.

His learned and faithful friend, the Rev. Dr. Patterson, had some time before advised him to commence a course of reading, and had made a list of books which should constitute a kind of short course in exegesis and theology: but he had never found leisure to begin it; and the longer he waited for the time to come when he could conveniently do so, the farther it seemed away.

But Mr. Moorhouse said, "You only need one book for the study of the Bible."

Mr. Moody responded, "You must have studied a great many books to come by your knowledge of it."

"No," was the reply. "Since I began to be an evangelist, I have been a man of one book. If a text of Scripture troubles me, I ask another text to explain it; and if this will not answer, I carry it straight to the Lord."

Here was a new scheme of education for the pulpit: every man his own theological seminary; the only text-book, the Bible; instead of Greek and Hebrew, the language of prayer; for professors and teachers, the apostles and prophets, with Christ and the Holy Spirit as Head over all. In this school even he might become a scholar

Mr. Moorhouse had been surprised to find that Mr. Moody's congregation did not bring their Bibles to meeting. "You should have God's own Word in your hands," said he; "so that you may know whether my words are right and true,"—and during his short stay with them, he introduced the fashion with which he was familiar at home, and which has been kept up by that congregation ever since, of a constant use of the Bible, not only in the pulpit, but also in the pew.

Mr. Moody was so much impressed with the power of this "man of one book," that he asked him to show them how to study it as he had done. Accordingly, Mr. Moorhouse appointed a meeting at Mr. Moody's house, at which fifty or sixty persons were present, and there held the first "Bible Reading" of which there is any record in America.

He had no idea of inaugurating a revolution in the method of preaching in America; but that was what he actually did. The beginning was small enough; but, already, the method of Bible study and Bible work which he showed to Mr. Moody and his little company of delighted friends that night, is coming into high favour and extensive use, not only by evangelists and lay helpers, but by the ministers themselves.

Every one had brought a Bible, as directed. After prayer for the enlightenment of the Holy Spirit, who had at first inspired the writing, and must now inspire the understanding of the Scriptures, the "boy preacher" led them on a voyage of discovery from Genesis to Revelation; tracing the promises, prophecy and history of REDEMPTION. On this theme they found the Word of God to be especially rich and full; it was, indeed, the centre around which all the Scriptures revolved; and so wonderfully did it become impressed upon their minds, that it seemed to them like a new revelation. Text after text was found and joined to the wonderful series, until they appeared like links of a long golden chain, holding a broken and ruined world together, and binding it fast to God's mercy-seat. This was Mr. Moody's first lesson in systematic theology.

But so great a revolution in his habits of study and preaching was not to be brought about all at once. He saw the land from afar, and desired exceedingly to go in and possess it. He gave up his plan for a course of reading, and, a second time in sight of the shores of learning, put boldly out to sea. His old habits generally ran away with him when he stood up to preach; but in his study he followed the new method.

His world was so full of wonderful and instructive scenes, that the stories of them seemed almost to tell themselves. It was hard for him to find time for a great deal of Bible in his hailstorm harangues; but he kept sturdily at it, trying to acquire the biblical method of preaching, in which was the hiding of the power that was to be revealed to him in days to come. From that time he ceased to urge people to begin their religious life by finding something to do for

Christ; but insisted that, first of all, they should let Christ do something for them. If they would only believe, Christ would help them to *be* and to *do.*

He began to understand the privilege and duty of entire consecration and perfect love. He ceased to teach that a holy heart must be attained by a life-long struggle with self, the world, and the wicked one; but urged sinners to accept it as a gift from the Lord Himself. Conversion was instantaneous; the warfare was to come afterwards. This, he discovered, was the doctrine preached by the prophet Ezekiel:–

"A new heart also will I give you, and a new spirit will I put within you: and I will take away the stony heart out of your flesh, and I will give you a heart of flesh."

He began to study the Bible on his knees.

In this he made rapid progress. Some of the hard words did indeed continue to plague him; but he soon found out that the longest words in the Bible, as everywhere else, were not apt to be of the most importance: so he followed the example of the worthy Scotch minister, who was accustomed to say to his congregation, when he came upon a Scripture passage which was too wonderful for him,—

"Brethren, this is a difficult text; a *very* difficult text; but, my brethren, let us not be discouraged by it. Let us look the difficulty boldly in the face,—*and pass on.*"

There were very few practical and saving doctrines in the Word of God through which he could not pray his way. Like his friend Moorhouse, he became a "man of one book"; that is, a Bagster's Bible. This he carried about with him continually, in order to use his leisure moments in studying it. His sermons began to be rich in the wealth of the Scriptures; and, beyond all doubt, it was this new acquirement which, with God's blessing, opened out before him his career of almost boundless usefulness, and placed the keys of the kingdom of heaven in his hand.

The Rev. Dr. Roy, his former pastor at Plymouth Church, mentions a sermon which he heard Mr. Moody preach on "The Compassion of Christ"; in which he seemed like a man inspired, and under which the great audience were moved like the forests swept by the winds.

When it was over, the Doctor inquired of him how he had prepared such a sermon. He answered, "I got to thinking the other day about the compassion of Christ; so I took the Bible and began to read it over, to find out what it said on that subject. I prayed over the texts as I went along, until the thought of His infinite compassion overpowered me, and I could only lie on the floor of my study, with my face in the open Bible, and cry like a little child."

The visit of that great English preacher, the Rev. Dr. Punshon, was another godsend to him.

The Doctor preached for him in Farwell Hall several times. His great sermon on "Daniel in Babylon" was especially blessed to Mr. Moody. The vivid picture of that fearless prince and prophet showed him that the characters of the Bible were actual men and women. It was not their different circumstances which made them different from other men, but only their perfect faith in God.

A new field was thus opened to him; and through that whole summer, after making the acquaintance of this hero, Mr. Moody studied and preached the biographies of the Bible. Abraham and Moses, Daniel and Paul, Noah and Samuel, David and John, one after another, were called to rise before his vision, and show themselves to his amazed and delighted congregations. Far and wide he preached these sermons; and all the time he sought to impress this truth upon his hearers: "Whatsoever YE shall ask in faith, believing, YE shall receive." "God is no respecter of persons; but IN EVERY NATION he that feareth Him and worketh righteousness is accepted with Him."

"Abraham believed God, and it was counted to him for righteousness."

"Daniel was taken out of the den, and no manner of hurt was found upon him, because he believed in his God."

He insisted, with the greatest emphasis, that the central power in religion was faith—faith in Jesus Christ—faith in the Christ of the Gospels; and so thoroughly did he give himself up to this great truth, that he began to feel the force of the "boy preacher's" prophecy, and to say to himself in his closet—"If I can only learn to believe as those men believed, what is there to hinder God from laying some great work on me?"

After this, his desire for Bible knowledge led him to leave his pressing work at home, and make a voyage to England; where he might have the help of certain brethren who had become mighty in the Scriptures, by becoming "men of one book." Not many months before, he had crossed the Atlantic, with his family, for the benefit of their health; and when some of his friends asked him why he went so soon again, he answered:—

"I am going to England to study the Bible."

It would appear that, during his short stay, he used his knowledge as fast as he acquired it; for, in those three months of Bible study, he preached about ninety sermons, besides attending many meetings for inquiry and prayer. But no great success attended him: God was only sending him to school.

After this it began to be his habit, in the social meetings, to say, "Tell us your experience in Bible language."

When any one expressed an opinion on any doctrine of religion, he would straightway inquire: "Have you God's Word for it?"

He began also to be impatient at those figures of speech and stock phrases which people sometimes use in speaking to anxious sinners. "Give them the words of Christ," he would say; "man's words are good for nothing, but Christ's words are spirit and life."

He gave up his reliance on exhortations and anecdotes, as a means of awakening sinners; and, though he continued to use them, it was only to explain or enforce some text of Scripture. The idea that people must first be interested and attracted by some worldly wisdom, and so made ready to hear the Word of God, he held to be a delusion and a snare. He would say to those who argued for this notion of the schools:

"Don't you think God knows best how to interest people?"

Thus, from being merely a point of departure, from which his sermons wandered into highways and by-ways, the Word of God came to be the entire plane of their projection, and a good part of their solid substance.

A very important help to Mr. Moody, and, through him and his friends, to tens of thousands of other Christian workers in America, was the introduction of the International Sunday School Lessons.

The idea of turning the thoughts and prayers of the whole English-speaking world upon the same passage of Scripture at the same time, appears to have come directly from God. The impetus to the study of the Bible which was given by it, is something which would have been incredible if it had been foretold. It is the most notable "advance along the whole line" which the Church militant has taken for more than a hundred years. It deserves to be classed with the great Methodist revival, and the first inauguration of Sunday-schools. It is on this account that, to the heavy and costly commentaries on the whole Bible, which were beyond the reach of the great mass of Sunday-school teachers, have been added many little books containing the ripest fruits of Christian scholarship, in exposition of the particular lessons so wisely selected by the International Committee.

Soon after the National Series—which preceded the International—came into use in Chicago, the Young Men's Christian Association devoted the Saturday noon prayer-meeting to the study of the Sunday-school lesson for the following day. As almost all its working members were also active Sunday-school workers, they entered studiously and zealously into this new exercise, which at once became very popular, and attracted large numbers of persons not hitherto connected with the Association.

The prayer-room of the first Farwell Hall, holding a thousand people, was filled to overflowing every Saturday; and after it was burned, and the meeting was removed to the lecture-room of the First Methodist Church, the interest became so great that it was found necessary to open the audience-room, which, week after week, was filled, even to the galleries and the aisles, with men and women, eager, like the Athenians, to hear some new thing; but, unlike them, anxious to hear it concerning the old truths of God's Word.

Mr. Moody seemed to communicate to the entire Association his own new and wonderful grasp of the Holy Scriptures. Pastors of the leading city churches put forth their best efforts in conducting these Saturday Bible meetings; while many a quaint and homely interpretation, from some unlearned but devoted heart, gave new freshness and vigour to the exercise.

It was the social meeting at Corinth over again, on a large scale. When they came together, many a one, if not every one, had a psalm, or a tongue, or a revelation, or an interpretation; and the apostle's charge, "Let all things be done unto edifying," was obeyed with wonderful fidelity and success. The skill in this Bible work to which Mr. Moody, Mr. Jacobs, Major Whittle, and others, attained, was one of the greatest spiritual acquirements recorded in the history of the Church in America; and their mastery of the Word becoming known abroad, they came to be in great request all over the United States and in Canada.

Encouraged by the remarkable favour which the Lord had shown him as steward of the Word of Life, Mr. Moody devised a plan for a Bible school; in which those who were willing to devote their time to the Lord's work, as evangelists, exhorters, Bible-readers, and the like, should receive a special and gratuitous course of training, both in the sense of the Scriptures, and also in the best methods of teaching and preaching them.

His departure for England, where the Lord has so signally blessed his labours, obliged Mr. Moody to commit this enterprise to other hands. And here, as always, God had a servant ready for the work.

Miss Emeline Dryer, an accomplished Christian lady, holding the highest educational position in the West, as the female head of the faculty of the Illinois State Normal University, had been moved by the Lord to come to Chicago, and devote herself to the sorrowful task of trying to help those lost women who are so far away from, and generally neglected by, all ordinary means of grace.

It was a picture fit for angels to gaze upon: a learned and honoured Christian woman, stepping down from her high position to become a teacher and evangelist in the reformatory institution known as "The Erring Women's Refuge."

The capacity and devotion of this heroic woman were not long in becoming known; and, after the Great Fire, her services were called into requisition in a wider sphere, as secretary of the Women's Aid Society.

This Society, like many others for missionary work, came naturally into fellowship and labour with the Young Men's Christian Association: and her ability having been proved for two years, during which she conducted the great Bible-class in Mr. Moody's church, and, at the same time, several girls' and mothers' meetings in various parts of the city, the Bible school was placed in her charge. It is now in successful operation, and is regarded by Mr. Moody as one of the most important of all his various projects for helping on the kingdom of God. It is supported wholly by voluntary contributions from some most judicious Christian people, who already see in it the beginning of a great school of Christ, equal in power and usefulness to Mr. Spurgeon's famous college in London.

The "Bible readings," which have been so much blessed of God, and so much enjoyed by Mr. Moody's audiences, both in America and Great Britain, have a striking history of their own.

It is a sad confession to make, in this late year of grace, that anything which can fitly be described as a Bible reading is new. But Mr. Moody has certainly introduced a method of handling the Word of God which has excited deep interest among thoughtful and judicious Christian people, and is regarded as a valuable contribution to the meagre stock of Scriptural exercises hitherto practised in our churches.

The use of Scripture in sermons has become lamentably small. The text is often used merely as a starting-point, or as the statement of a theme which is to be worked out with all the arts of rhetoric, and so much of logic as the author may be able to command; with here and there a quotation brought in as a kind of respectful notice due to the Bible, or as a suitable method of rounding off a period. Even in some most orthodox theological seminaries, young men are but poorly trained to know and use the Scriptures. Systematic and sectarian theology, ancient literature, homiletics, rhetoric, and elocution, leave little time for the reverent and prayerful study of the Word of God. These schools send out into the world their annual instalments of professional ministers, with heads more or less full of clerical learning; but, with all their study, there is one thing they have not learned: namely, how to "preach the Word."

The poverty of the American pulpit in this respect is becoming more and more apparent; and the Church is occasionally sending abroad for men to fill some of its highest pastorates; not because the ministry of America is deficient in piety or culture or eloquence, but because it is deficient in a thorough understanding of the Holy Scriptures, and in that particular use of them which is called "expository preaching."

Other evangelists have, of late, been led to become "men of one book"; and the fact that these persons, taken from the level of the people, wholly wanting in professional training, but mighty in the Scriptures, have been honoured of God in leading more souls to Him than any other class of men now living, is another showing of the truth of the Saviour's saying—"The words that I speak unto you, they are spirit and they are life."

This lesson Mr. Moody had partially learned of his

friend Mr. Moorhouse; but it was to be burned into his heart in letters of fire.

During a considerable part of the year 1871, he passed through a terrible struggle of soul with respect to himself and his work. He used to weep and pray in agony in his closet, and then, with a sorrowful face, go out to his public duties. He was constantly begging his friends to pray for him. Having made the acquaintance of two very aged women, who were remarkable for their lives of faith in spite of great afflictions, he used to go to them like a broken-hearted child, and ask them to teach him how to trust wholly in God.

One great torment of his soul was the thought that he was an ignorant man, and yet was looked upon as a religious teacher. He began to wonder if he were not one of those blind guides; and if, some time, he would not find himself in the ditch. If the devil had known just what was in store for this man, he could not have tempted him more cunningly or pressed him harder. But still he went on with his work. He dared not stop, though he was sometimes so mortified by his errors of speech and his lack of worldly wisdom, that he was almost ready to sink.

At last he reached the point where he was willing to give even his ignorance to Christ, and to be just as weak as Christ wanted him to be. Then he began to lay hold of the lines of power. Every promise was like the valve-lever of an engine in his hand.

The waves of fire which swept away his church, his home, and his beloved Farwell Hall, could not harm him now. But having no place among the miles of ashes where he could go on with his work, he went away to the Atlantic coast, trusting to God to bring him into some field of labour.

He reached Brooklyn at the time when Dr. Cuyler's new Mission Chapel was just completed; and on going to see it with a friend, he said,—

"I should like to hold some meetings here: the air of the place seems full of Heaven." This was repeated to the Doctor, and immediately he received an invitation to do as he had desired.

But the meetings dragged heavily. Few people attended, and none were awakened. At last, when the congregation had fallen to eighteen persons, a good lady said to him:—

"Mr. Moody, we have plenty of preaching in Brooklyn; but if you would tell us something about the Bible, perhaps it would be blessed to us."

It would appear that he had fallen into his old style of address at this new place: but he at once accepted the suggestion, and set about preparing some exercises in Bible study, after the manner of Mr. Moorhouse several years before, but with such improvements as his experience and skill suggested. Strangely enough, he had never made use of this particular method until now.

Telling them all to bring their Bibles, he appointed a study for the following afternoon. At once the power of God came down. Day after day the meetings increased. A great revival broke out, and spread from the Mission into the home Church. Sinners on every hand were inquiring what they must do to be saved.

From Brooklyn he went to Philadelphia, preaching

and reading "the Word"; and the Lord greatly blessed his labours there also.

When he returned to Chicago he at once commenced the "Bible readings"; and in a short time they became a favourite religious service, and were attended by large numbers of the most intelligent Christian people. Many pastors, learning the art from Mr. Moody, made use of it in their own pulpits; and several lay evangelists, who had been in doubt about their call to "preach," hailed this new method as something which was, without question, a fit and helpful thing to do.

The success of these "readings" in England, and especially in Scotland, where the people know very well how to handle a Bible, is God's own testimony to the saving power of His Word. Mr. Moody's addresses are mighty, Mr. Sankey's singing is heavenly; but the "Bible readings," are so little human and so much Divine, that they, more than anything else, have been used in awakening sinners and building up the saints.

These "Bible readings" consist in a careful and systematic grouping of Scripture texts, all relating to a single central truth; which, by this method, is vividly impressed upon mind and heart. After singing, and prayer, the congregation take their Bibles; and the leader reads the list of texts which he expects to use, asking, after each one, "Who will read this when I call for it?" Or the texts may be written out; or chapter and verse noted on a piece of paper, and the slips distributed to those who are to read them, if preferred.

The entire list of selected Scriptures being thus assigned to persons in the congregation, the exercise opens by calling for the text first in order. The one who has taken it reads it aloud; and the leader explains, illustrates, and enforces it briefly, and then calls for the next. Sometimes one person is appointed beforehand to find and read the texts as they are called for; and sometimes the leader reads them, asking all the congregation to turn to them and read with him. Thus the Lord is brought into the congregation to speak for Himself. No wonder He honours such a use of His Word!

The "Spiritual Songs" of Mr. Sankey are well adapted to open the hearts of the audience and prepare them to receive the good seed which is so bountifully sowed by Mr. Moody, through the mediums of his "Bible Readings" and preaching. Mr. Sankey's rich voice gives a great charm to his singing, and seems particularly suited to the nature of the songs and purposes for which he uses it, and its great reputation induces thousands to attend the meetings solely from a desire to listen to it. Eventually many of these persons become personally interested in the great subject presented to them so tenderly and sweetly by Mr. Sankey in his songs, and which is impressed upon them by the clear discussions of the "Bible Readings," and driven home and enforced by the powerful and faithful preaching of Mr. Moody,—and become converted. How large a share of the glorious results of the combined efforts of these two faithful co-workers for Christ will, at the last great day, when all secrets shall be made known, be attributed to the songs of Mr. Sankey, will only then appear; but certain it is, that many a redeemed spirit will remember how his bosom melted into tenderness as the clear enunciation of Mr. Sankey made plain the story of the love of Christ, in words which floated upon waves of liquid melody that filled the room, and how this tenderness deepened into sincere repentance under the convicting appeals and powerful personal applications of Mr. Moody.

It seems not out of place here to give one or two of the songs most used by Mr. Sankey. His favourites are the two called "Ninety and Nine," and "Jesus of Nazareth Passeth By." The first was found by him in an obscure Scotch newspaper; the last was written by Miss Campbell. Both were set to music by Mr. Sankey, who is reported to have said that these two had done more good than all the other songs in his collection. They are truly sermons in themselves.

NINETY AND NINE.

1. There were ninety and nine that safely lay
 In the shelter of the fold,
But one was out on the hills away,
 Far off from the gates of gold.
Away on the mountains wild and bare,
Away from the tender Shepherd's care.

2. "Lord, Thou hast here Thy ninety and nine;
 Are they not enough for Thee?"
But the Shepherd made answer: "This of Mine
 Has wandered away from Me;
And although the road be rough and steep
I go to the desert to find My sheep."

3. But none of the ransomed ever knew
 How deep were the waters crossed;
Nor how dark was the night that the Lord passed through
 Ere He found His sheep that was lost.
Out in the desert He heard its cry—
Sick, and helpless, and ready to die.

4. "Lord, whence are those blood drops all the way
That mark out the mountains track?"
"They were shed for one who had gone astray
Ere the Shepherd could bring him back."
"Lord, whence are thy hands so rent and torn?"
"They are pierced to-night by many a thorn."

5. And all thro' the mountains, thunder-riven,
And up from the rocky steep,
There rose a cry to the gate of heaven,
"Rejoice! I have found My sheep!"
And the angels echoed around the throne,
"Rejoice, for the Lord brings back His own!"

JESUS OF NAZARETH PASSETH BY.

1. What means this eager, anxious throng,
Which moves with busy haste along—
These wondrous gatherings day by day?
What means this strange commotion, pray?
In accents hushed the throng reply,
"Jesus of Nazareth passeth by."

2. Who is this Jesus? Why should He
The city move so mightily?
A passing stranger, has He skill
To move the multitude at will?
Again the stirring tones reply,
"Jesus of Nazareth passeth by."

3. Jesus! 'tis He who once below
Man's pathway trod, 'mid pain and woe;
And burdened ones, where'er He came,
Brought out their sick, and deaf, and lame.
The blind rejoiced to hear the cry,
"Jesus of Nazareth passeth by."

4. Again He comes! From place to place
His holy footprints we can trace.
He pauseth at our threshold—nay,
He enters—condescends to stay.
Shall we not gladly raise the cry?—
"Jesus of Nazareth passeth by."

5. Ho! all ye heavy-laden, come!
Here's pardon, comfort, rest, and home.
Ye wanderers from a Father's face,
Return, accept His proffered grace.
Ye tempted ones, there's refuge nigh;
"Jesus of Nazareth passeth by."

6. But if you still His call refuse,
And all His wondrous love abuse,
Soon will He sadly from you turn,
Your bitter prayer for pardon spurn.
"Too late! too late!" will be the cry—
"Jesus of Nazareth *has passed by.*"

CHAPTER XIV.

THE HOME AND THE TABERNACLE.

In the old family Bible already mentioned there is the following record, under the head of Marriages:—

"D. L. Moody to Emma C. Revell; 28th August 1862."

Matrimony is the oldest means of grace.

"Whoso findeth a wife findeth a good thing," says a high authority: a statement in which Mr. Moody has special reason to concur. The helpmeet of his home is a lady for some years a helper in his Mission. His first acquaintance with her dates from the little Mission Sunday-school in which he was offered a class provided he would gather it himself.

This book does not claim to be a biography, and has little to do with Mr. Moody's social or domestic life; but his home has been so blessed, and has added so greatly to his usefulness, that this record would be incomplete, in a very important particular, if no mention were made of it.

Not until after he had commenced a new home for his much-loved North Market Mission School, did he make a home for himself. As in every step of his life, he married and set up housekeeping by faith. A very small cottage satisfied his ambition as well as his wants. As might be expected, this was a most cheery and hospitable home. It was generally full of visitors, both old friends and strangers; and all the poor people of the neighbourhood soon learned the number on its door. The home, like its master, was full and running over with fun, sympathy, and religion. Mr. Moody would play practical jokes on his wife and his guests, laugh and jump and shout with the children,—the happiest child of them all: and in the midst of the merriment, some text of Scripture would flash upon him, or some subject for a sermon would present itself; and instantly he would say, "Get out your Bibles,"—and, in a trice, would turn the whole household into a Bible class.

If a person came in who was unconverted, he would leave everything else, and immediately inquire about his soul; and, if he found him at all under the influence of the Holy Spirit, almost before he knew it he would have him on his knees in prayer.

Whatever cares or troubles weighed upon his mind during the day, he always left them behind on coming home. That was his refuge,—a little world in itself; and into it the cares of his great work outside were seldom permitted to come.

Two children—a boy and a girl—were born to him; and a happier father or a more devoted mother it would not be easy to find. From their earliest understanding Mrs. Moody was accustomed to pray with them daily, and to teach them that they belonged to the Lord Jesus.

It would seem, from the stories which he tells of them, that they inherited his own intensity of life and feeling. One day he found his little boy with an elegantly illustrated Bible on his lap, in the act of digging out the eyes of a picture of Judas Iscariot with a pair of scissors. On being asked why he was doing such mischief, the little fellow referred to the lesson read at prayers that morning, which had been the betrayal of our Lord; and his indignation at the conduct of Judas had taken this form of expression.

Mr. Moody's habit of trusting in the Lord for daily bread sometimes brought the little household into great straits. After his marriage, the same as before, he refused all offers of salary from any source whatever, assured that the Lord, who had taken care of him when he was alone, would, no doubt, take care of his wife and children also. This confidence was fully justified; for, though sometimes almost in sight of it, they never came to actual distress.

One of the most remarkable gifts which the Lord sent to His faithful servant was a new and completely furnished home.

An old friend had erected a row of elegant houses; and one of these he privately set apart for Mr. Moody, free of rent, if his other friends would furnish it for him. The enterprise was undertaken with great spirit, and the house was fitted up from basement to attic in thorough and comfortable style. Soft carpets; handsome furniture and ornaments for hall and parlours, including life-size portraits of Mr. Moody and his wife; a book-case containing a large and serviceable library; dining-room, bedrooms, and kitchen all in order; china, silver, and linen for the table;—all articles required for housekeeping, were tastefully and lovingly arranged.

Early on New Year's morning Mr. Moody and his family were captured and carried off in a coach, they knew not why, or whither. It stopped before a fine-looking row, and he was conducted into a house, which, to his surprise, was full of his acquaintances and friends. After the greetings had been exchanged, and he was wondering what it all could mean, the Rev. Dr. Patterson, on behalf of the company, presented him with a lease of the house and the free gift of all it contained, as a token of love and respect for his simple and earnest Christian character, and of gratitude for his faithful labours, under which they and their city had been so largely blessed.

It was more like a dream than a reality. Like the Gospel, it seemed almost too good to be true. Hand in hand, speechless with wonder and weeping for joy, Mr. Moody and his wife made the round of the beautiful rooms—so much finer than they had ever hoped to possess; and when they had seen and admired them all, he tried to thank his friends for their kindness. In broken sentences he told them how good the Lord had always been to him, and that he had not trusted Him in vain.

When that company broke up, it was with the feeling that they had done all this under the Lord's own direction, who, in this way, had determined to honour the faith of His servant who had forsaken all to follow Him.

In this new home he had the pleasure of entertaining his old pastor, Dr. Kirk; here he received the visits of many of the most distinguished Christians of America; and here, as in the little cottage, there was always comfort for the sorrowing and help for the poor.

But this home, with all its precious memories, was of only short duration. On the 8th and 9th of October, 1871, a tidal wave of flame swept the city, leaving, on an area of one mile in width by four miles in length, but a single house remaining. Within this fated region had stood the second Farwell Hall, Mr. Moody's church, and his beautiful home—the New Year's gift from his friends. From the site of the Illinois Street Church, in every direction, as far as the eye could reach, only ruins were to be seen. All his parishioners were driven from their homes, saving nothing of their worldly goods except the trifle they could carry away in their hands.

Leaving his family at the house of a friend, beyond the reach of the flames, he at once began the work of feeding the hungry and sheltering the homeless, who swarmed by thousands in the churches, public buildings, and open lots about the city. The first and chief depository of supplies was in the relief department of the Young Men's Christian Association. These Mr. Moody distributed with a bountiful hand. It was his especial delight to give food and raiment to all who came to him hungry and half clothed. But some unworthy persons, taking advantage of his tenderness of heart, made spoil of the supplies intended for the really needy.

Hearing of this, and learning that complaints were made of his too bountiful distribution, he at once withdrew from the work of relief, and started for the east, with the double purpose of holding revival services and of raising a little money to build some poor barrack or shed, where he might again establish his church and school.

A cordial welcome awaited him from the Rev. Dr. Cuyler and his people, in Brooklyn, who gladly gave him sympathy and assistance. His revival work in that city has already been mentioned.

He next went to Philadelphia, holding religious services in the evenings, while the days were devoted to raising money for rebuilding his ruined church.

Some of the brethren, among whom was his old friend George H. Stuart, and Mr. Wannamaker, of *The Sunday School Times*, finding that his work of collecting progressed but slowly, said to him: "Mr. Moody, how much money do you need?"

"If I had a thousand dollars, I could build a great box that would hold my Sunday-school," was the reply.

"You shall have three thousand, at least," said they; and they were as good as their word.

The brethren at home had secured the use of a lot in the midst of the burnt district, not far from the ruins of their church, on which they proposed to build a rough structure in the simplest and cheapest manner. It was at first supposed that a roof forty feet by sixty would cover all the people who could be gathered in such a place. But Mr. Moody's faith looked forward to the speedy rebuilding of the city; and in his frequent despatches announcing the progress of his subscription-list, he continually urged them to "*build large.*" The new Tabernacle was therefore made to cover the entire plot of ground,—a hundred and nine feet in length and seventy-five in width. It was a great enclosure built of rough timbers and boards, and lined with heavy paper, to keep out the cold. It was a single story in height, with a flat roof of paper, gravel, and tar; supported by lines of posts and beams like a stable. But it harmonized so entirely with the waste of ruins surrounding it, that the poor desolate creatures, living in wretched hovels and holes under the sidewalks, felt a strong attraction toward it, and were very much at home within its walls.

The band of brethren left in charge by Mr. Moody were all without homes of their own, and some of them without the ordinary comforts of life. Having no money to give, they gave the labour of their hands, to help on with the Tabernacle; while those working-people who were too poor to spare any time by day, came at night, and builded the best they knew. The work was pressed forward with the utmost haste, encouraged by despatches and remittances from the absent pastor; and when it was ready for dedication he was sent for, to come home and meet again the remnant of his scorched and scattered flock.

There were but few buildings in sight of the Tabernacle when it was finished; save, here and there, a little shanty built on the sheltered side of a blackened and crumbling wall; and some of the brethren were anxious lest, from out this desolation, no consider-

MR. MOODY'S TABERNACLE, CHICAGO.

able number of people could be gathered. But, to their surprise and joy, on the day of dedication, crowds of children were seen picking their way among the ruins, and along the streets half blocked up with rubbish, coming from no one knew where, but drawn by the magical attraction of the promised reunion of their school. More than a thousand children were present at this first meeting, many of them accompanied by their parents. The great building was completely filled.

Thus, a second time, Mr. Moody's church became a Mission; and the new Tabernacle came to be a greater wonder and blessing than even the old North Market Hall. The work of saving the bodies and souls of men, women, and children went forward there successfully and joyfully. The place was kept open and warm night and day, as a shelter to any homeless wanderer who might choose to enter. Religious services, in great number and variety, were in almost continual progress, from early afternoon until late in the evening, by which many houseless wanderers were brought within the sympathy of this loving and zealous brotherhood, and shown the way to a home in the heart of Christ and the kingdom of heaven.

Mr. Moody, leaving his family with friends at the east, took lodgings in a little class-room in the great Tabernacle, with one of his faithful Sunday-school teachers as steward, cook, and man-of-all-work. His mornings were largely spent in searching out and relieving the families of his former congregation. Large quantities of clothing and provisions were sent to him for distribution; which, being stored in the

Tabernacle, made it a centre of interest to the hungry and destitute: a fact of which Mr. Moody was not slow to take advantage in trying to lead their hearts to Christ. He would say to some half-starved, shivering man who came to ask for assistance:

"Here, take these clothes; help yourself to these provisions,—all you can carry; and promise me to thank God for them, on your knees, before you eat the flour and potatoes, or put on the coat and trousers." Sometimes noticing the evident distress of one who had seen better days and was too proud to ask help, he would send a messenger after him as he went out from the meeting, to inquire, confidentially, if there was anything he could do for him.

But the constant aim of all his plans and labours was to save the souls of sinners. He would say: "What is the use of keeping these poor people's bodies a little longer out of the grave, and not trying to keep their souls out of hell?"

A hungry man was always more than welcome at his table in the little class-room. Hundreds of people, attracted by the bright lights and warm fires of the Tabernacle, came in to warm themselves; and some one was always on the watch, ready to make both hunger and cold a reason for offering Christ and salvation, as well as food and shelter.

During his absence, Mr. Moody had been gloriously baptized with the Holy Ghost; and the presence of such a man, among such a congregation, was one of the best benedictions Heaven could send them. He was full of hope and happiness, though, like them, he had suffered the loss of all things. It was St.

Paul's experience over again: "Poor, but making many rich; having nothing, and yet possessing all things."

Wave after wave of revival swept the Tabernacle meetings; crowds of people attended the almost constant service, weeping over their sins one day, and shouting over their pardon the next. Men and women, cast down and hopeless, coming to Mr. Moody for comfort and advice, seemed to absorb a portion of his overflowing gladness; and went out to bear their sorrows, and struggle through their toils, with a stronger and more hopeful heart.

A happier company than his great Sunday-school, thus literally sitting among the ashes, could hardly be found this side of heaven. The fire had taken away everything else, but it had left them Christ, and one another. In spite of all the troubles of the week, the Sabbath brought again the much-loved reunion; and, with hearts all melted together, with teachers more loving than ever, and with Mr. Moody at their head, who was such a fountain of good cheer and happiness, this Sunday-school was the one bright spot in their shadowed lives. They came through the cold and snow for miles, wretchedly clad, and pinched with want, to hear about Christ, and to sing the Sunday-school songs, which are always full of happiness and heaven. Mr. Sankey, with his harmonium, was on the platform to lead their voices, or to sing for them the songs with which he has since charmed so many thousands, on both sides of the sea. Miss Dryer, the faithful helper in the Bible work, was also there. On week-days she held "mothers' meetings," to which poor women came, from a distance of two or three miles, through the burnt district on foot. There were also sewing schools for girls, four or five afternoons a week; where little fingers were kept busy making garments, which, when finished, were given to the makers; and where singing, and prayer, and recitation of Scripture texts, and kind and helpful words from their teacher, made sewing schools an attractive means of grace.

The following is a list of the regular Sunday services at the Tabernacle, during the year following the fire:—

The Lord's Supper, every Sunday, at nine in the morning; preaching, by Mr. Moody, at half-past ten, at the close of which he waited at the door, to greet the people as they passed out. Then, dinner in the class-room; at which a number of the Sunday-school teachers were present, to talk over the work of the day. Immediately after dinner, a teachers' meeting, for the study of the lesson. At three o'clock the Sunday-school, with Mr. Moody for superintendent; following it, a teachers' prayer-meeting, also led by him; then supper, in the class-room; then the Yoke-fellows' prayer-meeting. Preaching again at half-past seven; after which Mr. Moody held a meeting for inquirers, which sometimes lasted far on into the night.

Thus did God cause His servant to pass through the fire, that He might bring him out, not burned but tempered. His faith had been tried, and had not been found wanting. Now he was ready for glorious service. But for those days of struggle and those nights of toil, he might not have been able to bear the success which was in store for him.

And now one last trial of his faith, before God puts the sharp sickle into his hand.

He is called to England. God wants him there. He announces his intended departure to his family who are to go with him, and to his church who are to be left behind. He appoints the day to give them his parting message and to bid them farewell.

But he has no money. He cannot pay his passage.

The last day arrives; to-night he is to go. No money!

He will not ask it of men; he can only ask it of God.

A few hours before he and his family are to take the train, a friend, who knows nothing of his needs, bethinks him that Mr. Moody will want some money "*after he reaches England.*" He goes to say good-bye, and places five hundred dollars in his hand.

Now he can go. One last trial, one last deliverance, and then the sea takes him on its bosom and bears him on his mission, whose history will be immortal, written in the glad memories of twice ten thousand souls, who at the Judgment Day will rise up to call him blessed. "They that be wise shall shine as the brightness of the firmament, and they that turn many to righteousness as the stars for ever and ever."

CHAPTER XV.

MOODY AND HIS CO-LABOURERS.

ONE of Mr. Moody's most valuable qualities is his genius for finding out and employing those who are specially qualified to assist him in his work. In this respect his generalship is of a very high order. He gathered about him a class of active and devoted Christian workers, who were in constant training, and ready at a moment's notice, like himself, to go on errands for the Master; and so acceptable were the labours of these lay evangelists, that they came to be in demand, to hold meetings in various parts of the city and in the country round.

Some of the men who took their first lesson of Mr. Moody at Farwell Hall, followed his example, left all things for Christ, and devoted their lives to evangelistic work. Others, still retaining their position as men of business, began to give large portions of their time as Christian helpers; their ample fortunes enabling them to enjoy the luxury of working for nothing, and paying their own expenses.

MR. FRANK ROCKWELL, who, for a long time, was the efficient superintendent of the Young Men's Christian Association, gives this account of his capture by Mr. Moody:—

"Twelve years ago, last December, I was a student in the Chicago Medical College. My health had failed from overwork, and I was going home to the country for a short vacation. On the evening before my intended departure, I went over to the little prayer-meeting, which Mr. Moody used to hold in an old shanty that had formerly been a saloon. I had never seen the man before; but I was interested in his meeting, and took some part in it. At the close he came straight up to me and said, 'Young man, who are you?' I gave him my name, and told him something of my plans, upon which he appealed to me thus: 'Give up your medicine, and go in for saving souls, and you will bless God for it through all eternity!'

"I was so much attracted by his hearty ways that, instead of going home, I went next morning to his office, in the rooms of the Young Men's Christian Association, which at that time was his only home. He immediately set me at work in the mission department, and afterwards gave me a share in the duties of the relief office, which he had organized a little while before.

"He had discovered that the County Agent, whose business it was to look after the poor, did not relieve all needy persons; and he also learned that the methods of relief prevented many worthy but modest people from pressing their claims for assistance. It occurred to him that if he could help these poor people to food, clothing, fuel, etc., they would be more easily brought within the reach of the means of grace; and, acting at once upon this idea, he established a system for comforting their bodies, as the first step toward saving their souls. He divided the whole city into districts, having reference to the location of the principal churches, and persuaded each congregation to appoint visitors from among their own members, who should visit the several districts monthly, and make reports of their work at the rooms of the Association. On the requisition of these visitors, fuel, provisions, and clothing, were supplied. The work of keeping the treasury full for this purpose, Mr. Moody took upon himself."

Experience, and the opportunity for doing good, were the only wages these visitors received; but their work was a blessing to their souls, as well as to the souls and bodies of the poor; and through them Mr. Moody gained such a thorough knowledge of the needs and sorrows of the city, that for a time he held in his single hand almost the whole of its charitable work of this description. The wisdom and efficiency of this system became so apparent that several small societies, which had been maintained by individual churches, were united with the relief society of the Young Men's Christian Association, under the name and charter of the Chicago Relief and Aid Society, of which Mr. O. C. Gibbs was the first superintendent. At the time of the Great Fire this society was the chief almoner of the world's overflowing charity.

CAPTAIN SIMMS.—Another man whom he initiated

into the order of lay evangelists, was Captain Simms, of the ship "Flying Mist."

This young sailor first made the port of Chicago in the summer of 1860. He was an avowed sceptic; believing that all religion was a delusion; and that all professors of it were either hypocrites or fools. His favourite theory was that every man had within his own nature the power to be as good, or as bad, as he pleased. He was correct in his habits, eschewing tobacco, and liquors. It was his constant boast that nothing could ever tempt him to intemperance; but, from drinking a glass of port wine and water, an irresistible appetite for strong drink seized upon him, and, in spite of all his self-righteousness, within two years he became a miserable drunkard.

Several times he was on the verge of delirium tremens; and, with his constitution almost ruined, he was given over to die. As a last hope, his friend, Captain McMillen, in order to take him away from his drinking companions gave him the berth of mate on board his vessel.

On this voyage, when his head was somewhat cleared, and his heart somewhat softened, the awful impression seized upon him that his boasted strength was a delusion, and that he was a man utterly lost, unless he could get help from heaven. Strangely enough, through all his dissipation he had clung to the doctrine of self-sufficiency, preaching it with every nerve trembling, and with brain confused with drink. But now the Spirit of the Lord had driven him from his refuge of lies, and, utterly broken-hearted, he gave himself up to God.

From that hour the appetite for liquor died within him!

When his ship returned to Chicago he went at once to the strangers' meeting at Farwell Hall, where he confessed himself a seeker of religion. Within a week he was soundly and happily converted, and began to tell his old companions the story of his new hope in Christ. To get rid of his doubts, he began to search the Scripture, asking the Lord to show him the right meaning of the words he read. One after another the great truths of the Gospel were opened to his mind; more especially the promises which encourage God's people to pray. His faith took such strong hold of these that he was able to put them in daily use, with respect to his temporal as well as spiritual needs. He seemed to be taken out of himself, and his life was "hid with Christ in God."

One thing for which he prayed was that God would send him tidings from his old home in Scotland. He had, at seven years of age, been brought by his father, a wild and reckless man, to America, who basely deserted him among perfect strangers. For seventeen years no word of his mother and his two sisters had ever reached him, though he had written to them again and again.

One day, having written a letter to a friend in the West, he noticed, on reading it over, that it contained no personal matter, and might be sent to any one else with equal propriety. At the same time he felt impressed to send it to an acquaintance at the East; which thing he did, having added these words: "Have you heard anything from my mother?" In a few days the answer came, enclosing a letter written by his mother eight years before; asking what had become of her lost boy. He at once despatched a letter across the sea to this new address; but, as he afterwards learned, the family had removed a second time; and the letter would have shared the fate of all the others had it not been for a citizen of that place, who, seeing the letter advertised in the post-office, forwarded it to its true destination.

In a few weeks his prayer was answered. A letter from his mother, with the picture of his two sisters, now grown to womanhood, came to strengthen his faith in God; and as no time was lost in bringing them to Chicago, where the mother, and the elder sister were soon brought to the Saviour, and where now the younger sister, who was in Christ before, is engaged in the Bible work which Mr. Moody organized just before his last departure for England. Captain Simms sails the "Flying Mist" in the summer, and labours as an evangelist in Chicago during the winter.

But the story is not yet all told.

One night, while Mr. Moody and the Captain were going home together from some revival meeting, they paid a visit to the saloon from which the Captain had been taken by his friend McMillen. After some words of Christian counsel to the sailors who were lounging there, they climbed up the steps to the sidewalk again, and presently came upon Captain McMillen himself, who, with some of his old friends. was taking an evening stroll.

Mr. Moody, on being introduced, immediately inquired of the strangers if they loved the Lord, and finding them all unsaved, he said:

"Well, boys, it is a bad thing to be without Christ. I may never have another chance to pray for you, so let us pray right here." And there at the street corner, at eleven o'clock at night, he knelt upon the pavement and prayed to God to save the captain and his friends. That prayer was speedily answered. Captain McMillen is now an active member of a Chicago church, and one of the boys who were with him is a worker in the Young Men's Christian Association.

JAMES MORRISON.—Another trophy from the sea is Mr. James Morrison, who sails as carpenter in the summer and does the work of an evangelist in the winter.

Two years ago last January, this wild young Highlander strayed into a place where Mr. Moody and Major Whittle were giving personal instruction to a number of inquirers, after the public exercises had closed. Setting four chairs together, Mr. Moody almost thrust him into one of them, seating the others beside him, and then said to his comrade:

"Here, Major; talk to these three fellows."

Among other instructions given them was the direction to read the fifty-third chapter of Isaiah before they went to bed. When they went home, Morrison, being the only owner of a Bible among them, read the chapter, partly out of curiosity to see what it was, and partly because he felt grateful for the kind interest which had been shown by those brethren in trying to save their souls.

Among his other employments, Morrison had been

a dancing master. He was wild and wicked, and among the saloons and sailors' boarding houses he was regarded as a brilliant and dangerous man. After the Highland fashion, he carried a *skean,* or long knife in his stocking; and his mates were afraid to quarrel with him, lest he should be the death of them with it. But by means of the little meeting, and the chapter out of the Bible, the whole current of his life was turned from sin and Satan unto God. Lying awake that night, he was impressed with the idea that two people were praying for him—Mr. Moody, and his old mother in Scotland. Then he said to himself, "I believe Christ is willing to save me if I could only get to Him; but where in the world am I to find Him?" And then these words came forcibly to his mind: "I that speak unto thee am He."

The next morning he said to his room-mates, "I am a Christian." He then began to feel as if he would like to find some other Christian; and starting, he presently met Captain Simms, to whom he told his new experience. That night he went to the meeting again, and, on being asked what was his state of mind, he answered again, "I am a Christian." Feeling it his duty, he next went to a house where he had lately drawn his *skean* and threatened the life of a man; and there he began to preach Christ. From one saloon and dance-house to another he went, saying to his old companions in sin, "I am a Christian." And so he spent the winter.

His Scotch training in the Bible and catechism was now of great use to him. He joined the Bible-class in Mr. Moody's Sunday-school, and began bringing his old friends with him. Every one who came was converted. When asked how it was that every one he brought was blessed, he answered, "I have been praying to the Lord to make me a 'fisher of men.'"

He is now in charge of the Young Men's Christian Association reading-room, in the great depôt of the Rock Island and Michigan Southern railways, still pursuing his Bible work among the poorest of the poor.

People are often "laid upon his heart," as he says; and to these he goes at once and asks them, "Are you saved?" One of these strangers whom he felt laid upon his heart, and whom he led to Christ, was a poor fellow, whom he met in the street, looking as if he were hungry. "I can tell when a man is hungry by his looks," says he, "for I have sometimes been very hungry myself." This young man proved to be the son of a Christian minister in Germany; but, his money being all gone, and his good clothes in the pawnshop, he had been turned out of his wretched boarding-house. He was ashamed to apply to his German society, and was almost desperate enough to end his own miserable life.

Being at one time sorely discouraged and tempted to give up his work, he said to Mr. Moody, "I do not think I am of any use to the Lord."

"It is a strange man for whom God has nothing to do," replied Mr. Moody. "I began work by bringing in children to the Mission Sunday-schools."

"I can do that," said Morrison; and, his hope and courage quickly returning, it was not long before he had a Mission Sunday-school of his own, after the manner of that in the North Market Hall. In its neighbourhood he is already acquainted with every family, and welcomed in almost every house. He says: "Mr. Moody had a wonderful acquaintance with the children, and with their parents also. I myself know as many as three hundred families, where I have been to find children for my school."

This man seems to be doing Mr. Moody's work over again, in a neglected region on the south side; for not only does he teach the children in the Sunday-school, but is becoming a sort of pastor also. In this work he finds much to cheer, and little to discourage him; for the missionary system of the Young Men's Christian Association has leavened the whole lump of the city, and such a region as The Sands used to be is now nowhere to be found.

Down in the dirtiest streets and in wretched hovels, he says, he sometimes finds a good friend of the Lord. In such a place, one day, he made the acquaintance of a poor old woman, who interested him greatly.

"How old are you?" he asked.

"Seventy-five years old," was the reply.

"Are you a believer?"

"Yes."

"How long?"

"Seventy-five years."

"What!"

"Yes. As early as I can remember, my mother told me that the Son of God came down into this world and died for me, and then went back to heaven, where He is waiting for me to come. And ever since then, I have been trying to go to Him."

This missionary says: "It is just as easy for me to get some of those poor outcasts to believe in Christ, as for the pastors of our fashionable churches to get their people to do the same. They are just as near the kingdom as any one else, and my work is as hopeful as theirs."

He was calling one day on the mother of one of his little Sunday-school girls, and made inquiries of her about her husband.

"Ah!" says the woman, "he is awful. Everything goes for tobacco and whisky, and sometimes we are half starved."

Feeling this man "laid upon his heart," he sought his acquaintance, and presently bringing out his Bible, he began to read to him the third chapter of John, beginning with the fourteenth verse—which particular passage Morrison says he has "read almost out of the Book." Under his instruction the man found the way to the Cross, threw away his liquor and tobacco, though it cost him a desperate struggle; and the last time he called upon the family, he found them neatly and pleasantly settled.

The happy wife was delighted to see him, and could hardly express her joy. "He is so different now, that I hardly know him: no more whisky, no more tobacco. And now, Mr. Morrison, I have so much money, I don't know what to do with it."

Thus was proved over again the wisdom of Mr. Moody's policy at the North Market Mission:—"Make these poor people Christians, and they will make gentlemen and ladies of themselves."

Morrison meets all kinds of ignorance and superstition; but his method is the same with them all. He finds some passage of God's Word which exactly meets their case, and holds them to it till they come out into light and grace. To hardened sinners he preaches the law, and tells them kindly but earnestly that they are going straight to hell. If a man is a sceptic, he urges him to believe on the Son of God, and drives him from one corner to another with texts of Scripture till he forces him to take refuge in Christ. It is all by the power of God's Word.

Down here among these low and ignorant people he finds the old wonders over again—visions, dreams, supernatural appearances, and the like. One wicked woman was scared out of her sins by seeing the devil standing, one night, at the foot of her bed: a very different result, no doubt, from what that personage intended.

This ex-dancing master speaks by authority when he says that club dancing is full of sin. He has been anxious for the souls of his old pupils in that fashionable art, but only one of them has been converted; the rest, he says, "are roaming yet."

CHARLES M. MORTON.—Among the men brought out and trained by Mr. Moody is Charles M. Morton, missionary at the Plymouth Bethel, connected with Mr. Beecher's church in Brooklyn. His was a very unpromising case, as will appear from this account he once gave of himself. He says: "I grew up without a knowledge of the Saviour, and scarcely knew or believed that there was a God. . . . When the War broke out, we shouldered our rifles and went to the front. Our lives then were wicked. I was a ringleader in drinking and in gambling, and it used to be my boast that I could blaspheme the name of God in more ways than any other man about."

Having lost his right arm, he left the army and went to Chicago, where he continued his life of sin till his money was all gone, and then applied to the Employment Bureau of the Young Men's Christian Association for work. Mr. Gibbs, who was then in charge, and to whom a soldier with an empty sleeve was always an object of tender interest, spoke to him about Christ ; and, having no chance of employment for a man with only one arm, he gave him a place as man-of-all-work about the Association rooms, which were then in the Methodist Church block ; and Mr. Rockwell, superintendent of the Mission work, gave him lodgings in his own room in the same building.

Mr. R. gives the following account of his conversion :—

"When Morton came to be my room-mate, he brought, along with his other small properties, a pouch of tobacco and a pipe ; and when I came home that evening I found him sitting with his chair tipped back, his heels on the window-sill, his hat stuck on the back of his head, smoking till all was blue. Taking up the Bible, I mentioned that I was in the habit of reading a chapter and offering prayer before I went to bed, and asked him if he had any objections.

"'Objections? no: none at all. You can pray as much as you like without disturbing me.' And, as far as I know, he did not stir from his place, or even stop his smoking while the reading and praying were going on. The next night he was in his old attitude, lost in smoke as usual; though, from the account he gave of himself afterward, I learned that this time he did take off his hat during the prayer, but must have put it on again very quickly, for I did not see the action.

"Feeling a deep interest in his case, I presented him at the noon meeting for prayers, and this I continued to do twenty-one days in succession. During this time he spoke with great freedom of his doubts concerning religion, saying it was only fit for foolish people, and declaring that Burns had written better things than any contained in the Bible. But, as I afterward learned, though he still concealed it all from me, he gradually became more attentive at prayers. On the third evening he stopped smoking; on the fourth he took down his feet from the window-sill; on the fifth he got down on one knee; on the sixth on both knees: but every time he was up and in his old place before I reached the 'Amen,' so I did not see how fast he was coming on.

"On the evening of the twenty-first day we had a little prayer-meeting down in a Baptist church in De Koven Street, and there we prayed for Morton till the heavens seemed to bend. It was late when I reached home, and I found him in bed; so I sat down beside him and said to him:

"'Charley, we have been praying for you to-night.'

"'Have you? I thank you, Frank,' said he, his voice choking with emotion; and then he turned away and buried his face in the pillow. About midnight he arose, and went into the prayer-room adjoining, where, after an hour of mighty wrestling with God, he felt his sins forgiven; and when he came back his infidelity had vanished, and he was a saved and happy man.

"A little while before his acquaintance with the Young Men's Christian Association, he and a comrade named Stewart had been on a drinking bout together, trying who would drink the most liquor before being overcome by it. While Morton was seeking and finding the Saviour at the Association, Stewart was doing the same thing at the church, and the very next time they met after their great debauch together, each was surprised and overjoyed to find the other happy in the love of Christ."

Mr. Moody, after his usual fashion, called out the young convert, and almost compelled him to take part in the Association prayer-meetings. The first time he was called on he was unable to utter a word, though he made a desperate effort to open his mouth in prayer. The next time he was able to talk with the Lord a in sentence or two. At length the real power and genius of the man began to appear; and Mr. Moody, who was quick to notice such marks of promise, took him over to his Illinois Street Church, and made him a kind of assistant pastor. His duty was to visit from house to house, hold cottage prayer-meetings and street meetings, and to preach in the Illinois Street Church on Sunday evenings, while Mr. Moody was holding service at Farwell Hall.

These two men used to attend a good many conventions together; and Morton became, like his leader, a very effective platform speaker, drawing largely from his own strange experience, and exhorting with great earnestness and power. It was while attending the National Sunday School Convention at Newark, New Jersey, in April, 1869, that he attracted the attention of some of the Brooklyn brethren, who were on the look-out for a man to take charge of the Plymouth Bethel. They invited him to Brooklyn, tested his quality, and installed him in the place where he has ever since remained. He is now regarded as one of the most successful home missionaries in America.

MAJOR WHITTLE.—Another of Mr. Moody's comrades, whom he was instrumental in leading into evangelistic work, is Major D. W. Whittle.

For several years, though holding an important business position, he gave a good deal of time to religious conventions, Bible readings, and revival meetings in various parts of the city. In April 1874, he resigned his position as manager of the Elgin Watch Company, and a salary of five thousand dollars a year; committed his fortunes wholly to the Lord, and commenced the life of an itinerant evangelist; thus fulfilling Mr. Moody's prophecy, who had for years insisted that he was a chosen instrument for the great work of God. The Major, who had made an honourable name as a soldier of his country, has come to higher honours as a soldier of Christ. The recent revival in the city of Louisville, Kentucky, was a mark of God's approval such as few men have ever received so early in their history as evangelists. Following the example of Mr. Moody, who had called the singing brother, Sankey, to his aid, Major Whittle joined company with Professor Bliss; and, by the invitation of twenty-four pastors of that city, they went down to Louisville together, in February 1875. People came to the meetings in crowds, until it became necessary to entreat those who already loved the Lord to stay away, in order that those who were seeking Him might have a place.

When the public exercises were over, those who desired personal instruction and prayer were invited to remain; and of these there were so many that the hall was marked off into twenty-four sections, each of which was put in charge of a pastor, who, with the help of his deacons and chief men, laboured and prayed with those who came into their division. At almost any hour an inquirer might find some helping hand holding open the door of the kingdom, and hear some loving voice earnestly persuading him to enter.

People would often stop Major Whittle and Professor Bliss in the streets, and beg to know what they must do to be saved. Saloons and theatres lost their patronage, and failed to pay expenses. The chief newspaper of the city freely gave the use of its columns for extended notices of the meetings. Leaders of society, and fashionable belles, as well as people of the great world of the poor, were among the converts. The whole city was revolutionized; and, from being the stronghold of those vices which flourish mostly in wealthy Southern society, it came to be a centre of spiritual life. Still later comes the news of a great revival under his labours at Memphis Tennessee.

J. H. COLE.—Another of the Farwell Hall evangelists, brought out by the Spirit and providence of God

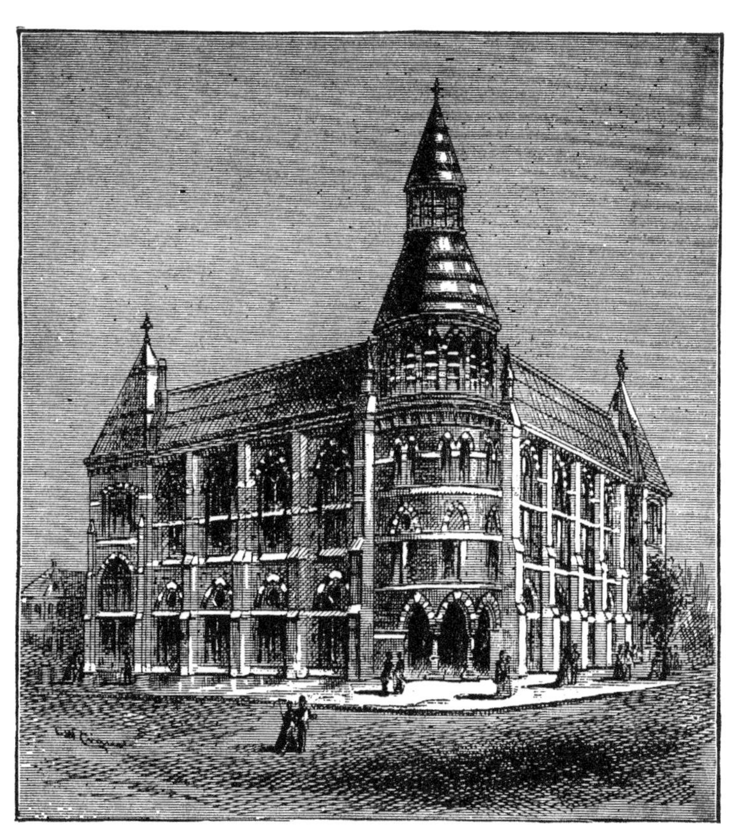

MR. MOODY'S NEW CHURCH, CHICAGO.

through the influence and example of Mr. Moody, is Mr. J. H. Cole. He was saved from a life of dissipation; and, being thoroughly in love with Christ and His work, was left by Mr. Moody in charge of the Farwell Hall meetings, at the time of his departure for England. The great revival in Barraboo, Wisconsin, during the last winter, was the special blessing of God upon his labours there. At their close, he was called to assist the brethren at Louisville.

Early in the month of May, Mr. Cole rejoined his old friend in London, who first assigned him to the charge of the Young Mens' meetings in the tent near the Bow Road Hall, at the East end of London, of which further mention will be made in Part II. His next work was a series of Childrens' meetings, which reached an attendance of nearly five thousand.

During the last month in London of the American Evangelists, while Messrs. Moody and Sankey were speaking and singing to the great congregations at Camberwell Hall, in the South quarter of the city, it was determined to hold a series of revival meetings in the Victoria Theatre, a second-class play-house, in one of the worst parts of London; and, with some misgiving on the part of Mr. Moody and his Evangelistic committee, but at the earnest advice of Mr. Farwell, who was then in London, Mr. Cole was placed in charge. Night after night the old theatre was filled with a crowd of people who had been accustomed to divide their spare time and money between the gin palaces and the cheap performances of this stage; attracted at first by the novelty of a religious service in a place which, by common consent, was given over to the devil and his friends, and held afterwards by the evident power of God which attended the simple and tender preaching of His word.

This brief success of Mr. Cole, taking into account the difficulties under which he laboured, was not less remarkable than that of Messrs. Moody and Sankey themselves; and, in the absence of those brethren, would have attracted great attention. On being asked how he prepared his sermons, he replied, "I pray to God for them." His method is, by necessity, a simple and Scripture one, since he is not learned in any other book but the Bible, and his chief power consists in the fact that he has learned how to pray.

For some time Mr. Moody had been desirous of leaving in London some permanent and practical memorial of the great revival there, and the work of grace at the Victoria Theatre, under the labours of one of his pupils, led him to appeal to the liberality of certain brethren, with a view to purchasing the old theatre and refitting it as a religious head quarters, in which to hold free religious services on Sunday, and open meetings every night in the week; with appliances for all sorts of Christian work,—in short, a London edition of the Chicago Farwell Hall. The appeal was successful; the place has been purchased for this purpose, and is to stand, in the midst of a moral waste such as seems naturally to surround a theatre,—to stand as a trophy and memorial of the tidal wave of salvation which swept over the British metropolis in the year of Grace eighteen hundred and seventy-five.

Mr. Cole, as well as Mr. Moody, has been urged to remain in England, and go on with his work so auspiciously begun; but thus far he has declined all such invitations, and after a series of meetings in Liverpool, is expected to return to America.

Mr. J. V. Farwell and Mr. B. F. Jacobs, though still at the head of large business concerns, have, for the past few years, given large portions of their time to evangelistic labours, and there are many other gentlemen, and ladies too, who have learned the secret of entire devotion to God, and who are becoming more and more useful in the church, and among the outcasts and the poor.

Thus, from the consecration of this one man to the Lord, and the influence of his example and his success, a great system of lay work has been inaugurated in the North-west, which has, to a considerable extent, been repeated in other parts of the Union.

The Chicago band are not more able or influential than the lay helpers of other cities; but the power of God seems to have accompanied their labours in a wonderful degree.

Why is this?

Evidently because they have learned the secret of using God's words rather than their own.

PART II.

MOODY AND SANKEY IN GREAT BRITAIN AND IRELAND.

IRA DAVID SANKEY.

CHAPTER I.

EARLY HISTORY OF MR. SANKEY.

IRA DAVID SANKEY was born in Edinburgh, in the State of Pennsylvania, in the year 1840. His father's family were originally from England; his ancestors on his mother's side were from the north of Ireland. Both his parents were members of the Methodist Episcopal Church; and he, with his four brothers and four sisters, was trained up for the Lord, to whom he was consecrated in his infancy. His father was an influential man in the State, being for a length of time a member of the lower, and afterwards of the upper house of the legislature of Pennsylvania, while his wealth and influence made him an exceedingly useful member of the Church, in which he was also leader and exhorter. When Ira was a lad of sixteen the family removed to New-castle, in the same State, where the father assumed the presidency of a bank, and the son entered an academy, where he completed his education.

His first religious impressions were received from the instructions of an old Scotch farmer in the neigh-bourhood, who used to take him to the Sunday-school when he was only six years of age. This humble man made a great impression upon the mind of the boy, on account of his sincerity and earnestness in the service of the Lord.

The habits of his father's household were puritanical. All its requirements were severe: the boys were not even allowed to whistle on a Sunday; but this influence seems to have been blessed to the children, who were early brought to the Saviour. Mr. David Sankey was often invited to attend religious meetings in the neighbourhood, to which he would sometimes take his son Ira, who thus became familiar with religious services of different kinds, in which, while yet a child, he rendered good service in singing. In the day-school and in the Sunday-school, at a very early age, his was a leading voice. He was full of music, and sensitive to musical impressions. Tunes which he once heard he could sing again; and before he was sixteen years of age he began to make tunes for himself.

During a series of revival meetings held in King's Chapel, in Edinburgh,—which was the place of worship regularly attended by the family,—he was first brought under conviction of sin, and made to feel the necessity of saving faith in Christ. The first few nights he attended as a matter of course, sitting by the stove with the other boys, whispering, and enjoying himself, as boys sometimes will under such circumstances, even in the house of God. But presently, an old steward of the church, who had taken a great interest in him, came and inquired if he would not go to the altar with other inquirers, and try to become a Christian. This he at first refused to do; but, evening after evening, his old friend returned with the same earnest inquiry; and at last he joined the large company of inquirers, and bowed at the altar in humble penitence of soul; which, before many days, was followed by the joyful sense of pardon and acceptance with God. The reality and genuineness of this first experience of religion he never had occasion to question, though the great attention given to moods and feelings and the too great neglect of biblical instruction of inquirers, did afterwards give him some trouble. Upon one point, however, he was decided, and his experience was clear: namely, he gave himself completely and unreservedly to Christ; and this matter being settled once for all, his subsequent experience of grace was like the shining light "which shineth more and more unto the perfect day." This was in his sixteenth year.

At the close of the series of meetings, he, with a large number of others, was received into the church at Edinburgh, as a probationer; but before the six months' probation had expired, the family removed to Newcastle, in the same State, where he was received into full membership at the Jefferson Street Methodist Episcopal Church. Here also he became prominent in the service of song. When about twenty years of age, he was elected superintendent of the Sunday-school which at that time numbered about three hundred and fifty scholars. It was here that he commenced his solo singing,—singing the Gospel, as he is now accustomed to call it,—and which, from the first, proved a very great attraction. Largely on this

account the school was filled to overflowing, not only with children, but with their parents, who came, not so much to study the Word of God as to listen to the songs and hymns, which Mr. Sankey sang himself with wonderful sweetness and impressiveness, and in which he led the school, until it became famous for its musical acquirements.

About this time he was appointed to the leadership of a class in connection with his own church, which was composed of from sixty to eighty men and women, who came together one evening every week, to speak of their religious experience, and to receive instructions from their leader in the way of holiness. The duties of this responsible office led him to examine carefully the foundations of his own hope in Christ. He soon became impressed with the fact that he, like too many others, had been living by feeling rather than by the Word of God. He had been accustomed to measure his state of grace by what he heard related in class-meetings and prayer-meetings, rather than by the texts of Scripture which are given for the purpose of defining the true condition of a child of God. The care of this large number of persons seemed to him a weighty responsibility; and in order that he might not lead them astray, he commenced the study of the Scriptures with more earnestness than ever, searching in them for the right instruction to be given to each individual member of his class, to suit their various requirements in trial and suffering and labour. In this work he was largely blessed. The class was conducted on strictly biblical principles; its members were rooted and grounded in love, resting not upon their own, or upon each other's experience, but upon the never-failing promises of the Word of God.

He would say to the class, "Tell us your condition in Bible language. The Scriptures abound with accounts of religious feeling of all descriptions. There is no state of grace which may not be described by a text." And the members being thus instructed, were accustomed to search for their portraits in the Bible, and also to inquire what words of counsel or of comfort it contained for their especial use.

No wonder that a class conducted on such principles should have been thoroughly established in the faith of the Gospel, and should have given a good account of itself in all kinds of religious work. During the winter of 1867 some active Christian young men came out from the city of Pitsburgh, Pennsylvania, to hold what they called a "Christian Convention," in Newcastle, with a view to organizing a Young Men's Christian Association in that town. The Convention proved to be a success. An Association was organized, in which Mr. Sankey became an active worker, and of which he ultimately became president.

In April 1861, President Lincoln called for an army of 75,000 men, for the purpose of putting down the Rebellion in the South. A regiment was raised in Newcastle and the vicinity, and Mr. Sankey was one of the first who enlisted. The call was for three months' service. At the expiration of his term of enlistment, he returned to Newcastle, and entered the civil service under his father, who had been appointed collector of the internal revenue for that district; and in this capacity he remained until he resigned all connection with the business world to join Mr. Moody in Chicago. His abilities as a Christian singer made his services in great request throughout all that region of country; and he was accustomed to spend much time in attending conventions, mass meetings, and other public religious assemblies, to conduct the music of the congregations, and to sing his admirable solos, which soon became very popular. Mr. Sankey's singing was a part of his religion. His talent in this direction was a special gift from God, and as such he cultivated it almost exclusively in the lines of sacred music.

For years he felt deeply impressed that there was a power in song which the Church had failed to appreciate, or even to understand. It seemed to him that he had a special mission in this direction, and accordingly he entered into this department of Christian work with the same earnestness and devotion as he would have taken up the work of preaching the Gospel, if he had felt himself called thereto. No singing master, or conservatory of music, ever placed a professional stamp upon him. His style was acquired in the Sunday-school, in the regular services of the house of God, in camp-meetings and conventions, and in the closet upon his knees. He was accustomed to pray over his singing as a minister prays over his sermon; and thus receiving the baptism of the Holy Ghost, he was able to go forth in the name of the Lord, singing psalms and hymns and spiritual songs, making melody in his heart unto God, and thereby leading thousands of others to understand, and join in, the service of praise as they never had done before. From first to last he was never a professional musician. All the services which he rendered were gratuitous. He asked nothing of men; but the Lord has rewarded him according to his works.

It was at the International Convention of the Young Men's Christian Association at Indianapolis, that he first met Mr. Moody; in connection with whom he was destined to such great success. During the Convention a prayer-meeting was appointed for seven o'clock in the morning, in the church adjoining the Academy of Music, where the Convention was held. The meeting was led by Mr. Moody. When Mr. Sankey entered he found the singing in the hands of a worthy old man, who was dragging through a long-metre hymn in slow and solemn style; worshipful enough, it may be, to those who are accustomed to that kind of singing, but inexpressively dull and heavy to a man like Mr. Sankey. The meeting dragged, like the singing. Everything was in long metre and slow time. No sooner had Mr. Sankey appeared, than some one, who knew his capacity, invited him to lead the singing for the remainder of the meeting; and under his direction so great a change came over it, that what began with heaviness ended with delight. At the close some one introduced him to Mr. Moody, whose first salutation was,—

"Where do you live?"

"In Newcastle, Pennsylvania," was the reply.

"Are you married?"

"Yes."

"How many children have you?"

"One."

"I want you."

"What for?"

"To help me in my work at Chicago."

"I cannot leave my business," said Mr. Sankey.

"You must," said Mr. Moody. "I have been looking for you for the last eight years. You must give up your business, and come to Chicago with me."

Mr. Sankey replied that he would think and pray over the matter, and see what the Lord would direct. It seemed no small matter for him to resign his profitable situation, break up his home, go to a strange city, and unite his fortunes with a man of whom he knew so little, but whom he understood to be wholly given to the work of the Lord, and ready to go at a moment's notice anywhere in the world on a mission in His name. He talked the matter over with his wife, to whom this cross seemed, especially heavy. But at length, feeling that the invitation from Mr. Moody was a call from heaven, he determined to go to Chicago for a week at least, and labour with him, hoping the Lord would there more clearly indicate His will. Before the close of the Convention, they held one meeting together in the open air, in the streets of Indianapolis. Mr. Moody preached, and Mr. Sankey sang; and the good results which followed seemed to indicate that the Lord would be pleased to have them join company, and work together. Their week in Chicago was so much blessed, and their spirits clave to one another in such Christian love and fellowship, that Mr. Sankey determined to break off all connection with the world, and to join this ardent brother who, he felt, was specially appointed of God to labour among the masses of people not generally reached by the ordinary means of grace.

During this week they worked together in church, in Sunday-schools, in saloons and drinking dens, speaking and singing as occasion served; and in all these various labours their souls were refreshed, and good was done. This was about six months before the Great Fire, which occurred in October 1871. That great calamity, which overwhelmed the whole of that portion of the city where Mr. Moody's mission had been located so deranged his plans, that he went for a tour to the Atlantic coast, and Mr. Sankey returned for a time to his family in Pennsylvania. But no sooner was the new tabernacle erected in the midst of the ruins, than the two brethren returned and commenced their work again together, taking up their lodgings in ante-rooms of the great rough building, and giving themselves, day and night, to comforting the bodies and trying to save the souls of the unfortunate people who thronged this place of refuge.

The great revival which signalised this work in the chapel among the ruins, has already been recorded in these pages. During Mr. Moody's absence on his second visit to England, in the spring of 1872, Mr. Sankey "held the fort," and carried on the meetings. When his friend returned from attending the Mildmay Conference in London—which was one of the principal objects of his journey—he found Mr. Sankey deeply impressed with the same spirit which had taken hold of him, and under the influence of which his preaching henceforth became more strictly biblical. Mr. Sankey began to search for hymns which clearly set forth the doctrines of the Word of God; and thus the Bible preaching was accompanied with Bible singing, in a manner which at once attracted the earnest attention of many devout persons in Chicago and the region round about. For a year these two brethren pursued this line of labour. Many churches were visited by them, and the Lord honoured His Word and brought many sinners to Christ by the ministry both of the speaker and the singer.

The solo singing was not new with the Christians of Chicago. It had been introduced several years before by Mr. Phillips, of New York, and had been greatly admired and enjoyed, but had not been considered so much a means of grace and salvation as a method of pious enjoyment. When Mr. Sankey began to sing his songs with a view to the awakening and conversion of sinners, many good people were surprised; some were shocked, and others openly opposed the innovation. However, it soon became evident that the Lord approved this method of bringing souls into His kingdom; and presently all opposition to it ceased.

After Mr. Moody's second visit to England, he seems to have contemplated returning to that country; and having at length determined to go thither again, he said to Mr. Sankey—

"You have often proposed that we should go out evangelising together; now go with me to England."

At the same time Mr. Sankey was considering a proposal from Mr. Phillips to join him in a tour of "evenings of song" on the Pacific coast; and he was in no small doubt and anxiety of mind which of these invitations to accept. On one occasion he stated the case to a friend, and asked his advice, which was given to the following purpose: "Don't go with Mr. Phillips. Two workers in the same line, and especially two singers, are certain not to agree. Go with Moody; then you can do your work, and he can do his and there will be no occasion of conflict between you." It was at length decided that Moody and Sankey should go to England together; trusting wholly to the Lord to direct and support them, and sharing together whatever God by His providence should give them for the expenses of their journey and the reward of their labours. They were, as aforetime, to take no salaries or stipends in any form. They were to ask no collections. They were to engage in no business, but to devote themselves solely to the work of God, and to rely upon Him for all things requisite and necessary as well for the body as for the soul.

On the 7th of June, 1872, Mr. Moody with his family, accompanied by Mr. Sankey, sailed from New York, and ten days after landed in Liverpool.

CHAPTER II.

MAKING A BEGINNING.—YORK AND SUNDERLAND.

"WHY do you go to England again so soon?" said one of Mr. Moody's friends to him, a short time previous to his last voyage.

"To win ten thousand souls to Christ," was the reply.

It was with a hope of great things in his heart, that Mr. Moody started on his third expedition to Great Britain; a hope which had been growing and strengthening for a long time, and which had now come so fully to possess him that he already claimed this great success as his own. When he arrived in Liverpool, on the 17th of June, 1873, he learned that two of his old friends, by whom he had been invited to England, had recently died: the Rev. Mr. Pennyfather, rector of the Mildmay Park Church in London, and Mr. Cuthbert Bainbridge, an eminent Wesleyan layman and extensive merchant, in Newcastle-upon-Tyne. A third invitation, from Mr. George Bennett of York, the secretary of the Young Men's Christian Association in that town, was the one he intended to accept first in order; but on telegraphing to that gentleman, that he had arrived, and was ready to commence his meetings, he received the reply that everything was so cold and dead in York, that it would take at least month to prepare for the intended revival meetings. The despatch concluded by asking Mr. Moody to name a date at which he might be expected. He immediately telegraphed back, "I will be in York to-night." At ten o'clock he reached the city, where no one, except his friend Bennett, had ever seen him, and very few had ever heard his name.

The situation was, surely, not very encouraging; but, after carefully looking it over, Mr. Moody declared that every man must make his own way, and that he was ready "to go in at once." Mr. Sankey, who had gone to Manchester, was telegraphed for, and the meetings opened immediately. The next morning applications were made to several ministers of the town for the use of their pulpits on the coming Sabbath; and two Wesleyan, a Baptist, and a Congregationalist place of worship, were reluctantly placed at their disposal.

The first of that long series of revival meetings which were destined to form an era in the history of England, Scotland, and Ireland, was held on Sunday morning, in one of the small rooms of the Young Men's Christian Association, at which eight persons only were in attendance. The other meetings, which they held on this first Sabbath, were much more encouraging; but during the week which followed, there seemed to be nobody to pray for them, and nobody to work with them. The congregations were small. The interest increased slowly. The preaching was chiefly to professors of religion, who, as Mr. Bennett puts it, "needed almost as much waking up as the famous Seven Sleepers themselves."

Considered as a revival, this first week's work was a most lamentable failure ; but during the second week a better state of things appeared, and something in the nature of an awakening commenced among the congregation in one of the Wesleyan chapels.

The inquiry meetings, which always followed each public service, were somewhat new and striking to the good people of York ; but they gradually grew in favour, as the number of inquirers at them increased : and throughout the two years' campaign, this peculiar exercise has been one of the great instruments of spiritual success.

Mr. Moody's manner of expounding Scripture at once attracted great attention; one of the first effects of his ministry was the awakening of believers to the earnest study of the Word of God. He directed them to bring their Bibles, when they came to the meetings ; taught them the best methods of Bible study : and here, as in many other cities, there sprang up such a demand for a certain edition of the Bible, with index and concordance, that the publishers were forced to increase their production, and still were unable to supply their orders without considerable delay.

His expositions of Scripture were so plain, that people who went to church with no particular religious impressions were often brought under the influence of the truth. Even while he was speaking, and without waiting for the personal instructions of the inquiry meeting, they would sometimes be enabled at once to take Christ as their Saviour: they would then go forth from the meetings, happy in the Lord, to invite their acquaintances to the same line of faith and experience with themselves.

The chief difficulty, however, in the way of their success, was the coldness with which Messrs. Moody and Sankey were received by the clergymen and ministers of the place. The common people heard them gladly; and if they had been encouraged by their spiritual guides, there seems to be no doubt but that a great revival, like the one enjoyed in Edinburgh,. or Glasgow, or Liverpool, might have followed the labours of the evangelists here. Their subsequent success has quieted all doubts, and removed all opposition; and now the frequent inquiry is, "Will they ever come back again?"

During the month of their stay in York, two hundred and fifty persons professed to find Christ. Many, who were already members of churches, were brought up into a higher spiritual life; and it is believed that a large number of others, who made no profession, were greatly benefited by the services.

The noonday prayer-meeting, which Mr. Moody inaugurated, is still kept up by the Young Men's Christian Association; and very much permanent good was undoubtedly done.

Mr. Moody closed his work in York with an all-day meeting, which, from its novelty, as well as its efficiency, attracted great attention, and was most highly approved. First there was an hour for confession and prayer; second, an hour for praise; third, a promise meeting, which consisted of testimonies, on the part of believers, to the fulfilment of promises in their own experience; fourth, a witness meeting, which was a succession of public confessions of Christ by young converts; fifth, a Bible lecture by Mr. Moody; and finally, a communion service, conducted by Mr. Moody and four ministers who were present, in the Presbyterian fashion.

The singing of Mr. Sankey was both a surprise and a pleasure in York. Such singing was never heard in that town before. His lodgings were in the very centre of business; and sometimes, when he would sit down to his harmonium, and sing and play for the friends who were entertaining him, the street would be filled with a crowd of people, listening with delight. One instance is related of a woman who was deeply convicted of sin while listening to one of these hymns in the street, and who, on asking and obtaining an interview with the singer, was led immediately to the Saviour. A great many instances of conversion, through the singing of Mr. Sankey, have been recorded; but this seems to have been the first, as well as one of the most striking, of them all.

Mr. Moody's meetings in York were chiefly held in chapels. He would not go to halls, and other public places, lest he should seem to be neglecting or opposing the regularly established forms of worship. As always in his own country, so now in England, he greatly desired to work inside the Church of Christ, and not to establish any new system of his own.

It was a sore trial to him to find the ministry, at

first, almost universally indifferent, or hostile, to him; but he never departed from his original purpose, and ultimately, his faith and his firmness were signally honoured by the opening of churches and chapels of every order for his meetings, in the chief cities of the United Kingdom, and the opening of the hearts of their ministers and elders to receive not only his message, but himself.

SUNDERLAND.

The Rev. Arthur Rees, of Sunderland—a considerable city, on the eastern side of England—after attending some of Mr. Moody's meetings in York, determined to invite him to labour with his own congregation, at Bethesda Chapel; and to this place came the American evangelists, and commenced their meetings on Sunday, the 27th of July.

Mr. Rees is an open-communion Baptist; holding certain other opinions of his own; who has gathered about him a very large congregation of earnest Christian people among whom there seems to have been a good deal of religious life.

It required no small courage to bring Messrs. Moody and Sankey to Sunderland; but Mr. Rees was fully equal to the occasion, and his judgment, as well as bravery, was abundantly justified by the revival which followed. In speaking of the coldness and opposition, on the part of the ministers of Sunderland, one gentleman says:

"Mr. Moody had one whole minister, three-fourths of one other, and nothing, or next to nothing, of all the rest to help him in his meetings."

But their want of faith in this strange man was certainly not without excuse. His method of operation was so different from anything they had ever seen in a religious way, that it is no wonder they failed to recognise in him a chosen prophet of the Lord. Besides, he came quite unheralded, except by the sharp criticisms which had preceded him from York; and accounts of the revival there which contained more reference to its strangeness than to its spirituality and power. Mr. Moody was not a clergyman, nor even a minister. No holy hands had ever been laid upon him; his only consecration to the holy office was the one which he had made himself. His blunt ways, and evident want of culture, offended those nice persons who had always associated religion with everything that was elegant and orderly.

From the first he drew large congregations of curious persons, who went to hear Moody and Sankey just as they would have gone to hear an actor, or a vocalist; and it was from among this careless crowd that the first trophies of grace were won. Still the work dragged heavily. No one in all the town, except Mr. Rees, gave them the least official notice; and it seemed likely, for want of the co-operation of influential persons, that the movement would come to nothing.

"We never can go on in this way," said Mr. Moody. "It is easier fighting the devil than fighting the ministers."

After they had been in Sunderland some time, the Young Men's Christian Association sent a delegation to wait upon them at their lodgings; and this is the account which one of them gives of the interview:—

"They had already been a week in Sunderland; but, as yet, I had not seen either of them. Ah! thought I, what a lift heavenward shall I get from these holy men! We were shown into a back parlour by the servant, and very soon the two evangelists sauntered in in a style neither ecclesiastical nor dignified. Turning to me, Mr. Moody asked, in true Yankee fashion, What was our business with him? He did not show us a seat; he did not offer us his hand: altogether an auctioneer-like reception,

"We represent the Young Men's Christian Association, Mr. Moody, and have come to ask if you will give us an address in Victoria Hall, on Sunday afternoon.

"Preach for you? Oh yes! I'll preach for you, replied Mr. Moody.

"We don't want you to preach for us; we want you to preach for Christ.

"Oh yes—yes! All right! I'll preach for you.

"Our committee, continued I, hope you will not misunderstand the reason of their not joining you earlier in your work. It is not for want of sympathy; but because you came to us in a sectarian connection, and have allied yourself with Mr. Rees; and if we were to join you, on sectarian grounds, we should injure our Institution, which has enemies enough already.

"After explaining his position, and that his connection with Brother Rees and his congregation had no sectarian significance, he said,—

"I go where I can do most good: that is what I am after. And when we left, he followed us out to the gate, saying, 'It is souls I want: it is souls I want.'

"Alas! I had mistaken the man; and whether he spoke of souls or anything else, it is all the same to me now.

"Well, Frank, what did you think of it? asked my companion, as we walked off from this strange interview.

"Think! It is money: that is what it is, James.

"However, I went to the meeting, being careful to keep out of sight; but when Sankey began singing, I felt it draw me, and very little more of it would have pulled me on to the platform.

"That was not a good afternoon for Mr. Moody. His eye blazed with mournful earnestness, as it ranged that crowd, looking for anxious faces; and its strange light lives in my memory yet, while all my prejudices and misconceptions are dead and rotten.

"On the following Sunday night, when I got to the rooms of the Young Men's Christian Association, I found the meeting on fire. The young men were speaking with tongues, and prophesying. What on earth did it all mean? Only that Moody had been addressing them that afternoon. 'What manner of man is this?' thought I; but still I did not give him my hand. . . Many of the clergy were so opposed to the movement that they turned their backs upon our poor innocent Young Men's Christian Association, for the part we took in the work; but afterwards, when the floodgates of Divine grace were opened, Sunderland was taken by storm.

"I cannot describe Moody's great meetings; I can only say that the people of Sunderland warmly supported the movement, in spite of their spiritual advisers; that there was a tremendous work of grace, when measured by its immediate effects, but far greater in its consequences, after the evangelists were gone away. All honour to these two brother-soldiers of the cross, who, like Jonathan and his armour-bearer, stormed this fortress of British unbelief alone!"

In order to avoid all appearance of sectarianism, Mr. Moody removed the meetings to the Victoria Hall; though on the Sabbath, and even during the week, extra and overflow meetings were conducted in a few of the Nonconformist chapels.

It appears that the Wesleyan ministers of Sunderland had special reason to hesitate about joining Mr. Moody, on account of his Calvinistic theology; of which, however, he brought out very little in any of his discourses, but which they scented in some of his exhortations and instructions to inquirers. But about this time, the president of the Wesleyan Conference, the Rev. William Morley Punshon, LL.D., came down from London to attend a special service; and, having been well acquainted with Mr. Moody in Chicago, and knowing him to be thoroughly in earnest, and truly catholic in his spirit, he exhorted his brethren to give him their hands. This good counsel, from such high authority, was of much value to all concerned; and some of the Wesleyan chapels were amongst those which were opened for the extra services.

Still the work went on but slowly. Here and there

a prominent minister openly opposed it, both by sermons and in the public press. It was so different from anything which had ever been seen in Sunderland, that some of the clergy felt quite certain it must have come originally from the devil. With such earnestness and courage did Moody press the battle, that some of his best friends began to be alarmed; even Mr. Rees himself, losing heart for a time, began to criticise the methods of work, and issued a little tract on "Religious Dissipation: a Word of Caution for Times of Revival," which he prefaced with this text, from Proverbs xxv. 16:—

"Hast thou found honey? Eat so much as is sufficient for thee, lest thou be filled therewith, and vomit it."

Poor Mr. Moody! His soul was among lions. Even the sweet singing of Mr. Sankey could not calm all the disturbances which were raised by his vigorous discourses. Still he would not withhold a single word of the truth as he understood it, to please even the most eminent ministers or the most cautious laymen. God had given him his message, and he had nothing to do but deliver it. This he did, though oftentimes with a heavy heart, cheered by occasional conversions, and the satisfaction of doing his whole duty.

One of the fly-sheets issued against him was called "Kindly Reflections upon the Present Religious Movement." It was divided into three sections: viz., First, "Good results,"—of which five were mentioned; Second, "Questionable procedures in the movement," of which there were fifteen; Third, "Probable evil results," which were set forth in such vast and gloomy proportions as to make many a thoughtful Christian "rejoice with trembling," if even they did not prevent his rejoicing at all.

The chief difficulty in the minds of his critics, appeared to be, the too rapid progress of the revival among people of all sorts and conditions, and the too great freedom with which salvation was offered to whomsoever would have it. The preacher seemed to be throwing about the Gospel promiscuously into the crowds, with the chance that some would be hit by it, with the hope that some would be saved by it, but with the certainty that a great many would trample it under their feet. None of their attacks, however, troubled Mr. Moody, so long as plenty of sinners came to his inquiry-meetings to find out what they should do to be saved.

The opponents also declared that "solo singing is not worship"; but Mr. Sankey kept on singing his solos, to the edification of those who had no compunctions of conscience concerning them. It was alleged that Mr. Moody used too much pressure, not only in trying to persuade sinners to repentance, but also in his efforts to drive Christians to work. Nevertheless the pressure was kept up; and the month of meetings came to its conclusion with results which, if they were far from satisfactory, were also far from being complete: for months afterwards, when the news of the great outpouring of the Holy Spirit upon Newcastle, Edinburgh, and Glasgow, under the labours of these same brethren, poured in upon the astonished Sunderlanders, they began to say with themselves, "We have made a great mistake. We have cast away a blessing." And when delegations of young men from the North came down to hold more meetings among them, the whole city was moved; wave after wave of revival power swept over the churches, bringing more souls to the Saviour in this overflow revival than all those who had been converted under the labours of Moody and Sankey themselves.

CHAPTER III.

THE BREAKING OF THE CLOUD.—NEWCASTLE.

AMONG the eminent ministers from neighbouring cities, who came to visit Mr. Moody's meetings in Sunderland, was the Rev. David Lowe, D.D., pastor of the John Knox Presbyterian Church at Newcastle-upon-Tyne. He arrived at the door of the place of meeting just as Mr. Moody was sending a large number of inquirers into a separate room for religious conversation: who, on seeing and remembering the Doctor's face, saluted him thus:—"Here, Brother Lowe, go in and talk to all those inquirers. There are so many, you will have to make them into a little congregation, and talk to them altogether." Such an introduction to the revival was most fortunate for the Newcastle pastor; and, on further inspection, he became so thoroughly satisfied with the genuineness of the work of grace, that he pressed Mr. Moody to come to him as soon as he should finish his work in Sunderland. To this, as to a call from God, Mr. Moody at once agreed; and, a few days after, commenced his labours at Newcastle, having spent a few days at Jarrow on the way. Among the friends that greeted him here were Mr. Thomas Bainbridge, (a brother of Mr. Moody's old friend), and Mr. Richard Hoyle, a gentleman who divides his time about equally between his place of business and his large and flourishing Mission at the Music Hall.

At Newcastle Mr. Moody set himself down before Great Britain, with the deliberate determination of conquering its prejudices against himself, and breaking his way into the confidence of its people, in order to bring to them the message which he bore from God.

"We have not done much in York and Sunderland," said he, "because the ministers opposed us; but we are going to stay in Newcastle till we make an impression, and live down the prejudices of good people who do not understand us."

During the first week, five of the principal chapels of the town were placed at his disposal, and meetings were held in them alternately; but, at length, Mr. Moody settled himself at the Rye Hill Baptist Chapel, which was a very large edifice with a very small congregation. At first the audiences were not large, but in a fortnight the great audience-room was filled to overflowing. Then crowds were turned away for want of room; and during the last few days the desire to attend the meetings of Messrs. Moody and Sankey became so general and so intense, that one of the brethren declared he was actually glad when they went away, because the immense crowds which could not find admission to their services were sometimes almost riotous from disappointment.

One after another, the leading ministers joined hands with the evangelists, greatly to Mr. Moody's delight. "I am always glad to see a minister come to our meetings," said he; "for he always brings a large reinforcement with him." Some of the clergy of the Established Church also gave their sympathy to the movement; and long before the close of these remarkable services, the outpouring of the Spirit of God upon the entire population of the place proved that the Lord had honoured the faith of His servant.

An impression, indeed, had been made so deep and overwhelming, that it will enter into the history of the religious life of the present century, and so far-reaching in its influence, that no thought can measure its breadth of blessing. Not only at Newcastle, but in all the towns and villages over a radius of fifteen or twenty miles, the revival flame was kindled. The committee who managed the meetings held a business session every Friday morning, at which they were oppressed with delegations from all quarters, asking that brethren might be sent by Mr. Moody to hold meetings in their neighbourhood; and presently, the number of assistants having been greatly multiplied, hundreds of those outside meetings were held, and almost invariably they were marked with wonderful religious power.

A minister from the hills of Northumberland came to them with the Macedonian cry, "Come over and help us." He did not ask them to send a minister, or even a lay preacher; but if they would only send some person who could tell them the story of the Newcastle revival, he felt sure the Spirit of God would attend even such a simple message. They promised that a man should be sent; and the pastor went back to his home among the hills, to publish the news far and wide that some one was coming from Newcastle to tell them about the revival. When the appointed time arrived, an immense congregation had come together to listen to the glad tidings; but by some delay or accident the speaker did not come. There was nothing for it, then, but that the minister should try to tell the story himself, though he had only paid one short visit to the place; but even this scanty information was so thrilling and effective, that it produced a deep impression, and a powerful work of grace immediately broke out, which swept through all that region of country.

During the progress of the revival, Mr. Moody became oppressed with the thought that the meetings were too much made up of people who were Christians already, to the exclusion of great numbers who were earnestly seeking the truth. On this account he began to divide his congregations into classes, giving tickets to the different meetings which were held for them, and thus reaching many persons who otherwise would have been unable to profit by his ministry. Two notable meetings for merchants were held in the Assembly Hall, the fashionable place for holding balls and grand public ceremonies. Meetings for mechanics were held at the Tyne Theatre; and since no place was ever large enough to hold the congregations which came together, three or four overflow meetings were usually in progress, at such places as could be obtained in the neighbourhood.

By an admirable system which the committee adopted, the name and residence of every inquirer was made a matter of record; and lest the instructions given them in the inquiry meetings should not be always of a suitable character, tickets were issued to ministers, and other intelligent and experienced persons, by which they were admitted to assist at these exercises. The inquiry rooms were as crowded as the churches.

The first converts were from among the educated classes of society. It seemed as if God were honouring the religious training which these persons had received, and by means of it, as well as of the burning words of the preacher, were bringing them to a saving knowledge of the truth. Afterwards the work became more general; but the great majority of those who professed to have been converted were those who had known the Scriptures from infancy, and had been regular attendants at the house of God.

Now the hearts of the evangelists were made glad. Mr. Moody preached more heartily than ever: Mr. Sankey sang daily with new joy and enthusiasm. Their spiritual condition seemed to rise on the rising wave of the revival, and all who were associated with them felt themselves to be rapidly growing in grace, as well as in the knowledge of the truth.

Mr. Moody's method of explaining the Scriptures was greatly enjoyed. He would throw a text at a sinner, who would seem to see it blazing as it came. He poured out the oil of joy and consolation upon anxious and sorrowful hearts, in a way that suggested the Good Samaritan Himself; and in his conversations with anxious persons he seemed to have come again into possession of the power he used to have in working for the dying on the battle-fields;—a strange, secret familiarity with heaven and heavenly things, which he was in some measure able to convey to those whom he was instructing. Thus sudden conversions began to multiply.

To those who had always been accustomed to see the work of grace going on gradually in the souls of inquirers, these sudden conversions were something of a stumbling-block; but Mr. Moody, as usual, when any question was raised, fell back upon the Word of God. He searched the Scriptures for records and examples, and astonished his cautious brethren by pointing out the fact that the great majority of Bible conversions were of this same sudden type.

The noon prayer-meeting, which was an important element in the revival, had been commenced previous to his coming, by way of preparation. The room in which it was first held being over-crowded, it was removed to the Music Hall, which was capable of holding a thousand people. This place was usually filled; though Newcastle is so busy a town that, under ordinary circumstances, a noon prayer-meeting could hardly be maintained at all. In the afternoons Mr. Moody gave a series of those Bible readings for which he has become so famous; and many merchants and professional men, though overwhelmed with the cares of business, arranged their day's work with a view to enjoying them. The very best people in the city came in crowds, at four o'clock in the afternoon, to hear Mr. Moody read and explain the Word of God; and of all his services those Bible readings are most pleasantly and profitably remembered.

During the last week the meetings were held in the Brunswick Wesleyan Chapel, where wonders of grace were wrought. It was here that the famous Jubilee Singers appeared; and their simple, spiritual songs added a new charm to the services, which were already overflowing with sweetness and joy. Ministers of all denominations vied with each other in helpfulness. Even the Established clergy felt their hearts warming towards this irregular brother from across the sea; and some of them not only attended the meetings, but went away and held similar ones for their own congregations. An instance of this, it is said, was reported to the Bishop of —— by a clergyman whose heart had remained cold through all those fires. It was evidently done for the purpose of bringing down the Episcopal cudgel on the offender's head; but, greatly to his amazement, he received, in response to his accusation, this laconic answer: "Go thou and do likewise."

The Scriptural method of dealing with inquirers is well illustrated in the case of a middle-aged man who rose in the noon meeting, trembling with emotion, and said, "I am a lost sinner, and want you to pray for me." He afterwards came to Dr. Lowe for personal instruction, saying he felt his soul in fetters, so that he could not come to Christ.

"Come to Christ, fetters and all," was the Doctor's reply.

"Yes," said the poor man; "but Satan is very hard on me. He seems to be throwing dust in my eyes."

"Never mind your eyes; but come to Christ."

"I stick fast," said the penitent man; "I cannot get off."

Upon this, the Doctor was somewhat at a loss to know what to do; but, after a few words of prayer, he opened the Bible at the fifth chapter of John, and said to the inquirer, "What you want is to believe in Christ, is it not?"

"Yes," answered he, "I need to believe in Christ; but I cannot see how I am to do it."

"Listen, now, while I read," said the Doctor. "'After this there was a feast of the Jews, and Jesus went up to Jerusalem.' Do you believe that?"

"Oh yes; that is in the Bible: of course I believe that."

"'Now there is at Jerusalem, by the sheep-market, a pool, which is called in the Hebrew tongue Bethesda.' Do you believe that pool was there?"

"No doubt of it," said the inquirer.

"'In this lay a great multitude of impotent folk.' Do you believe these impotent folk were really there?"

"Certainly."

"'Blind, halt, and withered.' Do you believe they were blind and halt and withered?"

"Oh yes."

"Well, do you not think you are very much like these folk, lying there by the pool, and waiting for the angel to come down and trouble the water?"

"Yes," said the poor man; "that seems to be very much my case."

"You are impotent?"

"Yes; I cannot help myself a bit."

"You are blind? You just now said the devil was throwing dust in your eyes."

"True."

"And you have had this infirmity as long as thirty-and-eight years, have you not?"

"Yes; just about that," said the inquirer.

"Now hear what Jesus said:—'And when Jesus saw him lying, and knew that he had now been a long time in that case, He said unto him, Wilt thou be made whole?' Now, my friend, that is just what Christ is saying to you: 'Wilt thou be made whole?'"

Quick as lightning, the truth flashed in upon the poor man's mind. He sprang to his feet, shouting, "I am free! Where is Mr. Moody?" And away he rushed to find him; threw his arms about him, nearly carrying him off his feet; seized both his hands and shook them joyfully, exclaiming, "I am free! I am free!"

Afterwards, in the meetings, he gave this testimony:—"I am a new man. When I used to be in any trouble I would try to drown my sorrow in drink; but now, if anything goes wrong with me, I go to my closet and pray."

In his meetings at Newcastle, Mr. Moody dealt little in law: he felt that the people wanted to be saved; therefore he told them how. It did not seem necessary to threaten them, but rather to point out God's great desire to bless them.

At the close of the meeting one night, two people were left kneeling in prayer after all the rest of the congregation had retired: one of these was a broken-hearted penitent, and the other a Christian friend who was trying to help him to the cross. The poor fellow seemed like a drowning man. He felt himself to be sinking, and dared not leave the place of prayer, for fear he might lose his soul. Mr. Moody and three or four friends gathered round him in a circle, in the dark hall, (the gas had all been turned off except one faint burner); and there they prayed in turn, one after another, for the poor man who knelt in the centre of the circle, trembling like a condemned criminal. After they had prayed once round, no one dared to speak; but, at length, one of them commenced to quote the promises of God's Word. Text after text he recited, until he came to this one: "I have no pleasure in the death of the wicked; but rather that he turn from the error of his way and live." Then he asked the inquirer this question: "Will you yield to be saved?"

"I will," said the poor fellow, reaching out his hand in the dark, and giving his questioner a tremendous grip: who then took him in his arms, and lifted him gently to his feet, quoting, at the same time, these words: "And this is the will of Him that sent me, that every one which seeth the Son and believeth on Him may have everlasting life; and I will raise him up at the last day."

This strictly Biblical method of dealing with inquirers, as may be supposed, resulted in thorough and intelligent conversions.

One Methodist brother, in speaking of the meetings, said, "We have had revivals before; and we were not much the better for them. But this revival is substantial, for it is along the track of God's own Word."

Of Mr. Moody Dr. Lowe says: "I find him not at all devoted to himself, but wholly devoted to his work. He is modest; ready to take a hint from any one; ready to let every man do his own work: and all the time full of anxiety to save somebody. I never knew a man whom I could splice on to as I can on to Mr. Moody."

More than one minister of the Gospel, who found himself without a satisfactory experience, gave himself to Christ anew, and came into a joyful sense of pardon and acceptance. Professed Christians, who had been members of churches for many years, and who had only a kind of doctrinal faith in the Saviour, and were without any of the "comfort of the Holy Ghost," came out into the light; while in the very lowest stratum of humanity, lost souls were searched for, and found and brought up out of their degradation and wickedness, into the high and holy fellowship of God's own people.

Two all-day meetings were held at Newcastle; one of them, a convention for Christian workers, at which all the North of England was represented. About twelve hundred persons were present, the most of whom were ministers and official members of churches. The exercises were novel, interesting, and powerful. Amongst others was a service of praise, led by Mr. Sankey. This was somewhat different from what had been anticipated; for, instead of singing his sweet songs for an hour, he laid before the congregation, in wise and aptly-chosen passages of Scripture, the duty and privilege of praising God. Mr. Moorhouse spoke on SEPARATION. The last hour was occupied by Mr. Moody in a most delightful address on HEAVEN.

One result of the visit of Messrs. Moody and Sankey to Newcastle is thus forcibly expressed by one of the brethren there:—

"Nothing is so remarkable in this revival as the utter demolishing of the old-fashioned prayer-meeting. Enter solemn minister and solemn people, scattered—six,—eight,—ten—over a great area. A long slow hymn. Long portion of the Word. Two elders pray two long prayers, in which they go from Jerusalem, and round about unto Illyricum, and a great deal farther.

"Now we have crammed meetings. All sit close together. The singing is lively—new songs, new tunes. A few words from the minister give the key-note. Prayers are short. A few texts from the Word of God are frequently interspersed. Brief exhortations. . . . All this comes from our brethren from America. Why have we not found out how to conduct a prayer-meeting before? We in this country have been bound hand and foot by traditions. In the far West of America, at Chicago, for instance, there were no traditions. The only people that had traditions there, were the Indians. The brethren have thoroughly solved this question of prayer-meetings for us. We thank them."

To reckon up the results of this month of revival in Newcastle, would be as difficult a task as to estimate the blessings of a month of summer sunshine. To say that converts were received into all the evangelical churches by hundreds; that the whole of the North of England was reached, and roused, by scores of Christian workers, who were trained in this short course of instruction, and sent out to tell the story of the cross; that the ministers preached better, and the members prayed better; that Bibles were often in the hands of people who had read them but little before; that the Sunday-schools blossomed out into real gardens of the Lord; that pastors ceased to look at each other out of the corners of their eyes, but grasped each other's hands in cordial fellowship; and that the tidings of this outpouring of the Holy Spirit upon Newcastle and vicinity were published by the press, and sent by letter and telegraph all over Great Britain, as the most remarkable current news;—to say this, is only to draw the outline of the heavenly picture. God was with His servants: and so bountifully did He pour down blessings upon them and their labours, that Mr. Moody might have thought again of what he said to his old employer, when he first struck out as an evangelist;—"God is rich, and I am working for Him."

CHAPTER IV.

MOODY AND SANKEY IN SCOTLAND.

ON Saturday, the 21st of November, 1873, after brief, though successful periods of labour at Carlisle, Bishop Auckland, Darlington, Shields, etc., Messrs. Moody and Sankey arrived in Edinburgh.

The record of the work of these brethren in Scotland is a history of one long-continued miracle of grace. Except God had been with them, they could have done nothing. All the circumstances were against them; and the men themselves were, apparently, most of all in the way of their own work.

The Scottish people are eminent for their knowledge of theology. Doctrinal discussions are as natural to them as kites and marbles to boys, or dolls and ribbons to girls; and the various dissensions, disturbances, and divisions which have taken place among them on account of theological opinions, form a voluminous and remarkable history. He who would edify a congregation of Scotchmen must come to them with the beaten oil of the sanctuary; and pour it out from vessels of a proper and traditional form. He should be a man of high attainments in learning; the stamp of some college should be upon him; and more than all, he should come with the endorsement of some eminent body of divines. All these things were wanting in Mr. Moody. If there were any great preacher in all the world who was likely to be rejected in Scotland, aside from the power of God which attended him, D. L. Moody was that man.

To increase the difficulty, his companion, Mr. Sankey did not sing according to the Scottish tradition. In the first place, he sang but few of the psalms at all; and those he did sing were not in the accepted versions. Much of his music was in a form which unpleasantly suggested the performances in places less religious than churches and chapels. But the chief abomination of all was the "kist fu' o' whistles," with which he accompanied his voice; and which, by universal consent, had been kept out of Scottish sanctuaries for more than three hundred years.

But the tidings of the glorious revival in Newcastle had awakened a deep interest in the minds of many ministers in all parts of Scotland, and especially in Edinburgh, that great centre of religious thought and life. There were devout men and women, who for several years had been, like good old Simeon, "waiting for the consolation of Israel." They had been praying that God would visit His people in Scotland with some such outpourings of His Spirit as had been recorded in their earlier history: and when they heard that these strangers were so wonderfully blessed in converting their English neighbours, they began, in spite of all their prejudices, to say, "May not God bless Scotland, as well as England, by means of these evangelists from America?"

It was under such impressions as these that the Rev. John Kelman, of Free St. John's Church, Leith, was induced to visit Newcastle, and examine this new wonder for himself; and so fully convinced was he that God was with these men, that, on his return, he spread the good tidings among his brethren in the ministry, and suggested that Messrs. Moody and Sankey be invited to Edinburgh.

At about the same time the Rev. J. H. Wilson, of the Barclay Church, Edinburgh, became deeply interested in the work of revival in the North of England, through accounts which he had received from some of his leading members, who had visited Sunderland while Moody and Sankey were there; and had desired their pastor to invite them to his church.

From these two ministers, the one in person, and the other by letter, Mr. Moody received invitations to hold some meetings in the capital of Scotland. These he accepted, though with some misgivings; saying to himself, "What can such a man as I do up there amongst those great Scotch divines?" But feeling sure that God was able with a worm "to thrash a mountain," he set his face northward, and late in November commenced that wonderful series of meetings in the Free Church Assembly Hall.

So great was the interest in the approaching revival services, that a daily prayer-meeting was appointed at three o'clock in the afternoon, to implore the descent of the Holy Spirit. These meetings were a prophecy of the glorious work which followed. They were commenced in Craigie Hall, which place soon became overcrowded, and they were transferred

FREE CHURCH ASSEMBLY HALL, EDINBURGH.

to the Upper Queen Street Hall, and finally, to the Assembly Hall, where they daily increased in numbers and power.

On Saturday, the 23rd of November, the Music Hall, where the opening services were held, was densely crowded, to hear Mr. Moody preach the Gospel and Mr. Sankey sing the Gospel, according to the quaint announcements which had been posted over the town. Mr. Moody was unwell, and the Rev. Mr. Wilson was forced to take his place as speaker; while Mr. Sankey conducted the singing in a very attractive and impressive manner. On the next evening something went wrong with Mr. Sankey's organ, so he was not able to appear; and Mr. Moody conducted the services without him. Both these meetings, however, were wonderfully blessed; and the alternate absence of the two leaders was set down by the devout brethren as a providential showing that the power and blessing were of God, and not of men.

From the first, no place in Edinburgh could contain the congregations which pressed to hear this speaker and singer. Three or four of the largest halls and churches were constantly in requisition, and even then it was necessary to attend an hour or two before the time appointed, in order to be sure of admittance.

"One of the first things which impressed us," says Mr. Kelman, "was the extraordinary voracity of Mr. Moody's faith. We had been accustomed to go to the meetings, hoping God would bless us. But Mr. Moody always said, 'We know He will bless us'; and so well assured was he that God delighted to give large things in answer to prayer, that he was continually asking for blessings which were out of all proportion to our faith. But the blessings would come; sometimes so largely, that we did not know what to do with them. We were often absolutely overwhelmed with the power and glory of God."

At one meeting, composed of sixty-six young men, who were inquiring what they must do to be saved, sixty of them were blessed before they left the place.

Mr. Moody's use of the Bible was greatly enjoyed by his brethren in Edinburgh. They also were mighty in the Scriptures; and their people had been diligently instructed in the Word of God. The texts of Holy Writ which were stored away in their memories seemed like the bones in the prophet's vision, waiting for some one appointed of God to come and breathe upon them. This Mr. Moody did; and straightway, in thousands and thousands of minds, the bones began to come together, "bone to his bone." The whole system of salvation rose up before their consciences. It seemed as if the sacrifice on these Scottish altars had been ready and waiting for the fire; and when this man of God began to preach and pray, the fire of the Lord came down. There were multitudes of souls that were like ships, waiting outside the bar for the flood-tide to carry them into the harbour; and now the great tidal wave had reached them, and was sweeping them into the Church.

The religious interest soon spread, not only through Edinburgh and Leith, but throughout the whole of Scotland. The Evangelistic Committee, which was raised for the management of the services, was here, as at Newcastle, pressed to send messengers bearing the glad tidings to distant towns and villages. The whole population were talking of Mr. Moody and his preaching, and of Mr. Sankey and his singing. The newspapers were filled with reports of their meetings. The London press began to take great notice of the movement; and before many weeks the news of this wonderful revival formed a part of the cable-telegraph despatches.

In thousands of Christian households, the deepest interest was felt by parents for their children, and by masters and mistresses for their servants; and so universal was this, that Dr. Horatius Bonar declares his belief "that there was scarcely a Christian household in all Edinburgh, in which there were not one or more persons converted during this revival."

Such a statement, on such authority, is perhaps the best suggestion of the blessedness of this work of grace. It was the reverse of the last great plague of Egypt. There was scarcely a house in which some dead soul had not been brought to life; and the wave of joy that swept through that community, so marvellously favoured of God, made it seem more like heaven than earth.

Tickets were issued by the committee of management to those who desired to labour in the inquiry meetings; but presently it was found that improper persons, more blessed with zeal than knowledge, were offering their services in this department: a new system was then established, by which it was necessary, in order to obtain a worker's ticket, for the applicants to pass a strict examination before the committee, as to their qualifications for this work. Thus all false doctrine was carefully barred out; and the converts, already familiar with the Word of God, came into the enjoyment of faith and liberty in such spirit and force, that many of them were able, at once, to join the host of home missionaries, and go into the regions round about, to tell the story of their own conversion, and to lead their friends to Christ.

The brethren had now proved themselves workmen needing not to be ashamed, "rightly dividing the word of truth." Large numbers of the most eminent ministers and professors in the churches and colleges of Edinburgh joined hands with the evangelists, and rejoiced in their success. But so great a benediction could not pass without attracting the spiteful notice of the powers below. Satan seemed to be alarmed, lest he should be driven bodily out of the Scottish capital; and accordingly stirred up two different kinds of opposition,—the one from an insignificant source, attacking Mr. Moody's personal character, and the other from the highest circles, denouncing the character of the work.

While the revival was sweeping onward in its grandest flight, a letter was received from Chicago, claiming to state, by authority, that, some time or other, Mr. Moody had not held the respect of his brethren in America; and saying things to his discredit, which filled the hearts of his friends with alarm. They at once despatched across the sea for information; at the same time telling Mr. Moody what had been spoken against him. He had relied solely upon

God to sustain him, and to open the way before him, and had failed to provide himself with any letters of credence or introduction; but his brethren in Chicago, as soon as they learned that their friend was in trouble, despatched the following testimonial, which, once for all, set the matter at rest:—

CHICAGO, *May 21st*, 1874.

WE, the undersigned, Pastors of the City of Chicago, learning that the Christian character of D. L. MOODY has been attacked, for the purpose of destroying his influence as an Evangelist in Scotland, hereby certify that his labours in the Young Men's Christian Association, and as an Evangelist in this City and elsewhere, according to the best information we can get, have been Evangelical and Christian in the highest sense of those terms; and we do not hesitate to commend him as an earnest Christian worker, worthy of the confidence of our Scotch and English brethren, with whom he is now labouring; believing that the Master will be honoured by them in so receiving him among them as a co-labourer in the vineyard of the Lord.

A. J. Jutkins, Presiding Elder of Chicago Dist.
C. H. Fowler, President North-western University.
Arthur Edwards, Editor *North-western Christian Advocate* (Methodist Organ), Chicago.
M. C. Briggs.
S. M'Chesney, Pastor of the Trinity M. E. Church.
W. H. Daniels, Pastor Park Avenue M. E. Church.
Sanford Washburn, Pastor Halsted St. Ch., Methodist Episc.
C. G. Trusdell, Gen. Supt. Chicago Relief and Aid Society.
Wm. F. Stewart, Sec. Preachers' Aid Society.
G. L. S. Stuff, Pastor Fulton St. M. E. Church.
T. P. Marsh, Pastor Austin M. E. Church.
Lewis Meredith, Pastor Oakland M. E. Church.
Arthur Mitchell, Pastor First Presb. Ch.
Glen Wood, Western Sec. American Tract Society.
C. D. Helmer, Pastor Union Park Congregational Church.
Arthur Swazey, Pastor Ashland Avenue Presbyterian Church.
Rev. N. F. Ravlin, Pastor Temple Ch.
A. G. Eberhart, Asst. Pastor.
David J. Burrel, Pastor Westminster Presbyterian Church.
David Swing, Fourth Presb. Church.
Edward P. Goodwin, Pastor of 1st Cong. Church.
L. T. Chamberlain, Pastor of New England Cong. Church.
Edward F. Williams; Edward N. Packard; John Kimball; W. A. Lloyd; C. A. Sowle; John Bradshaw; C. F. Reed; S. F. Dickinson; A. Wesley Bill; Albert Bushnell, Congregational Ministers.

T. W. Guildford, 2nd Baptist Ch.
W. A. Bartlett, Plymouth Cong. Ch.
R. W. Patterson, 2nd Pres. Ch.
W. W. Everts, 1st Baptist Ch.

State of Illinois, Cook County Ss.,
City of Chicago.

W. W. VANARSDALE, being first duly sworn upon oath, says that he is the Superintendent of the Young Men's Christian Association of the city of Chicago, Illinois, and that he knows the foregoing signatures to be genuine.

W. W. VANARSDALE.

Subscribed and sworn to berore me, this 26th day of May, A.D. 1874. } ISAAC H. PEDRICK, *Notary Public.*

Mr. Moody did not attempt to defend himself, but left his defence in the hands of the Lord, who straightway sent him this deliverance from his trouble, which also caused him to be still more honoured, trusted, and beloved.

Amongst his difficulties in Edinburgh was the statement which somehow or other got abroad, that he was not quite orthodox on the subject of the personality of the Holy Spirit; and a letter was written to the Rev. Dr. Lowe, of Newcastle, who had been intimately associated with him, asking if this statement were true. The Doctor at once replied; saying that, in one of Mr. Moody's Bible-readings at Newcastle, he himself had been appointed to read the texts of Scripture bearing upon this very doctrine; and, said he, "Mr. Moody charged me to be particular to bring out the doctrine of the personality of the Holy Spirit, by special emphasis upon the personal pronouns: "*He* shall testify of me"; "*He* shall lead you into all truth." After this there were no more accusations of heresy.

But the opposition on the ground of the faults in the meetings themselves was not so easily overcome. In spite of the utmost care and diligence on the part of Mr. Moody and his committee, there would occasionally be something which was to be regretted. It was not difficult to find fault with the unwonted enthusiasm of those exercises, so different from the staid and orderly religious assemblies to which Edinburgh had been accustomed. Then there was the same old difficulty;—sinners were converted too fast. Time was insisted on as a necessary condition to a thorough work of grace in the soul. It was presumed that if a sinner were converted quickly, he could not be converted thoroughly. Again, there were those who did not believe in Mr. Moody's idea of conversion at all. The transition from darkness to light, by the inspiration of the Holy Ghost, was something which they failed to comprehend.

Anonymous letters were written to Mr. Moody and his committee, abusing them on account of the organ; the inquiry meetings; "singing the Gospel," etc.

A pamphlet was issued, in which the revival was referred to in such terms as the following:—"Spasmodic convulsions"; "Man-made revivals"; "One-sided views of truth"; "Superficial experience"; "Arminianism"; "Plymouthism"; "Galvanizing"; "Sensational shocks"; "Temporary bustle"; "Unscriptural inventions"; "The tinsel of a superficial religiousness"; and the like.

It is not to be wondered at that learned and conservative men, in Scotland and elsewhere, who had been educated in theology as in one of the exact sciences, and had spent large portions of long lives in discussing theories of doctrine, while their hearts had not been melted by the heavenly fire, should fail to comprehend such marvels as were occurring in this great work of salvation. The revival was too much for them: they were not able to stand it. They were like ships when the monsoon falls upon them: they stood trembling, confused, and ready to sink: their protests in pamphlets and sermons were so many despairing outcries for help in their distress. Their hearts were not large enough to hold such a blessing; their heads were not clear enough to understand it. They were almost drowned in the floods; they were struggling and choking in this Gospel wave, which seemed to be filling Scotland, as the waters fill the sea.

Dr. Horatius Bonar felt moved to come to the rescue; which he did in a tract reviewing the criticisms that had been put forth, and showing, not only from Scripture, but also from the history of religion in Scotland, that this revival was like all the other great revivals from Pentecost down; and giving one of the distinguished opponents of the movement, who had poured out the vials of his wrath most plentifully, this brief but crushing rebuke:—After quoting a long list of hard names, which this opposing doctor had used, as above, he says, "Surely the vocabulary has been exhausted. We can hardly conceive of anything worse. All this is said by *one* brother against hundreds of brethren!"

Whether the folly of so small a minority attempting to disgrace and destroy the opinions and work of almost the entire evangelical pulpit of Edinburgh, began to dawn upon them; or whether the Spirit of the Lord Himself softened the hearts that opposed the revival—certain it is that, after a little, the opposition faded out, and the brethren went on their way rejoicing, increasing daily in favour both with God and men.

It was no unusual thing for persons to come thirty or forty miles to attend the meetings, or to beg for the sending of some one whose lips had been touched with the coal of this altar-fire, to speak to the villagers among the mountains; and long after the meetings had closed, and Messrs. Moody and Sankey had gone their way to Glasgow and Dublin, applications to the Edinburgh committee for evangelistic workers continued to be so numerous that it was impossible to supply the half of them.

The converts, who were numbered by thousands, were divided into classes, and placed under the care of the pastors to whose congregations they properly belonged. Great care was taken not to trespass upon denominational lines; but when a man who had attended a place of worship where the Gospel was not preached in its purity, or where there was great deadness in religion, came to be blessed in the meetings, he naturally sought for a Sabbath home with some congregation whose pastor was full of the revival. Thus the evangelical ministry were almost forced, by the sense of self-preservation, to join in the movement, although their prejudices might lead them in an opposite direction; and some such preachers, coming unwillingly under its influence, were brought to see their need of a better spiritual life, and were among the happiest converts of all.

Edinburgh is a city of wealth and leisure. Large numbers of persons who have either made or inherited fortunes, reside here; and among the very highest classes of Edinburgh society were found the heartiest admirers of, and most enthusiastic workers with, the evangelists from across the sea.

But there are also, in this centre of wealth and learning, a good many educated infidels, who have united themselves into clubs for the purpose of preaching their unbelief, in much the same way as Christians unite in churches to enjoy the fellowship of faith. Among the notable cases of conversion was the chairman of one of these infidel clubs. He came to a meeting, intending not only to ridicule it, but hoping also to raise a controversy with Mr. Moody, and thus practically break it up. In this, however, he was altogether unsuccessful, and would have been thrust out of the house for his interruption, if the speaker had not interposed in his behalf. He remained for some time after the congregation were dismissed; and Mr. Moody, seeing him, inquired if he wanted to be a Christian. He replied that he did not, and that he had a very poor opinion of Christians.

"Would you like to have us pray for you?" said Mr. Moody.

"Oh yes; I have no objection to your trying your hand on me, if you like; but I think you will find me a match for you."

Mr. Moody kneeled down beside the scoffer, prayed for him earnestly and tenderly, and then left him, promising to pray for him still further at home. It was not long before he was brought under deep conviction of sin, resigned his presidency of the infidel club, and earnestly and faithfully sought the Saviour.

At a subsequent meeting in Edinburgh, out of thirty persons seeking the Lord, seventeen were members of this infidel club,—one of them its chairman, the successor of him whose conversion has just been related ; and who has since become a successful evangelist.

CHAPTER V.

THE WORK IN SCOTLAND CONTINUED.

THE wide-spread desire to obtain the services of the American evangelists became exceeding embarrassing. Requisitions for them pressed in from all quarters, not only from ministers, but from magistrates and leading citizens of towns both large and small. It was not from curiosity to see these men who had turned Scotland upside down, but from an earnest desire to share in this great blessing of the Lord, and from deep anxiety lest the revival wave should pass them by. All Scotland was begging for their ministry.

While yet the work of salvation in the capital was little more than begun, the spirit of awakening seemed to have penetrated the whole country; and the brethren who at first had felt quite satisfied at receiving so great a blessing in their own city, now began to pray for a similar benediction over all the land. It seemed as if God were willing to give anything that might be asked of Him: more willing to give than His people were to receive.

During the last week of December, copies of the following call to prayer were sent to every minister in Scotland, excepting Roman Catholics and Unitarians; signed, as will be seen, by a great number of eminent ministers and professors, as well as by many distinguished private citizens:—

"A WEEK OF PRAYER FOR SCOTLAND.

"EDINBURGH is now enjoying signal manifestations of grace. Many of the Lord's people are not surprised at this. Not a few ministers and others have for some time been discerning tokens of special interest and expectation attending the ordinary ministrations of the Word; and in October and November last, many Christians, of various denominations, met from time to time to pray for some remarkable blessing. They hoped that they might have a visit from Messrs. Moody and Sankey, of America; but they very earnestly besought the Lord that He would deliver them from depending upon them, or on any instrumentality, and that He Himself would come with them, or come before them. He has graciously answered that prayer, and His own presence is now wonderfully manifested, and is felt to be among them. God is so affecting the hearts of men, that the Free Church Assembly Hall, the largest public building in Edinburgh, is crowded every day at noon with a meeting for prayer; and both that building and the Established Church Assembly Hall overflow every evening, when the Gospel is preached. But the numbers that attend are not the most remarkable feature. It is the presence and the power of the Holy Ghost, the solemn awe, the prayerful, believing, expectant spirit, the anxious inquiry of unsaved souls, and the longing of believers to grow more like Christ,—their hungering and thirsting after holiness. The hall of the Tolbooth Parish Church, and the Free High Church, are nightly attended by anxious inquirers. All denominational and social distinctions are entirely merged. All this is of the God of grace.

"Another proof of the Holy Spirit's presence is, that a desire has been felt and expressed in these meetings, that all Scotland should share the blessing that the capital is now enjoying.

"It is impossible that our beloved friends from America should visit every place, or even all those to which they have been urged to go. But this is not necessary. The Lord is willing Himself to go wherever He is truly invited. He is waiting. The Lord's people in Edinburgh, therefore, would affectionately entreat all their brethren throughout the land to be importunate in invoking Him to come to them, and to dismiss all doubt as to His being willing to do so.

"The week of prayer, from 4th to 11th January next, affords a favourable opportunity for combined action. In every town and hamlet let there be a daily meeting for prayer during that week, and also as often as may be before it. In Edinburgh the hour is from 12 to 1; and where the same hour suits other places, it would be pleasing to meet together in faith at the throne of grace. But let the prayers not be formal, unbelieving, unexpecting, but short, fervent, earnest entreaties, mingled with abounding praise and frequent short exhortations; let them entreat a blessing on all the means of grace enjoyed by our native land; and let them also embrace the whole world, that 'God's way may be known upon earth, His saving health among all nations.' If the country will thus fall on their knees, the God who has filled our national history with the wonders of His love will come again and surprise even the strongest believers by the unprecedented tokens of His grace. 'Call unto Me, and I will answer thee, and show thee great and mighty things which thou knowest not.'"

W. G. Blaikie, D.D., Professor, New College.
Horatius Bonar, D.D., Chalmers' Memorial Church.
Chas. J. Brown, D.D., Free New North Church.
H. Calderwood, Professor of Moral Philosophy.
Laurence G. Carter, Charlotte Baptist Chapel.
A. H. Charteris, D.D., Professor of Biblical Literature.
John Cooper, late of Fala, United Presbyterian Church.
Thos. J. Crawford, D.D., Professor of Divinity in the University of Edinburgh.
David Croom, United Presbyterian Church, Lauriston Place.
G. D. Cullen, Royal Terrace.
Alexander Duff, D.D.
William Grant, Bristo Place Baptist Chapel.
William Hanna, D.D., 16, Magdala Crescent.
John Kelman, Free St. John's, Leith.
Robert Macdonald, D.D., Free North Leith.
Hamilton M. MacGill, D.D., Secretary of Mission Board, United Presbyterian Church.
James MacGregor, D.D., Professor, New College.
W. Scott Moncrieff, St. Thomas' Episcopal Church.
John M'Murtrie, St. Bernard's Church.
John Morgan, Viewforth Free Church.
Maxwell Nicholson, D.D., St. Stephen's Church.
Samuel Newnam, Baptist Church, Dublin Street.
Robert Rainy, D.D., Professor, New College.
Wm. Reid, United Presbyterian Church, Lothian Road.
William Robertson, D.D., New Greyfriars Church.
James Robertson, United Presbyterian Church, Newington.
A. Moody Stuart, Free St. Luke's.
Andrew Thomson, D.D., Broughton Place United Presbyterian Church.

John Wemyss, Richmond Place Congregational Church.
Alexander Whyte, St. George's Free Church.
Ninian Wight, Congregational Church.
George Wilson, Tolbooth Parish Church.
J. H. Wilson, Barclay Free Church.
John Young, United Presbyterian Church, Newington.
J. H. Balfour, Professor of Botany.
Ja. Balfour, 13, Eton Terrace.
George F. Barbour, George Square.
Cavan, 12, Lennox Street.
John Chalmers, Castle Bank, Merchiston.
David Dickson, Merchiston.
William Dickson, 38, York Place.
F. Brown Douglas. 21, Moray Place.
Wm. Jas. Duncan, 29, Abercromby Place.
E. Erskine Scott, 25, Melville Street.
William Gibson, Lauriston Gardens.
John Gifford, 41, St. Andrew Square.
Robert Haldane, Charlotte Square.
George Harvey, President Royal Academy.
A. Jenkinson, Princes Street.
John Millar, 26, York Place.
David M'Laren, Redfern House.
Duncan M'Laren, Jun., Newington House.
Francis Outram, Bart.
Polwarth, Mertoun House.
Hugh Rose, 3, Hillside Crescent.

Mr. Moody pointed out that it was quite impossible for himself and Mr. Sankey to comply with all the requests sent in for assistance ; but he suggested that deputations should be sent out from Edinburgh ; mentioning several distinguished ministers and laymen, who, he thought, should go on such errands. These brethren, receiving such appointments, went forth gladly in the name of Christ, and returned with exceeding joy, to tell what the Lord had done through their word. Their reports formed one of the pleasing features at the daily prayer-meeting,—at which Mr. Moody insisted that all who had been engaged in these outside meetings should give an account of their work immediately on their return ; and the good news accumulated so rapidly, that the hearts and minds of the people were unable to take it in. The story seemed almost too good to be true.

Perhaps no meeting in Edinburgh was more remarkable than that which closed the year 1873. Mr. Moody had appointed what is called a watch-night service, at which the last hours of the old year were to be spent in the worship of God, and the new year was to be ushered in with prayer and praise. There were many misgivings about the possibility of keeping a large audience together from eight o'clock till twelve; but Mr. Moody's expectations were fully justified by the crowd which occupied the Free Assembly Hall for five full hours. A great many persons were obliged to stand throughout the entire service; and this they did without a word of complaint. After singing and prayer, Mr. Moody announced the order of exercises. "Anything that is worship," said he, "will be in order." Prayer was offered at intervals. Mr. Sankey and the Jubilee Singers introduced most beautiful and appropriate solos and choruses. Mr. Moody reviewed the seven utterances of Christ—"I will." As he read the verses containing them, one after another, the whole audience, at his request, read the verses in concert. So great was the variety and interest of the meeting, that every one who stole a glance at the clock wondered to see how quickly the hours passed by.

Soon after eleven the lecture closed; and the remainder of the year was given to prayer—sometimes silently, sometimes audibly. At five minutes before twelve all speaking ceased. The distant shouts of the revellers outside were the only sounds to be heard. Kneeling, with bowed heads, the whole great assembly, with one accord, prayed in silence; till presently the clocks of the city, one after another, struck the hour which marked the close of the old year and the coming in of the new. For five minutes more the deep and awful silence continued; and then Mr. Moody gave out the last two verses of the hymn,

"Jesus, lover of my soul."

After a brief prayer, the benediction was pronounced, and all began, like one loving family, to wish each other a Happy New Year.

Great as were the blessings received hitherto, those which followed the "week of prayer for Scotland" far exceeded them; and the brethren began to say: The Master of the feast has kept the good wine until now.

At first the work of grace had been principally confined to the middle and higher classes of society; but at the close of the fourth week special measures were adopted for the purpose of bringing the Gospel to the poor. In accordance with this design, a meeting was appointed in the Grass Market;—a spacious square in the old town of Edinburgh, which in former times was the scene of many martyr executions. On the south side of this square is the Corn Exchange, an immense building capable of holding six thousand persons. In this place a meeting was held, on Sabbath evening the 28th of December, for men only. The admission was by ticket. At the close a great number of anxious persons followed Mr. Moody to the Free Church Assembly Hall, where an inquiry meeting was going on; and seeing the multitudes, the door-keeper came up to Dr. Bonar, who, with others, was dealing with the inquirers, bringing the intelligence, which was alike startling and embarrassing, "that Mr. Moody had brought up the whole Grass Market with him." The body of the hall was cleared for these men—many of them young men ; and they pressed in to the number of not less than six or seven hundred. These could not be conversed with separately, and Mr. Moody accordingly addressed them all together. When those who wished to give themselves to Christ were invited to kneel, all of them, as well as every one else in every part of the house, kneeled down; while Mr. Wilson, and afterwards Mr. Moody, led their prayer in giving themselves to Christ.

Previous to the arrival of the men from the Grass Market, on this occasion, a service was held in the hall for women only. The hall, as usual, was densely crowded, and seventy or eighty inquirers remained behind to be spoken to.

Dr. Bonar, in referring to this meeting next day, at the noon hour of prayer, said;—"In all my life I never preached to such an audience. The vast multitude bowed under the simple preaching of the Gospel, and without any excitement were melted into tears of penitence, and the children of God to tears of joy."

Such were some of the revival services by which the week of prayer was preceded. What, then, must have been the blessings which followed it, which could be described as the best of the wine at the last of the feast?

On Sabbath, the 4th of January, 1874, the services in connection with the week of prayer were commenced. Meetings were held in the two Assembly Halls, as well as in churches in all parts of the city, including several of those in the Episcopal communion; and as an evidence of the increasing catholicity of spirit which the revival had brought about, it was noticed that ministers of different denominations, who had hitherto held themselves widely apart, joined in hearty work and worship together.

On Monday, the 5th of January, Mr. Moody paid a flying visit to Glasgow, to be present at the noon prayer-meeting in that city; which he reported, at the nine o'clock meeting in the Free Assembly Hall, the same evening, as an occasion of great spiritual power. "God is going to do a great work in Glasgow," said he. "In the last two hours of our meeting there I met with about seventy-five young persons anxious to know what they must do to be saved."

A great variety of exercises were crowded into this week, at different hours of every day and evening. At all of them there was a great number of inquirers; and sometimes it was necessary even to close the door of the inquiry room, lest the crowd should make it impossible to proceed with the instructions.

It was not only in the regions round about the Free Assembly Hall, and in other choice localities in Edinburgh and Leith, but also among the poor and neglected populations of the Canongate and Cowgate, that the revival tide was observed to be rising. God seemed, indeed, to be blessing all classes and conditions of men.

A merchant, whose place of business was in a neighbourhood where drunken men and women frequently passed his door, declared that the influence of the revival was plainly apparent among the lower classes; for, since it began, he had seen very few persons passing his place in a state of intoxication.

A confectioner, whose trade consisted chiefly in providing ball suppers, was disgusted with the revival; it almost spoilt his business.

Separate meetings for men, women, and children were held, all of which were marked by deep spiritual power. So profound an impression was made upon the whole community, that strangers coming into the city were at once impressed with the feeling that something very unusual was going on. It was as if the blessing of God pervaded the very air. No wonder, then, that multitudes came in all the trains from all parts of Scotland, to breathe in the heavenly influence, which came down upon Edinburgh even as upon Jerusalem at Pentecost!

During the last weeks which Messrs. Moody and Sankey spent in Edinburgh, the love and gratitude of the people went out towards them in a tide of Christian affection. In many a household thanksgivings were daily offered to God for sending these brethren to labour in that city.

The simple and Scriptural style of Mr. Moody's addresses won the hearts of the great masses of

Bible-loving Scotchmen; while his method of instructing inquirers at first astonished, and then delighted them. They had never seen so many people saved in so short a time. But now a new view of an old truth appeared to them, and they saw that what was necessary for becoming a Christian was, not a long period of instruction and repentance, but the simple act of trusting in Jesus.

Requests for prayer poured in continually—some of them even from foreign countries. One lady asked prayer for her own conversion, saying, "I have come from Switzerland to be present at these meetings. I have been well brought up, but am not a Christian."

Some time after the special meetings closed, a letter was received from New Zealand, asking prayer for a revival in that colony.

The Christian convention which was held on the 4th of January, in the Free Assembly Hall, was a memorable and delightful occasion. About a hundred and fifty ministers from all parts of the country, and of all denominations, came up to consult with their brethren from America, upon the best methods of conducting the various departments of Christian work. From eleven in the morning till four in the afternoon the exercises were kept up, varying in form and increasing in power. Such a meeting had never been seen in Edinburgh before; not on account of its numbers, but on account of the great variety of religious sentiment represented in it. Surely nothing but the overwhelming baptism of the Spirit of God could have swept away the barriers which had so long kept these brethren apart: and if there is one thing more than another which attests the Divine character of the revival in Scotland under the labours of these American evangelists, it is the great progress which was made towards Christian fraternity and unity.

Remarkable cases of conversion were continually reported. The accounts of the meetings formed a large portion of the reading matter in the public press. A periodical entitled "Times of Blessing" was started, to spread the good news. All the religious newspapers and magazines in the United Kingdom vied with each other in obtaining full and graphic reports of the wonders of the work of grace in Scotland.

Here, as everywhere else, Mr. Moody's instructions were remarkable for their strictly Biblical character. People were not thrust into the kingdom of heaven by means of enthusiasm and excitement, but they were taught to enter by the strait gate; and on this account it is, no doubt, that converts in that revival hold out so well.

A workman who had found the Saviour relates his experience thus:—

"Six months ago I heard an address from the words 'Whosoever believeth hath everlasting life.' I had been a bad character, and could not take it to myself; but when I went home that night, I dreamed 'whosoever' meant me. I got bang out of bed, and went away to the Bible to see the word 'whosoever.'" "But," said one, "did you not know it was in the Bible?" "Oh yes, but I went to see it with my own eyes, and I have been resting on it ever since."

Not less than three thousand persons have been received into the various churches in Edinburgh as a result of this great awakening. The pastors are still holding meetings for inquiry and instruction with the large classes of converts which at that time came under their care; and it is believed that a great number of persons, who attended these meetings from other towns and villages, have been received into their churches at home.

The farewell meeting of Messrs. Moody and Sankey at Edinburgh was held in the fields, on the slopes of Arthur's Seat; no building being at all adequate to accommodate the vast congregation. The whole city, one might almost say, came out to bid them good-bye and God speed. From this historic seat of Christian learning, which they had entered with so much trembling, they went forth, with the blessings of the whole community upon them, and with such joy in their hearts as only those can know who are honoured of God in leading many souls to Christ.

CHAPTER VI.

WORK IN SCOTLAND CONTINUED.—GLASGOW AND THE NORTH.

ON the 8th of February, Messrs. Moody and Sankey, having finished their course in Edinburgh with joy, began their work at Glasgow; where, for a month before their arrival, special prayer had been offered for the blessing of God upon their labours. A meeting of ministers and leading brethren was called for to make arrangements for the approaching revival services. This meeting was held in a large church of the Scottish Establishment, which had never been used for such a purpose before.

It was thought a strange thing that Dr. Andrew Bonar, of the Free Church, should be introduced by the pastor of this Established Church, and that many ministers of different denominations should be seated together on the platform!

This sight had a happy effect upon the congregation, and was a prophecy of the harmonious manner in which these brethren were to labour together; and in which the whole community was to be united in Christian fellowship and work.

The first meeting was held on Sunday the 8th.

An hour before the time a vast crowd had assembled, and four large churches in the vicinity were filled. During the whole time the services continued, these overflow meetings were a part of the regular system. While Mr. Moody was preaching in the principal place, Mr. Sankey assisted at another; and the ministers of the city were also actively engaged in conducting these extra services. Dr. Bonar, the Rev. Mr. Laing, the Rev. Mr. Wall, and others, rendered good service in this department of the work; and a share of the blessing always appeared to be given to them and their outside congregations.

It is held to be a most remarkable fact, that Mr. Moody, himself an unordained evangelist, not only obtained access to pulpits of various denominations, but was the means of bringing ministers of different orders together as they never had been brought together before. On his previous visit to Glasgow, in 1872, he scarcely produced a ripple on the surface of the Christian community; but this time God was with him; he had a message from heaven; and almost the whole population of the town, as if impressed with this fact, eagerly crowded to hear him.

The prediction which he had made at the Edinburgh noon-meeting, that God was about to send a great blessing to Glasgow, was now abundantly fulfilled. The month of prayer and preparation had not been spent in vain; and on his arrival, he was able to say to the people, with especial emphasis, "Come, for all things are now ready."

The same methods which had been so successful elsewhere, were repeated here. Meetings for young men, Christian workers, men's meetings, women's meetings, and conventions, were held with evident indications of the presence of the Holy Spirit. The whole community was alive with the revival. From this centre, also, spiritual influences radiated into the regions round about. In one instance five young men, who lived at a distant village, made a journey to Glasgow, were much impressed with what they heard, and went home to spread the good news. They invited others to go and hear for themselves. Then they began to hold meetings for prayer; and presently the revival wave reached their little village also.

One young man from a distance was humbled before God, and went home to tell what Jesus had done for him; and here, in a secluded hamlet, a shower of blessing descended. There was one place in particular for which prayer was offered at the noon meeting, which, it was stated, had been altogether won for the Lord. Previous to this it had been, to all appearance, utterly dead—one of the most barren and hopeless fields in which a minister could labour; but within two months from the time these prayers were offered for it, its pastor reported that, in the great congregation which assembled night after night for worship, he was not able to discover a single person who had not been under deep concern, or was not now resting in Jesus.

The small town of Dollar, where is an academy containing nine hundred pupils, gathered from all parts of the world, was a place in which great interest was felt; and efforts were made to secure a visit from the

American evangelists. Failing in this, the brethren there began to work among themselves; first appointing three nights of united prayer for the outpouring of the Spirit, and subsequently holding revival meetings for three weeks in the large academy hall. The result was an almost simultaneous awakening amongst the pupils in all the schools, as well as among the inhabitants of the town.

In one place, with a population of not more than two thousand five hundred, as many as fourteen hundred persons would come together for prayer.

The revival work in Glasgow and its vicinity was greatly strengthened by the assistance of ministers and others, who came down from Edinburgh to labour in, as well as to enjoy, the meetings. These brethren, with a large number of Christian workers who were raised up among the young men of the town, carried the work into the regions beyond, with ever accumulating interest and power.

The Glasgow noon prayer-meeting had been commenced during the week of prayer for Scotland. On the very first day, a soul was awakened; and from that time, never a day passed without tokens of the presence of the Lord. Requests for prayer continued to come in—sometimes from long distances in the country. One instance is mentioned of prayer being asked, by his parents, for a young man who had not been heard of for years; and from whom a letter was afterwards received, dated at New Zealand, saying that the prodigal had been longing to open communication with his friends at home, and had ridden a hundred and fifty miles to post that letter.

It was touching in the extreme to listen to the requests for prayer, from Highlands and Lowlands, from places well known, and from places whose names few had ever heard before; all of them crying out for the blessing of God, like dry and thirsty lands for showers of rain. Sometimes the thanksgivings almost outnumbered the requests. On one day thanksgivings were offered for the conversion of eighty-eight persons. The brethren, at first, regarded these simply as the fruit of the labours of the evangelists from America; but as news continued to come from all quarters, of the outpouring of the Spirit of God, they changed their minds, and began to say, "We are not alone; the Lord is blessing all Scotland." These revivals were evidently not "gotten up," but "brought down." It was the Lord's doing, and marvellous in all eyes.

Mr. Moody's success in Glasgow, as in Edinburgh, was, at first, amongst those who had received a religious education. To these persons his Bible-readings were peculiarly acceptable; and such crowds attended them, that admission had to be arranged by ticket. On Sunday mornings, at eight o'clock, addresses were given to Christian workers; and many Sunday-school teachers thought nothing of walking ten or fifteen miles at this early hour, to profit by Mr. Moody's experience and advice. One morning a man was found outside who was in great distress. He had come ten miles to attend that service, but had lost his ticket, and was not able to get in.

Dr. Andrew Bonar, in speaking of Mr. Moody, says: "There has been no evangelist with us from a distance, in whom we have had such confidence. He was so thorough, so Scriptural, so simple. My church," he went on to say, "is not very central; but I always sent my people and Sunday-school to his meetings, and they brought home a great deal of blessing with them."

The revival wave had now become so mighty that few were rash enough to oppose it, except those who hated all forms of piety, and were full of spite against Christ Himself. Everything seemed favourable to the awakening of sinners and the upbuilding of saints. Blessings abounded, and were easy to find.

One lady, who had been converted at the meetings, began to talk to her husband about Christ. At first he seemed to care little about it; but one morning she repeated to him, as well as she could, Mr. Moody's address of the previous evening, on Grace. When she had finished, he left the room, and in an hour came back happily converted.

"We don't know what to make of this work," said one; "it is so quick. Sinners seem to come into the kingdom of Christ almost without effort."

A distinguished gentleman had been converted; and one of his friends came to ask him this question:—

"Can you tell me in what you rest for salvation?"

"Yes, I can," was the reply; and opening the Bible, he pointed out these words: "God hath given us eternal life, and that life is in His Son."

Thus, as will be seen, the revival work in Glasgow was, like all the others, along the track of God's Word.

This charming little domestic scene is related by Dr. Bonar:—

"I called on a man and his wife in my parish, and said to the woman, 'I hear you have been getting some blessing.'

"We have been attending the meetings," was the reply.

"And have you not been blessed?"

"Yes; we have."

"Tell me something about it."

"Well, the other night my husband went out to a meeting; and when he was gone, I slipped out after him, heard just a little, and then came home and gave myself to Jesus. He was blessed too, that night; and when he came in he sat down very quietly, and looked at me,—and I looked at him. Then I said, Have you got anything? Yes, said he: have you? I think I have, said I. Well, that was just what I was wanting to tell you, but I didn't know where to begin. And now, said the wife, we are so happy together!"

The readiness with which inquirers came into the enjoyment of pardon and peace, was the chief distinguishing feature of the revival in Glasgow. The door of the kingdom of heaven seemed to be very wide open. Every church in the city was blessed; and some ministers who had been doing their work in a professional way came into an experience of grace, which gave them a new understanding of Christ and His Gospel. Five such cases are mentioned in Glasgow alone. In one church, fifty-four new communicants were received on the last Sabbath before Mr. Moody left—almost all of whom had been led by him to the Lord; while, six months afterwards, forty-eight others were received into the same communion, who dated their first impressions from his meetings. It is believed that not less than six thousand persons, in all, came to the inquiry rooms; some of whom had indeed been members of churches before, but were now for the first time brought out into light and joy.

The way in which God suited His blessing to Glasgow is matter of especial interest. Beginning with those who had been well instructed in the Scriptures, it wrought its work upon them; and, when they felt themselves saved, the Spirit of the Lord seemed to direct them to go out and labour for the great masses of the population which, here, as in other manufacturing communities, were outside the ordinary means of grace. Meetings were held in the streets and squares of the city; and invitations to attend them were distributed by young men of the different Christian Associations.

Fathers and mothers met to pray for the conversion of their children. Some young ladies held a prayer-meeting one night, at which forty were led to seek Christ. Children's meetings were also held, to which the little people crowded no less eagerly than their elders. On one occasion there was a great swarm of boys and girls crowding the passages near the pulpit. It was in vain to insist on their keeping back; and after a while, Mr. Sankey, who was especially popular with the children, seeing the situation, pushed aside the barrier and let the crowd of his little friends into the reserved seats, where they filled up the chinks between the ministers and the choir, like so many grains of sand. Better still, they swarmed into the great pulpit, and Mr. Moody allowed them to sit down all around him; every inch of the pulpit stairs being covered with them.

The conversion of one young girl, which was almost immediately followed by her triumphant death, was blessed to the awakening of six of her companions, who came to the services saying, "We wish to go to the meeting in the same church where Lizzie found Christ."

So deeply were the exercises pervaded by a sense of the Divine Presence, that, apart from the speaking and the singing, it was good to be there. One man who was so deaf that he could not distinguish a word of the preaching, went away deeply convicted of his sins, and afterwards was happily converted. The Lord was there, and he had heard Him speak.

At one of the noon meetings a gentleman brought to Mr. Moody a paper, signed by five hundred workmen in one of the ship-yards of Glasgow, petitioning for a visit from him during their noon intermission. Messrs. Moody and Sankey spent half an hour with them, to their great delight. Their rest for dinner was only three-quarters of an hour; but from this, a large number out of the two thousand men employed in that yard now find time every day for twenty minutes of prayer. "The ladies," as the men called the choir, were requested to go down and sing for them; this they consented to do, twice a week, for about two months; and by means of the singing, as well as the preaching and prayer, many of the workmen were led to the Saviour. "Once for all"; "Jesus of Nazareth passeth by"; "Free from the law"; "Hold the fort," etc., were found remarkably useful. Mr. Howie, the superintendent, says that scarcely a day passed without his having men coming to him anxious about their souls, who had been awakened by the singing at the yard.

Outside meetings of various characters were held—sometimes ten or fifteen each day. The highways and hedges were searched by the new converts for people whom they might compel to come to this feast of the Lord; and many a guest did they bring.

The story of the band of young converts, known as the "Ewing Place Young Men," is one of particular interest. On the evening of February 24th, a large number of young men, who were unable to obtain admission to the principal meeting, came together in the Ewing Place Church; where Mr. Moody, Professor Cairns, the Rev. J. H. Wilson, and others, met them at the close of the preaching in the City Hall. The spirit of conviction seemed overwhelming; and when those who were not saved, but who desired to give themselves to Christ, were invited to come forward to the three front lines of pews, which had been cleared for them, the pews were immediately filled: again three other lines were cleared, and quickly filled with inquirers: then three other lines were filled with the same class of persons,—in all, to the number of one hundred and one. This was the first time the so-called "altar services" were ever seen in Glasgow.

Very many of these young men were converted

before leaving the place ; and feeling the special tie of brotherhood which came of their similar experience, they joined themselves together into a band, for the purpose of making themselves useful in the work of the Lord. Every night, except Saturday, for the period of nine months, their prayer-meeting was attended by anxious inquirers; and "Ewing Place" became familiar, not only among the young men in Glasgow, but among earnest young Christians all over Scotland. Afterwards, the meeting was removed from Ewing Place Church; but the organization is still efficiently maintained.

The history of the Ewing Place Leaflet, inserted below, is interesting, as a glimpse at the work of these young converts in the lowest portions of the city.

"*Woe* unto them that rise up early in the morning that they may follow strong drink." Isaiah v. 11.

"*Woe* unto him that giveth his neighbour drink, and maketh him drunken." Habakkuk ii. 15.

"*Drunkards* shall not inherit the Kingdom of God." 1 Cor. vi. 10.

THE WATER OF LIFE.

Jesus says, "If any man thirst, let him come unto Me and drink." John vii. 37.

"And the Spirit and Bride say, Come. . . . And let him that is athirst come. And whosoever will, let him take the Water of Life freely." Rev. xxii. 17.

"Rock of Ages, cleft for me,
Let me hide myself in Thee;
Let the water and the blood
From Thy wounded side which flowed,
Be of sin the double cure,
Save me from its guilt and power."

Two young men were distributing copies of this leaflet near one of the largest grog-shops in Glasgow; but the manager of the place, not liking such quiet opposition to his business, had the young men arrested. They were brought before the magistrates, on the charge of obstructing the street, and fined ten shillings each, and costs. This produced a great excitement among the temperance and Christian people; and in response to the general desire to know the nature of the leaflet which the young men were fined for distributing, it was reprinted in the form of an immense placard, and posted all over the city: copies of the leaflet itself were also distributed in vast numbers; and thus the temperance movement was aided rather than hindered by this small persecution.

The great convention of Christian workers at the Kibble Crystal Palace, in the Botanic Gardens, on the 16th of April, was a most memorable occasion. The Palace, which can be seated for six thousand people, was filled to overflowing, while the platform was crowded with the most eminent ministers and evangelists from all parts of Scotland. The practical results of that convention, and of the revival at large, are still apparent in the vigour with which all departments of home-missionary work are now carried on. In this respect Glasgow is often cited as a model.

The last week, during which the meetings were held in the Kibble Palace, was in many respects the most remarkable of all. The building was crowded night after night, each time with a different audience. One evening the meeting was for warehouse girls, and those in shops who had been prevented from going to the other services, on account of their late hours of labour. On that occasion it is computed that about nine thousand young women were present. Mr. Moody preached; and afterwards an inquiry meeting was held in a neighbouring church. The next evening the Palace was packed with about seven thousand young men; and there were nearly as many more outside who were unable to obtain admission.

On Friday the meeting was for young converts, who were admitted by special tickets, of which three thousand five hundred were issued. The rest of the space was filled with Christian workers.

In speaking of this memorable occasion, one writer says: "Mr. Moody's subject was, 'What God is able to do.' He was grand, and so happy! The ministers were a sight! They became quite wrapt-up and excited. It was a treat to watch them. Moody talked a long time; Sankey breaking in with 'Daniel's band,' and 'More to follow'; but we could have listened long—all night, I believe." Mr. Moody, in speaking of it, said, "It seemed as if we were then receiving the Spirit as a seal on all our meetings." On Saturday a children's meeting was held.

But Sabbath was *the* day of days. In the morning the meeting was again for shop girls. The Palace was full at nine o'clock, and Mr. Moody preached from the text, "There was no room for them in the inn." On account of the heat the meeting was short, being over by a quarter to ten; and then followed a meeting for inquirers.

FAREWELL MEETING AT GLASGOW.

The evening meeting was announced for half-past six; but an hour before the time, the Palace was densely filled, and a much larger number were outside than inside. Every moment the throng increased; and when Mr. Moody arrived, the policemen on the ground estimated the number at not less than fifty thousand persons. Seeing the multitudes, Mr. Moody determined to preach from the carriage, in which he was driven through the crowd to a central and commanding position. The whole multitude closed around him in one solid mass, standing in perfect order and quietness, and eagerly listening to the words of him whose face they might see no more. When those inside the Palace learned of this change of programme, they immediately joined the masses outside; but even this great reinforcement made no perceptible difference in that vast congregation.

Over all this great assembly, Mr. Sankey's voice was heard distinctly while he sang "Nothing but leaves." Then Mr. Moody mounted the box of the carriage, and preached with marvellous effect. At the close of his discourse, he invited inquirers to meet him in the Palace; and this spacious inquiry room was quite filled. It was a great gathering of unhappy souls: some who were present remarked how sorrowful the faces looked. This meeting was kept up until half-past ten at night. Mr. Moody, Mr. Stewart, and others stated, simply and plainly, the way of salvation. Large numbers found peace in believing; but when, at the close, Mr. Moody asked all those to rise who were still unsaved, nearly two thousand rose to their feet.

It was remarked that this was a new audience, because they did not know how to sing the hymns.

From Glasgow, brief excursions were made to Gourock, Paisley, and Greenock, where the same Divine blessing attended them.

THE TOUR IN THE NORTH.

About the middle of May Messrs. Moody and Sankey paid another three days' visit to Edinburgh, and then turned their faces northward,—where, in Perth, Dundee, Aberdeen, Elgin, Inverness, Tain, and some other smaller towns, their coming was anxiously awaited.

In Dundee, the churches which were opened for their use were so inadequate, that meetings were held in the open air; at which the attendance was variously estimated at from ten thousand to sixteen thousand souls.

The two weeks of meetings in Aberdeen, commencing on the 14th of June, were on the same magnificent scale. No room was large enough for the congregations; and the outdoor meetings, in the delightful summer evenings of the North, were attended by multitudes varying from twelve thousand to twenty thousand people.

The revival at Inverness was signalized by many striking incidents. Messrs. Moody and Sankey visited that place in the first week of July, at the time of the annual wool fair; when hundreds of farmers from all over the Highlands, and wool dealers from Edinburgh and Glasgow, meet to transact the chief business of the year. Very many of these farmers spend their lives beyond the reach of churches and ministers, and the coming of the American evangelists was to them a God-send indeed. Some who had scarcely ever attended religious services before, received the Gospel literally as good news from heaven. Great numbers were converted, and, at the close of the fair, dispersed to their homes to awaken and bless those hitherto neglected regions. So great an impression was made at Inverness, that arrangements are now in progress for celebrating the first anniversary of the visit of Messrs. Moody and Sankey to that town. Well may their work be remembered, in view of such scenes as the following:—

An elderly gentleman and his wife, passing out of Dr. Black's Presbyterian church, were invited to go into the room where Mr. Moody was waiting to receive inquirers.

"No, not to-night," said the man, looking at his wife as if she were a hindrance to such a movement. But the brother who had given the invitation, seeing the embarrassment, said, "Let the lady also come in." They were the first inquirers to arrive. Mr. Moody, taking them into the pastor's study, gave them such instruction as their cases seemed to require; and before they left the room, both of them were rejoicing in hope of eternal life. Half-an-hour afterwards the lady returned, saying, "I want to see Mr. Moody; I want to tell him that my two sons have been at the inquiry meeting in another part of the church, and both have given their hearts to the Saviour."

This man was a comfortable farmer on one of the northern islands; his sons were settled near him:

and the whole family, thus blessed of God, returned to their island home to spread the Gospel, which they had heard with such blessed results, at the fair.

Northward still, even to the very end of Scotland—John o' Groat's House—Moody and Sankey went, preaching and singing everywhere to crowds of people, under the sky, the only roof large enough to cover them. Mr. Moody was everywhere regarded as a prophet of the Lord, sent to bless His people in Scotland; and Mr. Sankey, in spite of his organ, was received as an humble successor of the Psalmist himself. The brethren in the ministry gave them cordial welcome and hearty assistance. "The men"—that is, the leaders in the Highland churches—were, some of them, a little troubled about Mr. Sankey's hymns; so unlike were they to the psalms in Rouse's version. One of them came to his pastor and said, with no little anxiety: "I cannot do with the hymns. They are all the time in my head, and I cannot get them out. The psalms never trouble me that way."

"Very well," said the pastor; "then I think you should keep to the hymns."

People sometimes expostulated with Mr. Sankey concerning his organ, on the ground that it was sure to be a serious stumbling-block in the way of many whom he might otherwise reach with his singing. On one occasion a compromise was effected; the organ was used with the outdoor congregations, and left outside the sanctuary when the meeting was taken up within. On this occasion Mr. Sankey sang with such remarkable success that one of his friends congratulated him on this separation of the singer from his unsanctified musical machine.

That beautiful hymn, "The ninety-and-nine," which has been blessed to the awakening of so many souls, has a pleasant little history of its own. Mr. Sankey was anxious lest his singing should be a failure in the Highlands—the people there being so particular about what should be sung; and, accordingly, he searched for something specially adapted to their tastes. One day he found, in the corner of a newspaper,* the hymn above mentioned: the strange, wild melody to which it is set, came to his mind as an inspiration, and he sang it for the first time in the presence of a great congregation, without ever having written it out. This hymn, which seemed to be a special gift to this pastoral people, they received with peculiar pleasure: it was their favourite among all Mr. Sankey's songs; and, when he brought it down with him from the North, it became also a favourite all over Great Britain and Ireland.

Sometimes there was almost a strife to obtain the services of the evangelists even for a single day; and from such brief but impressive services, the most important results often followed. "The people of Scotland," said one of the Highland ministers, "hold strong opinions upon theology and church order, but they really love the Word of God and the Christian life, better than anything else; and it was this which, in spite of all differences, opened their hearts to receive Mr. Moody and Mr. Sankey."

* It appeared originally in *The Christian*, of Boston, United States, America; and was reprinted in England, in *The Rock*.

On their return from the North they were besought to hold farewell meetings in some of the places where they had laboured; and these meetings, especially in Aberdeen and Inverness, were scenes which will never be forgotten.

At a year's distance the fruits of that great awakening are gloriously apparent. Evangelistic services are held by the converts of this revival, all over the north of Scotland; and, by this means, the labours of Messrs. Moody and Sankey are multiplied a hundredfold.

CHAPTER VII.

THE WORK OF GRACE IN IRELAND.—BELFAST LONDONDERRY; DUBLIN.

FROM among the many invitations that pressed upon him, Mr. Moody next chose to visit the cities of Belfast, Londonderry, and Dublin.

On Sabbath morning, the 6th of September, the evangelists held their first meeting in Belfast, at Dougal Square Chapel, at eight o'clock in the morning. Long before the hour the place was crowded with Christian workers, to whom it was announced the address would be given. The second meeting, at eleven o'clock, was held in a larger church; while the evening meeting was adjourned to the largest place of worship in Belfast, capable of holding about two thousand people; but even here, not above one-fourth of the persons who came were able to obtain admission. Thus, at the outset, the work of the Lord in Ireland was marked with distinguished promise of success.

On Monday, a daily noon prayer-meeting was commenced; which also, next day, had to be adjourned to a more capacious building, holding about fourteen hundred people. This noon prayer-meeting was so largely attended, and so greatly blessed, that, in speaking of it, one of the Belfast brethren declares it to have been "the centre of the whole movement."

The crowds which pressed upon his ministry compelled Mr. Moody at once to divide his audience; and here, as in Scotland, men's meetings, women's meetings, young men's meetings, working women's meetings, and other special services, were held; all of them attended by anxious crowds of listeners; and, almost in every instance, several hundred earnest inquirers remaining for personal instruction. But even this plan did not meet the convenience of his would-be hearers: then two meetings were held at once, but they were no less crowded; and it became necessary, on the Sabbath, to preach in the open air.

After one of these great open-air meetings, held on the 27th of September, the whole of the following afternoon and evening were occupied as an inquiry-meeting; at which Mr. Moody and other Christian workers were employed from two till ten o'clock, in pointing the throng of anxious inquirers to the "Lamb of God, which taketh away the sins of the world."

On one occasion, two hundred young men, the very flower of Belfast, gave themselves to Christ. Still the interest increased. A service was held, one night, for persons who had not hitherto heard Mr. Moody; to which admission was had by ticket. For these tickets there were no less than three thousand applications.

The great revival in 1859 is still fresh in the memory of Christians in Ireland; but the awakening under the labours of the American evangelists is counted by them as the most remarkable of any they have ever experienced.

Mr. Moody always insists on quietness and order. None of those wild excitements, so frequently seen at such seasons, have ever appeared in connection with him; and this fact was noted as being in striking contrast with the revival of 1859.

One of the Sabbath evening meetings, exclusively for men, Mr. Moody declared to be, in his judgment, the most remarkable of any he had yet held in Europe. On the following Monday evening, at the close of his address, all who had recently been found by the Good Shepherd, as well as those who desired to be found by Him, were requested to retire to the adjoining lecture-room; to which invitation some six hundred men responded. These were again sifted by requesting those only who were deeply anxious to be saved, to adjourn to another room. Of these there were nearly three hundred. Then, after conversation and prayer, he invited all to rise who felt that they could, then and there, accept Jesus as their Saviour; and the whole company, except twenty or thirty, stood up to profess their faith.

The great mass meeting in the open air, on the 8th of October, was looked forward to with especial interest. Prayers were offered for its success in every particular; even that the Lord would give fine weather for the occasion.

The day was beautiful. The various railway companies ran special trains in connection with the meeting; and so large did the faith of the Irish brethren become, that they actually set out with the purpose of calling together an assembly of a hundred thousand people. "We want all Ireland for Christ," said they.

LONDONDERRY.

From the 11th to the 15th of October, Messrs. Moody and Sankey laboured in Londonderry, to which they had been invited some months before by a committee of the Young Men's Christian Association. In this place they were cordially received by ministers of all denominations; and all the churches were placed at Mr. Moody's disposal during his stay. The first Presbyterian Church, being the largest, was the one where the meetings were chiefly held; and here, as elsewhere, they resulted in the awakening of multitudes of sinners, and the encouragement of the ministers and the churches.

On the 15th they returned to Belfast, to hold their farewell services. The noonday prayer-meeting on this day was exclusively for sinners anxious to be saved. The admission was by tickets, which could be obtained on personal application only; but even with all these restrictions, about twenty-four hundred persons were admitted; and Mr. Moody addressed them in a manner so earnest and tender, that his words seemed to have come from heaven. This was the largest inquiry-meeting which he, or any of his brethren, had ever seen.

The meeting in the evening was for the young

converts. Admission was again strictly by tickets, which were only given on personal application. Two thousand one hundred and fifty converts' tickets were given ; and the congregation was made up to three thousand by ministers and Christian workers.

Mr. Moody's farewell address was from Romans xiv. 4: "God is able to make him stand." During the service, Mr. Sankey sang a hymn which had been composed by a dying youth in Belfast, beginning—

"Is there room? They say there is room."

The depth of spiritual interest which marked this concluding service, no words are adequate to describe. The joy of the speaker may be imagined, as he stood before this multitude of converts—a great harvest of souls gathered in in five short weeks. But who can picture, even to himself, the feelings of this grateful and affectionate congregation, when the man who had led them to Christ, in closing his last counsels, said to them, in a voice trembling with emotion ;—"Good-night. We shall meet in the morning when the shadows flee away"!

DUBLIN.

The brethren in Dublin had long been looking for the coming of the American evangelists, whose course had been marked by such a wonderful succession of blessings. As early as the previous May, Mr. Moody had promised a visit to the Irish capital. But, before he actually appointed his meetings there, he took council with the brethren, concerning a place in which to hold them. The largest churches and halls had everywhere been far too small for the congregations ; and this had affected him very painfully. He therefore made it a condition of his coming to Dublin, that the Exhibition Palace should be engaged for his meetings.

This is a magnificent structure, built some years ago by subscription, with a view to provide a place of innocent recreation ; which, it was hoped, would also be a great preventive of evil, if not a means of grace. In this respect, however, it had proved a mortifying failure.

God has never promised to save sinners by means of any sort of amusement.

But now this splendid structure was destined to be the scene of the most precious work of salvation ever experienced in Dublin.

Mr. Moody's condition was met. The Exhibition Palace was engaged ; and, on the 24th of October, he and his friend Mr. Sankey arrived, to commence their work. Their way had been prepared by months of earnest supplication, not only in meetings appointed for that purpose, and in the congregations on the Sabbath, but also at the family altars in hundreds of Christian homes : and in order that Dublin might understand what was to be hoped for, Mr. Smithson, of the Young Men's Christian Association, prepared a sketch of the revival in Scotland, which, in the form of a tract, was distributed to the number of fifty thousand copies.

Out of a population of two hundred and fifty thousand, there are only about forty thousand Protestants

EXHIBITION HALL, DUBLIN.

in Dublin; but the line of separation between Protestants and Papists was continually crossed and re-crossed; until Cardinal Cullen, seeing his flock straying, in such great numbers, into this heretical pasture, published an interdict forbidding such conduct. This, however, was far less effective than that prelate could have desired. The work of grace went on in Catholic, as well as in Protestant families. One instance is mentioned where a lady met seven young girls at an inquiry-meeting, five of whom had been brought up in the Roman Catholic Church. Singularly enough, the very first convert in this revival was a young man who had been brought up in the Romish faith.

Such events as these, which were constantly occurring, did not produce any unusual impression upon Mr. Moody's mind. He never could see any reason why a Roman Catholic should be converted to Christ in a different manner from a Protestant. Neither Protestantism on the one hand, nor Roman Catholicism ôn the other, was a condition of salvation; and he preached Christ to them alike—feeling that they all were sinners, and alike in danger of perdition: in precisely the same manner he taught them all to humble themselves before God, confess their sins, give their hearts to the Saviour, and believe unto eternal life. He only knew them as so many souls to be saved.

At one time, when some of the brethren were speaking, with glad surprise, of the many Roman Catholic converts, Mr. Moody interposed the remark: "Why should we distinguish between different kinds of converts? Are we not all one in Christ?" On this account, no doubt, it was that the Catholics in Dublin manifested so little hostility towards Mr. Moody and his work. He was a good Protestant, of course; but still more was he a Christian.

The Nation, a Fenian newspaper, in an article on the revival, says:—

> "With much regret we notice indications of an attempt to excite the hostility of our Catholic population against the religious services conducted by some Protestant missionaries from America. We trust we shall not appeal in vain to the spirit of tolerance, of honourable fair play, of respect of conscience in the breasts of Irish Catholics, when we call upon them to crush the slightest attempt at offensive demonstration against the religious exercises which some sections of the Protestant community are holding, under the auspices of the gentlemen we refer to. We Catholics should ever discriminate between the Protestantism of sincere men devoted to their own convictions, but seeking no unjust interference with ours, and the wretched kind of Protestantism which consists in wanton insult and aggression upon the Catholic poor. For this latter warfare on our homes and altars, we shall always have scorn and reprobation; for the former, we should always have respectful sentiments. Let Messrs. Moody and Sankey do all they can to make Protestants earnest in religion. Let us Catholics daily devote ourselves more and more energetically to the practical duties of our holy faith; and let us all, Protestant and Catholic, work and pray to keep the teachings and theories of the Huxleys and the Tyndalls far from the shores of Ireland."

The *Freeman's Journal*, another Catholic paper, noticed the movement in a less friendly manner, criticising Mr. Moody for "being too intimate with the Heavenly Host"; for "roaring too loudly and too furiously"; for "appealing to the imagination, and speaking in a noisy, rhapsodical, haphazard style"; but saying nothing to excite religious prejudices.

In an article entitled the "New Evangel," this paper did, indeed, attempt to make sport of Mr. Moody; but afterwards a member of its staff was converted in his meetings, and then it published fair articles upon the movement.

Mr. Sankey was in high favour with the Irish people. The sweetness and enthusiasm of his singing went straight to their hearts. In Dublin, more than anywhere else, instances of awakening and conversion under his singing were noticed.

A Dublin correspondent of the London *Times* says:—"There was no attempt made to win proselytes for any particular church, and not the faintest allusion to any of the distinctive characteristics of sects and creeds. The result was that Protestants and Roman Catholics, Jews, Presbyterians, Methodists, Moravians, Arians, and Quakers were all mingled in the great assembly, and all seemed equally impressed. The presence of over seven hundred and fifty clergymen of various communions, in answer to the invitation of the committee who had taken charge of the work, is a significant proof of the success of the movement. Let those who think they can do so, account for the movement, and explain what it is which brought together such immense congregations every day for nearly six weeks, and produced such extraordinary effects? The fact itself is memorable and suggestive."

Mr. Moody's Bible-readings were most highly valued. They were held, as usual, in the afternoon;

and were largely attended even by the busiest business men.

Among other remarkable meetings held in Dublin, was one for the soldiers of the garrison at Curragh; who came in large numbers, with many of the under-officers, to take part in the re-union at the Metropolitan Hall. Mr. Moody went straight to their hearts, drawing largely from his own experience in the Christian Commission during the Civil War in America, and making the men feel that he was almost a comrade; certainly a warm-hearted friend. His charming stories softened their hearts; and many of the veterans, who had often looked death in the face, wept like children while he spoke to them of the love and service they owed to Christ, the Captain of their salvation.

In the Great Exhibition Palace there was no lack of room. Mr. Moody insisted that it should also be made comfortably warm. "Let us get all the difficulties out of the way," said he. "It will not be easy to save these people while they are shivering with cold."

The powerful effects of the preaching and singing may best be understood from the fact that, out of the great congregations, sometimes as many as seven hundred inquirers remained for personal conversation; and these meetings, solemn and impressive beyond description, were often held till eleven o'clock at night.

It was not found necessary to preach those sermons which are generally used as a preparation for revival. The revival commenced immediately. Dublin had been waiting to hear the Gospel preached;

and its people, by crowds, when they heard it, eagerly pressed into the kingdom of Christ. From all over the island, multitudes came up to attend the meetings; many of whom went home happy in the love of Christ. One woman came a hundred miles to hear Mr. Moody preach, but was too late to obtain admission. The next day, however, she read a report of his sermon in a morning paper, and it was blessed to her salvation. One new convert wrote a letter to a lady friend, and this letter was the means of her conversion. Then she read it to her mother, who also was led to the Saviour: and afterwards her father and her brothers, all by reading the same letter, were induced to give their hearts to Christ.

The children's meetings which were held in the Exhibition Palace, were no less interesting than the other services. The little people came, not only from Dublin, but also by extra trains from Kingstown, Stillorgan, and other towns, and listened to the singing and speaking with faces beaming with delight.

There is in Dublin an organized society of atheists, who determined to try their hand at opposing Mr. Moody in a very cunning and mischievous way. Scattering themselves about in the hall during the preaching, they joined the crowds who, at the close, sought the inquiry rooms; and there, on pretence of seeking the light, attempted to turn these services into a debate, and to lead the anxious inquirers away from Christ, instead of to Him. Their scheme, however, was immediately discovered, and they were admitted to the inquiry room no more; unless they came, as some afterwards did, honestly asking what they must do to be saved. After this the greatest care was taken in the instruction of inquirers. They were organized into classes: Christian workers were appointed; women to converse with women, and men with men. No debate nor useless conversation were allowed; and the business of pointing souls to Christ went on in a correct and systematic manner.

One of the pastors found a poor woman with a little child in her arms, whose wretched and poverty-stricken appearance awakened his deepest sympathy; and who, upon his inquiring into her condition, said: "I am a convert. I was converted while Mr. Sankey was singing 'Jesus of Nazareth passeth by.'" While the minister was considering under whose care he should place this person, a lady came forward and said, "She is a good case. I know her. She is under my care. Give her a convert's ticket, if you please." This was another converted Roman Catholic.

The finances of the Dublin revival are worthy of special attention. Some days before Messrs. Moody and Sankey arrived, three or four gentlemen met at the office of Mr. David Drummond; and, after consultation and prayer, decided to send out a circular, saying that the American evangelists were coming; that the Great Exhibition Palace had been engaged for them; and that money would be wanted to meet the large expenses attendant upon the services. It was determined to ask for the sum of £1500; and circulars to this purpose were sent out to five or six thousand of the leading citizens of

Dublin. Only two instances of personal solicitation are mentioned; but the money came in so fast, that Mr. Drummond, who was the treasurer, was obliged to employ a clerk to keep the record. Old ladies would come in Bath chairs to bring half a crown. People in high life came in carriages, bringing cheques or gold. Even the poor desired to have some share in the work, and gave their pennies and half-pence. By some means the subscription became known to the prisoners in a certain gaol in the south of Ireland; and they, regretting their inability to be present, sent their good wishes, and a little collection which had been raised among them, to the amount of twenty-five shillings. From Protestants and Papists, masters and servants, the contributions poured in. No sum larger than £30 was received. A large part of the money was in silver and copper; but the full amount required was raised.

Having now come so near to the question of the support of Messrs. Moody and Sankey, the readers of this work will naturally desire to know something on that interesting topic. Here let it be said, once for all, that these brethren do not work for pay. They have never sought an invitation; never stipulated for any sum of money to be given them, either for their services or expenses. In every instance, Mr. Moody determined the question of going to, or passing by, a place, under the direction, as he believed, of the Spirit of God. The committees which invited him have held the matter of finance entirely in their own hands. They have raised the money as they pleased, and given him such sums as they judged suitable;

these he has shared with Mr. Sankey; and thus they have laboured together, taking what God sent them—which in many instances has been very little, and in no case very much. At Dublin the committee consulted together, and determined to give Mr. Moody a sum of money which, they afterwards were glad to learn, was in excess of what he had received hitherto: but even upon the proportion of this generous gift, the American evangelists will never become rich out of their present employment. Still in the secular press, and in the gossip of the streets and offices, these men are accused, by those who know nothing of them, of mercenary motives in their great work for Christ.

Only a little while ago a certain newspaper suggested that they were an advance-guard sent over by Barnum; and that the advertising scheme, no doubt, would presently appear. Another equally discerning party had heard of Mr. Moody's little device for setting children to study the Bible; which he calls "the Gospel clock." It consists of a grouping of twelve texts of Scripture in a circle, containing respectively, the same numbers of words as those which mark the hours upon a dial. A great many of these Gospel clock-faces have been arranged by the little people, to their no small profit and delight. But the individual referred to saw in it a suggestion of a different character. "I have it at last," said he: "Moody is a clock-maker in America, and this is the beginning of a system of advertising, by which he means to sell his wares."

In like manner Mr. Sankey has been assailed as an agent for the sale of that peculiar make of harmoniums which he uses to accompany his singing. But it is scarcely needful to say that no such charge can be properly made against him.

So mightily grew the word and work in Dublin that the evangelistic committee were forced to appoint a secretary to take charge of the applications for Christian workers, with which they were constantly besieged. Meetings were called together with the greatest ease, all over the north of Ireland. It was only necessary to announce a revival service, with perhaps a mention of the name of Mr. Moody or Mr. Sankey, or of the great revival in Dublin; and the people, for miles around, would come together, not knowing who were to speak, or whether there were to be any speakers at all. If some of the men were present who had been to the Dublin meetings, the crowd of listeners were satisfied with the simplest account of their experience and observation. If no such persons appeared, perhaps somebody had one of Mr. Sankey's hymn books, from which he could sing; and the song would be blessed to the awakening of sinners and the comfort of believers. From the smallest sowing of these seeds of grace, great harvests were gathered, all over the northern portion of the island. And still the work continues with such a power of blessing, that the brethren in Dublin almost begin to hope that all Ireland at last is to be saved.

The reason of all this is to be found, not wholly in the labours of Messrs. Moody and Sankey, but also in the earnest prayer which, for six months previous to their coming, had been offered for God's blessing upon their work. From March to October a daily prayer-meeting was held, to implore the descent of the Holy Spirit upon Ireland. The brethren there have received far more than they dared to ask; and still the rain of grace comes down, which maketh glad the valleys of the Lord.

The labours of the evangelists, which continued from the 24th of October till the 29th of November, closed with a three days' convention; attended by Christian workers and others from all parts of Ireland; and by about eight hundred ministers of all evangelical denominations. Mr. Moody himself went to the Archbishop of Dublin, and desired his assistance at this convention. He however refused to come, because of certain ecclesiastical difficulties; and so the convention went on without him. This must not be taken to signify that the Episcopal clergy refused to give their hands to the brethren from America. In Ireland especially, a goodly number of these servants of God not only listened to Mr. Moody's preaching, and were delighted by it, but learned many valuable lessons from him, which they have put to good use among their own congregations. His inquiry meetings at first were looked upon with suspicion; but now, in the Episcopal and Presbyterian churches of Great Britain and Ireland, this method of coming to close quarters is widely used, with very beneficial effect.

In many instances the zeal of the people outran that of their pastors. One lady in the country paid the expenses of several poor clergymen, and sent them to the Dublin convention. A minister from a distance, who was known to be opposed to such extra means of grace, was met by an acquaintance who saluted him as follows :—

"What! Mr. ———, are you here?"

"Yes," was the reply. "I was forced to come. My people would not let me stay away. It was, either come to the convention, or leave the parish."

Such cases, however, were rare. For the most part the ministers co-operated heartily in the movement; and the blessing of God upon their congregations has been one part of their reward.

The meeting for converts, on the second day of the great convention, called together two thousand persons, who, during the six months previous, had given their hearts to Christ. Mr. Moody spoke to them from Rom. xiv. 4: "Who art thou that judgest another man's servant? To his own master he standeth or falleth. Yea, he shall be holden up: for God is able to make him stand."

Mr. Moody's farewell addresses, like all his other discourses, are full of the words of Scripture, but almost empty of himself. The great temptation to deal in personal matters at such a time, with hundreds and thousands of people before him whom he had led to the Saviour, was always steadily resisted. He did not play upon their sympathies, but made the most of his last hour with them to impress yet once more upon their hearts the great lesson, that they were saved by faith in Christ. Christ was everything; the minister was nothing. The Word of God was everything; the words of the speaker were nothing.

Doubtless Mr. Moody's great and affectionate nature was thrilled to its centre with brotherly and Christian tenderness and love towards those souls whom he had been the means of saving. But now, as he bids them good-bye, he does not tell them that he loves them, but that Christ loves them. He does not tell them to remember him, but to remember the Lord and their duty.

From Dublin, the brethren returned again to England, leaving behind them thousands of grateful and happy souls, who will never cease to thank God for their coming; and laden with more heart-felt benedictions than ever went out of Ireland with any two men before.

CHAPTER VIII.

RETURN TO ENGLAND.—MANCHESTER, SHEFFIELD, BIRMINGHAM, LIVERPOOL.

THE return of the evangelists had been awaited with the deepest interest, and at the places where they were expected, special services of prayer had been held, for months together, in the hope that the same baptism of power, which had accompanied them through Scotland and Ireland, might also come with them to the chief cities of England.

During the whole of the last week in November, the committee at Manchester were busy with preparations for the arrival of Messrs. Moody and Sankey. As the time of their coming drew near the interest increased, until it became intense; and among other proofs of the Divine source of this feeling on the part of Christians, was the fact that believers of various sects and orders shared in it alike. This spirit of union found expression in a united communion service on Sunday, the 2nd of December: admission was by tickets; and so great a number of these were issued, that it was found necessary to divide the congregation between the two largest chapels in the town. During the first week the omens were good.

Large congregations greeted the speaker and singer, especially at the noon prayer-meetings, and the afternoon service for women.

The famous Free Trade Hall was taken for the noon meetings, which were attended by earnest audiences of from two to three thousand: a fact which in a busy, manufacturing city like Manchester, can only be accounted for on the theory of the general outpouring of the Spirit of God. The largest chapels were used for other services, but none were able to contain the crowds which flocked to attend them. Overflow meetings were in order, but it was quite impossible to bring the masses of would-be hearers all under the preaching of the Word at any given time.

The general interest expressed in the revival by all nonconformist ministers, and the harmony with which they laboured together, made the absence of the Episcopal clergy all the more noticeable; and before the end of the first week, Mr. Moody, who always desires the union of all who love our Lord and Saviour Jesus Christ in the good work to which he has devoted his life, caused the following circular to be issued:—

"Having come to Manchester with my friend Mr. Sankey, for the month of December, with the one object of preaching Christ, it has been matter of disappointment that not more clergymen of the Church of England have attended our meetings. As God has granted large blessings where unity has prevailed, we trust you will join in seeking a blessing for Manchester.

"*Manchester*, "D. L. MOODY.
"*4th December*, 1874."

So rapidly did the interest extend, that, within a

week, it was said, "Manchester is now on fire. The most difficult of all English cities to kindle by anything but politics, is now fairly ablaze; and the flames are breaking out in all directions."

Nothing was more striking than Mr. Moody's running commentaries on the Scriptures: the practical manner in which he dealt with Bible doctrines opened the way at once to the favour of this practical people. On two successive evenings, before immense congregations in the Free Trade Hall, Mr. Moody delivered his famous discourses on Heaven; which he followed up the next night, with his terrible sermon on Hell. Those who heard them will not soon forget the manifest presence of the Holy Spirit. They could almost feel the mighty rushing wind, as at Pentecost, shaking the place where they were sitting; and when the exhortation was urged upon sinners to flee from the wrath to come, large numbers of anxious persons pressed to the inquiry room, to be instructed personally about the question of their eternal fate.

Hitherto the revivals under the labours of Messrs. Moody and Sankey had been of a joyful type; but at Manchester, from the first, a deep solemnity pervaded the meetings. Mr. Moody put forth no effort to startle the imagination of his congregations, but sought in the simplest and most straightforward manner to lead their minds to Christ.

A writer, in speaking of the appearance of the assemblies under his sermons, says: "If you watch the audience, you can see faces change expression. You may read there shame, contrition, confession, hope, faith, peace, as the case may be. The truth comes home. There is a power. No man can do it. It is God's power. It is the Lord's doing."

The meetings in the Free Trade Hall on Sunday mornings, at eight o'clock, resulted in such an awakening among believers as had not been witnessed in Manchester for many a year. At that early hour, in the depth of winter, the great hall was crowded to excess with persons, most of whom had hitherto been careless about the work of the Lord; but who now were eager to learn the way in which they might do something for Him, who had done so much for them.

A scheme was organized at the suggestion of Mr. Reginald Radcliffe of Liverpool, by which every house in the city was to be visited. Hundreds of Christian men and women devoted themselves to this work; and their reports at the noon prayer-meeting constituted a feature of great impressiveness and value. The city was divided into fifty districts, each of which was placed under the charge of a superintendent, with a sufficient number of visitors to reach every house within its limits. A leaflet was prepared, containing the hymn "Jesus of Nazareth passeth by," and a short address by Mr. Moody. But this paper was to be used simply as an introduction, and to enable the visitor to come more easily to the question of personal religion.

The growing union among believers of various names became so notable, that a strong desire sprang up for its consolidation into some form by which it might become a permanent force and blessing. With this view, a meeting was held on one of the last evenings of Mr. Moody's visit, on behalf of the Young Men's Christian Association; at which the chairman intimated that it was contemplated to buy the old Museum and fit it up as the head-quarters of the Association. This Museum was a vacant building, situated near the Free Trade Hall, whose former use is indicated by its name. On this occasion Mr. Moody gave a spirited address, in which he spoke of the opportunities and duties of the young men of Manchester; and, at the close a collection was made, beginning with a gift from the chairman of £1000. Over £30,000 was ultimately raised, being the full amount required for purchasing and fitting up the building.

The spirit of consecration, so widely prevalent, led to special efforts to reach the neglected classes of society. One branch of this work was a mission among the mill girls, many of whom were brought to Christ. It is sometimes said, "A girl cannot be good in a mill": but one of these converts, as if to prove the error of this opinion, having first given her heart to the Saviour, spoke of Him to her companions, ten of whom were converted.

A young man in a large warehouse, who had been utterly regardless of Divine things, went to a meeting just to see what was going on; but when he heard Mr. Moody speak, he was almost struck dumb with amazement and alarm. Before long, his heart was quite melted. He went into the inquiry room, where a Christian minister pointed him to Christ; and having accepted the offer of salvation, he went his way rejoicing. In the warehouse where he was employed there were a large number of young men, to whom, in a frank and kindly manner, he told of the great change he had experienced. By his invitation several of them went to a meeting with him, and within three days eleven of the number were brought to Christ.

At one of the meetings in the Free Trade Hall a workman was brought under deep conviction by the singing of the hymn "Safe in the arms of Jesus." Indeed, the singing was often blessed to such results.

Requests for prayer at the noon meeting became so numerous that it was impossible to read them all, even in the most condensed form in which it was possible to arrange them. It was presumed that the Lord knew all about the people who desired the prayers of the congregation, and the petitions went up *en masse*, to which there seemed to be no lack of answers. Thanksgivings, also, were frequent. On one occassion, a minister returned thanks for the conversion of a friend for whom prayers had been offered twenty-five years; also for the salvation of several persons in his own congregation; and for the dispelling of the doubts of a young man who had travelled a hundred and fifty miles to attend the Manchester meetings.

On the same occasion, another minister rose to say he had never met with so much Scriptural teaching concerning the way of salvation as in Mr. Moody's addresses. Not only the ministers, but the common people as well, became impressed with a new understanding of the Word, and how to use it; even young boys were making themselves useful by

Bible readings in the cottages, where many persons would assemble to listen.

In speaking of the definite results of the work, which closed on the last day of 1874, one writer says: "I may be forgiven if I begin with the ministers of Manchester. If one class has been blessed more than another during these four weeks past, it has been the regular Christian ministry. I am sure I speak the sentiments of all my brethren who have thrown themselves heart and soul into the movement, when I say, that we have received nothing less than a fresh baptism of the Holy Ghost. If our dear brother, Mr. Moody, had accomplished nothing other than the awakening of the ministers of this great centre of population, his visit would not have been in vain. Next to the Christian ministry, I believe the great army of Christian workers have shared most largely in the blessing. Above all, drones have been rebuked, and recruits in large numbers have enlisted in the name of our Lord and King. The afternoon Bible readings have been greatly relished by thousands. At this, Mr. Moody surprised and delighted many of us ministers, by his wonderful acquaintance with the Word of God. He proved himself to be a very giant in Bible knowledge; and I have reason to believe that, in hundreds of cases, his immense audiences went home with souls hungering after righteousness, and determined to be better acquainted with the Word of Life."

The blessing received by the young men of Manchester, is indicated by the rise of the Young Men's Christian Association into increased activity; the purchase of the old Museum for its use, as above mentioned; and the addition of nearly five hundred names to the roll of its active members.

SHEFFIELD.

At nine o'clock on the last night of 1874, Messrs. Moody and Sankey commenced their two weeks' session in Sheffield. The service was held in the Albert Hall, which was crowded to excess; many having stood before the doors an hour before they were opened, in order to make sure of admittance. A large number of ministers occupied the platform The last three hours of the old year were spent in earnest exhortation by Mr. Moody; tender and impressive singing by Mr. Sankey; and solemn and silent prayer by the whole congregation.

A year of blessing had passed since that wonderful watchnight in Edinburgh, and a year of blessing was opening, in which even greater works were to be done. The vicar of Sheffield, with many clergymen of the Established Church, and dissenting ministers of various denominations, took part in the services of the week of prayer which followed.

It was proposed to divide Sheffield into districts, to be visited after the manner adopted at Manchester; but on account of the decided opposition of some of the Church clergy, who refused to allow their parishes to be canvassed in this irregular manner, the scheme was dropped. Such proof of a disposition, on the part of the managers of the movement, to conciliate all parties, and maintain Christian courtesy, checked the incipient division, and there was afterwards the most harmonious union between ministers of all orders, which had been seen anywhere in England. On one occasion an Independent minister preached to an immense congregation in the Sheffield parish church; while its rector addressed a great overflow meeting in the churchyard.

Mr. Moody gave some of his Bible readings with excellent effect; and all the services were marked by the evident presence of the Divine Spirit, and attended by immense congregations. The merits and demerits of the evangelists were discussed by excited groups at the street corners and other public places. The opponents of the movement attributed its success to skilful advertising, curiosity, novelty, etc.; but still the throng pressed to attend the meetings.

Sheffield has a population which is difficult to arouse,—sturdy, independent, unimpressible, like the metal on which they work; and the success of this movement is, therefore, the greater marvel. At first there was a feeling of disappointment, both respecting Mr. Moody's speaking and Mr. Sankey's singing; but presently Christian people began to look beyond the speaker and the singer, and then appeared the real power and blessing which accompanied them. The Sheffield Christians said, "This is a work of God."

At one of the noon prayer-meetings a telegram was handed in as follows:—"Three men were executed this morning at eight o'clock, at Liverpool. They all attributed the crimes for which they suffered to the evil influence of drink. Pray for the poor drunkards of Liverpool."

One of the preparatory meetings held in view of the approaching visit of the brethren from America, was blessed in the following singular manner:—An elderly man, who had been a devoted Christian, but had afterwards backslidden from God, feeling the torments of his conscience absolutely unendurable, sought to drown them in intoxication. Finding no relief even in this, he resolved to bring his life to an end, and was proceeding to carry out his design; when, passing near the lower Albert Hall, where a children's service was in progress, he entered; listened to the simple exercises; felt once more the love of the tender Shepherd; and at length, after having been almost torn to pieces by despair and remorse, came back again to Christ, and once more found rest and peace in Him."

BIRMINGHAM.

Birmingham has a population of nearly four hundred thousand people. It is noted for its intense political activity. The independence of its citizens has passed into a phrase—"the Birmingham spirit"—which, its own people say, may be interpreted to mean "every man for himself." It is a great manufactory of opinions in politics and religion, as well as of all manner of workmanship in brass and iron; and taking everything into account, it was thought that the American evangelists would find as much difficulty here as in any place which they had visited. But from the first, it might be said, the whole city was moved and went out to hear them. There were such crowds as never greeted a speaker in that town before; save when, on some exciting topic, Mr. Bright, Birmingham's distinguished member of Parliament, addressed the electors of his borough.

Early in the winter a meeting of the evangelical ministers had been called, at which it was resolved to invite Messrs. Moody and Sankey to Birmingham.

On Sunday, the 17th of January, 1875, they commenced their labours, with a meeting for Christian workers. It was held in the Town Hall, which is capable of seating five thousand persons. Twice during the day this place was densely crowded: and in the evening a service was held in Bingley Hall. This hall was built for the Birmingham annual cattle show. Its interior forms a square of about one hundred yards. Its covering consists of five parallel roofs, sustained by graceful iron pillars and girders; the windows are skylights; and at night it is well illuminated by gas. Two galleries sweep round the great enclosure, giving, with the platform, accommodation for ten or twelve thousand persons. But so great was the rush for admission that the immense building was thronged an hour before the time of service; and the doors had to be closed against thousands upon thousands,—a multitude so great that it was estimated to be capable of filling the hall two or three times over.

It would seem that so vast a congregation was favourable to the work, which had been greatly hindered in other places for want of a suitable building; but, at the close of Mr. Moody's address on Monday night, when he asked all those who were not Christians, but were anxious to be saved, to stand up, at first no one answered the appeal.

"What!" cried Mr. Moody, "is there no sinner in this vast assembly who wants to become a Christian?" Then a young girl, apparently about sixteen, rose in the body of the hall.

"Thank God, there is one at least!" he exclaimed immediately. Then, as if shamed by the courage of the girl, as well as convicted of their danger out of Christ, hundreds of men and women in all parts of the house rose in rapid succession; until Mr. Moody cried, "Thank the Lord, there are so many I cannot count them; but Jesus knows you every one." The inquirers were then desired to repair to the neighbouring church, where Mr. Moody and Mr. Sankey would meet them; and when they reached the place they found the church quite full.

During their two weeks in Birmingham, Messrs. Moody and Sankey were greeted by larger congregations than ever assembled to hear the Gospel in that town before. The whole community seemed to be awakened; and not only from the city, but from the regions round about, thousands flocked daily to the meetings: many from curiosity, some with hearts full of opposition, but most of them anxious to hear about Christ and heaven. In the counting-houses, shops, railway trains, omnibuses, in the streets,—everywhere, the topic of conversation was the sayings and doings of these two men.

The newspapers of Birmingham gave kindly notice of, and did good service to, the great revival. The *Morning News* says:—

"The spring-tide of blessing has rolled over Birmingham, and risen far above the ordinary high-water mark of years gone by.

The fishermen, who have learned the Divine art of catching men, instead of toiling all night and taking nothing, have had the fish leaping into the Gospel net, as it were, praying to be caught. When Bingley Hall began to fill up, it was a grand sight to see these rows and rows of people, not drawn out, as on the previous Monday, to hear the members of the borough expound their political views, but to meet the great sterling question, What shall I do to be saved? . . . When the first meeting on Wednesday was closed, it took almost an hour to empty the Hall sufficiently to enable Mr. Moody to deal with the inquirers. Mr. Moody's Bible readings were here received with especial favour. The same topics which had been blessed to the awakening of audiences of thousands of people, were here attended with the accustomed blessing. At the close of Mr. Moody's Bible reading on the blood, he said, 'If you wish to know the secret of our success for the last two years, it lies in this: that we have stood fair and square on the Bible doctrine of substitution. Ah! that is what is needed by a dying world.'"

At the convention with which the Birmingham meetings closed, Mr. Moody himself presided throughout the day—which was spent in considering topics of practical importance. It was attended by ministers from various parts of England, Scotland, and Ireland; especially from the cities where the evangelists had laboured. The Rev. Mr. Morgan of Edinburgh, the Rev. E. N. Keeling of Manchester, the Rev. Mr. Best of Dublin, and others, bore testimony to the Divine power which had accompanied the efforts of Messrs. Moody and Sankey in their respective cities.

"It has been a year of praise in Scotland," said Mr. Morgan. "There has been more heart-singing during the last twelve months than for a whole generation before."

"During the last two months," said Mr. Keeling, "there has been a unity among the Christian churches of Manchester which six months ago would not have been thought possible; and since Messrs. Moody and Sankey left us, we have had even more cause to be thankful than during their visit."

The Rev. Mr. Best said he believed the meetings in Dublin were larger than any held elsewhere; people were coming from all parts of the provinces, and staying in the city for days together, on purpose to attend the meetings. Mr. Sankey's hymns were being sung all over the country; and the names of the American evangelists would be remembered in connection with the religious history of Ireland.

Mr. Sankey conducted a service of praise.

Mr. Moody gave a lecture on Christian work.

The third hour was spent in answering the inquiry, How to conduct prayer-meetings? The fourth hour was occupied by the Rev. R. W. Dale of Birmingham, with an address on "How to reach the masses." The exercise known as the "question drawer" was conducted by Mr. Moody. All sorts of inquiries were poured in upon him; and the prompt and spirited answers he gave, marked this as one of the most interesting parts of the great convention. Some very searching questions were asked; the inquiry meetings in particular were criticised: some of Mr. Moody's methods excited opposition; but, after answering all objections in a skilful and patient manner, he gave this excellent advice,—"If things do not always please you, don't complain—*just pray!*"

A Christian lady invited one of her High-Church neighbours to attend one of Mr. Moody's services. She was very anxious about the impression it would make upon her mind; especially such things as standing up to be prayed for, going to the inquiry room, and the like: but what was her amazement, when the invitation was given, to see her friend stand up for prayers among the very first! When the meeting was over, the High-Church lady said to her friend: "I have had an ideal in my mind for years, of what a religious service ought to be, but I never have had the good fortune to see it till to-night."

People of ruder tastes were no less benefited. The artisans in the manufactories crowded to the meetings in large numbers. In one of the roughest trades, a man was heard to say;—"A dozen men were hit in our shop; and when Mr. Moody held his last all-day meeting for converts, and the foreman would not let us off, a good many of us laid down our tools, and started for the meeting. We were bound to have one last day with Moody and Sankey."

A young lady who had been converted, was sorely troubled what to do with her affianced husband; who was a wild young fellow, and quite a hopeless case in the way of religious impressions. One evening while he was paying her a visit, he noticed that she seemed to have something on her mind; and, on inquiring what it was, she told him she had become a Christian, and was in great doubt whether she could be happy with a man who had no interest in religion. In a manner half laughing and half crying, the young man relieved her anxiety as follows:—

"Don't be troubled, Mary; I have been to the

meetings too. I went down there the other night just to see what the fun was; and, before I had been there long, Mr. Sankey sang something that went straight to my heart. So now I am a Christian too; and we will go to heaven together."

The joyful news was told to the mother of the young lady, who came in just then; but instead of giving her approbation, she laughed at the young people for spending their time in talking of religion; saying, as they were about to be married soon, they had better be giving attention to housekeeping matters, and other practical things. But at length the mother was herself brought under deep conviction, which she was unable to shake off; and the good work progressing in the household, brought several of her children and other relatives into the fold of Christ.

Bingley Hall was Mr. Moody's especial delight.

"I must say," said he, "I have never enjoyed preaching the Gospel more, than since I came to Birmingham. We have reached so many people. I think, if we could, we would take up Bingley Hall and carry it round the world with us."

The number of those who were blessed of God under the labours of the American evangelists in Birmingham, may appear from the fact that at the converts' meeting, held just before they left, two thousand persons applied for tickets of admission; giving their names and addresses. About fourteen hundred of these professed to have been brought to Christ during those two weeks; the other six hundred being those who were still inquiring what they must do to be saved. These tickets were not given out indiscriminately; but every person who applied for one was conversed with by some member of the committee; and one gentleman expresses the opinion, from facts which have subsequently come to his knowledge, that there were three or four hundred other converts and inquirers, who at that time hesitated to apply for tickets; but who afterwards gave themselves to the Saviour, and united with some branch of His Church. These persons were all sent to the care of the pastors to whose congregations they properly belonged; where, in one instance at least, they were divided into little classes of two or three, and placed under the charge of some experienced Christian.

Since the departure of the brethren from America, the work has been going on. The following letter to one of the pastors gives such an insight into the work of grace among a certain class of people, that the readers of this volume will be glad to see it here, just as the poor girl wrote it; the names only being withheld:—

"*Back of* 65, *E——— Street.*

"SIR,—

"Im ill and cant cum to tel you how hapy I am so I get my dortor to write. Theres a young lady brings tracks to our house from your church and hers often beged me to cum to church somewere but I never went. On Sunday 25 her droped on me in high street and tuk me to youre chapel and by youre sermon I was just dun up. Wen it was over her cum to me agen and axed me to go to tother room and bles her swete face, I coud not say no so her tuk me and a young woman cryin near too me. After that I cum awa hers cum to our house agen next Sunday and i was misrable but did not lik to tel her as I'd got three shopmates and my son and dortor there but her axed me how I'd liked it so I just up and told her I'd never bin to the public all the week and never ment to go agen for i knowd you sed it was ronng but her said I must give it up for Christ's ak and ax him to help me. Then her spok of Christ's love and I axed her to sing the hym we'd had last Sunday but we'd got no buk so her sung come home out of Sankeys and red of the prodigal son. Then I axed her to pray which her did and I brok down then her seemed to give me to God—all tothers cried to. I cud not forget it her was the only one calm and I cum to chapell agen at night thinkin all time her'd giv me to God so in youre fust prayere I just giv myself and felt sur he'd have me for her'd told me so as well as you. God will pay you both. I've been a awful wicked siner and i feel if he cals me now I'll have to tell him I've done nothing for him tho hes done so much for me. I am hapy God bles you if I di my dortor will send you this. I thort of cuming to tell you.

"JOHN T——."

"My father died last weak and was buried on Saturday he was so happy. Im cuming to live at my brothers near your chapell and have promised our track lady to go to scool on a Sunday afternoon to a Bible class at the chapel hers been very kind and giv me a Bible and says her wants me to giv meself to jesus like father did. I hope you will excuse me havin wrote but father told me to thank you.

"E. T."

A week or two after, the poor girl wrote again:—

"*Moor Street.*

"GOOD SIR,—

"i am the dortor of john t—— who dide tother week and wrote to you and as I have giv meself to jesus to I thorth i would let you no it was the end of your sermon larst sunday nite mi brother as dun the same i wil tel you how he's ben a Catholick some time now but ever sinse he herd our track lady tother week he's ben in troble so he axed me to ax her if her woud mind caulin at his house to see him and her cum larst wensday and her torked and sung 2 out of her Sankys book to him and prayed and I went in then and he sed as how he'd found out as jesus ad dide for him and he knowd he did forgiv him and he seamed so appy. * * *

"ELLEN T."

LIVERPOOL.

Liverpool was one of the few cities in which Mr. Moody was well received on his former visit to England ; and his coming again was naturally looked forward to with the largest anticipations of blessing. No hall being large enough for the purpose, an immense, rude structure was built, in a central part of the town, called the Victoria Hall, capable of holding ten thousand people. The expense of this building was met by voluntary contributions. No direct solicitation was made; but a sufficient amount for the purpose was sent in, on the simple announcement that it would be required. In addition, as will appear, another large amount of money was given to aid the Young Men's Christian Association, on whose behalf Mr. Moody made a most memorable and successful appeal.

The record of the Liverpool revival is the record of those which preceded it; with the added feature of the great Victoria Hall, which was the first place erected especially for the revival meetings.

On his arrival, having refreshed himself with a week of rest after his labours in Birmingham, he found the great hall in readiness; and the Young Men's Christian Association eager to assist him. At the first meeting, which was for Christian workers, nearly two-thirds of the great congregation were young men. On the very first night, fifty young men were waiting in the inquiry room, ready to offer counsel and encouragement to those who might come desiring it; and throughout the entire month of meetings, and no less up to the present time, the members of this body, under the leadership of their efficient secretary, Mr. Nash, have done good service for the Master.

Among the ministers who heartily co-operated with the evangelists, was the Rev. Mr. Aitken, vicar of Christ's Church, Liverpool. This gentleman, who, for several years, had been a favourite and powerful missionary—and who, like his father before him, made preaching tours in various parts of England and Scotland—was a great reinforcement to the evangelists in Liverpool, having already rendered good service in connection with their meetings in several other cities. Even the great Hall was not sufficient to contain the vast crowds; and Mr. Aitken and many other ministers of the city were actively engaged in the conduct of overflow meetings, four or five of which, on some occasions, it was found necessary to hold, in order to reach the thousands upon thousands who were turned away from the great Victoria Hall.

The noon prayer-meeting, which was already in progress now, was thrilled with new life. It was held in the great Hall, and sometimes attended by as many as six thousand persons. Eighteen services a week were held in the Victoria Hall; and a large building in the neighbourhood, formerly used for a circus, was fitted up for the use of the overflow meetings.

Large numbers of clergymen were constantly in attendance from other places in which the evangelists had laboured; bringing tidings of the good work which was still going on; and sometimes accompanied by their unconverted friends, who had come by sea or land, to share in the great blessing which was now pouring down upon Liverpool. A gentleman from Dublin told of the conversion of a Roman Catholic priest, in the Dublin Exhibition Palace, during the singing of the hymn,—"Jesus the water of life will give."

The meetings in Dublin were reported as in successful progress; sometimes attended by six or eight thousand people: one-fourth of the whole being Roman Catholics; while in the inquiry room there were more Roman Catholics than of any other denomination.

The Gospel was not only preached in the halls and churches of Liverpool, but was carried into the streets and lanes of the city, and offered to the multitudes who, by sin, or poverty, or both, were kept from the ordinary means of grace. One Sunday afternoon, some young men went into a vacant stable, where they found a number of carters; to whom they spoke of the love of Christ, and whom they organized into a Bible-class. This simple beginning rapidly attained the size of a prosperous mission work. One of the carters who was converted, interested himself to secure the formation of a committee of working carters; most of whom had been converted at the Victoria Hall services; and meetings for this class of persons were held in the circus above mentioned, with an average attendance of about three hundred.

The sailors also had a night for them. Separate meetings were also arranged for the policemen, the boys in the ship-building yards, etc., thus taking account of the special fellowship of the trades, and bringing it into the service of Christ.

The elegant and commodious building now in process of erection for the Liverpool Young Men's Christian Association owes its completion, in large measure, to the interest which Mr. Moody always takes in young men. His appeal on its behalf was regarded as a masterpiece of solid sense and practical argument; some of the merchants and business men who listened to it, declared it would have done honour to the most eminent financier in England. From the Victoria Hall, where the address was given, the audience adjourned to the new premises of the Association. After prayer for God's blessing upon the new building and its uses, a memorial stone was laid by Mr. Moody; who made use of a silver trowel, presented to him for that purpose by the President of the Young Men's Christian Association. The block bears this inscription:

"This memorial stone was laid by D. L. Moody of Chicago, 2nd March 1875."

During the month at Liverpool the number of persons converted and awakened must have been numbered by thousands. The inquiry rooms were crowded throughout; and though no definite figures can be given, this was doubtless one of the most blessed harvest times of all their two years in Great Britain.

The following instance of the conversion of a

comic singer is related by Mr. Drummond:—This man was coming upon the stage one evening to sing a comic song, when a verse of a Sunday-school hymn which he had learned years ago, flashed through his mind, producing so deep an impression that he was unable to drive it away. He attempted to sing his song, but failed; and on retiring from the stage was summarily dismissed by the manager. For three weeks he plunged into the deepest dissipation, being scarcely sober for a single hour in all that time. During this debauch he wrote a comedy; which he finished off with a burlesque upon Messrs. Moody and Sankey, who had just then arrived in Liverpool; and in order to give greater point to his satire, he attended one of the services in Victoria Hall to hear them for himself. While thus watching for something of which to make sport, upon the comic stage, the Holy Spirit so impressed the truth upon his heart, that he remained to the after-meeting for inquirers, was instructed in the way of his duty, and that very night found peace with God. He has now entered into training for the purpose of becoming a missionary.

The Victoria Hall, as well as the Circus, is still in use under the auspices of the Young Men's Christian Association; whose members are conducting as many as forty meetings every night among all classes of people in various parts of Liverpool and Birkenhead.

Among the most striking events which have since occurred in connection with the Liverpool revival, must be recorded the important step taken by the Rev. Mr.

Aitken. This clergyman, being called of God to the work of an evangelist, in which he has been, of late, remarkably blessed, recently resigned his living, as so vicar of Christ's Church; and now, free from all clerical restraints, and relying wholly upon God for his support, is devoting himself to preaching in revivals and "missions."

CHAPTER IX.

THE LONDON REVIVAL.

ON the 9th of March, 1875, Mr. Moody entered upon his long contemplated work in London. A letter from him, which appeared in *The Christian*, urging the establishment of noonday prayer-meetings all over the country, attracted the notice of some brethren in London, who were interested in meetings of this description then being held in various parts of the capital. They came together to consult upon the establishment of one central meeting, which was finally located at Moorgate Street Hall. A committee of management was suggested, of which Thomas Stone, Esq., was made chairman; Robert Paton, Esq., honorary secretary; and James E. Mathieson, Esq., treasurer. At this conference, where various branches of the Church of Christ were represented, it was determined to address to Mr. Moody a formal invitation to come to London; although, in an indefinite way, it had been understood from the first that such was his ultimate intention. They at once opened communication with him; and, having received his promise to labour for the months of March, April,

May and June in the four different quarters of London, they set about the arrangements, which were planned on a magnificent scale. "If I come to London," said Mr. Moody, "you will need to raise five thousand pounds for expense of halls, advertising, etc., etc."

"We have ten thousand pounds already," was the reply.

The Moorgate Hall prayer-meeting, which was commenced in October 1874, was regarded as a work of preparation. It was kept up, with varying success, but without exciting any general interest.

During his week of rest between Birmingham and Liverpool, Mr. Moody, who was to pass through London, suggested that the ministers of the capital should be invited to meet him at the Freemasons' Hall. A letter was sent by the Committee, signed by Mr. Moody, to the two thousand pastors in London; and about twelve hundred responded to the invitation.

At this meeting, having been introduced by the chairman, Mr. Moody said that, in view of certain misapprehensions concerning himself and his friend Mr. Sankey, he had desired to meet the ministers of London, whose confidence and help he greatly needed; and, accordingly, he had invited them, not so much to speak to them himself, as to answer any questions which they might desire to ask. Upon this, a volley of sharp inquiries was poured in upon him for half an hour or more; and never was his skill, in conducting "the question drawer," more urgently needed or more successfully used. Ministers of all denominations were present; each one looking at this strange man from his own sectarian point of view, and anxious to know, first of all, what treatment his peculiar notions were likely to receive in the proposed revival meetings. Among the first inquiries were some concerning the finances of the movement. How was Mr. Moody paid? Was Mr. Sankey peddling American organs? What about the copyright of the singing books? etc. But Mr. Moody was not long in setting these matters at rest. He informed them that he had money enough for all his personal expenses in London; and didn't ask that city for a penny. Mr. Sankey was not selling organs; and as for the profits of the little hymn-book, which had been sold in such great numbers, he had indeed received a royalty upon them; but, in order that no one should say that this revival had the least flavour of a speculation about it, he then and there resigned into the hands of Mr. Mathieson, the treasurer of the London Committee, all right and title to the profits of the book in question.

A minister who announced himself as a "red-hot ritualist" inquired whether Mr. Moody would send back to a ritualist pastor any members of his congregation who might be converted in the revival? This question was somewhat embarrassing; but Mr. Moody replied, that his business was not to apportion the converts among the churches, but to lead as many souls to Christ as possible. Another minister wished to know exactly what was Mr. Moody's creed; suggesting that it should be printed and circulated, in order that the Christian public might know what sort of doctrine he preached.

"It is already in print, and in circulation," said Mr. Moody. "You may find it in the fifty-third chapter of Isaiah." "Are you going to institute efforts to reach and save the miserably poor?" said one. "Oh yes," was the reply, "and the miserably rich also."

One old gentleman was greatly disturbed lest Mr. Moody's frequent reference to the sins of dram-selling and intemperance should cause the revival to degenerate into a movement in aid of teetotal reform. Prejudices of all sorts were thrust before the face of this man; who cared nothing whatever for any of them,—desiring only to know how he might save the greatest number of souls; and, in order to this, how he might shape his course, without compromising his conscience, so as to gain the co-operation of the men who professed to be engaged in a similar work. In this respect, this famous meeting was not a great success; but it was useful as a striking picture of the spirit of contention with which the various branches of Christian work are carried on.

The British metropolis cannot be properly described as a city. It is a vast assemblage of cities; and its people, unlike those of the places where the evangelists had hitherto been labouring, had very few points in common. Each minister and congregation formed a separate community; watchfully caring for their own progress, but strongly tempted, by sharp competition, to leave all outside Christian enterprises to take care of themselves.

The magnitude of the attempt to reach and move the great metropolis may appear in the fact that in the north quarter of London, where the meetings

MEETING IN AGRICULTURAL HALL, ISLINGTON.

first commenced, the single parish of Islington, which is only about one-third of this north quarter, contains a population equal to Liverpool or Chicago; while in the whole of North London, as marked on Mr. Moody's map, there is nearly a million of souls.

The Agricultural Hall was naturally suggested as the point in the North at which to commence the work. This great structure has two principal uses; one for the Smithfield cattle show at Christmas, and the other for the great horse-fair in June. Under its arched roof of glass and iron is an area where thousands of cattle are exhibited in pens and stalls; and where horses in great numbers march in grand procession. Twenty or thirty hunters at once, are here put through their trials of jumping and running. These facts, better than any figures which may be given, will serve to indicate the immense size of the great hall of the Agricultural Society. This place had once before been used for preaching, by Mr. Spurgeon; though it was regarded as altogether too large for such a purpose. But Mr. Moody, with his experience of the Crystal Palace in Dublin, Bingley Hall in Birmingham, and the great Victoria Hall at Liverpool, was only too glad to find such an audience-room in which to preach the Gospel. After all the different estimates of the capacity of this place, it is enough to say that, during the first week of meetings here, the congregations averaged about eighteen thousand. But it was found impossible to make so large a number hear distinctly the preaching, or even the singing; and the size was reduced, by means of temporary partitions under the galleries, to the capacity of about fourteen thousand. In this shape it was constantly overcrowded; every seat being sometimes occupied for nearly an hour before the service commenced.

For each of the four quarters of London a local secretary was appointed; who, under the direction of the Central Committee, attended to the management and advertising of the services. There were also local committees for each denomination of Christians, in this case amounting to the aggregate of three or four hundred members; formed with a view to the thorough visitation of Islington, Hackney, Clerkenwell, Camden Town, Kingsland, Highbury, and all the region from the river on the south to the open country in the north; and bounded on the east and west respectively, by Regent's Park and Hackney Road. It was, however, found impossible to carry out such an extensive scheme, and the visitation was never completed.

The attitude of many of the pastors was at first one of observation and armed neutrality; though a few of the most honoured ministers, both of the Established and Nonconformist churches, gave their heartiest co-operation. Those cautious brethren occupied the platform by hundreds; but very few of them were willing to assist at the inquiry meetings, or in any way to identify themselves with Mr. Moody and his work. The movement was a new one. There were possible dangers attending it; and it was not until, by his earnest and simple preaching of the Word of God, and the manifest blessing of Heaven upon his labours, that the ministry, in large numbers, felt it safe to join hands with him.

The inquiry meetings were held in St. Mary's Hall—a spacious audience-room, when not compared with the vast hall itself; and this was densely filled, night after night, not only with penitent sinners and those who were pointing them to Christ, but also with persons anxious to see what was going on. So great a curiosity was the inquiry meeting thought to be, that the passages to St. Mary's Hall were blocked with such crowds as London only can show; pushing and elbowing and shouldering and crushing, to get a peep at those who had taken this first important step in coming out from the world and giving themselves to Christ. On this account it was found necessary to remove the inquiry meetings to one of the great galleries within the Hall itself; where the work of instruction might be protected from the overwhelming crowds of people, who seemed no less anxious to watch this novel exercise than to hear Mr. Moody preach or Mr. Sankey sing.

The Secretary for the North, and the Rev. H. C. Billing, vicar of the Church of Holy Trinity, Islington, with the assistance of seventy or eighty stewards or ushers, managed these great meetings with much efficiency and success. The stewards were Christian men who volunteered for this service at the public call of the Committee. They were received on the certificate of their pastors; and the service which they rendered in this humble way contributed in no small degree to the success of the work at the Agricultural Hall.

These stewards were afterwards organized into a fraternal society, which is still kept up; not only in remembrance of the revival, but from a strong desire to perpetuate the catholic spirit which sprang up in their hearts while, as representatives of different communions, they had cordially laboured together.

The number of those who were awakened under the preaching, as well as under the singing, increased from week to week. After the public service was over, Mr. Moody would often find, in one of the anterooms, a hundred men awaiting his instruction: Mr. Sankey, in another room, would address seventy or eighty women: in the gallery specially set apart for inquirers, there would be sometimes four or five hundred persons conversing, two by two, about the salvation of their souls; while here and there, in groups scattered about the great Hall, anxious sinners were eagerly listening while some Christian worker, who had been duly appointed to this task, pointed them to the cross of Calvary. Besides St. Mary's Hall, holding perhaps twelve hundred people, there were three other rooms of nearly equal size, in use as rooms of inquiry.

At first the congregations were composed of respectable, church-going people; but afterwards, efforts were put forth to reach the lower classes; and many wretched characters from the slums of London were brought to the meetings, and to Christ.

For the term of eleven weeks, including the one week of preliminary services held before Mr. Moody's arrival, the North London revival meetings were continued. Mr. Moody was here for five weeks, every afternoon and evening, except Saturday; and after his departure to East London, meetings were kept up for five weeks more, by the Rev. William Taylor, of California, the Rev. Mr. Aitken, of Liverpool, the Rev. Newman Hall, of London, and the Rev. Dr. Mackay, of Hull; with occasional brief assistance from Mr. Moody and Mr. Sankey, as well as from the local ministry of North London, and visiting clergymen from all over Great Britain.

The same methods which had been used elsewhere so successfully were the ones which were followed here. Many difficulties were continually arising out of the new circumstances of the case; but they were met and overcome with a wisdom which seemed to come down from above. Thus the Agricultural Hall was not only the scene of a great revival, but a school in which the committee, and the evangelists themselves, were prepared for the further labours which awaited them in the capital.

No less than twenty noonday prayer-meetings are regularly held in London: another meeting in connection with this work was also opened in Exeter Hall, on the 9th of March; and maintained, with evident marks of the Divine favour. Many eminent ministers and others came up to London from the towns and cities where the evangelists had laboured, and rendered good service in sustaining them.

From Exeter Hall, the noonday prayer-meetings were removed first, to Her Majesty's Opera House in the Haymarket; then to the Bow Road Hall; and finally to the Victoria Theatre, in the south of London. From first to last these meetings have been a notable feature of the London revival. The requests for prayer which continually poured in were too many to be read in order, and it was necessary to classify them thus:—Fifty requests for prayer for unconverted husbands by Christian wives. Ten requests for prayer for unconverted wives by Christian husbands. Two requests for prayer for unconverted ministers, by members of their congregations. Fifteen requests for prayer for prodigal sons, by broken-hearted parents. Eighty requests for prayer for children out of Christ. A minister requests prayer for his wife, who has been led astray by false teaching, and has become a sceptic. Requests for prayer, from Sunday-school teachers without number, for the conversion of their classes. Requests for prayer from ministers all over Great Britain, for revivals among their own people.

The minuteness with which some of these requests entered into private family histories was almost startling; showing that those who sent them were desperately in earnest. The different classes from which they came were also indicated. At Bow Road, in the East End, amongst a population where gin-palaces and wretched dwellings abounded, requests would come up for prayer on behalf of convicted dog-fighters, publicans, intemperate women, and persons who had been converted, but who were forced to live in wicked communities, like sheep in the midst of wolves. At the Opera House in the West End, the wealth and culture of its society were apparent not only in the wording of the letters, but also in the character of the requests themselves.

Prayer was sought for sons in the army and navy; for sons consecrated to the holy ministry, who had broken away from restraints and entered upon worldly lives; for absent relatives in India; for persons in danger of backsliding by reason of worldly prosperity; and those in danger of ruin by the vices of fashionable life.

One day, as if to bring the two extremes together, a poor woman in Newgate prison, condemned to death, sent a request for prayer to be read at Her Majesty's Opera House; on hearing which, the great congregation, largely composed of the nobility and gentry of London, seemed to be touched with pity, and joined in prayer for the soul of this poor criminal in a manner which showed that the Lord Himself was in it.

Bow Road Hall.

After labouring for five weeks at the Agricultural Hall, Messrs. Moody and Sankey removed to the tabernacle erected for their use in the East End of London; named from the thoroughfare near which it was located, Bow Road Hall. This immense structure, the plan of which was perhaps suggested by Mr. Moody's favourite Bingley Hall, in Birmingham, was designed to hold an audience of ten thousand people. But even this was too small. A large tent was then pitched near the building, in which overflow meetings were held; but it afterwards became more especially useful for the young men's meetings, which were conducted by Mr. Cole, of Chicago, Mr. Drummond, and others.

That class of persons towards whom the labours

of the evangelists in this part of London were chiefly directed, are possessed of strong prejudices, as well as great curiosity. The latter element contributed, during the first few days, to fill the great Hall; but the former produced such a reaction that, during the second week, the audiences fell off considerably; and it began to be a matter of no little anxiety whether the meetings here would ultimately succeed.

The conversion of a very wicked man under the labours of Mr. Henry Varley, after Messrs. Moody and Sankey had left the East, is related as a case in point. He was awakened and brought to Christ under a sermon from his countryman, and went home to his wife after the meeting, saying;—"Get down the Bible; we will have prayers." The poor wife was overjoyed. "I am a Christian, too," said she; "but I have been afraid to tell you of it for ten whole years." In relating his experience, he said, "I was determined not to be converted by these Americans, and I would not go to the meetings until after they were gone away."

It will also be easily understood that a population so familiar with gin-palaces, and all their infamous accessories, were not easily persuaded to attend Divine service. They might go to the Hall for once, out of curiosity, or to sit in judgment upon the discourse; for these people are notable critics—equal in self-assurance to the high-learned rationalists themselves—and if something were said which, in manner or matter, did not suit their fastidious tastes, they walked away grumbling, denouncing the speaker and the singer in terms more forcible than polite. But the reaction was only for a little. Mr. Moody's straightforwardness soon won their confidence. He did not address them in discourses elaborately divided into firstlies, secondlies, and thirdlies; with introduction figurative, historical, antithetical; but aimed straight at their common-sense, talking to them in the same language about spiritual things that they themselves used in every-day conversation. He opened his discourse on heaven after this fashion:— "If I were going to talk to you about the United States of America, you would all want to hear what I had to say; but now I am going to talk to you about heaven, some of you care nothing for it. And yet heaven is a great deal the better place of the two. A good many of you will never go to America, but every one of you may go to heaven if you will."

It must by no means be understood that the congregations at the Bow Road Hall were entirely composed of the humbler classes. Within easy reach there are spacious streets and comfortable mansions, as well as dirty alleys and tumble-down houses. The rich and poor often met here together; and the Lord, the Maker of them all, seemed equally willing to bless the one as the other.

The local committee, aided by a large force of voluntary stewards, kept everything in order; and maintained an effective system of advertising, which they judged to be as appropriate in this enterprise as in any other.

To some fastidious persons it might seem a curious sight to see a man promenading the streets with two huge boards suspended from his shoulders, the one before and the other behind, bearing the striking words, "Moody and Sankey at Bow Road Hall to-night!" in letters large enough to be read at the distance of a hundred yards. A bellman, ringing with all his might one minute, and shouting with all his might the next, in giving notices of the revival meetings, was one of the methods of announcement suggested by Mr. Moody himself; who never was too nice about the means of doing good, so long as the good were done. This last was a method he desired to bring into use, from having observed that he was failing to attract a suitable proportion of the poor and wicked into his meetings. The crowds, he thought, looked too amiable, and were too well dressed. It was the congregation from the Agricultural Hall following him to the East End. Sometimes, looking over the sea of faces upturned before his gaze, he would say,—"I see too many Christian people here. I know you. A great many of you were at my meetings in Islington. You are converted already. Now, I want you to get up and go out, and leave room for hundreds of those sinners who are waiting outside for a chance to come in and hear the Gospel." Under such an invitation large numbers of believers would actually leave the places which they had occupied, perhaps for an hour before the meeting began; and go out into the tent, or to some overflow meeting in the street, in order to make room for those who needed the Gospel more from having heard it less.

Those who have been familiar with Mr. Moody for years, and remember the *abandon* and heartiness with which he used to throw himself into the meetings among the poor people at the North Market Hall in Chicago, were able to recognise the same manner in him while he addressed his great congregations at the Bow Road Hall. He talked to them in a way which made them feel that he was not above them; that he was their brother, and was not ashamed to own it; and on this account they listened to him all the more attentively, and his word went home to them with greater and swifter force of salvation. It was a sight to make the angels glad, to see hundreds of persons, men and women, young and old, who, after one of his impetuous appeals, would rise in that vast audience, to signify their desire to be saved.

Many strange instances of the work of grace were constantly occurring. One day a notorious dog-fighter was awakened and brought to Christ; and afterwards, on account of his strange experience, was invited to relate it in Her Majesty's Opera House, at the noon prayer-meeting; where he was received with especial kindness, because of the depths from which the Lord had evidently lifted him.

Mr. Sankey's singing has been nowhere more abundantly blessed, except perhaps in Dublin, than it was at the Bow Road Hall. But while his voice and the accompanying influence of the Holy Spirit were able to awaken sinners, bring comfort to broken-hearted penitents, and lift the souls of believers into almost heavenly joy, they were not sufficient even to keep the peace, among certain of the amateur musicians who had been organized into a choir. The same old difficulties, which in this world of sin seem scarcely separable from ordinary companies of men and women set up to lead this part of Divine worship, were found even in the midst of this mighty revival; and Mr. Sankey was obliged to say to some of those over-sensitive individuals;—" Don't trouble yourselves with the thought that you are essential to the meetings here. They would go on without Mr. Sankey, and certainly they will go on without you." After this rebuke, he invited them down to one of the inquiry rooms, where they had a season of prayer together, which so calmed their troubled spirits, that, thenceforth, there was more harmony of all kinds amongst them.

After Mr. Moody's departure the meetings were kept up in the Bow Road Hall, as they had been at the Agricultural Hall. The Rev. Mr. Pym, the Rev. Mr. Aitken, Mr. Henry Varley, and others, occupied the speaker's desk; and during the last days of June and the first of July, the Jubilee Singers, returning for a second tour in England, were placed under the direction of the Central Committee, to help along the work. Their wonderful melodies, born of sorrow, and wrought out with toils and tears, were sometimes no less impressive than the spirited solos of Mr. Sankey himself. The same blessings attended them, and awakenings and conversions were frequent. One lady was brought to the knowledge of Christ through hearing them chant the Lord's Prayer.

The West End.

The Royal Opera House, in the Haymarket, was the place which seemed providentially appointed for

MR. MOODY PREACHING IN THE OPERA HOUSE, HAYMARKET.

Messrs. Moody and Sankey's meetings in the West End of London. The place had been for a long time vacant by reason of legal complications; and was only secured under certain embarrassments, which gave the Committee no little trouble and expense, but which did not in any wise hinder the revival. Some solicitude had been felt by many of Mr. Moody's friends lest the blessing which had attended him elsewhere might not follow him into the circles of wealth, nobility, and fashion; but Mr. Moody himself seems to have had no anxiety upon this point. With him, a sinner riding in a carriage emblazoned with a coat of arms, was just as much in need of a Saviour as the poor dog-fighter himself. It was his calling to preach the Gospel here, as he had preached it elsewhere; and his simple, manly earnestness, and utter forgetfulness of himself, soon won for him not only the respect, but the admiration of those cultivated noblemen and ladies, than whom no people in the world are more ready to honour genuine excellence, or acknowledge the influence of real genius or piety. To them Mr. Moody was a rare Christian. The fact that he was not a scholar was forgotten. He evidently knew Christ and His Gospel and, because of this, the best people in London, including members of the royal household, pressed to hear his Bible readings and addresses; wept over his touching stories illustrating the love of Christ to lost sinners; sang with heartiness and rapture the sweet hymns and songs which the revival had already made familiar; and some of them, joining hands with him as one beloved of the Lord, gave him not only their personal friendship, but added the weight of their names and influence to help forward with the work. It is quite evident that many of these wealthy persons must have added somewhat of the weight of their purses also; for, during the last week of the revival in London, it was announced that twenty-four thousand pounds (one hundred and twenty thousand dollars) had been expended in arrangements for the revival; and that four or five thousand pounds, in addition, would be required to cover their cost.

The grand tier, as the first gallery in the Opera House is called, had been, by time-honoured custom, reserved for the nobility; and it was noticed, in the rush for tickets, by which it was necessary to divide the crowds pressing for one of the five thousand seats in the building, that applications for places in the grand tier proportionally outnumbered those for seats in any other part of the building.

The local committee for the West gave personal attention to the management of the meetings in the Opera House; constantly assisted by the chairman and secretary of the Central Committee, and by other gentlemen of fortune and leisure, who, from the first, had given their whole time to labouring in, as well as enjoying, these blessed means of grace. By far the heavier part of their duties consisted in keeping people out after the House was absolutely full; and in arranging such an order of services as might best accommodate the thousands who continually pressed to hear the speaking and the singing. Three or four different meetings a day were held. First, the noon prayer-meeting, at which Mr.

Moody often presided; then a Bible lecture at half-past three o'clock—sometimes for women only, and sometimes for mixed audiences; another address or sermon at half-past seven; and, as soon as the House could be cleared, a meeting for men, at nine o'clock in the evening. After all these, except the noon prayer-meeting, inquirers were instructed in two large ante-rooms of the Opera House, both of which were frequently filled.

For several weeks Mr. Moody divided his attention between the Opera House and the Bow Road Hall. The fastest conveyance was selected from among the cabs about the region of the Haymarket, to convey him to the East, as soon as he should finish his discourse at the West.

One who is curious in such matters has remarked how readily he transformed, as well as transferred, himself from one meeting to the other. Instinctively, the few graces of diction and manner which were in him, came out, rather than were brought out, before his cultivated audiences at the West End; but somewhere on the road these were always dropped, and the old *abandon* and heartiness were sure to appear, the moment he reached the platform of the Bow Road Hall. This same difference was noticed in his discourses: also in the adaptation of his addresses to different congregations in the same places. If the meeting were one for women, he seemed to be conscious of the fact that there were a great many persons before him who were sorrowing over wayward sons or godless husbands. He did not fail to notice, although he did not speak of it, the many widows' weeds which were scattered through the congregation; and in his selection of the hymns and the Scriptures, as well as his topics for discourse, he manifested a tenderness bordering upon reverence, for those upon whom, in London, as everywhere else, the heaviest burdens of care and sorrow always come. He would ask Mr. Sankey to sing some comfortable or touching solo, and would give out for the congregation, "Jesus, Lover of my soul," or, "There is life for a look at the Crucified One," or, "Safe in the arms of Jesus." But when the women were gone, and the men came rushing in, leaping over the chairs and crowding to their places, he would seem to be transformed, and suiting himself to the spirit of his congregation, he would lead off the service with "Ring the bells of heaven," or "Hold the fort." In this way, without seeming to be conscious of it, he illustrated the true spirit of the declaration of the apostle: making himself all things to all men, hoping thereby to save some.

The London revival had now become a world-wide wonder. Every day the news of it occupied large spaces in the public prints. So great was the desire to hear and to spread the tidings of it, that several extra newspapers were started in the capital; and some of those which had been leading a precarious life leaped at once into large success.

The press throughout the English-speaking world were discussing the merits of Mr. Moody's preaching and Mr. Sankey's singing; some writers wondering how the men could do it; others, taking counsel of their own gross natures, wondered why they did it, and how much they made by it; others, seeing and feeling the Divine mission of the men, thanked God for raising them up, and besought Him to send forth more such labourers into the whitening harvest.

Still, although sinners by thousands were coming to Christ, some, who held high places in what they called the kingdom of Christ on earth, made use of the secular press to give faint praise and forcible rebukes to these irregular workers in the Lord's vineyard. The devils were fleeing—cast out by the power which accompanied their word; but the men were not following certain traditional lines.

The Archbishop of Canterbury felt moved to explain that, from what he had heard of Mr. Moody and his work, he had no doubt good was being accomplished; in which, of course, all Christians must rejoice; but it was not at all according to his sense of the high dignity of his office to sanction such irregular proceedings, or advise his clergy to co-operate in them. To this another eminent minister replied;—"I think it rather presumptuous for an archbishop to talk about sanctioning the work of Mr. Moody and Mr. Sankey. I should as soon think of asking him to sanction the kindly rain that falls upon the parched fields, after weeks and months of drought."

Another event which made no small stir, and which even agitated the great British Parliament itself, was Messrs. Moody and Sankey's meeting in the vicinity of the famous old school at Eton. One of the Eton boys had been happily converted at the revival meetings in London; and, feeling desirous that his schoolfellows should profit by the same precious Gospel which had been so blessed to him, he sought and obtained a promise from Mr. Moody, that, some time, he would go down to Eton and hold a service there. Mr. Moody had forgotten all about it, when, nearly a month afterwards, the young man claimed the fulfilment of the promise; and arrangements were made to hold the meeting in a tent which had been pitched not far from the school.

This famous college is a High-Church institution; and one or two of its patrons, who did not wish their sons to be subjected to any such irregular religious influence as the preaching of Mr. Moody, protested against the proposed service under its shadow. One honourable member of the House of Commons announced his intention of publicly questioning Mr. Gladstone, who had given a letter of introduction to the head-master, to one of Mr. Moody's friends. The House of Lords also took up the matter; and violent articles appeared in the newspapers, denouncing the Evangelists and their friends, for attempting to forward their interests or increase their reputation, by thus associating their work with the Eton school. The excitement became so great that Mr. Moody was waited upon by a committee, who begged him to withdraw his appointment. He replied: "I have never missed an appointment yet, during this trip; and I certainly shall not begin now."

The invitation which he had accepted had been signed by a large majority of the students in the college; and, to yield to the pressure against him was not at all congenial to his tastes or habits—in whom the quality of firmness, especially under impressions of duty, is developed to a remarkable degree. He was only anxious lest disturbances, which seemed likely to occur, should result in a fight, and that some of the boys might receive bodily injury; in which event he would be blamed as the cause of all the difficulty. However, the meeting, which evidently could not be safely held in the tent, was appointed to take place in the Town Hall; the Mayor, who was a nonconformist, bravely maintaining his position in favour of free speech, though set upon most vehemently with a view to obtain an order closing the Hall against Messrs. Moody and Sankey. At last, however, his courage failed; and hastily causing a notice to be printed, to the effect that no meeting would be held, he despatched it to the college, where it was distributed among the boys. This was at two o'clock. The meeting was to be held at four in the afternoon.

The private grounds of a gentleman at Eton were placed at Mr. Moody's disposal; and there he preached in the presence of about two hundred of the college boys, and twice or thrice that number of the citizens of the town. His text was,—"Behold I bring you glad tidings of great joy which shall be to all people." But why he should have been so belaboured in Parliament, and abused in the public press, for bringing glad tidings of great joy to a company of lads in Eton college, is still somewhat of a riddle to a large portion of the British public.

The *Times*, in its fatherly way, repeated, in substance, the famous advice once given by the town-clerk of Ephesus; with the further kind suggestion, to those who had rushed into print, and disturbed the solemn counsels of the nation on so small a matter, not to make themselves ridiculous. This good counsel was acted upon, and no more noise was heard.

SOUTH LONDON.—THE CAMBERWELL HALL.

From the Opera House, where the power and blessing of the Lord was increasingly felt to the last, the evangelists removed to the new hall erected for them near Camberwell Green. This building, like the one at the Bow Road, was an immense framework of wood, covered with corrugated iron; having the earth itself for the floor. It was smaller than the Bow Road Hall, having chairs for about eight thousand people. The meetings in it were under the direction of the committee for the South, with the constant assistance of the president, secretary, and treasurer of the Central Committee; who not only gave attention to the material interests, but also laboured in the rooms of inquiry. Here, as everywhere, the congregations overflowed; and outside meetings in the streets, and in a neighbouring Presbyterian church, were frequently held, by Mr. Moorhouse, Mr. Drummond, and others, with most encouraging results. On one of the last days, while a dense audience had gathered in the building and the service was in progress, the doors were actually burst open by the crowds outside, who attempted to force their way into the building. Fears were excited for the safety

EXTERIOR OF CAMBERWELL HALL.

of the structure, and a panic ensued; however, by the efforts of Mr. Moody, something like quiet was restored, and the meeting went on as usual.

The chief interest at the Camberwell Hall has centered in the inquiry rooms. These have been under the management of four leading pastors, of as many different denominations. The large list of helpers under their direction, having learned a great deal of wisdom in the first months of the revival, have seemed to be particularly blessed in this precious work.

Among the cases which came under his own care, one of the pastors relates the following:—

The son of a minister came to the inquiry room, saying he had attended a meeting just to please his little daughter, who, for some reason or other, had taken to prattling about the revival. A hymn sung by Mr. Sankey had awakened him, and, in spite of the infidel notions which for years he had professed, he quite broke down under it; though by reason of his great wickedness he did not dare to hope for salvation.

"I ran away from home," said he "and joined the French army. In my wild soldier-life I used to profess to be an infidel; but I was a hyprocrite: I believed and feared the Bible all the time.

"Do you think there is any hope for me?" he continued.

"Yes," said the pastor; and he quoted to him that text—"Whosoever believeth," etc. Then they knelt together, and the poor man poured out a most heart-breaking prayer for himself. All at once he stopped. "I almost feel as if I could venture on Christ," said he. "Do you think I may?" "Certainly; at once," was the reply. And then he began to thank God for His patience and long-suffering, in a way that showed his humble gratitude and child-like trust in the Saviour.

Among the converts are several Jews; a great many Roman Catholics; a large number of infidels and scoffers; as well as some choice young men, who will doubtless become evangelists and pastors; thus spreading, in untold circles of blessing, the influence of this marvellous work of grace.

In spite of the complaints that Mr. Moody was partial and one-sided in his views of religious truth, it came to be fully recognised that he knew and could teach certain things, better than any other man had ever done in Great Britain. The first of these was, the doctrine of substitution: "Christ died for us." The second was, the experience of regeneration. The third was, Christian work.

The great revival and its leaders furnished texts for sermons in some of the leading pulpits of England. Mr. Spurgeon discoursed upon his friend Mr. Moody in the Metropolitan Tabernacle; the Rev. Dr. Cumming announced that, on a certain Sabbath, he would attempt to show Mr. Moody's place in prophecy: but whether words were spoken for, or against him, they seemed only to help on the work.

It is to be noticed that the sharpest adverse criticisms came from those who knew least about him; while it often transpired that those who were bitterly opposed to everything of this sort, as they understood it; after hearing an address by Mr. Moody, or a song by Mr. Sankey, and seeing the effects thereof, came to be their personal friends and admirers, and gave a hearty co-operation in the movement.

A considerable number of persons followed in the wake of this great series of revivals; removing their residence as the place of meeting was removed. Some of these persons, eminent for their piety and zeal, were greatly blessed in winning souls to Christ. Mr. Moody himself mentioned a lady, whose name would at once be widely and honourably recognised, who had laboured in the inquiry room ever since the meetings at Edinburgh; and who, up to that time—the last week but one of the two years' campaign—had been the means of bringing a hundred and fifty souls to the Saviour. It was a frequent sight, in the inquiry room at the Opera House, to see eminent Christians, both lay and clerical, pointing out the way of faith and salvation to penitents who were eagerly listening to the best instruction which was possible to be had on such subjects. Distinguished clergymen, coming to the meetings for a few days, entered eagerly into this work. Those who were opposed to this revival, and to all revivals, made special complaint of the inquiry meetings, which they called "confessionals"; but such services, conducted by chosen servants of God, many of whom had for years been honoured pastors of large congregations, were not likely to bring any harm, certainly; but produced untold results for good. Far and wide, throughout all Christendom, the news of the great London revival was spread; and from across the continents and oceans came letters and despatches, begging for prayers on behalf of individuals and communities, or returning thanksgiving for prayers already answered.

The name of one gentleman is mentioned, a colonel in the army in India, who was so deeply interested in the revival in London, where he had two sons residing, who were still out of Christ, that, on only a three months' leave of absence, the most of which must be spent on the ocean, he came in person to London, with the hope of bringing those sons to Christ, by bringing them to the meetings of the evangelists from America.

CONCLUSION.

In an enterprise of such magnitude as that which is here imperfectly outlined, it is evident that no exactness in the matter of results is possible to be attained. At the Agricultural and Bow Road Halls, as well as at the Opera House, converts' meetings were held at the conclusion of the services; to which tickets were issued, after personal examination as to the experience of those who applied for them. The same course is about to be followed at the Camberwell Hall; and while it is impossible to say just how many sinners have been awakened and converted, and how many professors of religion have been brought to a better sense of their privilege and a better performance of their duty, it may be safe to close this record of the two years' revival in Great Britain and Ireland, with the statement, that God has honoured the faith of His servants even beyond their largest hope; and that, besides the multitudes who elsewhere

INTERIOR OF CAMBERWELL HALL.

have been blessed under their labours, Mr. Moody and his friend Mr. Sankey have had the unspeakable joy of winning, in London alone, more than the full "ten thousand souls for Christ."

If it has not already appeared in these pages that the power which attends the ministry of these two men, is of God; and that they are honoured, in this pre-eminent degree, because they speak and sing the simple Gospel of Christ, instead of any doctrines or fancies of their own, then the book has failed of the purpose for which it has been written.

Another manifest reason why such benedictions follow them seems to be, their catholicity of spirit. Mr. Moody would never ask, or even suffer himself to know, the sect to which a minister or worker belonged, save for the purpose of avoiding any seeming partiality or neglect which might accidentally occur; and his heartfelt desire to be a helper, and not a rival, of the ministry, is seen in the fact that, with very very few exceptions, all his meetings have been held at such hours, on the Sabbath day and evening, as would not conflict with regularly established services at the churches.

This man, so humble, so earnest, so forgetful of himself, and so full of faith in Christ, has fairly earned the favour which he has everywhere received; and the Lord Jehovah Himself, as if to show His approbation of such ministry of His Word, has taken this obscure home-missionary from among the ragged children on The Sands, and in the Old North Market Hall, and made his name a word of wonder throughout the Christian world.

CHAPTER X.

GLIMPSES INTO THE WORD.

THE peculiar aptness and power of some of Mr. Moody's running comments on texts of Scripture will appear in the following selections:—

I wish people would use their dictionaries more, and study the meaning of some of these Bible words. There is that word "repentance." Some people are saying, "Why don't Mr. Moody tell us more about repentance?" Well, what is repentance? Some one says it is a "godly sorrow for sin." But I tell you a man can't have a godly sorrow, or a godly anything-else, till after he repents. Repentance means right-about-face! Some one says, "Man is born with his back towards God, and repentance is turning square round."

"What shall I then do with Jesus which is called Christ?" Pilate has Christ on his hands, and now he wants to know how to get rid of Him. So it is with every convicted soul who is not ready to be saved now. Poor Pilate! Poor Herod! Poor Agrippa! How near they got to the kingdom of heaven, and yet never got in!

Do you think it was an awful thing for those Jews to choose Barabbas instead of Jesus? All you who are refusing to become Christians this afternoon are worse than they; for instead of Christ you choose Satan himself.

Judas got near enough to Christ to kiss Him, and yet went down to damnation.

A man once wanted to sell me a "Book of Wonders." I took it and looked it over, and could not find anything in it about Calvary. What a mistake! A book of wonders—and the greatest wonder of all left out!

Poor drunkard!—Come to Christ; Christ is stronger than strong drink!

We have three great enemies: the world, the flesh, and the devil. But we have also three great Friends: the Father, the Son, and the Holy Ghost.

"*Now* is the accepted time." The last night I preached in Farwell Hall, in Chicago, I made the greatest mistake of my life. I told the people to take that text home with them and pray over it. But as we went out the fire-bells were ringing, and I never saw that audience again. The fire had come. The city was in ashes; and perhaps some of those very people were burned up in it. There is no other time to be saved but *now*.

Naaman left only one thing in Samaria, and that was his sin—his leprosy: and the only thing God wishes you to leave is your sin. And yet it is the only thing you seem not to care about giving up. "Oh," you say, "I love leprosy; it is so delightful, I can't give it up. I know God wants it, that He may make me clean. But I can't give it up." Why, what downright madness it is to love leprosy!

Some people tell us it does not make any difference what a man believes if he is only sincere. One Church is just as good as another if you are only sincere. I do not believe any greater delusion ever came out of the pit of hell than that. It is ruining more souls at the present than anything else. I never read of any men more sincere or more earnest than those men at Mount Carmel—those false prophets. They were terribly in earnest. You do not read of men getting so in earnest now that they take knives and cut themselves. Look at them leaping upon their altars ; hear their cry—" Oh Baal ! oh Baal ! " We never heard that kind of prayer on this platform. They acted like madmen. They were terribly in earnest : yet did not God hear their cry ? They were all slain.

Look at poor old Pharaoh down there in Egypt, when the plague of frogs was on him. What an awful time he must have had ! Frogs in the fields, and frogs in the houses ; frogs in the bedrooms, and frogs in the kneading-troughs. When the king went to bed, a frog would jump on to his face ; when he cut into a loaf of bread, there was a frog in the middle of it. Nothing but frogs everywhere ! Frogs, frogs, frogs ! He stood it as long as he could ; and then he sent for Moses, and begged him to take them away. "When would you like to have me do it ?" says Moses. Now just listen to what he says. You would think he would say, Now ! this minute ! I have had them long enough ! But he says,—" *To-morrow.*" Kept the frogs another day, when he might have got rid of them at once ! That is just like you, sinner. You say you want to be saved ; but you are willing to keep your hateful, hideous sins till *to-morrow*, instead of being rid of them *now*.

You have all sinned and come short of the glory of God, but God comes and says, " I will pardon you. Come now, and let us reason together." " Now " is one of the words of the Bible the devil is afraid of. He says, " Do not be in a hurry ; there is plenty of time : do not be good now." He knows the influence of that word "now." " To-morrow " is the devil's word. The Lord's word is "now." God says, " Come now, and let us reason together. Though your sins are as scarlet, they shall be white as snow. Though they be red as crimson, I will make them as wool." Scarlet and crimson are two fast colours ; you would not get the colour out without destroying the garment. God says, " Though your sins are as scarlet and crimson, I will make them as wool and snow. I will do it now."

God says, "Ye shall find me when ye shall search for me with all your heart." Now, it won't take a great while for an anxious sinner to meet an anxious God. It won't take a great while for a man who is really in earnest about the salvation of his soul to find peace in Him. I never yet found a man with his heart really set upon this one thing,—to find God,—but that he soon found his way into the kingdom of heaven. The great trouble with men is, that they are not really in earnest. Men don't seek for God as they seek for wealth and position down here in this world. Suppose I should say to-night that I lost last night in this hall a diamond worth £20,000—which I didn't do; but suppose I should say I did, and that I would give any one £10,000 that found it. I would not give much for the sermon. You would be thinking about the diamond all the evening. You would be thinking, "I wish I could find that diamond. I should like that £10,000." And I can imagine, as soon as the meeting was over—and some of you would not wait for that—you would look about and search this hall. How earnestly you would seek for that diamond! Well, is there a man or woman in this audience who will say that salvation is not worth more than all the diamonds in the world?

Many go all round the world in search of honour or possessions. Salvation is worth thousands of times more; but you don't get it that way. God has but one price for salvation. Do you want to know what it is? It is without money and without price. Rowland Hill said that most auctioneers found they had hard work to get people up to their price, but that he had hard work to get people down to his. "The wages of sin is death, but the gift of God is eternal life." Who will have it to-night? I say to you, young man, will you have that gift to-night? Suppose I was going over London Bridge, and saw a poor miserable beggar, bare-footed, coatless, hatless, with no rags hardly to cover his nakedness,—and right behind him, only a few yards, there was the Prince of Wales with a bag of gold,—and the poor beggar was running away from him as if he was running away from a demon, and the Prince of Wales was calling after him, "Oh, beggar, here is a bag of gold!" Why, we should say the beggar had gone mad, to be running away from the

Prince of Wales with the bag of gold! Sinner, that is your condition. The Prince of Heaven wants to give you eternal life, and you are running away from Him. "The wages of sin is death, but the gift of God is eternal life."

Out in our western country in the autumn, when men go hunting, and there has not been any rain for months, sometimes the prairie grass catches fire, and there comes up a very strong wind, and the flames just roll along twenty feet high, and go at the rate of thirty or forty miles an hour.

When the frontier-men see it coming, what do they do? They know they cannot run as fast as the fire can run. Not the fleetest horse can escape from that fire. They just take a match and light the grass around them, and let the fire sweep it, and then they get into the burnt district and stand safe. They hear the flames roar; they see death coming towards them; but they do not fear, they do not tremble; because the fire has passed over the place where they are, and there is no danger. There is nothing for the fire to burn.

There is one mountain peak that the wrath of God has swept over; that is Mount Calvary, and that fire spent its fury upon the bosom of the Son of God. Take your stand here by the cross, and you will be safe for time and eternity.

Did any of you ever go down into a coalpit, fifteen hundred or two thousand feet, right down into the bowels of the earth? If you have, don't you know that it would be sheer madness to try to climb up the steep sides of that shaft and so get out of the pit? Of course, you couldn't leap out of it; in fact, you couldn't get out of it at all by yourself. But I'll tell you this,—you could get out of a coalpit fifteen hundred feet deep a good deal quicker than you can get out of the pit that Adam took you into. When Adam went down into it, he took the whole human family with him. But the Lord can take us out.

You should be in earnest about seeking God. He was in earnest when he gave His Son to die for sinners. Christ was *in earnest* when He hung upon the cross.

"I waited patiently for the Lord, and He inclined unto me; and heard my cry. He brought me up also out of an horrible pit, out of the miry clay, and set my feet upon a rock, and established my goings; and He hath put a new song in my mouth." Now in those three verses that little word *He* occurs three times: *He* heard my cry; *He* brought me up out of the pit; and *He* put a new song in my mouth. There is nothing there for the sinner to do—is there? *He* does it all. The great trouble people have now-a-days is to make a new song for themselves. Why, you cannot sing without God tunes your heart and voice! You cannot establish your own goings. You have tried that—have you not? How many times have you tried to get the control over your temper, or said, I will do this, and I will do that, and have failed every time? You can't do it yourselves. *He* must do the saving.

A good many people are complaining all the time about themselves, and crying out;—"My leanness! my leanness!" when they ought rather to say, "My laziness! my laziness!"

There is a large class of people who are always looking upon the dark side. Some time ago, I myself got under the juniper tree. In those days I used to fish all night, and catch nothing. One of the workers in our Mission came in to see me one Monday morning, full of joy, saying what a good Sunday he had. "Well," said I, "I am glad you have had a good day; but I have had a very bad one." He knew I had been in trouble of mind and so he said, "Did you ever study Noah?" "No," said I; "I have read about him, but I don't know that I have ever studied him." "Well," said he, "study him. It will do you good." So I began to study Noah, and I found out that he preached for a hundred and twenty years without making a single convert. "That is a good deal worse than my case," thought I; and that made me feel better at once. That day I went down to the noon prayer-meeting, and one poor sinner rose and asked us to pray for him. "What would old Noah have given for that?" thought I. I tell you, my friends, what we want is perseverance. When God sets us at anything, we want to keep at it, and leave all the consequences with Him.

I can imagine when Christ said to the little band around Him, "Go ye into all the world and preach the Gospel," Peter said, "Lord, do You really mean that we are to go back to Jerusalem and preach the Gospel to those men that murdered You?" "Yes," said Christ; "go, hunt up that man that spit in my face, and tell him he shall have a seat in my kingdom if he will accept of salvation as a gift. Yes, Peter; go, find that man that made that cruel crown of thorns and placed it on my brow, and tell him I will have a crown ready for him when he comes into my kingdom, and no thorns in it. I will give him a crown of life. Hunt up that man that took a reed and brought it down over the cruel thorns, driving them into my brow, and tell him I will put a sceptre in his hand, and he shall rule over the nations of the earth if he will accept salvation. Search for the man that drove the spear into my side, and tell him there is a nearer way to my heart than that. Tell him I forgive him freely, and that he can be saved if he will accept of salvation as a gift. Go to the men that drove the nails into my hands and feet, and tell them I forgive them freely, and that they shall have a seat in my kingdom if they will accept of it. Go ye into all the world, and preach the Gospel to *every* creature."

Many think they have been born again because they go to church. A great many say, "Oh! yes, I am a Christian; I go to church every Sabbath." Let me say here that there is no one in all London that goes to church so regularly as Satan. He is always there before the minister, and he is the last one out. There is not a church or a chapel, in London, but that he is a regular attendant of it. The idea that he is only down in the slums and lanes and alleys of London is a false one. The idea that he is only in public-houses—I will confess I think he is there, and that he is doing his work very well—but to think that he is only there, is a false idea. He is wherever the Word is preached; it is his business to be there and catch away the seed. He is here to-night. Some of you may go to sleep, but he won't. Some of you may not listen to the sermon, but he will. He will be watching, and when the seed is just entering into some heart he will go and catch it away. Now, I tell you, my dear friends, before you get home the devil will meet you and say,

"Don't believe it,—you can't be saved that easy"; and you will have a terrible struggle with him. But I'll tell you what to do when he meets you. Just quote Scripture to him, and he will flee away at once. That's what the Saviour did. He said to him, "It is written—it is written,"—and away went the devil in an instant; he couldn't stand Scripture. And that's the only way to conquer him. Say to him, "It is written, and I believe the Word of God before I believe you, devil,"—and depend on it he will leave you.

It is said of David's mighty men that they were right and left-handed. They were wholly consecrated; they could use their left or their right hands for the king. That is what we want in London. Men who are right-handed and left-handed for the King of Glory. Men who can use their eyes, and tongues, and ears, and everything for the Lord Jesus.

The most powerful sermon Christ ever preached was His discourse to Nicodemus. I believe there have been more souls born again by reading the third chapter of St. John's Gospel than by reading any other chapter in the Bible. And that beautiful and wonderful sermon was preached to *one man* only! If we Christians have the same mind that Christ had, not despising the day of small things, but each one of us doing what we can to bring some one to the Saviour, we shall see a great work accomplished.

When Jesus, along with His little band of disciples, came to the grave wherein Lazarus was laid, they found it covered by a stone. Jesus could have removed the stone Himself; but, notice, He bade His followers to remove the stone. And we find that after the Master had restored the dead man to life, He also said to them: "Loose him, and let him go." The Master could have loosed him; but He said to His disciples: "You loose him." What lesson does the Master mean to teach us by this? He means to teach His followers that, whilst He alone can speak the word of life to dead souls, He wants us to remove the stone, and to loose the poor souls and let them go. He would have us to be co-workers with Him.

When men going up in a balloon have ascended a little height, things down here begin to look very small indeed. What had seemed very grand and imposing, now seem as mere nothings; and the higher they rise the smaller everything on earth appears; —it gets fainter and fainter as they rise, till the railway train, dashing along at fifty miles an hour, seems like a thread, and scarcely appears to be moving at all, and the grand piles of buildings seem now like mere dots. So it is when we get near heaven: earth's treasures, earth's cares, look very small.

There are but few now that say, "Here am I, Lord; send me": the cry now is, "Send some one else. Send the minister, send the church officers, the churchwardens, the elders; but not me. I have not got the ability, the gifts, or the talents." Ah! honestly say you have not got the heart; for if the heart is loyal, God can use you. It is really all a matter of heart. It does not take God a great while to qualify a man for his work, if he only has the heart for it.

Read the 103rd Psalm, and mark how the Psalmist bids us "forget not all His benefits." Some one has said we cannot remember them all, but we must not forget them all—they are too numerous to keep them all in mind, but let us keep some of them in mind. Observe five things in the 3rd, 4th, and 5th verses of this psalm:—(1) "He forgiveth all thine iniquities." (2) "He healeth all thy diseases." (3) "He redeemeth thy life from destruction." (4) "He crowneth thee with loving-kindness and tender mercies." But there are very many crowned heads that are still not satisfied. God, therefore, does more,—(5) "He satisfieth thy soul." What more can we have than that?

"Except a man be born again, he cannot see the kingdom of God." I often rejoice Christ did not say this to that woman at the well, nor to that woman who was a sinner. If He had spoken it to them, people would have said, "Oh, that poor woman needed to be converted; but I am a moral character—I do not need to be converted. Regeneration will do for harlots, thieves, and drunkards; but we who are moral do not need it." But who did Christ say this to? He said it to Nicodemus. Who was he? He was one of the church dignitaries; he stood as high as any man in Jerusalem, except the high priest himself. He belonged to the seventy rulers of the Jews; he was a doctor of divinity, and taught the law. There is not one word of Scripture against him; he was a man that stood out before the whole nation as of pure and spotless character. And what does Christ say to him?—"Except a man be born again, he cannot see the kingdom of God."

There are some who say, "We don't have any sympathy with these special efforts"; and I sympathize with that objection. I believe it is the privilege of the child of God to make *continuous* efforts for the salvation of others, every day throughout the year.

Let no time be spent in arguments. I believe that is a work of the devil, to take off attention and cause delay. If a man comes to argue, we should go on our knees, pray with him, and then let him go. Job never fell until he got into an argument with his friends; he could stand his boils, and all his other afflictions, better than an argument.

Our Lord said on one occasion, "There is no man that hath left house, or brethren, or sisters, or father, or mother, or wife, or children, or lands, for my sake and the Gospel's, but he shall receive a hundredfold more in this present world, and in the world to come life everlasting." But Peter answering said, "Lo, we have left *all*, and followed Thee." So it always is. We make much of our sacrifices. What *had* the disciples left? A few old broken nets, and some boats. What did they get in exchange? The kingdom of God!

Many of the Bible characters fell just in the things in which they were thought to be strongest. Moses failed in his humility, Abraham in his faith, Elijah in his courage, for one woman scared him away to that juniper tree; and Peter, whose strong point was boldness, was so frightened by a maid, as to deny his Lord.

One reason why we don't have more answers to our prayers is because we are not thankful enough. The Divine injunction is, "Be careful for nothing; but in everything by prayer and supplication, *with thanksgiving*, let your requests be made known unto God." Some one has well said there are three things in this verse: careful for nothing—prayerful for everything—thankful for anything.

"And now abideth faith, hope, charity—these three; but the greatest of these is charity." Love is the greatest of God's gifts, and of all the Christian virtues. I don't think we shall require faith when we get to heaven. Before the throne of God we shall walk by sight, and not by faith. Nor shall we need hope there, as we shall have attained to the full measure of possession. Faith and hope will be past, but love will still reign. Therefore love is called the greatest.

A friend of mine was walking along the streets one dark night, when he saw a man coming along with a lantern. As he came up close to him, he noticed by the bright light that the man had no eyes. He went past him; but the thought struck him, "Surely that man is blind!" He turned round and said, "My friend, are you not blind?" "Yes," was the answer. "Then what have you got the lantern for?" "I carry the lantern," said the blind man, "that people may not stumble over me." Let us take a lesson from that blind man, and hold up our light, burning with the clear radiance of heaven, that men may not stumble over us.

I once heard of two men who, under the influence of liquor, came down one night to where their boat was tied; they wanted to return home, so they got in and began to row. They pulled away hard all night, wondering why they never got to the other side of the bay. When the grey dawn of morning broke, behold, they had never loosed the mooring line or raised the anchor! And that's just the way with many who are striving to enter the kingdom of heaven. They cannot believe, because they are tied to this world. Cut the cord! cut the cord! Set yourselves free from the clogging weight of earthly things, and you will soon go on towards heaven.

When it is dark and stormy here, strive to rise higher and higher, near to Christ; and you will find it all calm there. You know that it is the highest mountain peaks that catch the first rays of the sun. So those who rise highest catch the first news from heaven. It is those sunny Christians who go through the world with smiles on their faces, that win souls. And, on the other hand, it is those Christians who go through the world hanging their heads like bulrushes, that scare people away from religion. Why, it's a libel on Christianity for a religious man to go about with such a downcast look! What does the Master say?—"My joy I leave with you, my *joy* I give unto you." Depend upon it, if our minds were stayed upon Him, we should have perfect peace; and with perfect peace we should have perfect joy.

I have an idea there are thousands of crownless saints in heaven. They just barely get in at the doors. They have, indeed, been redeemed by the blood of the Lamb; but there is no reward for them. They have sought their own ease in this world; they have not sought to work for Christ here below; therefore, though admitted to heaven, they enjoy no distinguished reward. "They that be wise shall shine as the brightness of the firmament; and they that turn many to righteousness as the stars for ever and ever." But none of those that have lost heart, and have given up working for the Master here, will shine as the stars, or receive the great reward hereafter. For those careless ones there is no bright glory, no place near the throne; they have just got in at the gates—that's all!

Paul said he was the "chief of sinners"; and if the chief has gone up on high, there is hope for everybody else. The devil makes us believe that we are good enough without salvation, if he can; and if he cannot make us believe that, he says, "You are so bad the Lord won't have you"; and so he tries to make people believe they are either too good or too bad to be converted.

In those words which He read in the synagogue at Nazareth, shortly after His baptism by John, Christ tells us His mission to the world :—"The Spirit of the Lord is upon me, because He hath anointed me to preach the Gospel to the poor; He hath sent me to heal the broken-hearted, to preach deliverance to the captives, and recovering of sight to the blind, to set at liberty them that are bruised, to preach the acceptable year of the Lord." Our Saviour was reading from the passage in Isaiah lxi. 1; and He ceased reading and closed the book in the middle of a sentence. The verse continues, "And the day of vengeance of our God." Christ came to preach the Gospel. By-and-by He will come again, and commence to read where He then left off. There is an awful day coming, when those who scoff and jeer now will hold a very solemn prayer-meeting. Their prayer already stands recorded in Holy Writ. They will call upon the rocks and mountains to fall upon them and hide them from the wrath of God.

CHAPTER XI.

NEW STORIES FROM AN OLD BOOK.

ONE peculiar charm of Mr. Moody's preaching is the fresh and lifelike style in which he tells Bible stories. To him those Scripture characters are real men and women; and he makes them seem as real to his audience as to himself.

It is a little surprising at first to see those ancient worthies behaving themselves like citizens of London or Chicago: wearing modern costumes, speaking English in Mr. Moody's own vernacular, and permitting him to turn their heads and hearts inside out, in order to show his hearers what is going on in there. But when the effect of the shock has passed away, the force and moral of their story begins to be appreciated as it scarcely could be, if set forth with Oriental stateliness of language, and covered with the dust of remote antiquity.

Irreverent people sometimes laugh at the idea of Shadrach, Meshach, and Abed-nego, tumbling into Nebuchadnezzar's fiery furnace, in broadcloth coats and trousers, stove-pipe hats, and Wellington boots; or to hear King David telling his experience, like a man in a Methodist class-meeting, and not always in grammatical style. But there is no small advantage in having these men modernised; for thereby their trials and triumphs come home to men's own hearts, making them feel that the Scriptures are not out of date, but were written for the learning and encouragement of all ages and all people; and leading them to say: What God did for these old-time believers, He is just as willing to do for me.

In this chapter it is proposed to give some of those old stories in their new dress, as Mr. Moody tells them.

It must be borne in mind that he never tells a story merely because it is interesting, or to help fill up the time, but always to illustrate and enforce the Gospel.

STORY OF A BLIND MAN.

IN the 18th chapter of the Gospel of St. Luke, you will find Christ was going into Jericho; and as He drew near the gates of the city there was a poor blind man who sat by the wayside, begging people to give him a farthing, and crying out, "Have mercy on a poor blind man!" This blind beggar met a man who said to him, "Bartimeus, I have good news to tell you." "What is it?" said the beggar. "There is a man of Israel who can give you sight." "Oh no!" said the blind beggar; "there is no chance of my ever receiving my sight. I never shall see. In fact, I never saw the mother who gave me birth; I never saw the wife of my bosom; I never saw my own children. I never saw in this world; but I expect to see in the world to come."

"Let me tell you, I have just come down from Jerusalem, and I saw that village carpenter, Jesus of Nazareth; and I saw a man who was born blind, who had received his sight; and I never saw a man with better sight. He doesn't even have to use glasses." Then hope rises for the first time in this poor man's heart, and he says, "Tell me how the man got his sight."

"Oh," says the other, "Jesus first spat on the ground and made clay, and put it on his eyes"—why, that is enough to put a man's sight out, to fill his eyes with clay!—"and then He old him to wash his eyes in the Pool of Siloam, and he would receive his sight. More than that, Bartimeus, He doesn't charge you anything: you have no fee to pay; you just tell Him what you want, and get you get it, without money and without price. It does not need dukes, or lords, or influence; you just call upon Him yourself; and if He ever comes this way, don't let Him go back without your going to see Jesus." And Bartimeus said, "I will try it; there's no harm in trying it." I can imagine him being led by a child to his seat as usual, and that he is crying out, "Please give a blind beggar a farthing." He hears the footsteps of the coming multitude, and inquires, Who is it passing? What does the multitude mean? They tell him it is Jesus of Nazareth passing by. The moment he hears that he says, "Why, that is the Man that gave sight to the blind!" The moment it reached his ear that it was Jesus of Nazareth, he began to cry out at the top of his voice, "Jesus, thou Son of David, have mercy upon me!" Some of those who went before—perhaps Peter was one them—rebuked him, thinking the Master was going up to Jerusalem to be crowned King, and did not want to be distracted. They never knew the Son of God when He was here. He would hush every harp in heaven to hear a sinner pray; no music would delight Him so much. But the blind man still lifted up his voice, and cried louder, "Thou Son of David, have mercy on me!" and the prayer reached the ears of the Son of God, as prayer always will; and they led the poor blind man to Him. Well, when Jesus heard the blind beggar, He commanded him to be brought. So they ran to him, and said, "Be of good cheer: the Master calls you; He has a blessing for you." When Jesus saw him He said, "What can I do for you?" "Lord, that I may receive my sight." "You shall have it": and the Lord gave it to him. And now the beggar follows with the crowd, glorifying God. I can imagine he sang as sweetly as Mr. Sankey; no one sang sweeter than he when he shouted, "Hosanna to the Son of David!"—no one sang louder than this one who had received his sight. Then he follows on with the crowd, which we see pressing into the gates of the city. I can imagine when he gets into the city he says to himself, "I will go down and see Mrs. Bartimeus,"—having, of course, after all those years of blindness, a curiosity to see what his wife looked like.

As he is passing down the street, a man meets him, and turns round and says, "Bartimeus, is that you?"

"Yes; it's me."

"Well, I thought it was, and yet I thought my eyes must deceive me. How did you get your sight?"

"I just met Jesus of Nazareth outside the walls of the city, and I asked Him to have mercy on me; and He gave me my sight."

"Jesus of Nazareth! is He in this part of the country?"

"Yes; He is on His way to Jerusalem. He is now going down to the eastern gate."

"I should like to see Him," says the man, and away he runs down the street; but he cannot get a glimpse of Him, being little of stature, on account of the great throng round Him. He runs to a sycamore tree, and says to himself, "If I get up there and hide, without any one seeing me, He cannot get by without my having a good look at Him." A great many rich men do not like to be seen coming to Jesus. Well, there he is in the sycamore tree, on a branch hanging right over the highway; and he says to himself, "He cannot get by without my having a good look at Him." All at once the crowd comes in sight. He looks at John—"That's not Him"; he looks at Peter—"That's not Him." Then he sees One who is fairer than the sons of men. "That's Him!" And Zacchæus, just peeping out from amongst the branches, looks down upon that wonderful—yes, that mighty God-Man, in amazement. At last the crowd comes to the tree, and it looks as if Christ is going by; but He stops right under the tree. All at once He looks up and sees Zacchæus, and says to him, "Zacchæus, make haste and come down." I can imagine Zacchæus says to himself,—"I wonder who told Him my name. I was never introduced to Him." But Christ knew all about him. Sinner! Christ knows all about you; He knows your name and your house. Do not think God does not know you. If you would try to hide from Him, bear in mind that you cannot do so. He knows where each one of you is; He knows all about your sins. Well, He said to Zacchæus, "Make haste and come down." He may have added, "This is the last time I shall pass this way, Zacchæus." That is the way He speaks to sinners,—"This may be the last time I shall pass this way; this may be your last chance of eternity." He may be passing away from some soul to-night. Oh sinner! make haste and come down and receive Him. There are some people in this nineteenth century who do not believe in sudden conversions. I should like them to tell me where Zacchæus was converted. He certainly was not converted when he went up into the tree; he certainly was converted when he came down. He must have been converted somewhere between the branches and the ground. The Lord converted him just right there. People say they do not believe in sudden conversions; and that if a man is converted suddenly he won't hold out—he won't be genuine. I wish we had a few men converted like Zacchæus in London; it would make no small stir. When a man begins to make restitution, it is a pretty good sign of conversion. Let men give back money dishonestly obtained in London, and see how quick people will believe in conversion. Zacchæus gave half his goods to the poor. What would be said if some of the rich men of London did that? Zacchæus gave half his goods all at once; and he says, "If I have taken anything from any man falsely, I restore him fourfold." I think that is the other half. But to get Christ is worth more than all his wealth. I imagine the next morning one of the servants of Zacchæus going with a cheque for £100, and saying, "My master a few years ago took from you wrongfully about £25, and this is restitution money." That would give confidence in Zacchæus's conversion. I wish a few cases like that would happen in London, and then people would not go on talking against sudden conversions.

THE STORY OF MEPHIBOSHETH.

1 SAMUEL XX. 14, 15; and 2 SAMUEL ix.

THERE is a story, my friends, in the books of Samuel—away back as far as the time of the kings of Israel—which will help us to understand the Gospel. It is about a man of the name of Mephibosheth.

You remember what a hard time David had when Saul was hunting him to kill him, just as men hunt game.

Well: one day David and his good friend Jonathan were

taking a walk together in the fields. Saul was very angry, and was bent on killing David; but his son Jonathan was looking out for a chance to save him. It had been revealed to him that David was to be king after his father, instead of himself; but this did not hinder his love for David. It must have been real, true friendship, that could stand that sort of thing!

After they had agreed upon a sign by which David was to know whether it was safe for him to stay around the court of the king, where he could see his friend once in a while; or whether he must leave, and go off into the cave of Adullam, Jonathan says to him,—

"David, it has been revealed to me that you are to be king after my father. Now, I want you to promise me one thing: when you come to the throne, if any of the house of Saul are alive, I want you to be good to them, for my sake."

"I'll do that, of course," said David. So he made a solemn covenant to that effect, and then he went off to the cave of Adullam, to get out of the way of Saul, who was bound to kill him if he could.

But God took care of David. You never can kill or harm a man, if God is taking care of him.

About four years after that, David heard that there had been a great battle over by Mount Gilboa, and that the Philistines had beaten the Israelites with great slaughter, and that Saul and Jonathan were both dead. So he got his men together, and went out after the enemies of the Lord and of Israel; and it was not a great while before he had turned the tables on them, and set up his kingdom at Hebron.

It must have been pretty near fourteen years after that before David remembered his promise to his old friend Jonathan. It is a great deal easier to make promises than to keep them. How many broken vows has God written down against you to-night? But one day the king was walking in his palace at Jerusalem, where he had removed his capital; and all at once he happened to think of that promise. It is a good thing God does not forget *His* promises that way.

"That's too bad!" said David. "I forgot all about that promise. I have been so busy fighting these Philistines, and fixing things up, that I have not had time to think of anything else." So he called his servants in great haste, and said, "Do any of you know whether there is any of Saul's family living?"

One of them said there was an old servant of Saul's by the name of Ziba, and maybe he could tell.

"Go and tell him I want him, right away."

Pretty soon Ziba came; and David said, "Ziba, do you know whether there is anybody of the house of Saul in my kingdom?" Ziba said there was one he knew of—a son of Jonathan, by the name of Mephibosheth.

Oh how that name, Jonathan, must have smitten the heart of David! One of the sons of his old friend living in his kingdom for as much as fourteen years, and he had never known it! What would Jonathan think of him for forgetting his promise that way!

"Go, fetch him!" says David; "go quick. Tell him I want him. I want to show him the kindness of God."

Now, my friends, where do you suppose Mephibosheth was all this time? Why, he was down at Lo-debar. Did you ever hear of that place? There may be some sailors here: did you ever come across that port? When you have travelled on the railway, did any of you ever stop at that station?

Ah! yes: that is where the whole human race are until they come to Christ for salvation; away down at Lo-debar,—which means, *a place of no pasture.*

The king is in haste to keep his promise now. I seem to see them hurrying off; maybe they take the king's own chariot, and rattle away to find this son of Jonathan.

When they reached the little out-of-the-way place, I fancy there was a great commotion.

"Where's Mephibosheth? The king wants him."

Poor fellow! when he heard that he hung down his head He was afraid the king wanted to kill him, because he was of the house of Saul, his old enemy.

Ah! my friends; that's just the way sinners receive Christ's offers of salvation. They think God hates them, and wants to cut their heads off. But that is a great mistake. God loves them for Christ's sake, a great deal more than David loved Mephibosheth for Jonathan's sake. I never knew a sinner to take the Gospel right. They always think, at first, that it is too good to be true.

"Don't be afraid," said the servants. "The king says he wants to show you the kindness of God. He is in a great hurry to see you ; so get ready, and jump right into the chariot. Don't you see the king has sent his own chariot to fetch you?"

It did begin to look as if the king meant no harm to him. But poor Mephibosheth had another difficulty. He was lame in both feet. He was a little fellow when David came to the throne ; and an old servant, who was afraid that all the house of Saul were going to be killed, took him up and ran away to hide him. Somehow he managed to drop the lad, and lamed him in both feet.

And now I can see poor Mephibosheth looking down at his feet. Maybe the toes turned in,—or he was club-footed. And he says to himself, "I am not fit to go to the king. I am a poor cripple. I am not fit to be seen among the tall, handsome servants of the palace in Jerusalem."

That's just the way with a convicted sinner. He is all the time thinking of his own unworthiness, and saying to himself that he isn't fit to be saved.

"Never mind your lame feet, Mephibosheth ; so long as the king sends for you, it's all right." So they take him up, and put him into the chariot, and start for Jerusalem on a run.

As soon as the king sees him, he takes him in his arms, and cries out,—

"Oh Mephibosheth, the son of my dear old friend Jonathan! you shall have all that belonged to the house of Saul; and you shall live with me here in my palace!"

What a happy man he must have been to hear that! Sinner, that is just what God says to the soul that comes to him in Jesus Christ. He takes us in His arms ; He gives us a great fortune of love and grace ; and He promises that we shall live with Him in His heavenly palace for ever.

Some people think that Mephibosheth, like certain low-spirited Christians, after he went to live with the king, must have been all the time worrying over his lame feet. But I don't think so. He couldn't help it ; and if David didn't mind it, it was all right. So I think that when he dined with him in state, with the great lords and ladies all around him, he just stuck his club-feet under the table, and looked the king right in the face.

That is the Gospel, my friends. We are God's enemies, and the children of His enemies. We are lame, and blind, and wretched, and ragged, and hateful by reason of our sins. But the covenant of grace in Jesus Christ has been made; and now God sends for you, poor sinner, to come in Christ's name and eat bread at His table, and be in His house, and in His heart for ever. Will you come? Will you come *now?*

THE STORY OF BARABBAS.

I HAVE often thought what a night Barabbas must have spent just before the day when Christ was crucified.

As the sun goes down, he says to himself: "To-morrow!—only to-morrow! And I must die on the cross. They will hang me up before a crowd of people; they will drive nails through my hands and feet; they will break my legs with bars of iron; and in that awful torture I shall die before this time to-morrow, and go up to the judgment with all my crimes upon me."

Maybe, they let his mother come to see him once more before dark. Perhaps he had a wife and children, and they came to see him for the last time.

He couldn't sleep at all that night. He could hear somebody hammering in the prison-yard, and knew they must be making the cross.

He would start up every now and then, thinking he heard the footsteps of the officers coming for him.

At last the light of the morning looks in through the bars of his prison.

"To-day—this very day—they will open that door and lead me away to be crucified!"

Pretty soon he hears them coming. No mistake this time. They are unbarring the iron door. He hears them turning the key in the rusty lock. The door swings open; there are the soldiers.

Good-bye to life and hope! Death, horrible death now!—and, after death, what will there be then?

The officer of the guard speaks to him:—"Barabbas, you are free!"

He hears the strange words, but they make very little impression on him. He is so near dead with fear and horror, that the good news doesn't reach him. He hears it; but thinks it is a foolish fancy. He is asleep and dreaming. He stands gazing a moment at the soldiers, and then he comes to himself.

"Don't laugh at me! don't make sport of me! Take me away and crucify me; but don't tear my soul to pieces!"

Again the officer speaks: "*You are free!* Here—the door is open: go out; go home."

Now he begins to take in the truth; but it is so wonderful a thing to get out of the clutches of the Roman law, that he is afraid to believe the good news. And so he begins to doubt, and to ask how it can be.

They tell him that Pilate has promised the Jews the release of one prisoner that day; and that the Jews have chosen him instead of one Jesus of Nazareth, who was condemned to be crucified.

Now the poor man begins to weep. This breaks his heart. He knows this Jesus. He has seen Him do some of His miracles. He was in the crowd picking pockets when Jesus fed the five thousand hungry people.

"What! that just man to die—and I, a thief, a highwayman, a murderer, to go free!" And in the midst of his joy at his own release, his heart breaks at the thought that his life is saved at such a cost.

Sinner, that is the Gospel. Christ died for you, "the just for the unjust." "He was bruised for our iniquities, and by His stripes we are healed."

Come out of your prison; throw off the chains of sin. You were justly condemned, but Jesus died for you. Let your heart break in penitence; weep tears of love and joy.

ELIJAH AND THE PRIESTS OF BAAL.

LET us go to Carmel for a few minutes.

King Ahab had forsaken the God of Israel, and all the court people and "upper ten" had followed his example.

But there was an old prophet out in the mountains, to whom God said: "Go to Ahab, and tell him the heavens shall be shut up and there shall be no rain."

Away he goes to the wicked king. He bursts in upon him like a clap of thunder, gives his message, and hurries away.

I suppose Ahab laughed at the old prophet. "What! no more rain? Why, the fellow must be crazy!"

Pretty soon the weather gets very dry. The earth is parched, and begins to crack open. The rivers have but little water in them, and the brooks dry up altogether. The trees die; all the grass perishes, and the cattle die too. Famine; starvation; death! If rain doesn't come pretty soon, there won't be a live man or woman left in all the kingdom.

One day the king was talking with the prophet Obadiah.

You see he did have one good man near him, along with all the prophets of the false god. Almost anybody likes to have one good man within reach, even if he is ever so bad. He may be wanted in a hurry some time.

"See here, Obadiah," says King Ahab; "you go one way, and I'll go another, and we'll see if we can't find some water somewhere."

Obadiah hadn't got a great way before Elijah bursts out upon him.

"Oh, Elijah! is that you? Ahab has been hunting for you everywhere, and couldn't find you. He has sent off into all the kingdoms about, to have them fetch you if you were there."

"Yes; I'm here," says Elijah. "You go and tell Ahab I want to see him."

"I dare not do that," says Obadiah; "for just as soon as I tell him you are here, the Spirit will catch you away and take you off somewhere else; and then the king will be very angry, and maybe he'll kill me."

"No," says Elijah. "As the Lord liveth, I will meet Ahab face to face this day."

So Obadiah hurries off to find Ahab, and tells him he has seen the prophet.

"What! Elijah?"

"Yes."

"Why didn't you bring him along?"

"He wouldn't come. He says he wants you to come to him."

Ahab wasn't used to have people talk that way to him; but he was anxious to see the prophet, so he went. And when he sees him he is very angry, and cries, "Art thou he that troubleth Israel?"

"Not at all," says Elijah. "You are the man that is troubling Israel—going off after Baal, and leading ever so many of the people with you. Now, we have had enough of this sort of thing. Some people are praying to God, and some are praying to Baal, and we must have this question settled. You just bring all your prophets and all the priests of Baal up to Mount Carmel, and I also will come. We will make us each an altar, and offer sacrifice on it; and the God that answereth by fire, let Him be God."

"Agreed," says Ahab; and off he goes to tell his priests and get ready for the trial.

I fancy that was a great day when that question was decided. All the places of business were closed, and everybody was going up to Mount Carmel. There must have been more people on Mount Carmel than there are to-day at the races.* A better class of people too!

There were eight hundred and fifty of the prophets and priests of Baal altogether. I fancy I can see them going up in a grand procession, with the king in his chariot at their head.

"Fine-looking men, ain't they?" says one man to another as they go by. "They'll be able to do great things up there on the mountain."

But there Elijah marched, all alone: a rough man, clad in the skins of beasts, with a staff in his hand. No banners, no procession, no great men in his train! But the man who could hold the keys of heaven for three years and six months was not afraid to be alone.

Now says Elijah to the people, "How long halt ye between two opinions? Let the priests of Baal build them an altar and offer sacrifice, but put no fire under; and I will do the same: and the God that answereth by fire, let Him be God."

So the priests of Baal build their altar.

I am sure if God hadn't held him back, Satan would have brought up a little spark out of hell to set that sacrifice on fire. But God wouldn't let him.

Then they begin to pray: "Oh Baal, hear us! Oh Baal, hear us!"

Elijah might have said, "Why haven't you prayed to Baal

* This was given on Derby Day, at the Opera House, Haymarket, London.

for water this dry weather? You might just as well have asked him for water as for fire."

After a long time they begin to get hoarse.

"You must pray louder than that, if you expect Baal to hear you," says the old prophet. "Maybe he is asleep: pray louder, so as to wake him up."

Poor fellows! they haven't any voice left; so they begin to pray in blood. They cut themselves with knives, and lift their streaming hands and arms to Baal. But no fire comes down.

It is getting towards sundown.

The prophet of the Lord builds an altar. Mind; he doesn't have anything to do with the altar of Baal, but builds an entirely different one, on the ruins of the altar of the Lord which had been broken down.

"We won't have anybody saying there is any trick about this thing," says the prophet. So they bring twelve barrels of water and pour over the altar. I don't know how they managed to get so much water; but they did it.

Then Elijah prays: "Oh God of Abraham and of Isaac and of Jacob, let it be known this day that Thou art God in Israel."

He didn't have to pray very loud. God heard him at once, and—*down came the fire!!* It burnt up the sacrifice, burnt up the wood, burnt up the water, and burnt up the very stones of the altar. Jehovah is God: nobody can halt any longer.

Ah! but some of you say, "I too would have decided for God if I had been on Mount Carmel that day." My friends, Calvary is a great deal more wonderful than Carmel. The sacrifice of Christ on the cross is more wonderful than the sacrifice which was burned on that altar.

Decide for Christ now, with Calvary in sight. Choose *ye* this day whom ye will serve.

THE LEPER.

SEE that poor leper! Do you know what an awful thing the leprosy is? A disease so terrible that it separates its victim from all the world, and makes him an outcast, even from his home. Every one is afraid of him. His disease is so contagious, that to touch him, or even to breathe the air near him, is dangerous ; and so these poor afflicted wretches have to go away and live in caves and deserts by themselves. They sit by the wayside afar off, calling to the passers-by for charity,—who sometimes throw them a piece of money, and hurry away lest they also come into that terrible plight. Here is a poor man who finds the marks of what he thinks is this terrible disease upon his body. According to the law, he must go to the priest and be examined. Alas ! the priest says it is the leprosy —nothing else.

Now the poor man, with broken heart, turns away from the Temple, and goes to his house to say good-bye to his wife, and to take his children to his arms once more, before he goes away to spend the long years in the wilderness alone, or with other lepers like himself, until death shall come to deliver him from his sufferings. What a sorry house is that ! Surely this is worse than death itself. He goes out of his door with no hope of ever entering it again. He walks the street by himself, and if any one comes near, he lifts up his voice in that mournful cry, "Unclean ! Unclean !" Out of the gates of the city he goes, away from all his friends and acquaintances, carrying with him the sorrow of separation and the seeds of death. One day he sees a crowd passing along the road, but he dares not go near enough to inquire what it is. All at once he happens to think it may be that Prophet of Nazareth whom he has heard of—that same Man that, people said, could open the eyes of blind men, make lame men to walk, and who had even raised the son of the widow from death, over there at Nain. If only it were He ! At any rate he will take the chances, and cry out after Him ; and so he shouts, at the top of his voice, "Have mercy upon me!" All the rest of the crowd are afraid of him ; but Jesus, who is in the midst, hears some one calling ; and, just as He always did when anybody wanted anything of Him, He stopped to find out what it was. He is not afraid of the leper ; and so, while the rest of the crowd stand away by themselves, He calls the poor fellow up to Him and asks him what he wants ; and the leper, with his heart full of anxious hope, replies, "Lord, if Thou wilt, Thou canst make me clean." "I will," says Jesus : "be thou clean!" A strange sense of health and strength suddenly comes over the man. He looks at his hands, and finds the leprosy is all gone. He begins to pour out his heart in thanks to Jesus, who sends him away to the priests, saying, "Go, show thyself to the priest, and offer the gift that Moses commanded.

Now I seem to see that cleansed leper hurrying away to show himself to the priest, to be pronounced cured, according to the law; and then hastening to his little home, to see his wife and children once more. He bursts into the house, weeping for joy. He stretches out his arms to his wife and little ones, saying, "I am clean! I am clean! Jesus did it—Jesus of Nazareth."

Sinner, how glad you would be if Jesus had made you clean from the leprosy of sin!—and He is just as willing to cleanse you as He was to cleanse this poor leper. Come to Him just now. Ask Him to cleanse you, and hear Him say, "I will: be thou clean!"

THE WIDOW'S SON.

THINK of that poor widow at Nain! She is an old woman now; and her only son, who is the staff of her life, is sick. How she watches him; sits up all night to see that he has his medicine at the right time; sits by his bedside all day, fanning him, keeping away the flies, moistening his parched lips with water! Everything he asks for, she brings. The very best doctor in Nain is sent for; and when he comes and feels the pulse of the young man, and looks at his tongue, he shakes his head; and then the poor woman knows there is no hope for her boy. What an awful thought! My son, my only son must die: what will become of me then? Sure enough, the doctor is right; and in a little while the fever comes to its crisis, and the poor boy dies, with his head upon his mother's bosom. The people come in to try to comfort the poor woman; but it is of no use. Her heart is broken. She wishes she were dead too.

Some of you know what it is to look your last upon the faces of those you love. Some of you mothers have wept hot tears upon the cold faces of your sons.

Well: they make him ready for burial; and when the time comes, they celebrate the funeral service, and put him on the bier to carry him away to the grave. What a sad procession! Just as they come out of the city gates, they see a little company of thirteen dusty-looking travellers, coming up the road. There is One among them, tall and far fairer than the sons of men. Who can He be? He is moved with compassion when He sees this little funeral procession; and it does not take Him long to find out that that woman who walks next the bier is a poor widow, whose only son she is following to his grave. He tells the bearers to put down the bier; and while the mother wonders what is to be done, He bends tenderly over the dead man, and speaks to him in a low, sweet voice, "Arise!" And the dead man hears Him. His body begins to move: the man who was dead is struggling with his graveclothes; they unbind them, and now he sits up. He leaps off the bier, catches a sight of his mother, remembers that he was dead and is now alive again; takes her in his arms, kisses her again and again, and then turns to look at the Stranger who has wrought this miracle upon him. He is ready to do anything for that Man—ready to follow Him to the death. But Jesus does not ask that of him. He knows his mother needs him; and so He does not take him away to be one of His disciples, but gives him back to his old mother.

I would have liked to see that young man re-entering the city of Nain, arm-in-arm with his mother. What do you suppose he said to the people, who looked at him with wonder? Would he not confess that Jesus of Nazareth had raised him from the dead? Would he not go everywhere, declaring what the Lord had done for his dead body? Oh how I love to preach Christ, who can stand over all the graves, and say to all the dead bodies, "Arise!" How I pity the poor infidel, who has no Christ; who goes down to his death without any hope of resurrection! Is there a poor widow here to-night? Christ will have compassion on you. Your son is dead, maybe. Well, He will raise him up also at the last day, and you along with him; and give him back to you, and you to him, if you both have believed in Jesus, and given Him your hearts.

THE STORY OF NAAMAN.

I HAVE been reading to you about a person who was a great man in his own country—a very honourable man, one whom the king delighted to honour. He stood high in position, he was captain of the hosts of the king of Syria; *but he was a leper;* and that threw a blight over his whole life. There was no physician to help him in all Syria. None of the eminent doctors in Damascus could do him any good. Neither could any in Jerusalem. But I will tell you what they had in Syria: they had one of God's children there—and she was a little girl. Naaman knew nothing about her, though she was one of his household. I can imagine this little Israelite, one day, as she said to Mrs. Naaman, her mistress, that there was a prophet in her country that could cure her master of his leprosy. "Why!" says the mistress, "what are you talking about? Did you ever hear of anybody being cured of leprosy?" "Ah!" said the little girl, "it's true, I can assure you: we have got physicians down there that can cure anything." So at last some one told the king what the little maid of Israel had said. Now Naaman stood high in the king's favour, for he had just won a great victory. He was called a lord; perhaps he was a prince—a sort of Syrian Prince Bismarck, who stood near the throne. So the king said, "You had better go down to Samaria, and see if there is anything in it, and I will give you letters of introduction to the king of Israel."

Yes, he would give Naaman letters of introduction to the king. That's just man's idea. Of course, if anybody could help him it was a king. Of course the king had power both with God and man. Oh, my friends, it's a good deal better to know a man that knows God! A man acquainted with God has more power than any earthly king.

Away goes Naaman down to Samaria with his letter of introduction, and he takes with him a bag of gold and silver. That's man's idea again: he is going to pay the great doctor. And he took about £100,000 sterling, as far as I can make it out, to pay this doctor's bill. There are a good many men who would willingly pay that sum, if with it they could buy the favour of God, and get rid of the curse of sin. Yes, if money could do it, how many would buy salvation! But, thank God, it is not in the market for sale! You must buy it on God's terms, and that is "without money and without price." Naaman found that out. My dear friends, did you ever ask yourselves which is the worst —the leprosy of the body or the leprosy of sin? Why, for my own part I would a thousand times sooner have the leprosy eating my eyes out, and eating off feet and arms ; I would rather be loathsome in the sight of my fellow-men than die with the leprosy of sin in my soul, and be banished from God for ever. The leprosy of the body is bad, but the leprosy of sin is a thousand times worse. It has thrown the angels out of heaven ; it has ruined the best and strongest men that ever lived in the world.

There is one thing about Naaman that I like—and that is, his *earnestness of purpose.* He was thoroughly in earnest. A good many people say, "Oh, I don't like such and such a minister ; I should like to know where he comes from, and what he has done, and whether any bishop has ever laid his hands on his head." My dear friends, never mind the minister ; it's the message you want. Why, if some one were to send me a message, and the news were important, I shouldn't stop to ask about the messenger who brought it; I should want to read the news; I should look at the letter and its contents, and not at the boy who brought it. And so it is with God's message. The good news is everything, the minister nothing. The Syrians looked down with contempt on the Israelites ; and yet this great man was willing to take the good news from the lips of this poor little slave. Why, if I got lost in London, I should be willing to ask anybody which way to go—even if it were only a poor shoeblack. It is the way I want, not the person who directs me. But there was one drawback in Naaman's case : though he was willing to take the advice of the little girl, he was not willing to take the remedy.

The stumbling-block of pride stood in his way. The remedy the prophet offered him was a terrible blow to his pride. I have no doubt he expected a grand reception from the king of Israel, to whom he brought letters of introduction. He had been victorious on many a field of battle, and held high rank in the army —perhaps we may call him Major-General Naaman of Syria ; or he might have been higher in rank even than that. He had a letter of introduction from the king himself, and of course he would be received with high honours. But instead of the king rushing out to meet him, when he heard of Naaman's arrival and his object, he rent his mantle in a rage, and said : "Am I a God, that I can kill and make alive ?" But at last the king bethinks himself of Elisha the prophet; and he says, "There is a man in my kingdom who may be able to help you and cure your leprosy." Now I can imagine Naaman's pride reasoning thus: "Surely the prophet will feel very much exalted and flattered that I, the great Syrian General, should come and call upon him."

He drives up in grand style to the prophet's house; and, after awhile, as nobody seems to be coming out to meet him, he sends in his message: "Tell the prophet Major-General Naaman of Syria has arrived, and wishes to see him." Elisha takes it very coolly. He does not come out to see him; but, as soon as he learns his errand, he sends his servant to say: "Dip seven times in the river Jordan, and you shall be clean." What a terrible blow to his pride!

I can imagine him saying to his servant—"What did you say? Did I understand you aright? Dip seven times in Jordan! Why, we call the river Jordan a *ditch* in our country!" But the only answer he got was, "My lord says, Go and dip seven times in Jordan." I can fancy his indignation as he asks—"Are not Abana and Pharpar, rivers of Damascus, better than all the waters of Israel? May I not wash in them and be clean?" So he turned and went away in a rage. The fact was, Jordan never had any great reputation as a river; it flowed into the Dead Sea, and that sea never had a harbour to it. And its banks were not half so beautiful as those of the rivers of Damascus. Yes, it was a dreadful blow to his pride! The truth was, that Damascus was one of the most beautiful cities in the world; and it is said that when Mahomet first saw it, he turned his head away, for fear it should lead his thoughts away from heaven.

Naaman went off in a rage; he got very angry. But I don't think much of that; for, if you notice when a man turns away in anger, he generally cools down and comes back again.

He thought the prophet would have come out to him very humble and very solemn, and bid him do some great thing. Instead of that, Elisha, who was very likely busy writing, didn't even come to the door or the window: he merely sent out the message—"Tell him to dip seven times in the Jordan."

And away he went—saying "*I thought; I thought; I thought.*" I have heard that tale so often, that I am tired of it. I will tell you just what I think about it, and what I advise you to do—"Give it up. Take God's words, God's thoughts, God's ways.

A man to be converted has to give up his will, his ways, and his thoughts. I have often noticed that when a man says: "If ever I am converted, it will be this way or that," God leads him in quite a contrary direction.

Whilst Naaman was turning the matter over in his mind, and thinking what was best to be done, one of his servants came and said—and a very sensible remark it was: "My lord, if the prophet had bid thee do some great thing, wouldst thou not have done it? how much rather, then, when he saith to thee, Wash and be clean!" Yes, and there's a deal of truth in that. Why, if Elisha had said to him, "Go back to Syria on your hands and knees," he would most likely have done it. If he had said, "Go back all the way on one foot," he would have tried to do it. Or if he had said, "Give me a hundred thousand pounds for the medicine I prescribe, and thou shalt be cleansed," no doubt he would have done it. But to tell him merely to dip in the river Jordan seven times—why, it was absurd on the face of it! "Why, if there is such cleansing power in the waters of Jordan, does not every leper in Israel go down and dip in them, and be healed?" "Well," says the servant, "you have come a hundred and fifty miles; and now don't you think you had better do what he tells you?"

His anger is cooling down; and he says, "Well, I think I might as well try it." That's the starting-point of his faith; but still he thought it a foolish thing, and could not bring himself to believe that the result would be what the prophet had said.

Naaman's will was conquered at last. He got to that point where he was willing to obey; and the Scripture tells us "to obey is better than to sacrifice." So he goes down to the river and takes the first dip; and as he comes up, I can imagine him looking at himself, and saying to his servant, "There! there I am, no better than I was when I went in. If one-seventh of the leprosy was gone, I should be content." Down he goes a second time, and he comes up puffing and blowing, as much a leper as ever; and so he goes down again and again, the third and fourth and fifth time, with the same result—as much a leper as ever. When he comes up the sixth time, he looks at himself, and says, "Ah! no better. What a fool I have made of myself! How they must all laugh at me! I wouldn't have the generals and aristocracy of Damascus know that I have been dipping in this way in Jordan for all the world. However, as I have gone so far, I'll make the seventh plunge." He has not altogether lost faith; and down he goes the seventh time, and up he comes again. He looks at himself, and shouts aloud for joy. "Lo, I am well! My leprosy is all gone—all gone! My flesh has come again as that of a little child. I never knew such a thing. I never felt so happy in all my life. I thought I was a great and a happy man when I accomplished that victory; but, thank God! praise God! I am the happiest man alive." So he comes up out of Jordan and puts on his clothes, and goes back to the prophet, and wants to pay him.

That's just the old story: Naaman wants to give money for his cure. How many people want to do the same now-a-days! Why, it would have spoiled the story of grace, if the prophet had taken anything! You may give a thank-offering to God's cause, not because you can be saved, but because you are saved. But the prophet refused to take anything; and I can imagine no one felt more rejoiced than Elisha did. So Naaman starts back to Damascus, a very different man than he was when he left it. The dark cloud has gone from his mind; he is no longer a leper, in fear of dying from a loathsome disease. He lost the leprosy in Jordan when he did what the man of God told him; and if you obey the voice of God, even while I am speaking to you, the burden of your sins will fall from off you, and you shall be cleansed. It is all done by the power of faith.

MR. MOODY'S ADDRESS ON THE PENITENT THIEF.

I AM going to take for my text this morning, *a man;* the last one whom Jesus saved before He went back to heaven; and the fact that He saved such a man at all, ought to give every one of us a great deal of hope and comfort. This man was a thief, a highwayman, a murderer, perhaps; and yet Christ takes him with Him when He ascends to glory: and if He is not ashamed of such a man, surely no class of sinners need to feel that they are left out.

It is a blessed fact, that all kinds of men and women are represented among the converts in the Gospels, and almost all of them were converted suddenly. Very many people object to sudden conversions; but you may read in the Acts of the Apostles of eight thousand people converted in two days. That seems to me rather quick work. If all the Christians here this morning would only consecrate themselves to the work of Christ, they might be the means of converting as many as that, before the week is out. Now let us look at Christ hanging on His cross between two thieves,—the Scribes and Pharisees wagging their heads and jeering at Him, His disciples gone away, and only His mother and one or two other women in sight, to cheer Him with their presence, amongst all this crowd of enemies. Hear those spiteful Pharisees calling out to Him, "If Thou be the Son of God, come down from the cross, and we will believe on Thee"; and the account says that the two thieves cast the same in His teeth.

So then the first thing that we know of our man is, that he is a reviler of Christ. You would think that he ought to be doing something else at such a time as this; but hanging there in the midst of his tortures, and certain to be dead, in a few hours, instead of confessing his sins and preparing to meet the God whose law he had broken all his life—instead of that, he is abusing God's only Son. Surely this man cannot sink any lower, until he sinks into hell!

The next thing we hear of him, he appears to be under conviction. Nobody is ever converted till he is convicted. In Luke xxiii. 39, 40, we read: "And one of the malefactors which were hanged railed on Him; saying, If Thou be the Christ, save Thyself and us. But the other, answering, rebuked him, saying, Dost not thou fear God, seeing thou art in the same condemnation? And we indeed justly; for we receive the due reward of our deeds: but this man hath done nothing amiss."

Now what do you suppose it was that made this great change in this man's feelings, in these few hours? Christ had not preached him a sermon—had given him no exhortation. The darkness had not yet come on; the earth had not opened its mouth; the business of death was going on as usual; the crowd were still there, mocking, and hissing, and wagging their heads: and yet this man, who in the morning was railing at Christ, is now confessing his sins. "We indeed justly." No miracle had been wrought before his eyes. The Son of God had not come down from the cross. No angel from heaven had come to place a glittering crown upon His head, in place of the bloody crown of thorns. What was it, then? I will tell you what I think it was. I think it was the Saviour's prayer,—"Father, forgive them, for they know not what they do."

I seem to hear this thief talking with himself in this way:—

"What a strange kind of man this must be! He says He is King of the Jews; and the superscription on His cross says the same thing. But what sort of a throne is this! He says He is the Son of God. Why does not God send down His angels, and destroy all this great crowd of people who are torturing His Son? If He has all power now, as He used to have when He worked those miracles they talk about, why does He not bring out His vengeance, and sweep all these wretches into destruction? I would do it in a minute, if I had the power. Oh! if I could, I would open the earth and swallow up these tormentors! But this man prays to God to "forgive them." Strange! strange! He must be so different from the rest of us. I am sorry I said one word against Him when they first hung us up here. What a difference there is between Him and me! Here we are hanging on two crosses, side by side; but all the rest of our lives we have been far enough apart. I have been robbing and murdering, and He has been visiting the hungry, healing the sick, and raising the dead. Now these people are railing at us both. What a strange world is this! I will not rail at Him any more. Indeed, I begin to believe He must be the Son of God; for surely no son of man could forgive his enemies this way."

That is what did it, my friends. This poor man had been scourged, and beaten, and nailed to the cross, and hung up there for the world to gaze upon; and he was not sorry for his sins one single bit—did not feel the least conviction on account of all that misery. But when he heard the Saviour praying for His murderers, that broke his heart.

I remember to have heard a story, somewhere, of a bad boy who had run away from home. He had given his father no end of trouble. He had refused all the invitations which his father had sent him to come home and be forgiven, and help to comfort his old heart. He had even gone so far as to scoff at his father and mother. But one day a letter came telling him his father was dead, and they wanted him to come home and attend the funeral. At first he determined he would not go, but then he thought it would be a shame not to pay some little respect to the memory of so good a man after he was dead; and so, just as a matter of form, he took the train, and went to the old home, sat through all the funeral services, saw his father buried, and came back with the rest of the friends to the house, with his heart as cold and stony as ever. But when the old man's will was brought out to be read, the ungrateful son found that his father had remembered him along with all the rest of the family in the will, and had left him an inheritance with the others, who had not gone astray. This broke his heart. It was too much for him, that his old father, during all those years in which he had been so wicked and rebellious, had never ceased to love him. That is just the way our Father in Heaven does with us. That is just the way Jesus does with people who refuse to give their hearts to Him. He loves them in spite of their sins, and it is the love which, more than anything else, brings hard-hearted sinners to their knees.

Now this man confessed his sins. A man may be very sorry

for his sins; but, if he does not confess them, he has no promise of being forgiven. Hear him: "We are suffering justly," he says. I never knew any man to be converted till he confessed. Cain felt bad enough over his sins, but he did not confess. Saul was greatly tormented in his mind, but he went to the witch of Endor rather than to the Lord. Judas felt so bad over the betrayal of his Master, that he went out and hanged himself; but he did not confess,—that is, he did not confess to God. He came back and confessed to the priests, saying, "I have sinned in that I have betrayed the innocent blood." It was of no use to confess to them. They could not forgive him. What he should have done was to confess to God; but instead of that, he went right away and hanged himself. How different is the case with this man! He confesses his sins to Christ, and Christ has mercy on him at once.

Just here is one of the great difficulties with a great many people. They don't like to come up face to face with their sins. They don't like to own that they are sinners. They excuse themselves in every way. They think they are not very bad sinners; that there are a great many worse than they are; and so they try to cover up the great fact which this penitent thief confesses openly. My friends, you never will be saved, so long as you try to cover up your sins.

We have heard a great deal about the faith of Abraham, and the faith of Moses; but this man seems to me to have had more faith than any of them. He stands at the head of the class. God was twenty-five years toning up the faith of Abraham; Moses was forty years getting ready for his work; but this thief, right here in the midst of men who rejected Him—nailed to the cross, and racked with pain in every nerve, overwhelmed with horror, and his soul in a perfect tempest—still manages to lay hold upon Christ, and trust in Him for a swift salvation. His heart goes out to the Saviour. How glad he would be to fall on his knees at the foot of that cross, and pour out his prayer to Him who was hanging on it! But this he cannot do. His hands and feet are nailed fast to the wood; but they cannot nail his eyes, nor his heart. He can, at least, turn his head, and look upon the Son of God; and his breaking heart can go out in love to the One who is dying beside him—dying for him, and dying for you and me.

And what does Jesus say in answer to his prayer? That prayer was a confession of Christ. He calls Jesus *Lord*, and begs to be remembered in His kingdom: that must be a kingdom in heaven, for surely there was no chance of a kingdom on earth, as things looked at that time.

Christ fulfilled His promise to the thief—"Whoso confesseth me before men, him will I confess before my Father and the holy angels." He looks kindly upon him, and says, "To-day shalt thou be with me in Paradise." And now the darkness falls upon the earth; the sun hides itself; but, worse than all, the Father hides His face from the Son. What else is the meaning of that bitter cry, "My God, my God! why hast Thou forsaken me?" Ah! It had been written, "Cursed is every one that hangeth on a tree." Jesus is made a curse for us. God cannot look upon sin: and now His own Son is bearing, in His own body, the sins of all the world; and so He cannot look upon Him.

I think that is what was heaviest upon the Saviour's heart, away there in the Garden, when He prayed, "If it be possible, let this cup pass away from me." He could bear the unfaithfulness of His friends, the spite of His enemies, the pain of His crucifixion, and the shadow of death; He could bear all these: but when it came to the hiding of His Father's face, that seemed almost too much for even the Son of God to bear. But even this He endured for our sins; and now the face of God is turned back to us, whose sins had turned it away; and looking upon Jesus, the sinless One, He sees our souls in Him.

In the midst of all His agony, how sweet it must have been to Christ to hear that poor thief confessing Him! He likes to have men confessing Him. Do you not remember His asking Peter, "Whom do men say that I am?" and when Peter answered, "Some people say you are Moses, some people say you are Elias, and some people say you are one of the old prophets," He asks again, "But, Peter, who do *you* say I am?" and when Peter says, "Thou art the Son of God," Jesus blesses him for that confession. And now this thief confessed Him—confesses Him in the darkness. Perhaps it is so dark he cannot see Him any longer; but he feels that He is there beside him. This poor thief did as much for Christ in that one act as if he had lived and worked for Him fifty years. That is what Christ wants of us—to confess Him; in the dark as well as in the light, when it is hard as well as when it is easy; for He was not ashamed of us, and carried our sins even unto death.

Just look a minute at the prayer of this penitent thief. He calls Jesus *Lord.* That sounds like a young convert. "Lord, remember me when Thou comest into Thy kingdom." Not a very long prayer, you see, but a prevailing prayer. Some people think they must have a form of prayer,—a prayer-book, perhaps—if they are going to address the Throne of Grace properly. But what would that poor fellow do with a prayer-book up there, hanging on the cross, his hands nailed fast to the wood? Suppose it were necessary that some minister, or priest, should pray for him, what is he going to do? There is nobody there to pray for him, and he is going to die in a few hours. He is out of reach of help from men; but God has laid help upon One who is mighty, and that One is close at hand.

Then look at the answer to his prayer. He got more than he asked. He only asked to be remembered when Christ came into His kingdom. But Christ says to him, "I will take you right up with me into my kingdom to-day." The Saviour wants us all to remember Him in His old kingdom,—to remember Him in the breaking of bread and in the drinking of wine,—and then He will remember us in the new kingdom.

Now think of this, my friends. The last the world ever saw of Christ, He was on the cross. The last business of His life was the saving of a poor penitent thief. That was a part of His triumph. That was one of the glories attending His death. No doubt Satan said to himself, "I will have the soul of that thief, pretty soon, down here in the caverns of the lost. He belongs to me. He has belonged to me all those years." But Christ snapped the fetters of his soul, and set him at liberty: Satan lost his prey. "The Lion of the tribe of Judah" conquered the lion of hell.

You know that in the British Colonies, before the time of Wilberforce, there used to be a great many slaves; but that good man began to agitate the question of setting them free; and all the slaves in the Colonies, when they heard of it, were very anxious to know how he was getting along. They knew the Bill was before Parliament; and with them it was a question next to that of life itself. But in those days there were no telegraphs and no steamships. The mails went by the slow sailing-vessels. They would be from six to eight months in making a voyage to some of the more distant of the Colonies. The slaves used to watch for the white sails of British ships, hoping to hear good news, but fearing they might hear bad ones. There was a ship which had sailed immediately after the Emancipation Act had been passed and signed by the king; and when she came within hailing distance of the boats which had put off from the shore at the port where she was bound, the captain could not wait to deliver the message officially, and have it duly promulgated by the Government; but, seeing the poor anxious men standing up in their boats, eager for the news, he placed his trumpet to his mouth, and shouted with all his might, "Free! free!"

Just so the angel shouted when this poor bondman of Satan's, almost in the jaws of the pit, was taken in hand by the Saviour Himself; delivered from the bondage of darkness, into the liberty of His dear Son; free—free from sin—free from the curse of the law—free now, in a little while, from the bonds of the flesh as well.

What a contrast! In the morning he is led out a condemned criminal; in the evening he is saved from his sins. In the morning he is cursing; in the evening he is singing hallelujahs with a choir of angels. In the morning he is condemned by men as not fit to live on earth; in the evening he is reckoned good enough for heaven. Christ was not ashamed to walk arm-in-arm with him down the golden pavements of the eternal city. He had heard the Saviour's cry, "It is finished." He had seen the spear thrust into His side. Jesus had died before his very eyes, and hastened before him to get a place ready for this first soul brought from the world after He had died.

You have heard of the child who did not like to die and go to heaven, because he did not know anybody there. But the thief had one acquaintance: even the Master of the place Himself. He calls to Gabriel, and says, "Prepare a chariot; make haste: there is a friend of mine hanging upon that cross. They are breaking his legs. He soon will be ready to come. Make haste and bring him to me." And the angel in the chariot sweeps down the sky, takes up the soul of the poor penitent thief, and hastens back again to glory; while the gates of the city swing wide open, and the angels shout their welcome to this poor sinner "washed in the blood of the Lamb."

And that, my friends, is just what Christ wants to do for every sinner here. He wants to save you. That is the business on which He came down from heaven. That is why He died : and if He gives such great and swift salvation to this poor thief on the cross, surely He will give you the same deliverance, if, like the penitent thief, you will repent, and confess, and trust in the Saviour.

Somebody says that this man "was saved at the eleventh hour." I don't know about that. Perhaps it was the first hour. It might have been the first hour with him, I think. Perhaps he never knew Christ until he was led out to die beside Him. This may have been the very first time he had ever learned the way of faith in the Son of God.

But how many of you gave your hearts to Christ the very first time He asked them of you? Are you not further along in the day than even that poor thief?

A little while ago, in one of the mining districts of England, a young man attended one of our meetings, and refused to go from the place till he had found peace in the Saviour. The next day he went down into the pit, and the coal fell in upon him ; and when they took him out he was broken and mangled, and had only two or three minutes of life left in him. His friends gathered about him, saw his lips moving, and, bending down their ears to catch his words, this was what they heard him say: "It was a good thing I settled it last night."

Settle it this morning, my friends, once for all. Begin now to confess your sins, and to pray the Lord to "remember you when He cometh into His kingdom."

MR. MOODY'S SERMON ON "THE BLOOD."

EXODUS xii. 1-18.

MY friends, it was the blood that did it. Just so it is now. God says, "When I see the blood I will pass over you. The blood shall be a token unto you." And I tell you, my friends, the greatest question that can be before you to-night is this: Have you got the token? Have you got the blood? Are you sheltered behind the precious blood of the Lamb? That is the question. If you are thus sheltered, and if you have the token, then you are perfectly secure and safe.

There is a legend told in reference to that night on which the Lord slew the firstborn of the Egyptians; and it runs thus: —There was a little child, the firstborn in the house of an Israelite; and you know God said that, in every house where the blood was not upon the doorpost, the firstborn should be smitten by death. This little girl was sick, but she was afraid that the blood was not upon the doorpost; so she asked her father if he was sure he had put the blood upon the doorpost; and the father said, "Yes, he was quite sure: he had ordered it to be done." But the little girl said the second time, "Father, are you quite sure that the blood is there?"

"Yes, my child," answered the father; "be quiet, and sleep." But the child could not sleep. She was very sick and very restless; and as night came on, and it grew darker and darker, and nearer and nearer to the time when the angel should pass over Goshen, she got still more nervous and restless and uneasy; and at last she said, "Father, take me in your arms and let me see the blood upon the doorpost"; and the father, to satisfy the child, took her to the door to show her the blood; and lo and behold! it was not there: the man to whom he had given instructions had forgotten to do it. And then the father, in the sight of the child, had the blood put upon the doorpost, and the child lay down and went to sleep.

That, of course, is only a legend; but, my friends, it might have been true. Now, when we see that we have the blood, it satisfies us. I don't believe the sinner will ever be saved until he has the blood. May God give you it to-night!—because it is that which atones for our sins, and that which is the token of our redemption.

People say: "If I were only as good as that minister, who has been preaching for fifty years, I should feel *so* safe. If I could give as much money to poor people as So and So gives, I should feel *so* safe for heaven; and that it was all right with me." Let me say to you, my friends, if you are behind the blood of Jesus Christ, you are just as safe as any man or woman in the world. It is the blood. It is not our righteousness. It is not our good deeds. It is not our benevolent works. Works may come in, and a reward be had for them; but they don't help us to salvation. They don't save us from the curseof death.

"It is to him that worketh not, but believeth." And so we must be sheltered behind the blood, and know that we are there, before we can be safe. Then, the moment we are safe, it will be time enough to talk about work.

My friends, the first thing is to know you are sheltered behind the blood. You go to a railway station, and you buy a ticket, and get into a carriage; and the guard comes round and cries, "Tickets," and you put your hand in your pocket and pull out the ticket, and present that to the man; but the guard does not look to see if you are a white man or a black, learned or unlearned, great or small. He does not know, perhaps, who you are, or what you are; but he looks for the token. Oh! my friends, God says, "If you have got the token, I will pass over you." Have you got the token? Young lady, have you got the token? Young man, have you got the token? That is the question—the solemn question.

I can imagine some of these lords and dignitaries of Egypt riding through Goshen the day before the passover. They could hear the bleating of the lambs all through the province, for every man had either his lamb ready to kill, or was killing it; and they were throwing the blood upon the doorposts. I imagine

I can hear those Egyptians saying, "Men! what are you doing? Why are you putting blood upon your houses? Why are you disfiguring your doorposts? We would not have blood upon our houses." "Ah!" say the Hebrews, "it is going to shelter us to-night. It will be worth to us, at midnight, more than all Egypt." And I can further imagine these great men going away and laughing together, and thinking that these Hebrews had gone clean mad. But, ah! that night, at midnight, they changed their minds. There was a wail that went up from every house. From the palace of the king down to the lowest hovel, death had come and taken his victim. He entered the palace of the rich and the hovel of the poor, and laid his icy hand upon the firstborn;—the only thing that could keep death out, was death. And so it is with us. The death of Christ is our life. People say we ought to preach up Christ's life and moral character. I don't know how many letters I have received, urging me to preach the life of Christ and not His death. But Christ died for our sins. He didn't say we were to preach His life to save men. Christ's death is what gives us liberty. God didn't say, Tie up a living lamb, and "when I see that I will pass over you." If that had been done, death would have passed over the living lamb and taken his firstborn. It was death that kept death off; and the only way to meet death, is by death. Death has come, and I must either have some one to die for me, or die myself. That is the lesson that God is trying to bring out—the great doctrine of substitution. These little lambs were typical of the coming of the Lamb of God. They foreshadowed the scene at Calvary; and they went on being offered until Jesus Christ Himself should come.

And then, there are one or two other verses we ought to notice. "Thus shall ye eat it; with your loins girded, your shoes on your feet, and your staff in your hand; and ye shall eat it in haste; it is the Lord's Passover." Now, there are many people who are just satisfied with getting to Calvary; but forget to feed upon the Lamb, and are thus deprived of much spiritual power. They are satisfied with the work done at Calvary, and they forget the work of the Holy Ghost in them. They forget to eat of the Lamb. Now Christ is the Bread of heaven, and we are to feed upon Him, and get spiritual power. Then it is that we really become strong.

The Israelites had a long journey before them; and they were to feed upon the lamb. And then it says in the fourth verse: "And if the household be too little for the lamb, let him and his neighbour next unto his house take it according to the number of the souls: every man according to his eating, shall make your count for the lamb." Christ is enough for any family—He is enough for every family here to-night. He is enough for every soul, if you will only take Him and feed upon Him. Then in that second verse it says: "This month shall be unto you the beginning of months: it shall be the first month of the year to you." Everything dates from Calvary; and not from the cradle. Some people seem to think they start from the cradle to heaven; but we start from the cross; everything begins with the blood. "This shall be the beginning of months." Men have wrought for these four thousand years, making bricks without straw, for Egypt's king. Those four thousand years have rolled into the past; and now, when a man comes to Christ, all that is done in the past is wiped away: he has been the devil's own, but now he is the child of God.

If you give yourselves to God to-night, everything will date afresh from now, and you will become a citizen of a better world.

I must direct your attention to Exodus xxix. 16; and there you will read of the blood again: "And thou shalt slay the lamb, and thou shalt take his blood and sprinkle it round about the altar." Now the high priest had to take the blood and sprinkle it round about the altar. There was no way for a man to come to the altar but by the way of the blood; and there never has been any other way, since Adam fell, but this way. Any man who attempts to come to God now, without coming through Jesus Christ, as his Mediator, is just deceiving himself. He will have no fellowship with God unless he comes by the way of the blood. That was kept up until Christ came; then they could come and make their wants known through Jesus Christ, but not till then. Turn to Exodus xxx.; and there you will find: "And Aaron shall make an atonement upon the horns of it once in a year, with the blood of the sin-offering of atonements: once in the year shall he make atonement upon it throughout your generations: it is most holy unto the Lord." Make atonement! At-one-ment. If you want to become at one with God, you must become so through the blood. It is the only tie by which God and we can be linked together. When God made Adam, He surrounded him with everything that was good; and with a golden cord bound him unto Himself. And Christ came back to re-link man to God, and heaven; and it is just done by that one word—the *blood.* Atonement, by Christ means the sinner and God made one.

There may be some one who says, "Why does God demand blood? I don't see why He should demand blood." There may be some of you saying, "It seems very strange." So it does; and so it appeared to me. I could not understand why it was that God demanded blood; but the whole thing is plain enough now. Will you turn to Leviticus xvii. 11: "For the life of the flesh is in the blood; and I have given it to you upon the altar to make an atonement for your souls: for it is the blood that maketh an atonement for the soul." Now, my dear friends, do you see why He demands the blood? God said to Adam, "In the day that thou sinnest thou shalt die"; and the moment Adam sinned he died. He was not taken out of this clay temple, but he died spiritually. That is where many people make the mistake. They seem to think the body is the most important part of them. My friends, it is only the house that we live in. The life that God had given to Adam, that he might commune with His Creator, was forfeited the moment he fell. The moment he believed and received that devil's lie into his mind, and broke the law of God, he fell out of communion with God; and the moment that God came down after him, where did He find him? Why, He found him out of the fellowship—out of communion. Adam had gone and hid away from his loving Father: and ever since, God has been trying to get Adam's sons into fellowship and communion with Him; but the only way that He can be just, and justify the sinner, is, that the sinner should believe that "His Son died for our sins, according to the Scriptures." God's word must be kept. "Heaven and earth may pass away, but God's word shall never pass away." This, then, tells us why God demands the blood. "The blood is the life of all flesh." Now, it is really life that God demands. This life has been forfeited. You have sold yourselves for nought, but you shall be redeemed "without money." Life, then, is gone. Your life, my friends—the old-

Adam life—is not worth crossing the street after. God stamped it with death, and said it should never come into His presence. Now, if I don't get life, it is said, I must perish. That is what the apostles preached,—"Christ died for our justification. Christ rose for our sins." Now how can God be just, and justify the sinner? I will tell you: because God Himself came down in the form of sinful flesh, and took upon Him our nature, and died that we might live. There is the doctrine of substitution. Why, people say, "I don't believe in the doctrine of substitution." Well then, if you don't believe in that, you don't believe in the Bible. I tell you, take the doctrine of substitution out of that Bible, and I would not carry it home with me. If it does not teach that, it teaches nothing.

From the fall of man, all the language of that book has rung out this one thing: "The seed of the woman shall bruise the serpent's head." It has run along down through the ages ever since Adam fell.

Isaiah took up the strain, and sang, "He was wounded for our transgressions, He was bruised for our iniquities; and the chastisement of our peace was upon Him, and by His stripes we are healed." Take the doctrine of the substitution out of this Bible, and what are you going to do with that verse? You break away from your moorings. You break away from all our hope.

Take the history of those first two worshippers we have on record—Cain and Abel. Now Abel believed in the doctrine of the substitution, but Cain did not. I seem to hear Cain saying to himself, "I am not fond of shedding blood. I don't see why Abel must be always killing something for an offering to God. It seems to me much better to bring some of the fruits of the earth." But, my friends, the Bible says that "God had respect unto Abel and his offering; but unto Cain and his offering He had not respect." There are a great many Cainites in the world in these days. Take care, my friends, not to disobey God, and neglect the blood of His Son, lest He, as in the case of Cain, reject both your offering and yourselves. You insult the Almighty by offering the work of this frail body to atone for sin. Can you atone for sin yourselves? People say: "I believe God is so merciful, that that settles the question for me." Suppose a man robbed me of a thousand pounds, and said: "I have nothing against Mr. Moody; I have very warm feelings towards him." That is not the question. The question is: "Have I anything against him?" So men say they have done nothing against God. That is not the question. The question is, my friends, Has God anything against you? And you never will have peace until that is removed, and God is reconciled: and the moment you accept of His Son, then there is reconciliation—and there is no reconciliation until that is done. Now God does not demand payment of you. If Christ died for my sins, I have not got to die.

"The wages of sin is death." What is it? Death! Have you sinned? Yes. Have we all sinned? Yes. Then we must receive the wages. We must either receive them, or some one else must receive them for us. Then Christ comes right in, and says: "I will take your place." Christ died for the ungodly. Well, I am ungodly, and I will take the benefit of that death.

There is a woman in our country who was hoping to be saved, because she thought that she was a respectable sinner. Some sinners don't think they are like other sinners. When people talk to me in this strain, I know they are *great* sinners. She heard a sermon, which showed her clearly that Christ died for the ungodly; and she said, "I must be ungodly: He died for the ungodly": she awoke to the fact that she was unlike God, and the light of eternity flashed into her soul.

My friends, take your place amongst the ungodly. I am tired of people making out that they are not bad sinners,—whereas they are bad from the crown of the head to the sole of the foot. They are bad, and God says it: and let God be true and every man a liar. The glorious truth of the Gospel is that "Christ died for our sins." Ask me my hope of eternal life, and I reply, "*Christ died for my sins.*" Take that away, and I don't know what will become of me. No one else can save me. Those ministers cannot do it: they have as many sins of their own as they can attend to; and if you cannot get rid of your sins yourself, or any one else for you, you are shut up to this: "Christ must save us, or we must perish." If God turned Adam out of Eden for that one sin, do you think He is going to allow us into heaven with ten thousand sins? I must give my life to atone for my sins, unless I can find some one else who will take my place. Now, thank God, I have found Jesus; and every man and woman out of Christ here to-night can find the same Substitute.

There is a story told of the great Napoleon, that, when he sent out a draft for recruits, a man was drafted who didn't want to go into the army; but he had a friend who thought a good deal of him, and this friend offered to go in his place. He was found to be a good healthy man, and he was taken. A battle was fought, and the man was killed and buried on the field. Some time afterwards another draft was made, and by a mistake this man, whose substitute the other had been, was drafted the second time. When they went to take him, he said,—

"You cannot take me."

"Why not?"

"I am dead."

"You are not."

"Yes, I am. I died at such a battle, and you will find me buried on such a battle-field."

The man declared that he was dead, and they declared that he was alive;

"See if I was not drafted at such and such a time." They looked, and found that he had been drafted; and found another name against his: and then they said that he had got a substitute.

"I know that," said he; "and he died for me, and you cannot take me."

They said they would, take him and they did. Upon this he appealed to the emperor,—who decided they could not take him, for another man had died in his place.

There were hundreds of such cases during our war, where men bought substitutes; and others served through love—the father for the son, and the son for the father, and brothers for brothers. One wealthy man hired another to go to the war for him, and he was killed. The wealthy man went down South, and built a monument over his substitute's grave; and on it he put this inscription: "HE DIED FOR ME." Ah! my friends, go to the tomb of Jesus, and say over it, "He died for me." Yea, you can go further, and say, "He rose for me, and He is at the right hand of God for me; and I have life in Him, and the hope of eternal glory. Death cannot touch my spiritual nature; I am safe for time and eternity."

My friends, what will you do with the precious blood to-night? Will you trample it under your feet, and send back an insulting message to God, that you don't care for His Son, or for the blood that flowed from Calvary? or will you find refuge and shelter behind the blood to-night? Do you say there is no beauty in it? Young lady, will you get up and leave this place, laughing and making light of the Son of God, and the offer of mercy? Young man, will you turn with contempt from the Saviour, and refuse a share in the great salvation He offers to you—bought at the price of His blood?

Some men seem to think it is noble to fight against such a Saviour; others have not the moral courage to lift up their voices for Him. It seems to me cowardice not to confess Christ, after what He has done for us. A good many years ago, when the Californian gold-fever broke out, there was a great rush to the place. There was a young man who left a wife and little boy, and went to California. He told his wife that, as soon as he succeeded in business, he would send for her and his child. They watched and watched for the letter to come, bringing the money; but no news came. He was not very successful, and it was a long time before the money came to take them to the Pacific coast. But at last the letter did come; and that wife and little boy were full of delight. They thought they were going to see him whom they loved. They went to New York, and took their passage in one of these beautiful Pacific steamers. They sailed out of the harbour: but they had not been out to sea long, when, one beautiful day, when everything seemed calm and still, all at once there was a cry of "Fire! fire!"

The pumps were set to work; but in spite of everything, the flames increased. There was a magazine of powder on board; and the captain knew the moment the fire touched it, all would perish. The lifeboats were lowered, and the strongest of the passengers and crew sprang into them, and left the rest to die. Among the number left, were that poor mother and her boy. The last lifeboat was pushing away: it was her last hope. She bent over that ship, and begged them to take her boy and herself: but no,—the crew said "they didn't dare take any more." She pleaded with them until at last one of the men said, "Let us take them;" but the other men cried out against it. At last they promised to take one of them, and shouted this to her. What do you think she did? Did the mother leap into the boat and leave the boy to perish? But you, mothers, know that she would not do that. No true mother would do that. This mother seized her darling boy; she pressed him to her heart, handed him over the side; and, as she dropped him into the boat, she said, "My son, if you live to see your father, tell him that I died in your place:" The boat pushed off, and in a little while that vessel was blown up, and that mother perished. Young men, what would you say of that son, who is now grown up, if he should speak disrespectfully of such a mother as that? You would say he would not be fit to live.

Ah! Christ has done more than that for you. He left a life of glory to endure a life of shame; while we were without strength, He died for us. He did not die for His friends alone; He died also for His enemies. I want you all to come to Him to-night. Won't you believe on Him and be saved?

POPULAR EXCUSES.

"And they all with one consent began to make excuse."—LUKE xiv. 18.

SOME people are always making excuses for not doing their duty, and especially for not coming to Christ. If I asked you to come to Christ, you would be ready to give some reason for not accepting the invitation. I never saw an unsaved man in my life but had some excuse—never! and if you don't have one ready, Satan will be right by you to help you to make one. He is good at that sort of thing. That has been his occupation the last six thousand years—helping men to make excuses.

Just bear in mind, these men were invited to a feast, and not to a funeral. They were not invited to go to prison. They were not invited to a hospital, or to a madhouse; but they were invited to a feast. Now, when a man prepares a feast, there is a great rush to see who will get the best seats; but when God prepares His feast, the chairs would all be empty, if His disciples did not go out to compel people to come in. No sooner did the King send out His invitations than the excuses began to rain in. "And they all wth one consent began to make excuse."

All at it, and always at it. Did you ever stop to think, my friends, what would take place if God should take every man at his own word who wants to be excused? If He were to say, "I will excuse you," and with the next breath take them all out of the world? If every one in this audience should be taken at his word, who makes excuses in this respect, and if God should say, "Cut him down, let him cumber the ground no longer, hew him down," there would be a very terrible state of things in London. If every man in London, and every woman, who wants to be excused, and is saying so,—if God should take them at their word, and say, "I will excuse you," oh! my friends, there would be a great many shops not opened to-morrow. The public-houses, for instance, would be closed ; for I never saw a publican in my life but what wanted to be excused. He knows he cannot go on with his hellish traffic, if he accepts this invitation. He would have to stop that at once. Many of your cabmen do not want to come to the feast, because they would have to stop their business on the Sabbath. There would be a great many of your princely merchants that would be gone. They do not want to accept the invitation, because they think, if they do, they cannot make money so fast. They are carrying on some business which would then have to be stopped, because they accepted this invitation. There would be a very sad state of things taking place. Those that were left would have to be busy burying the dead. It would be a very solemn time, if God should take men at their word, and just excuse them. You let some terrible disease lay hold of a man, and half his excuses are gone at once.

Every kind of excuse is given ; but that man does not live who can give a good excuse.

Let any man get an invitation from Queen Victoria to go down to Windsor Castle, to some banquet ; and there is not a man but would consider it a great honour to receive such an invitation. But only think of the invitation that I bring to-night ! It comes from the King of kings. The marriage supper of the Lamb is going to take place, and God wants every man in this assembly to be present. I cannot speak for the rest of you ; but if I know my own heart, I would be rather torn limb from limb—I would rather have my heart torn out of me—than be absent from that marriage supper. I have missed a good many appointments in my time, but, by the grace of God, I mean to make sure of keeping that one.

These men all began to say, "I pray thee have me excused." Let us take up that first man's excuse. What was it? He had bought some ground, and he must needs go and see it. Why did he not, if he were a good business man, go and look at the ground before he bought it? It was not going to make the ground any better for him to go and look at it. He had not made a partial bargain and might withdraw. He was not afraid that some one might step in ahead of him and get the ground from him, and so he would lose it: it was not anything of this kind;

but he had bought the ground, and must needs go and see it! It is a strange time to go and see ground, just at supper time! I think the ground would have looked all the better after he had been to the feast. But the fact is, my friends, he did not believe it was a feast; and that is the trouble to-day. Men do not believe the Gospel is a feast.

The second man is approached by the messenger, who says, "My lord has made a great feast, and he wants to have you come to it." "Take back to your lord the message, that I cannot be there. I have bought five yoke of oxen, and I have got to go and prove them." Why did not he prove his oxen before he bought them? That is the time to prove oxen; but now he has bought them, let them stand in the stall. The trade is already closed; the bargain is already made; the oxen are bought. They are his, and now he can go and prove them at any time. A queer time to prove oxen, at supper time! He had better have proved them in the morning, and so have been ready to go to the feast in the evening.

The third man had married a wife, and therefore he could not come. Why not take his wife along with him? A young bride likes to go to a feast—no one better. He might have taken her: and if she was not willing, then let her stay at home. You smile, you laugh at this, but you can see plainly what these excuses were. They were simply falsehoods, just manufactured to ease their consciences. That boy down in the audience sees how absurd these excuses were; for the fact was, they did not want to go to the feast; and it would have been a good deal more honest for them to have said; "I don't want to go to your lord's feast, and I will not go."

Now, I would just like to take up some of the popular excuses of the present day. I do not doubt but there are hundreds of you who say to-night, "If I could accept that invitation Mr. Moody, I would like to be a Christian; but, sir, I have tried, and I find it is a very hard thing." Well, now let us look at that excuse. Do you mean to say that God is a hard Master? Do you say it is a hard thing to serve God? and do you say that Satan is an easy master, and that it is easier to serve him than God? Is it honest,—is it true? If it is, then I must confess that I have not read my Bible right; because I read it this way:—"The way of the transgressor is hard." If you doubt it, young men, look at the convicts in that prison; right in the bloom of manhood; right in the prime of life. He has been there for ten years, and must remain there for ten years more,—twenty years taken out of his life, and the thought that when he comes out of that miserable cell, he comes out a branded convict! Do you think *that* man will tell you "the way of the transgressor has been easy"? Go and ask the poor drunkard,—the man who is bound hand and foot, and is a slave to the infernal cup, and is hastening on to a drunkard's grave and to a drunkard's hell,—ask him if he has found the way of the transgressor easy, and the devil an easy master. Go ask the libertine—go ask that gambler—go ask the most abandoned man you have got in London,—ask them all, if they have found the devil an easy master. Suppose we were to take the most faithful follower of the devil, and put him into the witness-stand, and let him testify; do you think the most faithful follower of the devil would tell you that he is an easy master? Why, there is not a young man here but knows in his heart the devil is a hard master. The best way to settle this question is to find out by the testimony of those that have served both masters. I do not think any man has a right to judge until he has served both masters. If I heard a man condemn a master, I should be very apt to ask if he had served him; and if he had not, he could not very well testify. I am speaking to many to-night who have served both masters. Many of you have served Christ; and many of you, before you were brought into the fold of Christ, served the devil. I would like to ask the young men here to-night that are Christ's,—that have served Christ,—I would like to ask you, who have been brought into the kingdom of God and found Christ,—is Jesus a hard Master? [Loud cries of No.] I thought you would say *no.* I knew you would. I never heard a man say, "I have served Christ for five years, or more, and found Him a very hard Master." You never will say that. One of the greatest lies that has come out of the pit of hell is, that Christ is a hard Master. It is a lie, and has been so from the foundation of the world. Oh, young man, I beg of you, do not believe the devil when he says that God is a hard Master. It is false, my friends; and to-night let me brand that excuse as one of the devil's own lies, that he has been retailing up and down the earth for six thousand years.

Look how poor Adam suffered, because he believed the devil's lies! Look at poor Judas! Did he find the devil an easy master? See him throwing down the thirty pieces of silver! Why, he got so tired of the devil's service that he hanged himself twenty-four hours after he entered it.

Then there is another very popular excuse. I can imagine a good many would say; "Well, Mr. Moody, the fact is, I want to be saved." Of course you do! You would not be coming here at this time—at some inconvenience, many of you—if you did not want to be saved. But you say, "The fact is, Mr. Moody, I don't know that I am elected. If I thought I was elected I would come. I know that I cannot come unless I am elected; and I really want to come very much, but I don't know that I am one of the elect." Now, I have heard that till I have got sick and tired of it. I want to say to every unconverted man in this hall to-night that you have no more to do with the doctrine of election than you have with the government of China. I am not saying this in haste; I weigh well my words. I say that no unconverted man has anything to do with the doctrine of election. You have to do with the word *whosoever*. Now, the invitation is, "*Whosoever* will, let him come to this feast." To-night, my friends, let me say that you are invited, every one of you; and if you don't come, it will be because *you won't*, not because God does not want you, or has not given you the power to come. With the invitation there comes the power. Christ said to the withered man, "Stretch out thy hand." The man might have said that he had not the power; but with the invitation there came the power. And so it is here. Suppose I walked up the street to-night, and I stepped up to the door of this Camberwell Hall to go in, and a man stopped me, and I said to him, "Why not let me in?" "Where's your ticket?" "I have got none." "But no one is admitted without a ticket." "Then I cannot go in, I suppose?" "No; it is for a certain class—those that have got tickets." I go along farther—up to the Exeter Hall; and there is an anniversary meeting of some society. I step in, and a policeman pushes me back. I say, "I want to go in"; and he says, "You cannot go in here unless you have got a ticket. None but members can be admitted to-night." I do not happen to be a member of the society, and I cannot go in.

I go along a little farther, and come to another meeting; and there, perhaps, they are Quakers. The policeman stops me, and says, "Nobody admitted but Quakers." I am not a Quaker, and cannot go in. Farther on I find a soldiers' meeting. I cannot go in because I am not a soldier, and none but soldiers are admitted. But I go farther on, for I find written up in great big letters, "*Whosoever will*, let him come in." In I go: that means *me*. Now God has headed His invitation with *whosoever*, in great burning letters; and if you will go in, God will receive you to-night. He wants you to come this hour—this very minute. "*Whosoever will*, let him take of the water of life freely." I have an idea that the Lord Jesus Christ saw how men were going to stumble over that doctrine of election; for, after He had been back in heaven for thirty or forty years, and John was in the Spirit on the Lord's Day, in the Isle of Patmos, Jesus came to him and said, "John, write this," and he wrote. Again He said; "John, before you close the book, put in this—The Spirit and the Bride say, Come. And let him that heareth say, Come. And let him that is athirst come. And *whosoever* will, let him take the water of life freely." That for ever has settled in my mind, the doctrine of election.

Another excuse is: "I can't understand the Bible. Men are giving that as the reason why they do not accept the invitation to be at the marriage supper of the Lamb. Now, I want to say I never met a sceptic or infidel who had read the Bible through. I heard a man say the other day to another man, "Have you read such a book?" "Yes." "What is your opinion of it?" "Well, I only read it through once, and I would not like to give my opinion without reading it more carefully." But men can give their opinion about God's Book without reading it. They read a chapter here and there, and say, "Oh, the Book is so dark and mysterious!" and because they cannot understand it by reading a few chapters, they condemn the whole of it. The Word of God tells us plainly that the natural man cannot understand spiritual things. It is a spiritual book, and speaks of spiritual things; and a man must be born of the Spirit before he can understand the Bible. What seems very dark and mysterious to you now will all be light and clear when ye are born of the Spirit.

You say, "If that is so, how am I to understand how to be

saved?" I will tell you. When God puts salvation before a sinner, He puts it so plain that a man who runs can read, and a wayfaring man, though a fool, need not err therein. There are a great many things in the Book which are dark and mysterious; but when it comes to the plan of salvation, God has put it so plain that that little girl ten years old can understand it, if she will. You understand what it is to come. "Come unto me, all ye that labour." You know what it is to take a gift. "He came unto His own, and His own received Him not. But as many as received Him, to them gave He power to become the sons of God." "The wages of sin is death, but the gift of God is eternal life." You know what it is to believe in a man. Well, "believe in the Lord Jesus Christ, and thou shalt be saved." You know what it is to put trust and confidence in a man. Now, put your trust and confidence in the living God, and you are saved. You are saved by casting yourself unreservedly upon the Lord Jesus Christ. When God puts salvation before a man, He puts it so plain and simple that if he is willing to come as a little child, he can come.

Suppose I should send my little boy, five years old, to school to-morrow morning, and when he came home I should say, "Can you read, write, spell? Do you understand all about arithmetic, geometry, algebra?" The little fellow would look at me, and say, "Why, Papa, why do you talk that way? I have been trying all day to learn the A B C." Supposing I replied; "If you have not finished your education you need not go to the school any more,"—what would you say? You would say; "Moody has gone mad." Well, there is about as much sense in that as in the way that infidels talk about the Bible. They take it up, read a chapter, and say; "Oh, it is so dark and mysterious, we cannot understand it." This blessed Book is given to be a lamp to our feet and a light to our path, to guide the way to those eternal mansions. It never was given to keep men out of the kingdom of God. That is the devil's work—trying to make you believe the Word of God is not true. I tell you the only way we can overcome the enemy of our souls is by the written Word of God; and the devil knows that, and so he comes up, and says; "It is full of lies; it is dark and mysterious; it contradicts itself: don't you believe it." He knows the moment a man goes to the Word of God and believes it, he finds liberty to his soul, and gets beyond Satan's reach; he gets a weapon in his hand with which to conquer the devil; he overcomes the enemy of his salvation. The devil does not want you to find that out, and whispers this lie; and you believe it rather than the Word of God. Young man, your mother is right: the Bible is true, and you had better accept it.

Keep this in mind: you will never stand up before the bar of God, and say, the Bible kept you out of the kingdom. It may sound very well here, now; you may be satisfied to give that for an excuse down here, to-night; but you will not be satisfied to give it in the Courts of Heaven;—you will not stand up in the great Judgment Day, and say the Bible kept you out of the kingdom.

Then there is another class. Some people say; "I haven't any doubt about the Word of God; but the fact is, there are some men in the Church who are hypocrites; therefore I don't purpose to go into the Church." I am not asking you to come into the Church—not but what I believe in churches—but I am asking you to the marriage supper of the Lamb; I am inviting you to this feast; we will talk about the Church by-and-by. We want you to come to Christ first; then we will talk to you about the Church. But you say; "Here are some hypocrites." So there are; and I can imagine you saying; "Oh yes—there is a man up here in one of the churches that cheated me out of £5 a few years ago; you are not going to catch me in the company of such hypocrites." Well, my friend, if you want to get out of the company of hypocrites, you had better get out of the world as quick as you can. One of the twelve apostles turned out to be a hypocrite; and there is no doubt there will be hypocrites in the Church to the end of time. But "what is that to thee?" says Christ to Peter: "follow thou me." We do not ask you to follow hypocrites, we ask you to follow Christ; we do not ask you to believe in hypocrites, we ask you to believe in Christ. Another thing,—if you want to get out of the company of hypocrites you had better make haste and come to Christ. There will be no hypocrites at the marriage supper of the Lamb; they will all be in hell, and you will be there with them if you do not make haste and come to Christ. That excuse would sound strange, would it not? We very often hear men give it down here, but it would sound very strange before Jehovah—a man saying, "I know You invited me to be at the marriage supper of Your Son, but I did not accept it because I knew there were some hypocrites that professed the Gospel."

There is another class who say; "I know there are hypocrites, but they don't have any influence over me." If I could go to the door as you go out to-night, and take you by the hand and say, "My friend, why not accept of the invitation to-night?" you would say, "I pray to be excused to-night; I have not time. I have got some very pressing business to-morrow morning to attend to, and I have to go home to bed as quick as possible, to get my night's rest. You will have to excuse me." And the mothers here would say, "I have to go home and put the children to bed; you really must excuse me";—"very pressing business";—"no time." Thousands of men in London say they have not time. Thanks be to God! it don't take time: it takes decision. But what have you done with all the time God has given you? Your locks are turning grey, your eye is growing dim, and that temple of your body is coming down: what have you done with all those years? Is it true you have not time? What did you do with the three hundred and sixty-five days last year? No time?—what have you done with it all? Have not you had time to accept of this invitation? Why, men spend fifteen or twenty years to get an education, that they may go out to earn a living for this frail body that is soon to be eaten up with worms; or five years to learn a trade, that they may earn a living; and yet they have not five minutes to seek their souls' salvation! You "have no time." Is it true? You know it is a lie; and if you go out to-night unsaved, it will not be because you have not time, but because you won't accept the invitation. God says, "Seek *first* the kingdom of God." That is the first thing to do. Supposing you do not get so much money to-morrow, and get Christ, is not that worth more than money? Better for a man to be sure of salvation than to have the wealth of the world rolled to his feet!

But there is another excuse coming up from some one in the gallery. A man says, "My heart is so hard." Well, that is just the very reason you ought to come. If you had not a hard heart you would not need a Saviour. Can you soften your heart? Can you break your heart? Did not God invite the hard-hearted? Did not Christ come to seek and to save that which was lost? It is just because men's hearts are hard that they need a

Saviour. That is no excuse at all. God invites you, and you won't stand up and tell the Great King you did not accept His the invitation because you had a hard heart. He invites "whosoever"; and you can come along with your hard heart.

In the North there was a minister talking to a man in the inquiry room. He said, " My heart is so hard, it seems as if it was chained; and I cannot come." "Ah!" said the minister, "come to Christ, chain and all"; and he just came to Christ, and Christ snapped the fetters, and set him free right there. If you are bound hand and foot by Satan, that is the work of God to break the fetters; you cannot break them. Thanks be to God! He can break the fetters and set the captive souls free to-night. I do not care how hard the heart is: the Lord can save to the uttermost; He bids you come just as you are. Oh, this old excuse—"I am so bad!" Away with it!

Paul said he was the "chief" of sinners; and if the chief has gone up on high there is hope for everybody else. The devil makes us believe that we are good enough without salvation, if he can; and if he cannot make us believe that, he says, "You are so bad the Lord won't have you"; and so he tries to make people believe, because they are so bad Christ won't have anything to do with them. God invites you to come just as you are. I know a great many people want to come, but they are trying to get better and to get ready to come. Now mark you, my friend, the Lord invites you to come just as you are; and if you could make yourself better you would not be any more acceptable to Him. Do not put these filthy rags of self-righteousness about you. God will strip every rag from you when you come to Him, and He will clothe you with glorious garments. When our war was going on, we would sometimes go to the recruiting office and see a man come in with a silk hat, broadcloth coat, calfskin boots—his suit might be worth $100; and another man would come in whose clothes were not worth a pound; but they both had to strip, and put on the uniform of the country. And so when we go into Christ's vineyard we must put on the livery of heaven, and be stripped of every rag of our own. However bad you are, come just as you are, and the Lord will receive you.

Some say; "I would like to become a Christian; but I have a prejudice against these special meetings, and against Americans, and against a layman too. If it was a regular minister, if it was *our* regular minister, I would accept the invitation." If that is your difficulty, I can help you out of that. You can just get up, and go out of the hall, and run right over to your minister, and have a talk with him; your minister would be most glad to see and talk and pray with you. And if you say you do not want to be converted in a special meeting, there are regular meetings in all the churches throughout London. But if you say: "There is a great awakening here in London," and you do not want to be converted in that way; then jump into a train, and go to some town where there is no revival. We can find you some place where there is no revival, and some church where there is not much of the revival spirit. If you really want to go, don't give that for an excuse. How wise the devil is! When the Church is cold, and everything is dead, men say, "Oh, well, if there was only some life in the Church I might become a Christian,—if we could only just have a wave from heaven!" Then when the wave does come, they say, "Oh no; we are afraid of excitement, and afraid of these special meetings. We are afraid there will be something done that won't be just in accordance with our ideas of propriety." My friend, it is God who is working. He prepares the way.

There is another class here who say: "I would like to come; but then I do not feel." That is, I think, the very worst excuse, and the most common excuse we have. I wish sometimes the word could be abolished,—feel! feel! You go into the inquiry room. "Well, Mr. Moody, I do not *feel* this and that." Why, supposing my friend Mr. Stone should invite me to go to his house to-morrow to dinner, and I say to Mr. Stone, "I should like to go very much, but I don't know that I feel right." "Well," he says, "what do you mean? Do you mean you don't want to go to my house?" "Oh no, I want to go." (That is what men say: "Oh yes, we want to be saved.") "What do you mean, Mr. Moody? Do you mean that you do not know you will be well to-morrow? Do you think you will be sick?" "Oh no, I expect to be well to-morrow, if I live." "Well, what do you mean by feeling?" "Well, I do not know just how I'll feel. I would like very much to go to your house to dinner to-morrow, but I don't know that I will feel just right." "I don't understand you, Mr. Moody; I am not talking about feeling; I invite you to come to my house to dinner." "Well, I would like to come very much, but the fact is, I do not know how I will feel to-morrow." I can imagine my friend saying, "What has come over Moody? I think the fellow has gone mad. I asked him to my house to dinner, and he says he would like to come, but he does not know that he will feel right; he talked about feeling all the time." Of course you would say he has gone mad. But that is the way people talk now. You speak to them about coming to the kingdom of God, and they say; "I do not know that I feel just right." Away with your feelings. God is above feeling. We cannot control our feelings? If I could, I would feel good all the time—never catch me feeling bad at anything! I am sure if I could control my feelings I never would have any bad feelings; I would always have good feelings. Bear in mind, Satan may change our feelings fifty times a day, but he cannot change the Word of God; and what we want is to build our hopes of heaven upon the Word of God. When a poor sinner is coming up out of the pit, and just ready to get his feet upon the Rock of Ages, the devil sticks out a plank of feeling, and says; "Get on that"; and when he puts his feet on that, down he goes again. Take one of these texts—"Verily, I say unto you, he that heareth my word and believeth on Him that sent me hath everlasting life, and shall not come into condemnation, but is passed from death unto life." My friend, that is worth more than all the feelings that you can have in a whole lifetime. I would a thousand times rather stand on that verse than on the best frame of feeling. I took my stand there twenty years ago. The dark waves of hell have come dashing up against me; the waves of persecution have surged around me; doubts, fears, and unbelief have assailed me; but I have been able to stand right there. It is a sure footing for eternity. It was true eighteen hundred years ago, and it is true to-night. That Rock is higher than my feeling. What we want is to get our feet upon the Rock, and then the Lord will put a new song into our mouths.

There is another class, who say they cannot believe. Not long ago, a man said to me; "I cannot believe." I said, "Who?" "Well, I cannot believe." I said, "Who?" He stammered and stuttered, and I said; "Who cannot you believe, —God?" "Oh yes, I believe God: I cannot believe myself." "Well, you do not want to believe yourself. Your heart is deceitful above all things, and desperately wicked. Put no confidence in the flesh. Don't believe yourself; call yourself a liar, and let God be true. Believe in God, and say as Job said; 'Though He slay me I will trust Him.'" Some men seem to talk as if it was a great misfortune that they do not believe. Bear in mind, it is the damning sin of the world. "When He, the Holy Ghost, is come, He will reprove the world of sin, and of righteousness, and of judgment: of sin, because they believe not on me." That is the sin of the world—"because they believe not on me." Why, that is the very root of sin—the very tree, and all the fruit! This is the tree that brings forth this bad fruit—it is the tree of unbelief.

I wish I had time to go on with these excuses; for they are as numerous as the hairs on our heads. But if I could go on and exhaust them all, the devil would help to make more. You can just take them, tie them up in one bundle, and mark them lies—the whole of them. Not one of them is true. If your excuse is a good one, if it will stand the light of eternity do not give it up for anything I have said. Hold it firm, take it to the bar of God, and tell it out to Him. But if you have an excuse that won't stand the piercing eye of God, I beg of you, as a friend, give it up—let your excuses go. Let them go to the four winds of heaven, and accept of the invitation now. It is a very easy thing for a man to excuse himself into hell, but he cannot excuse himself out.

I wish I had time to call your attention to, who will be at the marriage supper of the Lamb. Lift your eyes heavenward to-night, mothers; you have loved children that have gone on before you; they will be at the marriage supper of the Lamb; they will sit down with Abraham, Isaac, and Jacob, in the kingdom of God: will you be missing? Fathers and mothers who have loved ones that have gone on before you! if you could hear them, they are shouting from the battlements of heaven; "Come this way." Young man, you have a sainted mother there,—a loved father there: they are beckoning you heavenward to-night. They have been gathering from the time the holy Abel went up: for six thousand years, gathering out of the four corners of the earth. The purest and best of earth are here; they are in heaven: and God wants you and me to be there. Blessed is he that shall be at the marriage supper of the Lamb!

Dare you make light of the invitation? Suppose you should just write out an excuse to the King of Heaven: "While sitting in the Camberwell Hall July 10th, 1875, I received a very pressing invitation from one of Your messengers to be present at the marriage supper of Your only-begotten Son. I pray Thee have me excused." Would you come up and sign that? Would you take your pen and put your name down to that excuse? I can imagine you saying, you would let your right hand forget its cunning, and your tongue cleave to the roof of your mouth first. I doubt whether there is a man in this room who could be made to sign this excuse: but what will you do? Many of you will get up and go out of this hall, making light of the preacher, laughing at everything you have heard, paying no attention to the invitation. I beg of you, do not make light of this invitation. It is a loving God that invites you; but God is not to be mocked. Go, play with the forked lightning, trifle with any pestilence, any disease, rather than with God. God is not to be trifled with.

Just let me write out another reply: "To the King of Heaven. While sitting in the Camberwell Hall July 10th, 1875, I received a pressing invitation from one of Your servants to be present at the marriage supper of Your only-begotten Son. I hasten to reply, By the grace of God I will be present." Who will sign that? (Many replies of "I will!" "I will!") Who will set to their seal to-night that God is true? Be wise to-night and accept of the invitation. Make up your mind now: do not go away till the question of eternity is settled.

THE PROPHET DANIEL, IN MR. MOODY'S VERSION.

TO those who have heard or read the stately and brilliant oration of Dr. Punshon on "Daniel in Babylon," by which this line of address was first suggested to Mr. Moody, this rendering of the story in modern and homely language will be especially interesting. The contrast in style will be striking, but the power and effect of the two discourses will be found almost identical. A diversity of gifts; but the same spirit.

WHEN we come to the life of such a man as Daniel, the first thing we ask is: What was the secret of his success? Well, my friends, I'll tell you what I think was the secret of this man's success;—He knew his God.

A great many professing Christians never get on intimate terms with their God, and so they never amount to much. But Daniel, from his boyhood, knew and trusted in, the God of Abraham, and the God of Isaac, and the God of Jacob; and that was what put such courage into him.

There is another very important thing about Daniel: he was able to say *no!* at the right time.

I tell you, my friends, it would be a great thing for our young men to be able to say NO! when the devil comes up to them and begins to coax them away from the God of their father and mother.

We don't know just how old he was when we hear of him

first: probably about seventeen. The king Nebuchadnezzar had given orders to take some of the best and brightest boys among the Hebrew captives and bring them up among his wise men. They were to be taught the language and the learning of the Chaldeans, and to be fed with meat and wine from the king's table.

"But Daniel purposed in his heart that he would not defile himself with the portion of the king's meat, nor with the wine which he drank." There was something in the law of his God forbidding him to eat meat or drink wine which had been offered to idols; and Daniel knew that the king's meat and the king's wine had been offered to idols, so he determined not to touch it.

If he had been like a good many of our modern Christians, he would have said something like this: "Well, it can't be helped. I don't like to defile myself this way; the law of God forbids it; and if I were only home in Jerusalem I never would do it in the world. But I really don't see how we are going to help it. We are slaves. Besides, it is the king's special order; and if he should hear of our disobedience, our heads would come off in no time. Really, we can't be expected to run such a risk as that."

That's it: the devil told him to do in Babylon as the people of Babylon do. But Daniel had the courage to stand up to the law of his God, and say *no!*

Consequences? Never mind the consequences. There wasn't any such word in his dictionary when it came to obeying the law of his God. He was bound to do it, let the consequences be what they might.

Do you hear what it says here in this eighth verse of the first chapter? "Daniel purposed in his *heart*." That's the trouble with a great many people: they purpose to do right, but they only purpose in their heads, and that doesn't amount to much. If you are going to be Christians, you must purpose to serve God away down in your hearts. "With *the heart* man believeth unto righteousness."

So when the servant who had charge of them came to bring them their dinner, Daniel and his three young friends told him they couldn't eat that meat and drink that wine, because it was against the law of their God.

Look at that! Daniel doesn't try to dodge the question at all; he gives the true reason right out at once.

I am afraid some of you, if you had been in his place, would have tried to hide behind some excuse. You would say you weren't very well; or that meat and wine didn't agree with you. Not so with Daniel. He tells that heathen the true reason why he can't eat the king's meat or drink the king's wine, and I have no doubt the man respected him for it.

"But," says he, "it won't do at all. If you don't eat it, the king will find it out. He'll see you some time looking lean and thin, and he'll ask what the matter is, and then I shall lose my head as well as you."

"Just try us for ten days," says Daniel. "Give us pulse to eat and water to drink, and see how we get along on it."

So the servant tried them on the pulse and water, and at the end of ten days they were the fattest and best looking of the whole crowd.

Some people think wine makes them look better, and that they can't get along without it. Look at their red noses and bloated faces!

I tell you, all the stimulant a person needs is the Word and the Grace of God.

There was a soldier down in Tennessee when I was there,—a great strong, hearty fellow, who was a teetotaler. One day, when the army was going on a long march, a man offered him a drink of whisky.

"I am a teetotaler," was his reply.

"Never mind that. You're in the army now; besides, you need some stimulant to help you on this long march."

Taking out a pocket Bible, he held it up before the face of his tempter, and said,—

"That is all the stimulant I want."

Just so with Daniel. He took God's side in this question, and held to God's terms, and God made him strong and healthy; gave him favour with those who saw his honesty, and, above all, peace in his own soul.

The next we hear of him is about two years after.

I seem to see the officer coming in and laying his hand on Daniel's shoulder, and arresting him in the king's name.

"What's the matter?" says Daniel.

"Why, haven't you heard?" says the officer. "The king had a dream last night, and when he woke up he couldn't remember it; so he called all his wise men together, and asked them to tell him his dream, and then interpret it for him. Nobody could tell it. The king was so angry that he commanded that all the wise men should be put to death. You belong to that school; so you will have to die."

"It seems to me the king is rather hasty," says Daniel—cool and calm as a summer morning. "Just let him give us a little time, and I'll show him his dream and the interpretation also."

He knew his God and trusted in Him. All secrets belong to God.

That night Daniel and his three friends had a little prayer-meeting together. I have no doubt they read the story of Joseph; how the dreams of old Pharaoh were revealed to him; and how he came to be a great man in Egypt afterwards. And then they went to sleep.

I don't think many of you would have gone to sleep with such danger as that hanging over your heads. But Daniel slept; and in his sleep the king's dream was revealed to him.

The next morning there was a great stir all about the palace. It had got out that a young Hebrew captive was going to tell the king his dream, and save the lives of all the wise men of Babylon; and everybody was anxious to know all about it.

I can see the young man brought into the presence of the mighty monarch. He stands there without the slightest fear. His God, in whom he trusted, has made him master of the situation. The king looks at him, and says, "Young man, can you tell me my dream and the interpretation of it?"

"My God can!" answers Daniel; and he begins.

"In your dream, O king, you saw an image——"

"*That's it!*" says Nebuchadnezzar, his face lighting up all at once; "you've got it! I remember it all now."

"Yes," says Daniel; "my God revealed it to me last night in a dream." You see he doesn't take any credit to himself for it, but gives the glory to his God.

"The head of this great image was gold, his breast and his arms were silver, his belly and his thighs of brass, his legs of iron, and his feet part of iron and part of clay. And then, O king, you saw a stone cut out without hands, which struck the image upon its feet, and crushed it to pieces till it became like the dust of the summer threshing-floor."

"That's all right," says the king. "Now can you tell me the interpretation of it?"

Now I imagine some of you would have tried to soften down the interpretation a little. It was a pretty hard thing for Daniel to stand up there before that great monarch, and tell him his kingdom was to be like the dust of a summer threshing-floor: but he did it.

"Thou art this head of gold. And after thee shall arise another kingdom inferior to thee; and another third kingdom of brass, which shall bear rule over all the earth. And the fourth kingdom shall be strong as iron. Afterwards it shall be divided, and become part strong and part weak. And in the days of those kings shall the God of heaven set up a kingdom which shall never be destroyed; it shall break in pieces and destroy all those kingdoms, and it shall stand for ever."

The king was greatly pleased with Daniel, and made a great man of him; and, for his sake, put his three friends into office. You see Daniel didn't forget his friends when he got into a good place himself.

Well: not long after that—maybe it was the dream that put it into his head—Nebuchadnezzar made a great image, and set it up in the plains of Dura. It was about ninety feet high and about nine feet wide. Some people say it was made of solid gold. I rather think the king intended that image to represent himself. He was going to have a universal religion, and he was going to be the head of it,—there are some such people now-a-days,—and so he gave orders to have all the nobility and great officers of his kingdom brought together to worship the golden image which he had set up.

I don't know where Daniel was at this time. Perhaps he was away in some other part of the kingdom on business; but his friends, Shadrach, Meshach, and Abed-nego, were there to represent him. Their enemies were there too. A faithful servant of God is sure to have enemies, watching for a chance to get him out of the way.

It was a great day when the image was unveiled. I seem to see it flashing in the sunlight; the vast throng of worshippers standing around it; and the king, at the head of a splendid procession of his lords and ladies, coming across the plain with banners flying and music playing: really, it must have been a trying time for those three men, who were so much out of fashion as not to bow down to the great idol when everybody else was doing it.

But the law of their God and the law of the king were in conflict. The king said, Bow down! God said, No!—and it didn't take them a minute to decide what to do.

Some people would have said, "There's no great harm in bowing with all the rest; but then you needn't *worship*, you know: just bend your knees a little, but don't say any prayers to the idol."

Not a bit of it. These men were not going to compromise their consciences; and their enemies knew it very well. The hour has arrived; everything is ready; the king makes a sign with his hand, and the cornets and sackbuts, and all the other instruments, give a great blast, and the whole multitude fall down on their faces before the great image which Nebuchadnezzar the king has set up. No; not all! There are three pairs of stiff knees in that kingdom—three men who will not bow to the false god. Their enemies have taken care to put them in the front rank, near to themselves, where they can watch them, and so find occasion to accuse them to the king.

I seem to see these fellows looking out of the corners of their eyes, when, by the king's command, they ought to have been worshipping the idol; and I hear them saying to themselves, "Aha! we have got you now!" and so they go to tell the king.

"O king! live for ever. Do you know that there are three men in your kingdom who will not obey you?"

"No: who are they?"

"Three of those Hebrew captives: they don't bow down along with the rest of us; and we thought you would like to know it."

"Bring them to me," says the king, in a great rage; "I will see whether these fellows are going to disobey my orders like this."

It is quite likely he would have ordered their heads to be taken off at once, if he had not remembered that they were particular friends of Daniel.

Now they stand face to face with the great king.

"What is this I hear of you?" says Nebuchadnezzar. "They say you disobey my orders, and do not bow down and worship my golden image. Now, I will try you once more; and then, if you don't bow down, into the furnace you go."

We do not know who the speaker was on that occasion; perhaps it was Shadrach. He stands there with his two friends, looking calmly at the king, and thinking of the fiery furnace without trembling in the least, or feeling the slightest fear. And this is what he says,—

"We are not careful to answer thee in this matter, O king. The God whom we serve is able to deliver us from the burning fiery furnace, and He will deliver us out of thine hand, O king. But whether He deliver us or not, we will not bow down."

"Who is this God of yours, that is able to deliver you out of my hands?" says the king, in a towering rage. "Go and heat that furnace seven times hotter than ever, and take these fellows up, and thrust them into it. Be quick about it. I will not have such rebels in my kingdom."

So some of the king's servants hurry away to the furnace to stir up the fire, and others seize Shadrach, Meshach, and Abed-nego, and take them away; and when the furnace doors are opened, they come near to cast them into the fire,—which is so hot that it burns the servants to death, but does not harm the men who are cast down headlong into it. Then the king goes and looks into the furnace; and what is his astonishment at seeing four men, instead of three, walking in the midst of the fire, as safely as if they were in the king's garden!

"Did I not tell you to cast in three men?—and lo! I see four walking about in the fire; and the form of the fourth is like the Son of God."

The Lord Himself was with His three faithful servants. The great Palestine Shepherd looked down from heaven, and saw those three sheep of His flock about to be cast into the fire: and He made haste, and came down Himself, to see that they suffered no harm. Ah! Jesus is always with His people. Though they pass through water, they shall not be drowned; though they pass through the fire, they shall not be burned. The fire burned off only the devil's bands: it did not singe a hair of their heads.

Does not Christ say that the hairs of our heads are all numbered? There is wonderful care and love in that.

Did you ever know a mother who loved her little child so well that she would count the hairs on its curly head? But the Lord loves His children so well that He counts their hairs—every one; and not one of them comes to any harm, so long as His child is faithful to Him. There was not even the smell of fire upon their garments; and the king's counsellors, and princes, and governors, and captains, and all together, saw these men upon whose bodies the fire had no power.

My friends, let us remember that it is always safe to do what God wants us to do. If our way to heaven leads through fire and water, it is all the same: it is all right. That is the proper way for us to go.

And now King Nebuchadnezzar orders these men to come out; and he restored them to their places again. He has found out who was the God that was able to deliver His servants out of the hands of the king; and I am quite sure that, from this time, neither the king nor anybody else in Babylon ventured to say anything against those men, or against the God whom they worshipped, and who had delivered them out of the fiery furnace.

The king himself makes a decree, "that every people, nation, and language, which shall speak anything amiss against the God of Shadrach, Meshach, and Abed-nego, shall be cut in pieces, and their houses shall be made a dunghill, because there is no other God that can deliver after this sort." So the king promoted these men; and, instead of being burned to death in the furnace, they came to be more honourable than ever.

The next thing that we hear of the king is, that he has had another dream. He seems to have been a great man for dreams. This time he saw a great tree which "reached unto heaven, and the sight thereof to the end of all the earth; . . . and, behold, a watcher and an holy one came down from heaven, and cried aloud: 'Hew down this tree, and cut down his branches, shake off his leaves, and scatter his fruit: let the beasts get away from under it, and the fowls from its branches. Nevertheless, leave the stump of his roots in the earth. . . . Let his heart be changed from man's, and let a beast's heart be given unto him, and let seven times pass over him: to the intent that the living may know that the Most High ruleth in the kingdom of men, and giveth it to whomsoever He will.'"

The king seems to have been as much puzzled by this dream as by the other; and nobody could tell him what it meant, until he sent for Daniel. Even he was troubled about it at first; but presently the Lord showed it to him; and then he preached such a sermon to the king about his pride, and the necessity of repentance, that the king's face turned pale, and his knees began to shake, and it was not long before he lost his reason, and wandered away from his palace, out into the woods and the deserts, and became more like a beast than a man. But at last the Lord had mercy on him. His counsellors and princes gathered about him again, and brought him back to his palace. But the king's heart was softened. I think he became truly converted to God; and from this time we don't hear him saying any more: "Is not this great Babylon that I have builded?" But we hear him blessing the Most High, and praising and honouring Him whose dominion is everlasting, and whose kingdom is from generation to generation.

And now the king makes one more proclamation, different from all the others. Up to this time he has been telling other people what to do; now he begins to speak of his own duty, and he says, "I, Nebuchadnezzar, will do this—I will do that." "I will praise and extol and honour the King of Heaven, all of whose works are truth." He has found out his own duty. His heart is softened; and although we do not hear anything more of him, I have no doubt that Daniel and he used to walk the streets of Babylon, arm-in-arm, and talk over their experiences together; and when the king died, I feel quite sure that he went safely to heaven, to be welcomed by the God of Daniel; and through the long eternity King Nebuchadnezzar will rejoice that that young man, Daniel, took his stand for God when he came down to Babylon, and did not follow the fashion of that wicked capital, though it might have cost him his life.

The next thing we hear of Babylon is, that the grandson of Nebuchadnezzar, a wild young prince, called Belshazzar, has come to the throne. On a certain occasion he makes a great feast to a thousand of his lords. They come together in a great banquet-chamber, and they drink and carouse all night long. They do not care for the armies of Cyrus, which are besieging the city. They trust in its high walls and its gates of brass, and feel themselves perfectly safe. At last, when the head of the young king has been quite turned with wine, he orders the golden vessels, which his grandfather captured from God's temple at Jerusalem, to be brought into the banquet-hall, that they may drink wine out of them in honour of the gods of Babylon. But while they are doing this impious thing, behold, a hand appears, writing with its fingers upon the wall—the doom of the kingdom of Babylon.

Drunk as he is, the miserable king is frightened.

"Bring in the wise men," says he. And the wise men come in haste, and stare at the writing, but not one of them is able to read or understand it. No uncircumcised eye can read God's handwriting.

Somehow or other, the news of this strange affair reaches the ears of the king's mother; and she sends a servant to him, telling him that, in the days of his grandfather, there was a man in Babylon who could interpret dreams, and reveal secrets, and do all manner of strange things, and maybe he would be able to read the writing.

It seems that Daniel had been lost sight of for the last fifteen years; but now there is special work for him to do; and so they find him out, and bring him in and ask him to read the writing. "*Mene, Mene, Tekel, Upharsin*"*:* and the meaning of it was clear as daylight to him.

Now I have no doubt that a good many courtiers, if they had seen such writing as that upon the wall of the king's palace, would have softened the meaning of it a little, and not have given it in its full strength, for fear of offending the king. But that was not Daniel's fashion at all. He reads it just as God writes it. "*Mene:* God hath numbered thy kingdom, and finished it. *Tekel:* Thou art weighed in the balances, and art found wanting. *Peres:* Thy kingdom is divided, and given to the Medes and the Persians."

Ah! poor miserable Belshazzar! Even now the soldiers of Cyrus have turned away the waters of the Euphrates, and are coming into the city along the empty banks. The soldiers are battering away at the doors of your palace, and before morning your blood shall be spilled upon the stones, along with the wine which you have been drinking, out of the vessels from God's holy temple at Jerusalem. You are weighed in God's balance, and found wanting.

My friends, suppose God should begin to weigh some of you to-day; suppose you were to step into the balances now, don't you think you would be found wanting? Get into the scales, take along with you your education, and your wealth, and your dignity, and your fashion, and your fine clothes, and everything you have that is splendid,—and the Lord will put the ten commandments in the other, and up you will go like feathers —"weighed in the balances and found wanting." Only they who have Christ in their souls can stand the test of God's weighing. Dare you step into the balances to-day?

Some one will ask me, "Mr. Moody, dare you step into the balances to-day, and be weighed? Do you know that you would be saved, if the Lord should bring you to judgment?" Yes; thanks be to God, Christ is able to save me—even me; and He will save all of you who will cast off your sins, and take Christ instead.

After a while, Darius, the Mede, comes to the throne of Babylon. He must have met Daniel somewhere in his travels, for no sooner does he set up the kingdom than he puts him into a place of great power. He chooses a hundred and twenty princes, whom he places over the kingdom; and over these princes he appoints three presidents, and he makes Daniel the president of the presidents: so that he really is the first man in the kingdom, after the king. His business was to "see that the king suffered no damage"; that is, he was to keep watch of the accounts, to see that nobody cheated the king. This must have been a very difficult place, and Daniel must have had his hands full. He had to watch those hundred and twenty rascals, who were all the while trying to steal something off the revenue; and to go over their accounts again and again, so as to be certain that they were correct to a penny.

It was not long before Daniel became very unpopular with the princes. I seem to hear them talking amongst themselves in this way:—

"There is that miserable old Jew, Daniel: if we only had him out of the way, we could make no end of money. We would very speedily be rich; we would have our country houses and our city houses, and our fine horses and chariots, and we would live in the very highest style, off the revenues of this kingdom; but that old fellow watches us as narrowly as a cat watches a mouse. We can't cheat him—even to a shilling." "Why," says one, "I never saw such a man in all my life. I gave in an account the other day that was only a few pounds short; and did not he send it back to me, and make me pay the difference? I wish he were back in Jerusalem, where he came from."

However, the king trusted Daniel; and he was such a thoroughly good and honest man that they really could find no way to revenge themselves upon him. They talked it over together again and again, and all agreed that there was no chance of getting him out of the way, unless they could find something in his religion by which they could bring him into trouble.

"We shall not find any occasion against this Daniel, except we find it against him concerning the law of his God." What an honour! Nothing wrong with him—even in the eyes of these bad men—except that he was too faithful to his God!

How many of you are likely to be complained of on that account?

Finally, they hit upon a plan which they thought might possibly succeed. One night they are closeted together in secret; and one of the princes says to the rest: "I think I have got a plan that will work. You know King Darius is very popular, and he is very proud of it. The people praise him a great deal, and he likes it. Now suppose we ask him to establish a royal decree, 'that whosoever shall ask a petition of any god or man for thirty days, save of the king, he shall be cast into the den of lions.' That will be putting the king in the place of the gods, and he is most likely to be flattered by that of anything I can think of: then, if once we can get that old Hebrew into the lion's den, we shall make a good deal more money than we have been able to do with him watching us all the time."

This notion seemed to please the princes very well. They drew up the document immediately. It would not do to let Daniel hear of it, before the king should sign it; and so they appointed a committee to take the decree down to the palace the very first thing in the morning. There were some lawyers among these hundred and twenty princes; and I seem to see them drawing out the law with great care, making it firm and binding—laughing to themselves, and saying: "The laws of the Medes and Persians change not. If once we can get Darius to stamp this document with his signet-ring, Daniel is done for, sure enough."

So the committee go down to the palace next morning to obtain his signature. They begin by flattering him. If a man wants another to do a mean thing, he always begins by appealing to his vanity.

"O king, we have been thinking how popular you are in your kingdom, and what you might do to make yourself even more famous than you are; and we have come to the conclusion that, if you would publish a decree that nobody in the kingdom, for thirty days, should pray to any other god except yourself, it would turn the hearts of all the people towards you even more than now. We should then have a universal religion, and the king would be at the head of it."

Darius felt flattered by this proposition. He turned it over in his mind, and presently said,—

"That seems sensible."

"All right," said the princes. "We thought you would like it; and in order that there might not be any delay, we have the document here already drawn up. Now if you will please to stamp this with your signet-ring, we shall have it published right away."

The king takes the document, reads it over, stamps his seal upon it; and the committee go away laughing, and saying, "Ha, ha! old Hebrew, we will have you in the den of lions before night."

The princes lost no time in publishing the new decree of the king. I can imagine some one of Daniel's friends, who had seen the document, going up to his office in great haste, to give him warning that there was some trouble brewing.

"Have you heard the news, Daniel? Those hundred and twenty princes have gone and got Darius to publish a decree that nobody shall pray to any other god, except him, for thirty days. That is a conspiracy against you. Now I want to give you a little advice; and that is, to get out of this town in a hurry.

But Daniel says he can't leave his business. He is afraid these hundred and twenty princes will cheat the revenues while he is away. His duty is right there, and he is determined to stay there and attend to it.

"Well then, had you not better pray more secretly? You

have a habit, that is all well enough in ordinary times, of going up to your chamber, where the windows open towards Jerusalem, and saying your prayers there three times a day. And sometimes you pray pretty loud, and people out of doors can hear you. Now just shut your windows while you pray, for the next thirty days; for these princes are sure to have some spies watching you at your prayers. You had better stop up the key-hole of your door also, for these mean fellows are not above peeping in to watch you. It would be still better, Daniel, if you would not kneel down at all, but say your prayers after you get into bed."

Ah! how many young men have gone to Oxford, or Cambridge, and lost their peace of mind and their hope in Christ, because they were afraid to pray before their room-mates!

And what does Daniel say to such advice as this? He scouts it. He tramples it under his feet. No man shall hinder him from praying. No king shall frighten him out of his duty. He attends to his morning's work; looks over the accounts as usual; and when twelve o'clock comes, he goes to his chamber, puts the windows wide open, kneels down and prays, not to Darius, but to the God of Abraham, Isaac and Jacob. His windows are opened towards Jerusalem, and his face is turned that way; for Jerusalem is dearer to him than his life, and the God of his fathers is his sure defence. I can seem to see him kneeling there – that old man, with his white locks and beard, praying at the probable cost of his life; but he does not seem to be troubled by the danger; neither is he angry at the command of the king or the manifest wickedness of those hundred and twenty princes. He prays for the king, his friend,—who, he is sure, has done this wickedness in some thoughtless moment. He prays for his enemies, the princes, who are wickedly seeking to destroy him.

Those men have taken care that two witnesses shall be underneath Daniel's windows at the time when he usually goes to pray. "Hark!" says one to the other. "Did you hear that? The old man is up there praying, sure enough! Listen: he is not praying to King Darius."

"No," says the other; "he is praying to the God of the Hebrews."

So they listen till the prayer is finished, and then they hurry away to the princes, to give their evidence against Daniel;

and the princes lose no time in laying the matter before the king.

"O King Darius! live for ever. Is it not written that the laws of the Medes and the Persians change not?"

"It is," said Darius; "anything that is stamped with the king's seal cannot be changed."

"That is what we thought," said the princes. "Did you not make a decree that no man should pray to any other god than to the king?"

"Yes, I did," said Darius.

Then they tell him that the chief of the presidents—this Daniel, the Hebrew—has refused to obey the king's command. Poor Darius!

"What a mistake I have made!" says he. "I might have known that Daniel would not obey such a command as that. I had quite forgotten about him when I made it." There is not a man in all Babylon who is so troubled as the king. The account says that "he laboured till the going down of the sun to deliver Daniel." But the command had gone forth, the law had been made, and it could not be changed, even for the sake of Daniel himself.

If Darius had loved his friend only as much as Christ loves us, he would have gone down into the den of lions for him. Our Darius, our King, counted not His life dear unto Himself, but freely delivered it up for us.

At sundown the king's officers go for the old man, to take him away to the lions. They bind his hands behind his back, and lead him along the streets of Babylon towards the den. The whole city goes out to see the sad procession. The princes look out of their windows, and rub their hands, and laugh over the success of their wicked plot; and the people look on in wonder, to see such a sweet-faced old man led away to die like a criminal; and poor Darius walks the chamber of his palace, wringing his hands in agony, saying, "Ah me! I have destroyed my friend."

But Daniel walks with a firm step. His old knees don't shake a bit. The wind of the evening plays with his white locks, and with a smile upon his face he goes to meet the lions. He has served his God now for seventy long years, and he feels sure that God will not desert him in this great hour of trial. I can imagine him saying, "My God can bring me out of the jaws of the lions just as easily as He saved my three friends from the furnace of fire. But even if they eat me, I shall only die for my God." And when they put him into the den, God sent one of His angels to shut the mouths of the lions.

At the hour of the evening prayer, Daniel kneels in the den; and if he can get the points of the compass down there, he prays with his face towards Jerusalem; and then, taking one of the lions for his pillow, he lies down and sleeps, as sweetly as any man in Babylon. The king sits up all night, thinking what his folly has cost him—even the life of his most faithful servant. But he remembers that the God of Daniel has done strange things for them who trusted Him. He has heard of Shadrach and his friends coming out of the fiery furnace; and he knows that Daniel went into the den feeling that his God would go with him and save him. At the first dawn of day he orders out his chariot, and you can hear the wheels rattling over the pavements of Babylon before the people are up. Away he goes, with his horses on the run, to the door of the lion's den; springs out of the chariot; looks down into it, and with a voice trembling with anxiety, cries out, "O Daniel, servant of the living God; is that God whom thou servest continually, able to deliver thee from the lions?"

Hark! There comes up a voice out of the den. It is the voice of Daniel; to whom this morning is like the morning of the resurrection. He has been down to the gates of death, and yet he is alive.

"O king! live for ever. My God hath sent His angel and shut the lions' mouths, that they have not hurt me."

Oh how glad King Darius was to hear the voice of his friend once more! He has him brought up out of the den, takes him up in his arms, into his chariot; and away they go, home to the palace, to breakfast together and talk over this wonderful deliverance.

Then King Darius published another decree. The experience of Daniel had thoroughly converted him; and now he declares "that, in every dominion of his kingdom, man shall tremble and fear before the God of Daniel, who worketh signs and wonders in heaven and earth, and hath delivered His servant from the power of the lions."

We have not time, this morning, to follow the history of this man any further. Three times a messenger came down from heaven, to tell him that he was greatly beloved of the Lord The Spirit of God was with him, and the hand of God protected him.

May the God of Daniel be with us—the courage of Daniel be in us! May we have grace to confess the Lord, to go through the fire and amongst the lions, if need be, for the sake of His truth; and at last, after all the trials of this life are over, may we be so happy as to sit down with Daniel and all the ancient worthies, in the kingdom of our God!

"WHAT MUST I DO TO BE SAVED?"

Mr. Moody's Last Sermon in London. Preached in Camberwell Hall, Sunday Evening, July 11th, 1875.

I SUPPOSE you do not want to hear a sermon on this last night so much as you want to know how to be saved. I want, if I can, to answer that question, "What must I do to be saved?" There is no question that can come before us in this world that is so important; and I think that there is not a man in this audience to-night who does not feel interested in it. I heard a man, when he was going out the other night, saying: "I do not believe in sudden conversion. I do not believe what the preacher said to-night, that a man could come in here a sinner, and go out a Christian." Now, I want to say that I do not believe in any other conversion. I do not believe that there ever has been a conversion in the world that was not instantaneous, and I want you to mark this: not but what many cannot tell the day nor the hour when they were converted. I will admit that: they may not know the time; but that does not change the great fact that there *was* a time when they passed from death unto life; that there *was* a time when they were born into the kingdom of God. There must have been a minute when their name was written in the Book of Life. There must have been a time when they were lost, and a time when they were saved; but we may not be conscious when the change takes place. I believe the conversion of some is like the rising of the sun, and of others like the flashing of a meteor. But both are instantaneous, really, in the sight of God. There must be a time when life begins to rise; when the dead soul begins to live.

Now, this evening I want to take up some of the Bible illustrations. In the first place, there is the ark.

There was a minute when Noah was outside of the ark, and another minute when he was inside. And, bear in mind, it was the ark that saved Noah: it was not his righteousness; it was not his feelings; it was not his tears; it was not his prayers. It was the ark that saved him. If he had tried to make an ark of his feelings, or of his prayers, or of his life, he would have been swept away: he would have been drowned with the rest. But, you see, it was the ark that saved him.

When I was in Manchester, I went into the gallery one Sunday night, to have a talk with a few inquirers; and while I was talking, a business man came in, and took his seat on the outskirts of the audience. I think, at first, he had come merely to criticise, and that he was a little sceptical. At last I saw he was in tears. I turned to him, and said, "My friend, what is your difficulty?" "Well," he said, "Mr. Moody, the fact is, I cannot tell." I said, "Do you believe you are a sinner?" He said, "Yes; I know that." I said, "Christ is able to save you"; and I used one illustration after another, but he did not see it. At last I thought of the ark, and I said: "Was it Noah's feelings that saved him? Was it Noah's righteousness that saved him, or was it the ark?" "I see it, now," said he; "I see it." He got up and shook hands with me, and said: "Good-night: I must go. I have to go away by the train to-night; but I was determined to be saved before I went. I see it now."

A few days after, he came and touched me on the shoulder, and said, "Do you know me?" I said, "I know your face, but do not remember where I have seen you." He said, "Do you not remember the illustration of the ark?" I said, "Yes." "It has been all light ever since," said he. "I understand it now. Christ is the Ark; He saves me; and I must get inside Him." When I went down to Manchester again, and talked to the young friends there, I found he was the brightest light among them.

Let me take another illustration. There was the blood in Goshen. God says, "When I see the blood I will pass over you." Now He does not say, "When I see Moses' feelings, or the feelings of the people, I will pass over you"; or, "When I see you praying and weeping, I will pass over you"; but, "When I see the blood I will pass over you." It was the blood that saved them, not their righteousness. And a little child by that blood in Goshen was just as safe as Moses or Aaron or Joshua or Caleb. It was the blood that saved them. Look! there is the Jew taking the hyssop. He dips it in the blood, and strikes it on the doorpost. One minute it is not there : the next it is there. The moment the blood is there they are saved. God says, "When I see the blood I will pass over you." Some people say, "If I were only as good as that minister I should feel so safe"; or, "If I were only as good as that mother in Israel who has been praying fifty years for the poor and unfortunate, should I not feel very safe?" My friends, if you are behind the blood, you are as safe as any man or woman who has been praying for fifty years. It is not their righteousness and good works that are going to save them. They never saved any one. God says, "When I see the blood I will pass over you." And when I am sheltered behind the blood, then I am saved; and if I am not sheltered behind the blood, I am not saved. That was instantaneous, was not it? God says, "When I see the blood, it shall be a token, and I will not enter." Death came down and passed over Egypt; and where the blood was on the doorpost he passed by; but where the blood could not be found, in he went and took the victim away. The great palaces could not keep out death; wealth and position could not keep out death. He went and took the Crown Prince of Egypt; he took the richest and the poorest, the highest and the lowest. Death makes no distinction, except a man is behind the blood. My friends, be wise to-night, and get behind the blood. The blood has been shed. The blood is on the mercy-seat; and while it is there you can be saved. God is imputing to His Son your trespasses and sins. He says, "I will look at the blood on the mercy-seat." Press in, my friends; make haste and get in to-night; for the Master of the house will rise up by-and-by and shut to the door, and then there will be no hope.

Take another case. When Israel went over Jordan, God told Joshua to have six cities of refuge; three on each side of Jordan. They were to be built on a hill, where they could be seen at a great distance, and the gates were to be kept open day and night. All obstacles were to be kept out of the way, the highway was to be kept in repair, the bridges and everything in good condition, so that nothing should hinder a poor man flying to the city of refuge. If a man killed another in those days, it was considered a great disgrace if the nearest relative did not take vengeance. "An eye for an eye, and a tooth for a tooth." If a man killed another, the next kinsman was bound to put him to death. But if he could escape to a city of refuge he was tried, and if it was found he had not intentionally killed the man, he might live. Now for my illustration. Suppose I have killed a man. I am out away in the woods working, and my axe slips out of my hand, and kills the man working with me. I know that his kinsman, his brother, is not far away. The news will soon reach him that I have killed his brother. What shall I do? I start for the city of refuge, over there away on the hill, ten miles off. I run—and we are told that in those days there used to be signposts with the word "Refuge," written in great red letters, so that a man might read as he ran; he need not stop. I have been told that there was a finger pointing towards the city, and a man who could not read might see the hand. A man does not have to learn to read before he can be saved. I see that hand; it is pointing to the city of refuge. The gate is wide open, but it is ten miles away. I leap over the highway. I do not look behind, to the right hand or to the left. I do not listen to this man or to that man, but, like John Bunyan, I put my fingers in my ears. The avenger has drawn his sword, and is on my track. I leap over into the highway; and, pretty soon, I can hear him behind me. Away I go, over that bridge, across that stream, up that mountain, along that valley,—but I can hear him coming nearer and nearer. There is the watchman; I can see him on the wall of the city. He gives notice to the inhabitants that a refugee is coming. I see the citizens on the wall of the city watching, and when I get near I hear them calling, "Run, run! Escape, escape! He is very near you! Run! escape!" I press on; leap through the gate of the city; and at last I am safe. One minute I am outside, and the next I am inside. One minute I am exposed to that sword; it may come down upon me at any minute: the next minute I am safe. Do I feel any difference? I feel I am behind the walls: that is the difference. It is a fact. There I am. The avenger can come up to the gates of the city, but he cannot come in. He cannot lay his sword upon me. The law of the land shields me now. I am under the protection of that city; I have saved my life; but I had no time for lingering.

A great many of you are trying to get into the city of refuge, and there are enemies trying to stop you. But do not listen to them. Your friends tell you to escape. Make haste! Delay not for a single moment!

In our country, before the war, when we had slavery, the slaves used to keep their eye on the north star. If a slave escaped to the Northern States, his old master could come and take him back into slavery. But there was another flag on American soil, and if they could only get under that flag they were for ever free. It is called the Union Jack. If they could only get as far north as Canada they were free; therefore they kept looking towards the north star. But they knew if they only got into the Northern States, there might be some one ready to take them back. So it is with every poor sinner who wants to come to Christ. Many men do all they can to hinder him; others will cheer him on. Let us help every man towards the north star. A man has escaped: perhaps he swims across the Mississippi river, or crosses the Ohio river in a little canoe. The master hears of it, and he takes his hounds and sets them on his track, and begins to hunt him down. The slave hears the hounds; and he knows that his master is coming to take him back to slavery. The line is a mile or two away. He escapes as fast as he can. He runs with all his might for the frontier, over hedges and ditches and rivers; away he goes for Canada. By-and-by he comes in sight of Canada. He can see that flag floating in front of him; and he knows that if he can only cross the line before his master and the hounds overtake him, he will be free for ever.

How the poor black man runs! leaping and bounding along; and at last, with one bound, he goes over the line. He is free! One minute he is a slave; the next minute he is a free man, under the flag of Queen Victoria, the British flag! (cheers)—don't cheer, my friends, but come to Christ—and your laws say that no man under that flag shall be a slave. One minute he is a slave; the next minute he is a free man. One minute it is possible for his old master to drag him back; the next minute he shouts, "Free!" If Christ tells us that we are free, we are free. My friends, Christ is calling to-night. Get out of the devil's territory as quick as you can. No slave in the Southern States had so hard a master as yours, nor so mean a master as Satan. Take my advice to-night, and escape for the liberty of your soul.

I can imagine some of you saying; "I do not see how a man is really going to be converted all at once." Let me give you another illustration. Look down there. There are two soldiers. Now, if you bring those soldiers up to this platform, and ask them how they became soldiers, they will tell you this—that one moment they were citizens, and the next minute soldiers. What was it that made them soldiers? It was when they took the Queen's shilling. The moment they received that shilling they ceased to be citizens, and they became soldiers. Before they received that shilling they could go where they pleased; the next minute they came under the government and under the regulations of the army, and they must go where Queen Victoria sends them. They did not have to wait for the uniform. The minute they received the shilling they became soldiers. What made them soldiers? Receiving the shilling. What makes a man a Christian? Receiving Christ. "He came unto His own, and His own received Him not: but as many as received Him, to them gave He power to become the sons of God."

Now, the gift of God is eternal life. Who will have the gift to-night? When I was down in Manchester I asked that question, and a man shouted in the meeting, "I will!" Who will have it now? Is not there some man here in London, as there was in Manchester, who will say that he will have the gift? Is it not a wonder to have to plead with so many to take the gift? "The wages of sin is death; but the gift of God is eternal life." Who will have the gift now? (Many responses of "*I* will"; "*I* will.")

I can imagine one man down there who says; "How about repentance? How about getting into the ark or the city of refuge before repentance?" My friend, let me ask you what is repentance? It is right-about-face! I think these soldiers understand that expression. Some one has said that every one is born with his back to God, and that conversion turns him right round. If you want to be converted, and want to repent, I will tell you what you should do. Just get out of Satan's service, and get into the Lord's. Leave your old friends, and unite yourself with God's people. In a few days, if nothing happens, I expect to go to Liverpool. If, when I am in the train, my friend Mr. Shipton says, "Moody, you are going in the wrong train,—that train is going to Edinburgh,"—I should say, "Mr. Shipton, you have made a great mistake; somebody told me the train was going to Liverpool. You are wrong, Mr. Shipton; I am sure you are wrong." Then Mr. Shipton would say, "Moody, I have lived here forty years, and I know all about the trains. He must have been very ignorant or very vicious who told you that train goes to Liverpool." Mr. Shipton at last convinces me, and I get out of that train and get into the one going to Liverpool. Repentance is getting out of one train and getting into the other. You are in the wrong train; you are in the broad path that takes you down to the pit of hell. Get out of it to-night. Right-about-face! Who will turn his feet towards God? "Turn ye, for why will ye die?" In the Old Testament the word is "turn." In the New Testament the word is "repent." "Turn ye, for why will ye die, O house of Israel?" God does not want any man in this audience to perish, but He wants all to be saved. You can be saved now if you will.

There is another illustration I wish I had time to dwell upon; and that is about *looking*. There is that serpent in the wilderness. "As Moses lifted up the serpent in the wilderness, even so must the Son of man also be lifted up, that whosoever believeth on Him should not perish, but have everlasting life." Look here! Just give me your attention for a few minutes. "Believe on the Lord Jesus Christ." How long does it take a man to believe? Or, if you will, how long does it take a man to look? Some people say they believe in educating people to be Christians. How long do you educate children to look? You hear the mother say, "Look," and the little child looks. It does not take a child three months to learn to look. Look and live! You need not go to college to learn how to look. There is not a child here but knows how to look. Christ says, "Look unto me; for I am God, and there is none else."

There is the brazen serpent on the pole. God says to the children of Israel, who are dying of the bite of the fiery serpents—"Look, and live!"

Now, there is nothing in looking at a piece of brass which can cure the bite of a serpent. It is God who cures it, and the looking is the condition. It is obedience; and that is what God will have.

One moment the poor sufferer is dying; the next there comes

a thrill of life through his veins, and he lives: he is well. My friends, look to Christ, and not to yourselves. That is what is the matter with a great many sinners; instead of looking to Christ, they are looking at the bite.

It is not looking to the wound; it is looking to the remedy. Christ is the remedy of sin. What you want is to look from the wound to the remedy—to Jesus, the Author and Finisher of our faith. Who will look to-night, and live? Turn your eye to Calvary; believe on the Lord Jesus Christ and be saved.

NOTE.

THE last of the revival services in London occurred on Sunday evening, July 11th, at the Camberwell Hall. It was not, as was contemplated at the time the "Conclusion" was written, a converts' meeting; but an address to an audience of men only. When, near the close, Mr. Moody asked, "Who will accept Christ to-night?" large numbers of voices all over the vast congregation eagerly responded, "I will!" "I will!" And when, at the very last, those who wished to be Christians were requested to rise, a multitude—perhaps a thousand or more—rose to their feet; indeed there seemed to be nearly as many people standing as sitting.

A Thanksgiving and Farewell Meeting has been held this day (Monday, July 12th), at the Mildmay Conference Hall, Mildmay Park,—the building erected by the late Mr. Pennefather. Here a large number of ministers and Christian workers assembled, to talk of God's goodness, and rejoice over the blessings of the two years' revival. Among the striking facts brought out, was a statement, by Rev. Dr. Andrew Bonar, that, in Glasgow, during the past year, seven thousand souls had been gathered into the various churches. The work in the four sections of London was reported as still progressing under the labours of the pastors; "hundreds of whom," said Dr. Fraser, "have come into a better enjoyment of their work. The great secret of this wonderful revival seems to be, that, with hearty downrightness of speech, our brother has *preached the Word of God.*"

www.ingramcontent.com/pod-product-compliance
Lightning Source LLC
LaVergne TN
LVHW021316110826
845150LV00003B/586